AGEING IN SOCIETY

The British Society of Gerontology was established in 1973 to provide a multi-disciplinary forum for researchers in the field of ageing. Its members – researchers, teachers and practitioners – are drawn from the broad range of social sciences. The Society's aims are succinctly expressed as being to encourage the research and study of human ageing and later life, and the application of this knowledge to the improvement of the quality of life.

Also published by Sage Publications in association with the British Society of Gerontology:

Researching Social Gerontology
edited by Sheila M. Peace

AGEING IN SOCIETY

An Introduction to Social Gerontology

edited by
John Bond and Peter Coleman

SAGE Publications
London · Newbury Park · New Delhi

SAGE Publications Ltd
28 Banner Street
London EC1Y 8QE

SAGE Publications Inc
2111 West Hillcrest Drive
Newbury Park, California 91320

SAGE Publications India Pvt Ltd
32, M-Block Market
Greater Kailash – I
New Delhi 110 048

British Library Cataloguing in Publication data

Ageing in Society: an introduction to social gerontology.
   1. Man. Ageing. Social aspects
   I. Bond, John II. Coleman, Peter.
   305.26

ISBN 0-8039-8282-8
ISBN 0-8039-8283-6 Pb

Library of Congress catalog card number 90-061930

Typeset by Sage Publications, London
Printed in Great Britain by Dotesios Printers Ltd, Trowbridge, Wiltshire

CONTENTS

LIST OF FIGURES AND TABLES

Figures

Tables

ACKNOWLEDGEMENTS

We would like to thank the contributors for their part in the development and completion of this volume. This enterprise would have not been possible without the support of the British Society of Gerontology, particularly Hilary Todd and Anthea Tinker who as Chairwomen of the Publications Committee encouraged and cajoled the manuscript towards its completion. We would especially like to thank Debbie Buck who word processed the final manuscript; Barbara Ingman for the production of the figures and diagrams; and Penny Fowler and Senga Bond for their assistance in proof reading.

LIST OF CONTRIBUTORS

John Bond is Senior Lecturer in Sociology in the Centre for Health Services Research at the University of Newcastle upon Tyne. He has previously been a Senior Research Officer in the Scottish Health Service where he was employed to undertake a large survey of services for elderly people. In Newcastle he has recently completed an evaluation of the three experimental NHS nursing homes and is currently working on a multi-centre study of the resource implications to families and personal health and social services of physical and mental frailty in elderly people. He has written a number of articles and papers on ageing and health and with his wife is joint author of an introductory textbook on sociology for health care professionals.

Roger Briggs is Professor of Geriatric Medicine at the University of Southampton. He has previously worked in the National Health Service in London, Brighton and Leicester, and studied neurochemistry at the Institutes of Psychiatry and Neurology, London. He currently teaches students of medicine, nursing and allied professions (including social work) as well as providing a clinical service as a consultant geriatrician. His interests include basic and applied research in dementia.

Peter Coleman is Reader in Social Gerontology at the University of Southampton, a joint appointment between Geriatric Medicine and Social Work Studies. A psychologist by discipline, he obtained his PhD in London in 1972 on the subject of the functions of reminiscence in later life, and then worked for five years at the Institute of Applied Psychology at Nijmegen in The Netherlands. He teaches social work, medical, psychology and nursing students, and established and continues to run a post-qualifying course in ageing, health and social care. His research interests are predominantly in the field of adjustment to ageing. His publications include *Ageing and Reminiscence Processes: Social and Clinical Implications* (1986) and *Life-Span and Change in a Gerontological Perspective* (as co-editor 1985).

Mike Featherstone is Reader in Social Studies in the Department of Administrative and Social Studies at Teesside Polytechnic. He is chairperson for the Centre for the Study of Adult Life. His publications include *Surviving Middle Age*, 1982 (with Mike Hepworth), *Postmodern*

Culture? (1990) and numerous articles in the sociology of ageing, sociological theory and the sociology of culture. He is founding editor of *Theory, Culture & Society*.

Jeffrey Garland is a Principal Clinical Psychologist with Oxford District Health Authority's Mental Health Unit. Based at the Radcliffe Infirmary, he heads the psychology service to the Department of the Psychiatry of Old Age. A founder of PSIGE, the special interest group of the British Psychological Society's Division of Clinical Psychology, he has contributed, on service development and on carer support, to a number of texts. His current research interest is in the development of memory and counselling for people over 50 reporting concern about everyday remembering.

Mike Hepworth is Senior Lecturer in Sociology at the University of Aberdeen. He is a member of the Executive Committee of Age Concern Scotland and a founder member of the Centre for the Study of Adult Life, Teesside Polytechnic. His publications on the social imagery of ageing include co-authorship of *Surviving Middle Age* (with Mike Featherstone), and he is currently working on a cultural and interactional analysis of the stigmatised elements of 'deep old age'.

Dorothy Jerrome is a social anthropologist working in The Centre for Continuing Education at the University of Sussex. Her interest in the ageing process has developed over the last fourteen years, during which she has taught a wide variety of groups – professional, undergraduate and postgraduate, and community-based. She is a founder member of the Sussex Gerontology Network. Her research has concentrated on peer relationships in later life and she is currently concerned with counselling older people.

Malcolm Johnson has been Professor of Health and Social Welfare and Director of the Department of Health and Social Welfare at the Open University since 1984. Previously a Senior Fellow at the Policy Studies Institute in London, Secretary (Research and Policy) to the Personal Social Services Council – an advisory body to the government, and lecturer in Sociology at the University of Leeds, he has published more than 70 books, monographs, articles and chapters. He has also served on many academic and public bodies including being Convenor of the British Sociological Association Medical Sociology Group, Secretary of the British Society of Gerontology, Scientific Adviser to the Department of Health and Social Security, Vice Chairman of the DHSS Working Party which produced the Code of Practice on Residential Care and Chairman of the Advisory Council of the Centre for Policy on Ageing. Professor Johnson is the founding editor of the international journal *Ageing and Society*.

Chris Phillipson is Professor of Applied Social Studies and Social Gerontology at the University of Keele. His publications include

Capitalism and the Construction of Old Age (1982), *The Impact of Pre-Retirement Education* (with Pat Strang, 1983), *A Manifesto for Old Age* (with Joanna Bornat and Sue Ward, 1985), *Ageing and Social Policy* (ed. with Alan Walker, 1986), *Drugs, Ageing and Society* (with Bruce Burns, 1986) and *The Sociology of Old Age* (with Graham Fennell and Helen Evers, 1988). He is currently conducting research on old age abuse along with issues connected with the training of care workers involved with older people.

Alan Walker is Professor of Social Policy and Chairperson of the Department of Sociological Studies at the University of Sheffield. His books include *Disability in Britain* (ed., with Peter Townsend, 1981), *Unqualified and Underemployed* (1982), *Community Care* (ed., 1982), *Social Planning* (1984), *Ageing and Social Policy* (ed. with Chris Phillipson, 1986) and *The Caring Relationship* (with Hazel Qureshi, 1989). He has published numerous articles on retirement and old age. He is currently engaged in the evaluation of the Sheffield Neighbourhood Support Unit's innovation in the care of elderly people and a project on the employment of older workers in a period of economic expansion under the second ESRC Ageing Initiative.

1

AGEING IN THE TWENTIETH CENTURY

Peter Coleman and John Bond

Interest in the scientific study of human ageing has grown steadily throughout the twentieth century, culminating in recent years in a spate of academic books and the development of postgraduate courses in social gerontology. Introductions to the study of human ageing have typically emphasised changes in demography focusing on 'the ageing of populations'; a trend which has characterised industrial societies throughout the twentieth century but which in recent decades has become a worldwide phenomenon. The increase in the number of older people in society and the increase in the proportion of the population who are elderly has resulted in the study of human ageing focusing on old age in general and the problems or challenges of old age in particular. The products of much of such academic work has reinforced the predominant negative perceptions of old age present in society; views which are held by lay and professional people alike.

In this first chapter we will consider the demographic characteristics of an ageing population and highlight different approaches to the interpretation of these data from the perspectives of some of the scientific disciplines studying human ageing. This multidisciplinary approach will evolve throughout the subsequent chapters of the book.

DEMOGRAPHIC CHANGES IN THE TWENTIETH CENTURY

The ageing of populations

An unfortunate trend in recent years has been the increasing tendency to depict the growing numbers of older people in the population as a problem. Old age throughout this century has been seen as a 'social problem' (MacIntyre, 1977) and this predominant perspective is evident through the language used by policy makers and health and social service planners. Dramatic terms such as 'disaster', 'burden', 'rising tide' and 'impending crisis' are characteristic of many recent publications. While there is no denying the poor quality of life experienced by many elderly people (Townsend, 1989) or the challenge that planners and professionals face in providing health and welfare services for the growing numbers of frail elderly people, it is disappointing that the joys and triumphs of old age in the latter half of the twentieth century are not promoted with such energy. Perhaps this tendency reflects a perspective from the media that good news is not news.

Throughout the twentieth century the proportion of people aged 60 or over has increased in all countries of the world. This trend started earlier in industrialised countries but countries from the Third World are experiencing the same changes in population structure. In 1960 it was estimated that about half of the world's population aged 60 or over were living in Third World countries. By the year 2000 about two in three of the estimated 600 million people aged 60 or over will be living in Third World countries. The increase in the elderly population will be most marked in Asia, particularly China and India (WHO, 1989).

The improvement in life expectancy throughout the world is the result of a reduction in child mortality which reflects improvements in public health and medical advances in the prevention of many fatal infectious diseases in childhood. Increases in the life expectancy of older people reflect improvements in the quality of life in the second half of the twentieth century and to a limited extent some of the achievements of medical science. However, future improvements in health and life expectancy are likely to come in the future, as in the past, from changes in the physical and social environment which leads to disease, rather than from improved treatment of diseases once they have occurred (McKeown, 1979).

The challenge of increasing numbers of very old and frail people has only been taken seriously by planners and policy makers in the last two decades, although the demographic evidence from Britain shown in Table 1.1 has been available for much longer. For much of the century service planning was based on the numbers of people aged 65 or over and it is only in recent years that the numbers of people aged 75 or over and 85 or over have been used as a basis for planning. The increase in the proportion of the population aged 65 or over started in the early part of the century and was mirrored by a much sharper growth in the numbers of very old people. In Britain the number of people aged 85 or over, of whom one in five will have dementia (Report of the Royal College of Physicians of London, 1981) and three in five a limiting longstanding illness (Office of Population, Censuses and Surveys, 1982), rose from 200,000 in 1951 to 500,000 in 1981 and is expected to increase to 1.1 million by 2001 (Office of Population, Censuses and Surveys, 1984a). Similar increases have occurred and are expected in the United States and other industrialised countries (Guralnik et al, 1987).

Gender differences in longevity

An important feature of human ageing is the greater longevity of women than men. This has not changed with the rise in the numbers of elderly

Table 1.1   *Elderly people in Britain 1851–2001*

	Census date									Predictions	
Number (millions)	1851	1871	1891	1911	1931	1951	1961	1971	1981	1991	2001
65–74	0.7	0.9	1.1	1.5	2.4	3.6	3.9	4.6	5.0	5.0	4.6
75–84	0.3	0.3	0.4	0.5	0.8	1.5	1.8	2.1	2.6	3.0	3.0
85 or over	–	–	0.1	0.1	0.1	0.2	0.3	0.5	0.6	0.8	1.0
Proportion of total population (%)											
65 or over	4.8	4.6	4.8	5.1	7.4	11.0	11.7	13.3	15.1	15.9	15.2
75 or over	1.4	1.1	1.5	1.5	2.0	3.5	4.1	4.8	5.9	6.9	7.1
85 or over	–	–	0.3	0.2	0.2	0.4	0.6	0.9	1.1	1.4	1.8
Total number (millions)	20.8	26.1	33.0	40.8	44.8	48.9	51.3	54.0	54.3	55.4	56.4

Source: Office of Population Censuses and Surveys (1984c)

people in the population. Table 1.2 shows the gender structure of the elderly population in Britain in 1981. The gender ratio of people aged 65–69 is 121 (ie. for every 100 men there are 121 women) but this rises to 325 for people aged 85 or over.

This imbalance in the numbers of elderly men and women has a number of obvious consequences. Many women are left to live alone in old age. This is heightened by the tendency of women to marry men older than themselves. Over 80 per cent of women over the age of 75 are single, widowed or divorced. It also means that institutions like residential homes, who cater predominantly for very frail elderly people, are mainly occupied by women. Continuing-care institutions typically have fewer than one man to every three women (Bond et al, 1989a).

Definitions of old age

Administrative definitions of old age predominate throughout the literature on ageing. The age of 65 as the standard retirement age for men within the UK may still seem a convenient age limit for defining 'old age', 'later life' or what recently has come to be called the 'third age' (Laslett, 1987), although fewer and fewer people are actually retiring at this age. It has also been convenient to refer to elderly people as 'pensioners' since women at the age of 60 and men at the age of 65 are entitled to draw an old age pension. But is the use of chronological age a useful way of defining the later stages of human ageing? Other cultures have used different social definitions of old age such as grandparenthood or physical fitness. For the planners it may be more helpful to relate service needs to functional age. Although the prevalence of disability

Table 1.2   *Gender structure of the population of elderly people in Britain, 1981*
(thousands)

	Men	Women	Gender ratio[1]
65–69	1206	1461	121
70–74	954	1311	137
75–79	595	1006	169
80–84	271	629	232
85–89	98	296	302
90–94	26	102	392
95 or over	5	25	500

Source: Office of Population Censuses and Surveys and Registrar General Scotland (1983)
[1] Gender ratio = number of women per hundred men

and physical and mental frailty increases markedly with age (Martin et al, 1988) many 90-year-old people are as functionally able as people of 50 or 60.

People aged 85 or over would appear to represent the majority of elderly people, in the sense that a considerable proportion are physically or mentally frail. But it is important to emphasise the variability in this association between chronological age and disability, an association which is also dependent on factors in earlier life that may have influenced the health of individuals in later life. A lot too is unclear. We are not able to predict whether the next generation of elderly people will be more or less healthy than the present generation. Certainly factors such as the increased prevalence of smoking among younger women, the changing employment patterns of both men and women and general dietary changes in the course of the twentieth century will have their repercussions, but it is difficult to be sure about quite what their impact will be.

Predicting changes in human ageing

It is nevertheless very important for society to look ahead to the situation that awaits people in 10, 20, 30, 40 or 50 years time. The nature of political processes often makes people very short-sighted, since considerations are short-term. Yet in planning human services it is essential to look further. In Japan, for example, it is now evident that by the end of the year 2025 about one-fifth of the population will be over the age of 65 and this will be greater than any other country in the world. Presently the proportion of people aged 65 or over is relatively small (only 9 per cent in 1980). The rapid diminution in child mortality after the Second World War when birth rates were very high, followed by lower birth rates when prosperity increased, have contrived to create this rapid demographic change. The Japanese are very concerned as how to manage this transition, and rightly so. Will the pension system be adequate? Will traditional family care patterns need more external support to survive? It is better to be thinking ahead than to be caught unprepared.

Other countries too face similar changes, most dramatically China if the present policy of limiting families to one child each is adhered to for many years. The ageing of populations is an international trend in which industrialised countries have most experience but by the middle of the next century this experience will be worldwide. Some degree of planning is therefore essential for all countries.

A longer-term perspective does not only apply to societies and governments. It also applies to individuals. We need to educate individuals to think of their whole life course, to give them a time perspective which does not stop at young adulthood and the acquisition of a job, marriage and the formation of a family. All of us should be thinking beyond this, to middle and later life and to the ultimate point of any life career, death, and to consider the changing roles which we have to negotiate throughout the life course.

Demographic disaster or not?

The view that sees the rising numbers of elderly people as a disaster should be combated with vigour, otherwise it will be a self-fulfilling prophecy. Increased negative attitudes towards people in the later stages of life may be the result. The veteran American gerontologist Cowgill has argued that although the ratio of elderly people to the labour force is rising 'this does not mean that the total dependency load is increasing'. The increased numbers of frail elderly people who are dependent on society are more than offset by the declining numbers of dependent children. 'We have fewer dependent persons per worker in the United States than we had a century ago, and modernised countries characteristically have decisively lower dependency loads than less developed countries.' (Cowgill, 1984, p. 223).

Certainly adjustments have to be made within the new form of society, which will have a much more rectangular age distribution with equal numbers of people in each range rather than a pyramidal structure with rapidly declining numbers at the peak. There is no reason to think that such societies are not viable. Greater changes are likely to occur in the post-industrial society than the age of the population. The policies and attitudes of society will need to alter to accommodate such changes. People of all ages should be valued not only for their past contribution to society but also for their present and potential contribution. Elderly people have more to offer than many younger people give them credit for.

CHANGES IN THE STRUCTURE OF SOCIAL NETWORKS

Just as societies need to look forward in order to plan effectively for the future, so a historical review assists society to understand the present situation. Many people will sense that things have changed but often miss the basis for such change. Of course, in this respect the older we get as individuals the more often we harp back to the 'good old days', something which the youth of yesteryear also found difficult to cope with. As individuals look backwards at their life experiences they often appear to see the past through 'rose-tinted spectacles'. This is probably true of the way that people in general, but also politicians and planners in particular, view the structure of social networks and the support of very frail elderly people.

It is often observed that families do not care for their elderly relatives as they used to. Comparison is made with the situation people claim to remember in the post-war years. Well-documented studies of family life in this period (Townsend, 1957; Young and Willmott, 1957) describe the close reciprocal relationships of families and conclude that elderly people were well integrated in family life. More recent studies of elderly people suggest that this situation is not to be found in many places in modern Britain. For example, Abrams' (1978) survey of older people in various parts of the country undertaken in the late 1970s showed quite substantial numbers expressing loneliness. Over half the men and one-third of women who were living alone were not only lonely but 'shaken' by the extent of their loneliness. However, as Rossiter and Wicks (1982) report, this notion of family care is central to government policy on supporting elderly people at home in the community.

Changes in family size

Many close-knit communities such as those researched in East London were damaged by the post-war housing developments. However, the structure of families also changed markedly from this period onwards. There are now far fewer children per elderly person in the 1980s than there were 20 or 30 years ago. This reflects changes in family size which occurred much earlier this century when family size decreased quite sharply.

Victorian and Edwardian families were typically large – six, seven or eight children per family was quite normal – and elderly people alive during the post-war period in East London had borne their children in those times. If we consider only those aged 75 or over in 1960, to take a specific point in time, we can see that they had brought up children in the era before the First World War. Not only did they have many children, but they were likely to have more surviving children than previous generations, because of improvements in public hygiene, medical treatment and living conditions at the end of the nineteenth century. It is true that many of their sons would have been killed during the awful carnage of the First World War, but this also had the consequence that there were later more single daughters available to care for their elderly relatives. In retrospect, we can see that the post-war years were advantageous for elderly people in some ways. Also, the solidarity of working-class people living in East London was a positive product of urbanisation. In earlier periods of history there was probably less contact between families because travel was not so easy between the rural communities.

The situation only 25 years later is a very different one. Those who were over the age of 75 in the 1980s had their children in the period after the First World War and typically had smaller families. Indeed, nearly one in three surviving elderly people aged 75 or over have no surviving children. Wicks (1989) has recently estimated the ratio of elderly people aged 75 or over to women a generation younger and has shown that in 1901 there were 2.77 women for every elderly person. In 1986 this ratio was 0.84.

Changes in family structure

In addition to a decline in the size of families, the actual structure of the family has influenced the availability of family support. Geographical mobility has increased markedly in the post-war years. Few people live in the area where they were born or brought up. Again, according to Abrams (1978), of those elderly people who did have children, 40 per cent did not have one living within six miles. (Bond reviews the living arrangements of elderly people in Chapter 8.) The increasing participation of women in the work force has made it much harder for the typically one available daughter or daughter-in-law to provide support to elderly relatives. The impact of divorce cannot be underestimated. It has resulted in the weakening of connections between the generations, where complex patterns of family relationships have often taken the place of simple ties.

All this is not to say that individual bonds of affection and responsibility felt by children toward their parents have diminished or that other forms of intimate relationships have not emerged for many elderly people. But it does suggest that contacts with other than family members are likely to be relatively more important nowadays – especially contact between peer groups, people of the same age and position in life who also often share similar interests. (Jerrome explores the role of intimate relationships more fully in Chapter 9.) It also has important implications for the concept of community care advocated by successive governments. Care by the community cannot always be care by the family. (Johnson considers community care again in Chapter 10.)

ATTITUDES TOWARD OLD AGE

Understanding ageing

In recent years we have become aware how unnecessarily negative some of our attitudes to older people are. Concern is understandable when one thinks about issues like funding a proper pension system and providing adequate health services, but our attitude should not be only one of concern. Ageing is not only about becoming very frail and needing care. In fact, as already stressed, this is typically only a characteristic of older people at the end of their lives.

There is a widespread feeling for a greater understanding of ageing. This is reflected in some of the books that have been written for a popular audience, such as *A Good Age* (Comfort, 1977), *To the Good Long Life* (Puner, 1974) or the telling title *Ageing for Beginners* (Stott, 1981). All these books reflect, in part, the need for reassurance, to counter a sense of confusion and uncertainty about growing old. Long life should not be something to be afraid of, but an achievement to be enjoyed. New situations which face us as a result of the changing population and family structures and the inadequacy of our public services should be seen as challenges, not problems.

Central to society's problem-oriented approach to ageing is the question of attitudes. Comfort forcibly makes the same point:

> Unless we are old already, the next 'old people' will be us. Whether we go along with the kind of treatment meted out to those who are now old depends upon how far society can sell us the kind of pup it sold to them – and it depends more upon that than upon any research. No pill or regimen known or likely, could transform the latter years of life as fully as could a change in our vision of age and a militancy in attaining that change. (Comfort, 1977, p. 13)

Old age as a difficult period of life?

In Chapter 4 Coleman addresses directly the question of whether for individuals old age is a particularly difficult period of life. Certainly it is perceived to be difficult. Evidence for high levels of depression and loneliness are often cited in support of such observations. However, the claim is sometimes made that for the individual old age is nowadays more difficult than in the past.

A number of reasons have been put forward in support of this view. The first point that is often made in this context is the demographic one. Since contact with older people is much more frequent nowadays they are no longer so special. Old people have lost their 'rarity' value, the achievement status which was previously obtained merely by reaching the Third Age. Although there is some truth in this observation, numbers probably have little to do with declining levels of respect for elderly people. People were probably never respected just because they were old but because of the qualities associated with age.

Indeed, we have to beware of the idea that the rising numbers of elderly people in the population this century is somehow unnatural and abnormal. Furthermore, it is not entirely unprecedented. The researches of social historians (Laslett, 1976) have revealed that there have been 'precursor modern' societies with sizeable numbers of elderly people in them. The best recorded evidence is available for some of the Italian city states, such as Arezzo and Venice, of the Renaissance period and afterwards, when the proportion of the population aged 65 or over seems to have reached 10 per cent, 'modern' age population structures according to World Health Organisation definitions. This probably says something about the standard of living in Italian society at that time. Old age does not appear to have been a notable social problem in Italy during this period. On the contrary, the most revealing records, the artistic works of the period, show striking pictures of elderly men and women full of character and involvement in the life around them.

The second point has also been raised before, that family relationships are less strong and that this results in greater isolation of elderly people. The research evidence suggests that there has been a decline in family relationships as a result of changes in family size. But there is a danger of exaggerating the extent to which this has happened, and in creating a false myth about family life in the past. Again, we have to thank the social historians for demonstrating that in English society in particular, many elderly people always seemed to have preferred to maintain their own households in old age. Often for reasons of poverty or disability this was not possible, but a preferred pattern of life was to live close to but separate from their children. Even widowed people often maintained their own households (Laslett, 1976).

This deeply embedded emphasis on the value of independence in English life has its dark side of course, the greater danger of isolation. But it is not something new. Public criticism of family care of elderly people has a long history in Britain (Thane, 1985). Take, for example, the following quotation cited by Thane (1985):

> The duty of providing support for parents in old age or infirmity is so strongly enforced by our natural feelings that it is often well performed even among savages and almost always so in a nation deserving the name of civilised. We believe that England is the only European country in which it is neglected. (Report of the Royal Commission on the Poor Laws, 1834)

Although this was written over 150 years ago, it could have been written today. The aim of the resulting new Poor Law was to encourage greater family responsibility in the care of very frail relatives. So even at this time it was felt that families could do more than they did. Yet as Thane points out, the beliefs that family attitudes to the old were declining were entirely mythical. An obvious index of family neglect of elderly relatives is their presence in institutions. But over the last three centuries the proportion of elderly people living in institutions has remained remarkably low and stable. As far as historians can tell, elderly residents comprised people who were without close kin or community ties (Thomson, 1983). There was, however, the problem in some families of being unable to support their parents because of their own poverty, and this awareness eventually led to the innovative social security legislation at the turn of the century.

A further reason suggested by some, that old age is more difficult now than in the past, relates to the age of death. Documented changes in the survival curve show that deaths in earlier periods of life have drastically diminished which means that deaths in advanced age have risen sharply. As Briggs shows in Chapter 3, the life expectancy curve has changed its shape to become more rectangular.

An important point to make is that for the individual the experience of death has come to be concentrated in later life. Many people will live through to middle age experiencing only the death of their grandparents among those close to them. Later in middle age their own parents will die, but it is only in later life that death will be experienced as a constant pattern as siblings, friends and other contemporaries die. A statistic worth considering is that of those aged 50 in Britain, only 5 per cent of their cohort will be dead.

This is a very different situation from the one that was customary in the last century when death still appeared almost a random occurrence and the experience of death of people close to one was a common experience through childhood and young adulthood as well as in later life. The development of a standard pattern of life expectancy must make the experience of old age different, as the instance of bereavement and the burden of coping with loss are concentrated on older people. Coleman returns to these issues again in Chapter 5.

CHANGES IN ATTITUDES TOWARD ELDERLY PEOPLE

Modernisation theory

Probably the most significant theory to have been developed on historical changes and attitudes to old age is the so-called *modernisation theory* (Cowgill and Holmes, 1972). This argues that modernisation as a historical process resulted in lowering the status of elderly people in society. In particular, it explained how respect was lost for old age, and held that the term 'old' acquired a negative connotation as a result of the process of industrialisation. In medieval and Renaissance times, despite the negative image portrayed by Shakespeare's Jacques in *As You Like It* on the last stage of life – 'sans eyes, sans taste, sans everything', old age had its proper place in the cycle of life, deserving respect especially for the enhancement of qualities of wisdom borne of experience. Indeed, Anglo-Saxon texts in particular portrayed old age as the most favoured period of life and, in fact, rather pitied youth and its follies (Burrow, 1986). According to early versions of modernisation theory, the mass of industrialised societies remained fairly constant in its respectful attitude to the old. As summarised by Fischer it was:

non-literate in its culture, agrarian in its economy, extended in its family structure, and rural in residence. The old were few in number but their authority was very great. Within the extended family the aged monopolised power, within an agrarian economy they controlled the land. A traditional culture surrounded them with an almost magical mystique of knowledge and authority. (Fischer, 1978, pp. 20–21)

Modernisation altered all this in various ways:

First, the development of modern health technology multiplied the numbers of the elderly, and contributed to the ageing of the population and its work force. That situation, in turn, created pressures towards retirement, forced people out of the most valued and highly regarded roles, deprived them of utility, curtailed their income, and lowered their status. Second, modern economic technology created new occupations and transformed most of the old ones, which also meant loss of jobs, incomes, and status by the aged. Third, urbanization attracted the young to the cities thus breaking down the extended family in favour of the nuclear conjugal unit. Finally, the growth of mass education and literacy meant that 'there can be no mystique of age' and no reverence for the aged on account of their superiority of knowledge and wisdom. (Fischer, 1978, pp. 20–21)

More recent historical research has not denied that some such change has occurred in industrial societies but has placed its origins earlier back than was originally postulated by Cowgill and Holmes. Fischer has amassed considerable evidence to show that in North America at least attitudes were changing already at the end of the eighteenth century. He noted eight indicators of change:

1. In the early American churches and meeting houses people were seated by age, and seats of highest honour went to the oldest rather than the richest inhabitants. That practice was ended between 1775 and 1836 and was replaced by putting up the seats to auction to the highest bidder.
2. Mandatory retirements for officials as for example, judges, began in 1777 in New York and that practice intensified up to 1818 and then continued throughout the whole nineteenth century.
3. A distortion in age statistics from local census data in New York State was observed such that men tended to overstate their age in the eighteenth century but to understate it in the nineteenth century.
4. In dresses one can see a definite shift from an age-oriented fashion (powdered wigs, long coats) in the eighteenth century to a youth-oriented fashion (natural hair, tight-fitting waistcoats).
5. In the nineteenth century there developed a new language of ridicule for the old. Former words of respect disappeared, neutral words grew more negative.
6. In paintings, specifically family portraits of the eighteenth century, construction was hierarchical in age composition – the *pater familias* was enthroned above the family. In the nineteenth century he was sitting on the same plane with the rest of the family, egalitarian in age composition.

7. A change in legal procedures took place between 1775 and the end of the century. Partible inheritance replaced the impartibility in the legal codes in most states.

8. There is a change in the naming practices. There was a decline in the proportion of children named after their grandparents at the end of the eighteenth century.

At present the controversy centres on the correct interpretation of these changes. According to Stone (1977) these changes are an indication of the growth of egalitarianism and individualism rather than the lowering of respect for elderly people *per se*. The end product, though, seems the same, a loss of respect due to the older person.

In Fischer's own account the displacement of veneration for elderly people by contempt as they lost their privileged powers was followed in its turn by pity, as elderly people were seen no longer as the defeated enemy but as individuals in need of help. One perspective on the current situation would claim that it is with this set of attitudes of patronising contempt that we are still entrenched. Certainly the discomfort of mid-twentieth-century attitudes toward old age is highlighted by the Churchillian epigram 'All would live long but none would grow old'.

There are also signs, however, of a new respect for elderly people. Cowgill, now himself in retirement, has argued:

> there has been a reversal of that trend (loss of respect) within the United States, dating from about 1960. All social indicators show that the welfare and status of the elderly in the United States have moved upwards since that time. (Cowgill, 1984, p. 225)

There are many indicators of such change in Britain as well, which go beyond mere awareness of the problems of elderly people. One striking activity throughout the country, for example, is the growth of interest in oral history, a recognition of the valuable records older people hold within themselves and that they hold in virtue of having lived for a long time. Local projects to write up the history of particular areas of the country flourish on this basis. The development of pressure groups like the Gray Panthers in the United States also helps contribute to a new awareness of the place of older people in society, not primarily as individuals needing help, but as people having much to offer and wanting to give. The aim of the Gray Panthers is explicitly to fight against segregation of the old, shut away out of harm's way, and to achieve full integration, challenging what they see around them and contributing to social movements, for the welfare of the young as well as the old, and to work for peace (Kuhn, 1986). However, although there may be movement for a more positive attitude toward ageing, Featherstone and Hepworth in Chapter 12 provide a substantially negative view of images of ageing. Others would argue that although the Gray Panther Movement is a significant political force in American politics, it is very much a white middle-class pressure group which has had little impact on the majority of elderly people who are deprived. Walker in Chapter 11 highlights the relevance of continuing poverty and inequality in Britain.

Contemporary attitudes towards elderly people

Ordinary attitudes expressed towards elderly people still leave a lot to be desired. Stereotypes abound of elderly people as inflexible, hypochondriacal and self-preoccupied. Such views are also held by professionals, for example those who are not prepared to undertake groupwork with older people 'because they don't really want to listen to one another', or refuse the chance of providing therapy, 'because they can't change'.

Stott in her book *Ageing for Beginners* cites a number of such examples, including a striking quotation from a fellow journalist writing in *The Guardian*.

> Whenever I pass a group of old men or old women I can hear the keening note in their voices as they list for each other the iniquities of today ... the elderly are remarkably conformist, no matter how unique each of them might have been in their youth, which is why younger people have difficulty in regarding them as individuals ... old age has a vested interest in decline, a profit motive in refusing to acknowledge improvement. (Tweedie quoted in Stott, 1981, p. 3)

Stott's reaction is to reject such images, as reflecting the fears and anxieties of the young and the middle-aged. Better, she argues, to cultivate positive images of people ageing well. This is an understandable reaction but also rather escapist. The observations that Tweedie quotes do reflect something of reality. What is missing in them is not so much fact, but understanding. There is a lack of sensitivity in the observation, a lack of any real appreciation of how difficult life in old age can be, and why people react the way they do, so wrapped up in themselves or so critical of younger generations.

The fault is often in ourselves. We may have unrealistic expectations of old age, still possessing our childhood's view of our grandparents and archetypal notions of old age, characterised by wisdom and gentleness. We are disappointed – and resentful – when we find out that old people cannot all be like that. We find it difficult to empathise with people in life situations that we are not mature enough to comprehend.

Certainly the psychiatrists in Britain who have pioneered the development of specialist mental health services for elderly people have dispelled the notion of old age as a time of tranquillity. That is a rare state indeed. Adjustment is maybe a greater task in later life because of the lack of supports available to us in earlier life. We all have personality flaws that make us liable to fail. In earlier life these are often absorbed in work and the family, in competing and loving, in striving and receiving comfort. In old age we are often left alone without support, without a partner, a job, a role or money to spend. We may face infirmities and considerable isolation. It is no wonder that adjustment difficulties appear enhanced. In fact, of course, many elderly people are remarkably well-adjusted. But because of our lack of imagination, we do not appreciate their achievement. It is a shame that we have to grow old ourselves before we realise.

This point was demonstrated over 20 years ago by Carp (1969). She tested the possibility that behavioural characteristics commonly perceived as those of old age were not in fact specific to the later years of life by comparing a group of 350 elderly people with a similar number of college students. In the comparison, the students had higher index scores for characteristics such as neurosis, negativism, and unrealistic and unfavourable views of themselves, neglect of personal hygiene, dissatisfaction, social ineptness and drug taking. She also made the point that whereas such symptoms as unusual nervousness, irritability, depression, unaccountable outbursts of rage, personality change, apathy or withdrawal are in the younger person considered clear indication for counselling and psychotherapy, in the elderly person they often do not arouse interest, but are considered normal and acceptable. It is this kind of dullness that we must fight against.

We require much greater imagination in our thoughts and feelings about old age. One of the functions of this book is to stimulate such imagination. In the chapters that follow a number of authors from differing disciplines and perspectives critically examine existing ideas about ageing, present some new ideas and at the same time attempt to develop within the reader a critical and questioning eye. The study of human ageing is a challenging field and this book provides just a short introduction. Much remains to be done.

SOCIETY AND AGEING

In this chapter we have chosen to introduce the reader to two dominant themes in social gerontology. The first theme stresses old age as a social problem emphasising the increasing numbers of elderly people across the world. The second theme stresses the negative quality of public attitudes to old age. These themes and others will emerge in subsequent chapters of the book but in focusing on only two we wanted to establish within the reader the critical and unaccepting perspective necessary for the successful study of human ageing. By using both historical and life-span perspectives we have highlighted a positive view of human ageing. In the chapters that follow this positive tone will be challenged. However, some of the conclusions which will stem from the data presented will we hope support our optimism.

In Chapter 2 Bond, Briggs and Coleman introduce the reader to some of the perspectives used in the study of human ageing by sociologists, clinicians and psychologists. The purpose of this chapter is to emphasise the variety of theoretical ideas available to a student of social gerontology.

Biological, psychological and sociological perspectives tend to focus on different aspects of the ageing process. They make different assumptions, use concepts in different ways, pose different questions and arrive at different explanations of the ageing process.

In Chapter 3 Briggs, a physician with a special interest in the health care of elderly people, reviews the major biological changes which are associated with human ageing. He describes the various changes people may experience when they reach the Third Age and summarises the common diseases of old age, emphasising that for the majority of elderly people the experience of morbidity and disability may only be a relatively short experience occurring during the terminal phase of life.

In Chapters 4 and 5 Coleman, a psychologist, provides an insight into some of the psychological perspectives on human ageing. In Chapter 4 he reviews some of the major research findings from studies of age differences in intelligence and cognitive ability, and of personality change. He argues that when studying human ageing we should be concerned with the whole life course. In Chapter 5 Coleman looks at adjustment in later life and describes how elderly people have adjusted to awareness of being in the last stage of life and how they cope with change and loss. He examines the relationship between the social scientist's concept of demoralisation and the psychiatrist's concept of depression within the context of the meaning they have for the elderly individual. In this chapter he also reviews the function of reminiscence in the daily lives of elderly people and its role in therapy.

This clinical theme is taken up by Garland in Chapter 6 where he provides a clinical psychologist's perspective on environment and behaviour. He reviews the major factors affecting psychological well-being and highlights the significance of stress as a major mismatch between the demands of the environment and the individual's perceived ability to cope. Reflecting the way individuals shape their own environments Garland reviews the requirements of institutional living and the guidelines for practice in residential and other continuing-care institutions.

In Chapter 7 Phillipson examines from a sociological perspective the impact of retirement on individuals and groups. He highlights the contradictory feelings often expressed about leaving work and the variety of meanings attached to retirement. In providing an analysis of the future of retirement Phillipson assesses the key issues for social policy.

From a sociological perspective Bond, in Chapter 8, argues that the geographical location of elderly people and their living arrangements are strongly influenced by their structural position in society at earlier stages of the life cycle. He describes the living arrangements of elderly people and discusses the various policy options available in the future.

An anthropologist's view of intimate relationships among elderly people is provided by Jerrome in Chapter 9. Again the significance of relationships throughout the life course is emphasised. Jerrome describes the role of the family in old age and returns to the effects of social change on family relationships and the older person's social network.

Johnson provides in Chapter 10 a sociological critique of the concepts of dependency and interdependency which reinforce the negative stereotypes of old age. He provides statistical data about the prevalence of 'dependency', emphasising the continuity of experience with other age groups and highlighting the 'independence' of a majority of older people.

In Chapter 11 Walker focuses on the evidence that poverty and inequality remain a substantial part of human ageing. Using comparative, contemporary and historical data on the distribution of income and wealth, he documents the causes of poverty and inequality in old age.

A sociological perspective on the images of ageing is provided by Featherstone and Hepworth in Chapter 12. They pick a theme from this chapter by comparing the images of ageing before the industrial revolution with those which have emerged through the processes of industrialisation and modernisation. They lead into the final chapter in which Bond and Coleman consider the implications of current images of ageing for the 20-first century.

This introduction to social gerontology and the study of human ageing is a multidisciplinary enterprise. As with all introductions it has been necessary to be selective in the choice of material included. Many texts on human ageing have highlighted the effects of human ageing on different social divisions such as class, ethnicity and gender. By focusing on such sub-groups we would have been unable to emphasise the wide diversity of experience in human ageing. Nevertheless these social divisions are important and they have been introduced where appropriate at various points in the book.

2

THE STUDY OF AGEING

John Bond, Roger Briggs and Peter Coleman

The study of ageing is a multidisciplinary enterprise. Each discipline brings its own theoretical perspectives and methods. The purpose of this chapter is to introduce the reader to this variety of perspectives and to highlight both their different and complementary nature. Biological, psychological and sociological theories of ageing tend to focus on different aspects of the ageing process without necessarily contradicting each other. We show that they make different assumptions, use concepts in different ways, pose different questions and arrive at different explanations of the ageing process. Perspectives are not right or wrong, simply different.

To illustrate the complementary nature of the different theoretical perspectives we will examine the approaches adopted by each perspective towards the study of mental illness, particularly dementia. The chapter will not only identify differences in biological, psychological and sociological perspectives but will highlight differences in view within each of these broad disciplines. To begin with though, a brief word about theory.

THEORY IN THE STUDY OF AGEING

The word theory often gives rise to difficulties because it is used to describe everything which is not practical. When theory is used, as in psychological or sociological theory, then it refers to a set of conjectures or tentative explanations of reality.

Each one of us uses theory constantly. We carry in our heads our personal theories or models which represent the world about us. To do this we use selected concepts and the relationships between them. It is because we do not all share the same theories that we see the world differently. In other words facts do not speak for themselves; rather facts are interpreted in the light of some particular theory. It is because we have particular ideas about the nature of 'illness', 'old age' or the 'role of women' that we have different views about the way that society should care for sick old people.

Some facts are more generally accepted than others, and this may involve a process of accumulating particular knowledge which produces convergent theory. For example, we now take for granted the fact that the world is spherical. Yet at the time of Columbus' famous voyage it was certainly not taken for granted and many believed the world to be flat. It is by testing our hypothetical explanations that we accumulate knowledge and what may begin as scientific facts gradually become accepted into common-sense knowledge. Today we are in a position of uncertainty with some of the theories which are evolving about the origins and antecedents of psychiatric illness in old age. It is accepted theory which will influence the kinds of interventions produced; those holding different theories will produce different ideas about what is appropriate. For example, the prevalence of pervasive depression in people aged 65 or over is about 20 per cent (Gurland et al, 1983). A number of theories have been suggested as to the cause of depression in old age. Clinical work has suggested that there are changes in the ageing brain, psychologists have suggested changes in older people's self-concepts and sociologists have suggested changes in the social relationships of older people. These theories have led to pharmacological interventions, psychotherapy and the promotion of day centres and lunch clubs.

We cannot ignore theory, we can only choose from the alternatives. However, theory is not static but dynamic, constantly changing. Theory development therefore is best understood in a historical context, and fashions in the acceptability of different theories can be interpreted equally within a broader political or social context. The acceptability of different explanations of the influence of race on intelligence is a recent example of the fit between theories and the acceptability of broader ideas about the nature of people and society.

The role of theory

It would be a mistake to regard theories as right or wrong. There are, rather, theories which are more or less useful or profitable. No one theory is a completely accurate representation of reality but some provide better insight into a particular phenomenon than do others. The usefulness of any theory depends on how it functions:
1. to explain past events,
2. to predict future events, and
3. to generate new theory.

One function of theory is to provide explanations of what facts already exist about some phenomenon. Often facts appear trivial and disjointed yet they may be linked by some theoretical explanation. One example of this is the similar responses observed (facts) to bereavement, to retirement and to amputation. In all cases they may be explained by response to the loss of something valued. This kind of theorising is possible because of an existing system of relationships connecting different facts. When they are linked theoretically this adds to our understanding of otherwise disparate phenomena. By using theory we are able to summarise specific features which are generalisable beyond the immediate field of study. By the same token theory should be able to predict future outcomes.

Finally, good theory should lend itself to generating new theory capable of more parsimonious explanation and prediction. One aspect of this is that good theory should generate testable hypotheses which give rise to empirical testing. Theory therefore should point to areas yet to be explored and indicate which facts to observe while defining them clearly. In this way, new findings and empirical generalisations emerge which are then used to amend existing theory if this is then warranted.

BIOLOGICAL PERSPECTIVES

What is ageing?

We are all so familiar with the human and social effects of ageing and senescence on people around us that most of us do not think of ageing in 'biological' terms. However, just as birth and development can be seen from biological as well as social and psychological viewpoints, so too can senescence and death at the other end of the lifespan – in birds, bees or humans. Most living organisms show an age-related decline in functional capacity which can be studied at various levels ranging from the intact organism, be it plant or animal, through its component organs and their cellular constituents, down to molecular structure.

The terms 'ageing' or 'senescence', which are often used inter-changeably, imply decline and deterioration. Thus the growth of children over their initial years is thought of as 'development' rather than ageing, since the changes are beneficial rather than deleterious. Although the culmination of senescent decline is in the death of the individual organism, not all 'cell death' is damaging to the organism as a whole: indeed, it may be 'programmed' as part of the organism's biological economy. For example, the cells on the skin or lining the gut wall of a human have a short lifespan, since as they die they are sloughed off and replaced by new, dividing cells in a constant cycle of regeneration.

Ageing processes have been defined by Maynard-Smith (1962) as 'those which render individuals more susceptible as they grow older to the various factors, intrinsic or extrinsic, which may cause death', recognising that death may arise from a decline in the individual organism's ability to maintain its intrinsic function in the face of physiological stress from an extrinsic source such as 'accident' or disease. According to Comfort (1960), ageing is 'an increased liability to die, or an increasing loss of vigour, with increasing chronological age, or with the passage of the life cycle'. The four criteria proposed by Strehler (1962) have been widely accepted:

1. Ageing is *universal*, in that it occurs in all members of the population (unlike disease).
2. Ageing is *progressive*, a continuous process.
3. Ageing is *intrinsic* to the organism.
4. Ageing is *degenerative* (as opposed to developmental or 'maturational' changes).

It should be noted that ageing and death are fundamental, intrinsic biological properties of living organisms including humans, and that senescent changes are by definition deleterious. The biologist is concerned with measuring the nature and extent of ageing changes, trying to understand how these changes are caused and controlled, and learning how the effects of ageing can be manipulated or mitigated.

Biological theories of ageing

Programmed ageing

As already discussed, most organisms (including plants) undergo a process of ageing. It is possible that some primitive forms of algae and amoebae may carry on reproducing by simple cell division virtually indefinitely if the environment in which they are maintained is suitable, but more complex cells and organisms appear to have a limited lifespan and reproductive capacity. Natural selection and the process of evolution operate by modifying the characteristics of 'new' members of a species – in other words, it is reproduction and the early part of life which are of biological significance in terms of evolution. Survival into 'old age' is a rare event in the wild, most individuals being removed by accident or predation before the development of senescence. Thus natural selection may have allowed the accumulation of genes which operate to the 'good' of the organism in early life (when most individuals survive) even though these same genes lead to physiological decline later in the lifespan (when few surviving individuals remain to be affected). One could argue that the human being is not 'built' for old age in the industrialised world any more than is the rat for a laboratory – both artificial environments far removed from the world in which natural selection has operated for millennia. Various genetic mechanisms have been postulated to account for ageing phenomena and the determination of lifespan, and these view ageing as 'programmed'.

Many events during growth, development and reproduction are regulated by 'signals' from nerves or hormone-secreting glands. A key area of the brain in the control of such hormones is the hypothalamus, which is closely related to the pituitary gland. Various 'clock' theories of ageing have suggested that ageing changes are controlled by some kind of pacemaker whose main function is to direct the timetable of development until sexual maturity and reproductive ability are achieved. Thereafter, in the absence of a programme, the functions of the hypothalamus and pituitary become deranged and lead to physiological decline. While such 'clock' and 'pacemaker' theories are attractive, at least in highly complex organisms such as mammals, they are difficult to apply to simpler forms of life.

The cells which make up mammals can be thought of as essentially two types: 'fixed' cells, which after development do not divide further and have to serve the organism for the rest of its lifespan (for example, brain cells) and 'dividing' cells which carry on replacing themselves throughout lifespan (for example, skin or gut-wall cells). It should be noted that both types of cell will need to continue to make new molecules such as proteins, a process under genetic control, for the metabolism, function and repair of the cell and, in the case of the dividing cell, for replication. Hayflick and Moorhead (1961) showed that a variety of dividing cells from human tissues were only capable of a certain number of cell divisions: they could not replicate indefinitely when cultured, dying off after a period. A reproducing cell must make accurate copies of itself – too serious an error might be lethal to the cell or transform it to a 'malignant' cell (potentially cancerous). However, it is only through the natural selection of occasional 'good mistakes' that evolution has been able to operate. Thus there must be a balance between expending cellular energy on maintaining accuracy in cell division, and allowing some faulty copies: it has been proposed that the *Hayflick phenomenon* (of limited numbers of cell divisions) is an example of genes 'switching off' the mechanisms which maintain accuracy, thereby conserving energy but allowing errors to accumulate and cause senescence (Kirkwood, 1977).

Unprogrammed ageing
It should be noted that all these theories of 'programmed ageing' rely on the concept that genetic mechanisms are involved and that these mechanisms make evolutionary sense. Other mechanisms involved in ageing may be 'unprogrammed', due to random damage affecting molecules concerned with cell structure, function and metabolism. For example, large molecules like collagen and elastin (the proteins which make up connective tissue such as cartilage) may have their structure and physico-chemical properties changed by a process known as 'cross-linkage'. Similar changes can cross-link the strands of DNA, the molecule which carries genetic information.

Many normal metabolic processes within cells, such as oxygen utilisation, generate toxic by-products known as 'free radicals'. These substances are mopped up by several defence mechanisms which have evolved to protect the cell. However, free radicals may cause damage to membranes which surround cells and also cause breaks in the strands of DNA.

Orgel (1970) pointed out that errors involved in the transfer of genetic information from DNA – in the process of cell replication or the synthesis of proteins – could have serious consequences. Such errors in protein synthesis might themselves lead to further defects in protein synthesis and genetic information processing, introducing yet more error-containing proteins in a vicious cycle of 'error catastrophe' leading to cell death.

Explaining biological ageing

It can be seen that no single theory can explain all the causes of ageing, nor is there any reason why one cause should operate to the exclusion of all others. In general terms, it seems reasonable to suppose that:

a) the fundamental property of 'life' is the replication of genetic material;
b) such replication has an inherent risk of error due to random physico-chemical interactions ('non-programmed'); and
c) the process of natural selection would ensure a balance between catastrophic error and extinction on the one hand and too little error to allow necessary change on the other, so that ageing ('programmed') represents a stable evolutionary strategy.

Finally, we should remember that ageing processes evolved at a time when few animals (or human beings) lived far into their lifespan: in those circumstances, the risk of accidental death or starvation was too high to warrant expending excessive energy on the maintenance of highly accurate, potentially immortal, cells. Rapid and prolific reproduction were more likely to preserve the gene pool, a more important goal than the prevention of senescence in the individual. Now that most of us reach old age, evolution may take humans in a different direction in generations to come.

PSYCHOLOGICAL PERSPECTIVES

In our everyday lives we may think more about the psychological aspects of ageing than we do about biological ageing. However, the study of ageing, within the discipline of psychology, has hitherto played a relatively minor role. Recent emphasis on the interdisciplinary study of ageing and the increased awareness that psychological ageing must be placed within a historical, environmental and biological context, have served to make the study of ageing a model for other areas of psychological research where interdisciplinary links need to be made.

Experimental psychology

Psychology has diverse roots which can still be seen reflected in the different research methods employed by psychologists (Riegel, 1977). It was first cultivated as a laboratory-based science in the second half of the nineteenth century with a focus on analysing human intellectual functioning and ability, 'cognitive' processes by which the person gains knowledge or becomes aware of his environment. Perception, discrimination, memory, learning and reasoning have remained key topics. Although the first proponents of this new science were predominantly German, 'experimental psychology' subsequently developed most strongly in the United States and Britain where the findings began to be put to practical use.

The first distinct contribution to the field of ageing is generally credited to Sir Francis Galton (1822–1911), a half-cousin of Darwin. He was concerned above all to find some understanding of the hereditary basis of intelligence, and was particularly involved in measuring individual differences in motor performance and discrimination tasks. But he also launched the first large-scale collection of empirical data across the whole age span.

A major influence on psychology's development was the creation of the intelligence (IQ) test in the first part of the nineteenth century. Again this was the result of an American psychologist named Terman adapting techniques already developed by Binet and Henri in France to analyse more complex performances of judgement and knowledge. The success of the IQ measure as a means of selection gave psychologists a reputation for measuring absolute individual capabilities that has been hard to live down. When, during the Second World War, the occasion arose for testing large groups of young adults with the same instruments used on similar groups in the First World War, the results clearly indicated that a considerable improvement in performance with historical time had taken place, attributable to changes that had occurred in education, communication and welfare. But the full significance of the implications for the dependence of psychological characteristics on social factors was not recognised at the time.

Similarly, the age differences that were observed on psychological tests received little critical examination. The markedly poorer performance by older people on a whole range of tasks was taken at face value, and explained as being due to the apparently inevitable process of biological degeneration. Well before the end of the nineteenth century a picture of psychological ageing as a regressive movement was well established (Labouvie-Vief and Blanchard-Fields, 1982). Cognitive 'disorganisation' was thought to follow the reverse order of development with higher order abilities degenerating first. The model presented of psychological development and ageing was a unitary one, a sequence of growth and rapid build-up of abilities in early life followed by a period of relative stability followed by a long period of decline. Within this context the psychological study of ageing was seen as of limited interest and was not surprisingly a rather unpopular field of research. At best, research on older individuals could be seen to provide an additional dimension to investigations of the explanatory power of general theories of cognitive functioning.

More recently as cognitive psychology has developed to take account

of people's functioning in the real world as opposed to the laboratory (eg Neisser, 1982), older people's mental functioning has become
a more attractive topic to researchers. Closer links are being made
between research findings and the practical relevance that they may
have (Rabbitt, 1988).

Developmental psychology

On the continent of Europe somewhat different traditions of psychology
flourished. The notion of human development received more serious
consideration. Whereas in Anglo-American orientations both young and
old were compared against an ideal standard of functioning, the young
as not yet attaining it and the old as falling away from it, continental
philosophers and subsequently psychologists gave more credence to the
idea of developmental stages. Thus Jean-Jacques Rousseau (1712–1778)
insisted that children should be considered and evaluated by standards
independent of those of the successful young adult. Children were not
just immature adults but their qualities deserved separate recognition
and cultivation.

The idea of human development as a progression in qualitative leaps
from one stage to another is best represented in psychology in the work
of Jean Piaget (1896–1980) on the cognitive development of children (eg
Flavell, 1963). He divided this development into separate stages which
he termed sensorimotor, pre-operational, concrete operational and formal
operational intelligence. Piaget himself did not look beyond childhood,
but his methods and interpretations have been used to propose further
stages of cognitive development in adulthood.

Thus Riegel (1973) argued that adults come to accept contradictions as
a fact of life. Whereas during the stages of concrete and formal operations
thought becomes increasingly noncontradictory, the 'mature' adult comes
to a new apprehension and an effective use of contradictions in operations
and thoughts. Instead of making premature choices between apparently
logically incompatible alternatives, the more adult thinker is prepared
to endure such tension. Contradictions form the basis for innovative
and creative work, and for the discovery of new principles. Therefore
the developmental task of being an adult in Riegel's view requires the
ability to live with complexity and tolerate a high level of ambiguity.
This 'dialectical-operations' stage of cognitive development is achieved
through giving greater acknowledgement to the importance of intuitive
thought, such as insight and understanding based on hunch, sensing and
immediate apprehension rather than reasoning alone.

Ideas on the development of personality
The most well-known contributions to developmental psychology from
continental Europe have come in the field of personality study. Whatever
one may think of the detail of his theories, Sigmund Freud (1856–1939)

revolutionised thinking about human behaviour by proposing a dynamic model for human motivation and opened up interest in much broader fields of psychology than cognitive performance alone. He stressed that people did not always act in rational ways nor were they necessarily aware of the bases of their action. Freud and his immediate followers were not strictly speaking psychologists but clinicians involved in the treatment of mentally disturbed people, but in a short period of time at the turn of the century they produced a wealth of ideas about human motivation, often conflicting and so broad ranging that they have not yet been properly examined.

Freud himself was not interested in ageing and his description of developmental stages is limited to the very early periods of life. But his one-time colleague Carl Jung (1875–1961), who broke away from Freud to establish a rival school of 'psychoanalysis', did give much greater importance to what he called the second half of life. For him mid-life was a crucial turning point when the individual was provided with opportunities for new developments. These were less to do with involvement in the outside world but more interior processes that he referred to with the term 'individuation'. A person could achieve a new balance in personality, a man accepting his 'feminine' as well as 'masculine' aspects for example. Jung laid great stress on the value of symbolic and religious experience in creating a state of harmony between the individual and the world around, and derived evidence for his theories from his wide-ranging knowledge of other cultures and societies.

Another of Freud's associates Alfred Adler (1870–1937) also came to stress different aspects of human motivation. Disagreeing with Freud's stress on the overriding importance of sexuality he proposed that the prime motivating force in all people's lives is a feeling of inferiority. All individuals have this feeling to some extent because of the inferior position they once occupied as children, when power and privilege were exerted by adults. Some feel this more strongly than others, for example as a result of physical defects or heavy-handed parenting. Adler saw subsequent developments of an individual's lifestyle as a means of compensating for feelings of inferiority. In extreme examples this could take the positive form of remarkable achievements by people with handicaps, but could also be expressed negatively in excessively self-assertive behaviour. Adler himself saw the most successful resolution of problems of inferiority to be in involvement with others, in the development of 'social interest'.

The relevance to gerontology of Adler's thinking lies in the fact that feelings of inferiority and loss of self-esteem can become major issues in late life, as a result for example of physical decline, loss of status, beauty and other abilities. At the same time possibilities for friendship and close relationships may be diminished. In Adlerian terms rigid, rejecting attitudes on the part of older people and even disengagement can be seen as problems resulting from a fear of inferiority. The perspective of an Adlerian approach to therapy is essentially constructive. Inferiority feelings and neurotic lifestyles can be overcome by helping the individual to develop a wider interest in others and cultivate a sense of belonging.

Although the early psychoanalysts contributed interesting ideas on personality development, these have proved difficult to investigate in practice. As clinicians they cited their own observations on patients, but these are open to the criticism that they are not independently verifiable observations and refer in any case to a biased sample of people who are not necessarily representative of the general population.

The establishment of acceptable methods of research has remained a major problem for the study of personality development. Although the observations and interpretations of the psychoanalysts can be criticised for their unrepresentative nature, the standard methods of experimental psychology – laboratory-based research on randomly selected individuals – also does not in general provide a suitable basis because of the artificiality of the situations that can be studied in this way. In the last 25 years ethology, a branch of zoology dealing with the study of animal behaviour by means of observation in its natural setting, has had a growing impact on the study of human psychology. The challenge is to develop naturalistic methods of observation and systematic recording of human thought, feeling and behaviour. Psychologists have also been learning from the methods of anthropologists who are well experienced in recording activities and customs in different societies.

Erik Erikson's stages of life
Of all the pioneer theorists on personality development the most influential to the study of ageing has been Erik Erikson. His pervasive impact on adult personality research is well acknowledged (eg Ryff, 1984). In his book *Childhood and Society* (Erikson, 1965) he provided a framework for the whole lifespan in terms of a series of tasks to be fulfilled. Thus the child's or rather baby's first psychological task in life is described as developing a sense of trust rather than a sense of mistrust. The ensuing childhood stages are characterised in terms of 'autonomy', 'initiative' and 'industry'. In adolescence the issue is the development of 'ego identity' versus 'identity diffusion' – Erikson is probably best known for his formulation of the concept of 'identity crisis' – and in early adulthood the development of 'intimacy' versus a sense of 'isolation'.

In middle age the issue becomes one of 'generativity', again a word coined by Erikson himself. He describes it as 'primarily the interest in establishing and guiding the next generation'. This can mean a focus on one's own family but it can also include broader interests and concerns in the society in which one lives. The opposite state Erikson calls 'stagnation' for which he offers a succinct illustration. 'Individuals who do not develop generativity often begin to indulge themselves as if they were their own one and only child.'

The task of the last stage of life, old age, for Erikson is to attain 'ego integrity', an assured sense of meaning and order in one's life and in the universe, as against despair and disgust. This involves 'acceptance of one's one and only life cycle as something that had to be and that, by necessity, permitted of no substitutions' (Erikson, 1965, p. 260). Despair may be expressed in a feeling that one has failed and does not have the time to attempt another life or an alternative road to integrity, and also in a disgust with other people, especially the young.

Erikson himself was a Dane who emigrated to the United States, and the influx of many other psychologists from continental Europe, especially following the rise of Nazism, created in the United States a flourishing interest in developmental psychology. In Britain too, notable contributions have been made, most especially by John Bowlby who demonstrated the catastrophic consequences of maternal deprivation in early life for personality development (Bowlby, 1965). However, Erikson has been one of the few psychodynamic theorists until recently to take an explicit interest in late life. It is no wonder, therefore, that his statements about old age are so often quoted.

Life-span developmental psychology

Erik Erikson can be rightly considered one of the precursors of what has come to be known as life-span developmental psychology (Sugarman, 1986). This appears at present to provide a fruitful context for the study of the psychology of ageing. Although the product of work carried out within this perspective is still small, its influence can be expected to grow (see also Baltes et al, 1980).

It is unfortunate in some ways that discussion of the relevance of Erikson's theory to ageing often focuses on the last stage of 'integrity'. His theory is in fact much more sophisticated than brief presentations often imply. It is not the case that at each stage the 'task' is either left unresolved or resolved, thus allowing the way forward to further development. A solution may be only relatively successful, and this will have repercussions on all subsequent stages. Thus major unresolved residues of earlier difficulties can play a salient part in late life, and make the issues somewhat different for each individual according to his or her own past experience. Erikson's ideas in fact should not be seen as a fully worked out theory but more as a model or framework within which to describe psychological development.

The emphasis on the integrity of the lifespan is Erikson's lasting contribution and one that is vital to an understanding of old age. In order to understand people in late life it is necessary to see them in the context of their whole life history with the problems both successfully and unsuccessfully resolved from earlier periods in life. This approach to human development and human ageing contains a number of important implications. The first is that the situations of older individuals will vary according to their histories. The courses of development of different people are likely to diverge the longer they live, and the more experiences they absorb. Rather than growing more alike as we age, we therefore become more individual.

A second important point is that development occurs on a number of different fronts. There is no reason to think that intellectual development, physical development and social development follow the same trajectory. Indeed, the varying importance of different aspects of life may be an essential feature of the life course. Jung expressed a similar thought more poetically: 'we cannot live the afternoon of life according to the program of life's morning, for what in the morning was true will at evening be a lie. Whoever carries into the afternoon the law of the morning ... must pay with damage to his soul' (Jung, 1972, p. 396). In other words, each phase of the day, life has its own characteristics and potentialities which must not be ignored.

A third characteristic of the life-span approach is the recognition of reciprocal influences between the person and the environment. Again, this is a feature of human psychology emphasised by Erikson. An individual's development depends on the right psychosocial circumstances being available, for example in the characteristics of his (her) parents and the wider society. This success in turn creates the circumstances for another's successful development. Erikson gave considerable stress to the interdependence of the generations, with the old needing the young as much as vice versa. This is a very important point as psychology has traditionally put its emphasis on measuring individual characteristics while tending to neglect the environment around.

It must also be admitted that some of these points were already recognised by the first people who gave thought to developing a study of human lifespan in the eighteenth and nineteenth centuries. In particular, they raised the issue of 'cohort differences', that the development of people growing up in a certain period of historical circumstances will differ from those in another, which thus makes invalid 'cross-sectional' comparisons of people of differing ages at the same point in time (Baltes et al, 1977). It is sad in retrospect to realise how these same points were missed by those who exploited the new techniques of psychological measurement developed earlier in this century. Indeed, it is only recently that methods have been developed which provide possible solutions to these theoretical problems. We explore further the relationship between theory and method later in this chapter.

SOCIOLOGICAL PERSPECTIVES

Sociology has provided a number of different perspectives from which to study ageing. Three broad approaches are delineated here: structuralism, symbolic interactionism and ethnomethodology. A fuller account of these three sociological perspectives is provided by Cuff and Payne

(1984) and the following discussion is based on an account of different sociological perspectives used in the study of health and illness (Bond and Bond, 1986).

Structuralism

Structuralism as a broad approach is based on the assumption that all our social behaviour, our attitudes and values, are the result of the organisation and structure of society in which we live. A major refinement of this, however, is to view the components of social structure as in consensus with each other or, alternatively, to view them as in conflict.

Structural functionalism – a consensus perspective

All sociological perspectives have in common a focus on the ordered nature of society – that is, a belief that in most situations the range of possible actions is fairly limited and we have a fair idea of how we would behave as well as being able to predict, within limits, the behaviour of others. The notion of order is relevant to situations as diverse as the golden wedding party and the stability of whole societies. It is at the societal extreme that the consensus perspective is situated, based on the assumption that, in the main, societies can be regarded as stable and generally integrated wholes which differ by their cultural and social structural arrangements. This perspective in sociology owes a great deal to an analogy with the natural and biological sciences. When sociology first emerged as a discipline separate from philosophy there was a thrust towards scientific method modelled on the natural sciences. Comte, a French philosopher, believed that sociology was about adapting and applying methods of physical science to social life, to make 'law-like' statements about the determinants of human behaviour and to reshape society by being able to predict and hence control its workings.

The emphasis on societies as integrated wholes was also based in part on the crude analogy between social and biological organisms. The analogy arises from the fact that both social and biological organisms have, on the one hand, a propensity to survive against all odds and, on the other hand, a propensity to decay. Most, if not all, biological organisms are systems made up of a number of distinguishable interrelated parts. Each of these parts affects and responds to changes in other parts of the organism. This analogy does not mean that the social system mirrors the biological system in terms of structure, but that the different parts of the social system are also affected by and respond to changes in other parts of the system. Different parts of the biological system fulfil different functions and roles; hence the sociological analogy, functionalism. Some functions are more essential for the organism's survival than others; so, too, individuals and institutions fulfil a variety of functions and roles. When the human organism loses an eye it adapts to change in circumstances; in the event of heart failure the body eventually dies.

The human organism is therefore an open and adaptive system which, however, is not immortal. Likewise, in its simplest form structural functionalism describes society as an adaptive and open system whose different parts function to keep it unified and relatively unchanging.

In the study of ageing the structural functionalist perspective has offered two theories. On the one hand, there is *disengagement theory* which emphasises the phasing out of old people from certain roles in order that society can continue to function. On the other hand, *activity theory* emphasises the need to keep old people active in order to integrate them into society, again so that society can continue to function.

Disengagement theory   Disengagement theory was first expounded by Cumming and Henry (1961) in *Growing Old*:

> Disengagement is an inevitable process in which many of the relationships between a person and other members of society are severed and those remaining are altered in quality. (Cumming and Henry, 1961, p. 211)

As the individual grows older he and society will prepare in advance for the ultimate 'disengagement' which is caused by incapacitating disease or death. The theory states that the process of disengagement is the method by which society prepares for the structure of its members so that when the inevitable arrives it does not disrupt the orderly functioning of society.

Three criticisms have been levelled at the theory. First, by implication the theory suggests that disengagement is desirable and therefore condones a policy of indifference towards the problems of older people (Shanas et al, 1965). Second, disengagement is not inevitable and non-engagement in old age reflects the lifelong pattern of social interaction for some people. Third, the data presented in *Growing Old* have been incorrectly interpreted since cultural values and the economic structure combine to create a condition in which a large proportion of older people are disengaged (Rose, 1965a).

Activity theory   Activity theory takes a different perspective in explaining the process of ageing. Havighurst (1963) argued that successful ageing can be achieved by maintaining into old age the activity patterns and values typical of middle age. Happiness in old age is achieved by denying the onset of old age and where the relationships, activities or roles of middle age are lost it is important to replace them with new ones in order to maintain life satisfaction. Indeed, there is a considerable amount of data to suggest that, in North America at least, the level of activity individuals have developed over a lifetime tends to persist into their later years (Riley et al, 1968).

The central criticism of activity theory is its idealistic nature. It would appear unrealistic to expect, for all but a small minority, that people can maintain the level of activity associated with middle age through to old age in view of the limitations imposed by biological changes alone. Activity theory is also unrealistic because the economic, political and social structure of society prevents the older worker from maintaining a major activity of middle age, namely 'productive' employment.

Structuralism – a conflict perspective
Conflict theorists tend to regard themselves as radical critics of the consensus theorists, with their emphasis on maintaining the status quo. As such they are sometimes regarded as political rather than sociological, most strongly exemplified in the Marxist perspective.

Marxism is essentially a historical interpretation of the evolution of societies or social systems. It explains social change historically by examining the evolution of modern industrial society from ancient economies based on slavery, through the medieval economy based on serfdom, to the capitalist economy based on waged labour. Marxism is also deterministic in that it predicts the evolution of capitalist society to socialist society. Like other forms of structuralism it is synthetic in its approach to social change, being concerned with the whole of society rather than with specific aspects (Lefebvre, 1968).

Some aspects of Marx's social philosophy are central to his sociological theory (Bottomore and Rubel, 1965). For Marx all societies are *stratified* into distinct *groups* and *classes*. Underlying Marxist theory is the notion that power and authority are linked closely to the economic organisation of society. In capitalistic societies the power of relationships is exemplified by the conflict between owners of capital (*the bourgeosie*) and the working class (*the proletariat*). The relationship between these two groups is characterised by exploitation.

Marxism sees society as a product of the *conflict* between these two social groups or social classes, and predicts that the struggle will be resolved through revolutionary rather than evolutionary social change. Societies pass through definite stages of development, with each stage containing contradictions and conflicts that lead to social change. But society and history are not seen as external to man. It is through man's own activity as a member of a social class with his distinctive class consciousness that the social and historical world is created and changed.

The main criticisms of Marxist sociological theory have been about the position that only changes in the economic base can change society. Weber (1930, first published in German in 1904) argued that many factors must come together to produce social change and proposed that it was the religious ideals of Calvinism which transformed people's behaviour and produced capitalism, by turning their religious zeal into economic production through hard work rather than detaching themselves from work to pursue their religious interests.

Weber's other criticism of Marxism was over the derivation of the power available to social groups. He did not agree that power derived solely from economic relations, the relations to private property and the means of production. For Weber social status or prestige also played an important role in power relationships.

In the study of ageing the conflict perspective is represented by the theory known as the political economy of old age.

The political economy of old age   Political economy is understood to be the study of interrelationships between political structure, economic structure and social structure or more specifically, between government organisations, the labour market, social classes and status groups. The central focus of this perspective is on the interaction between the economic and political structure in society and the way they effect the distribution of resources and social goods (Pratt, 1976). In Britain, Townsend (1981), Walker (1982b) and Walker and Phillipson (1986) have taken a political economy perspective which has as a central concept the idea of structured or structural dependency. Structural dependency describes the development of a dependent status resulting from the restricted access to a wide range of social resources, particularly income. This is reflected in the large numbers of elderly people who live in poverty (Townsend, 1979; 1989). A review of secondary data on earnings, incomes and assets, housing circumstances and benefits in kind shows that about one in four elderly people have incomes which are equal to or below the State Poverty Line, ie the supplementary benefit rate appropriate to each family (Walker, 1980, see also Chapter 11). It has long been recognised that elderly people feature in the lower levels of the income distribution because they are usually not in 'productive' work. Society tends to reward present work; it does not reward past work and therefore it does not reward old age. Elderly people are discriminated against by economic and social policies which benefit the young employed and the well-off. Thus, poverty in old age and the dependent status of elderly people are related to low resources and restricted access to resources through the life cycle.

We can illustrate this relationship by considering the effects of retirement on a person's access to resources. Prior to retirement manual workers – the majority of elderly men – experience reduced economic status (Townsend, 1979). Increasingly early retirement schemes are pushing elderly workers into less skilled jobs and into unemployment. After retirement the inequalities resulting from low pay, unemployment, disability and for women, sex discrimination, are carried forward into old age. The decline in the real value of savings and pensions means that the worse-off are the very old. Retirement also restricts access to social resources in the form of a reduction in social relationships once the retiree is away from the world of work (Phillipson, 1982).

Symbolic interactionism

In some ways symbolic interactionism is an embracing term given to a number of characteristics which identify a broad sociological and social psychological perspective. Many of the core ideas in symbolic interactionism characterise a rather different frame of reference known as action theory, which evolved from Weber's simple idea that sociologists should proceed to *understand* those they study. This is achieved by attempting to look upon the world as they do; by appreciating how the world looks to them. To this is added learning the ideas, motives and goals which make people act. By learning these things about individuals, the sociologist should gain an understanding of why they act in certain ways in order to achieve particular ends in the face of their individual circumstances as they see them.

This approach, emphasising understanding the individual, is very different from that of structuralism with its emphasis on social structures and facts which exist independently of individual members of society. Although structural functionalist theories are built on the elements of individuals' social action, they are set within the broader social systems which govern individual social actions. The emphasis is therefore on understanding social action by reference to social systems rather than on social action as generated through individuals in their particular circumstances. Thus, *social action* is attractive to a broad range of social theories but is difficult to study empirically while linked to broad social structures rather than small groups. It has been left to those within the broad perspective of social interactionism to translate their theoretical position into empirical studies.

The main ideas of symbolic interactionism were provided by Mead (1964) in Chicago earlier this century, and the major contributions to this perspective have continued to be American. At the heart of Mead's approach is the assumption that there is a difference between animal *reaction* and human *conduct*. Conduct requires the possession of *mind* which is distinctive to the human species. To this is added the concept of *self*. Individuals both undergo experiences and are aware of doing so.

Mead (1964) regards human action as very different from human behaviour. Behaviour is limited to a stimulus–response relationship. The concept of action depends on individuals' ability to plan their actions, reflect on past experience and reflect on themselves in the same way as they look upon other kinds of objects in the environment. It is the capacity for self-consciousness which makes human beings different from animals, and central to this is the ability of the individual to take the same attitude towards himself as others take towards him. In this sense he becomes an object like any other object; to look upon oneself as an object is to see oneself as others do.

For different individuals the same object will have very different meanings which will depend on such factors as previous experience and current purposes. Individuals will also experience the many different meanings they hold for others, reflected back at them. In order to handle this complexity, individuals construct pictures of themselves according to the general, typical and predominant views of themselves as shown by others. This is carried out largely through the medium of language, which Mead refers to as the *significant symbol*. Through such exchanges individuals learn the ways of acting which others expect and the self-consciousness necessary to engage in social life. The meanings of all objects are similarly derived from the social interaction of the individual with other members of society. Such meanings are handled in and modified through an interpretative process used by other people in dealing with the things they encounter.

It is explaining such processes that is the hallmark of symbolic interactionist approaches – providing an understanding of how and why things are as they are, by finding out about the circumstances of people's lives. As Blumer (1969) contends, these circumstances do not exist *in themselves* as stimuli to which the individual reacts. Rather, what constitutes circumstances depends on the purposes, plans and knowledge that the individual has *in mind*. Social action therefore has to be interpreted as the mindful action of individuals initiated to bring about certain purposes.

Symbolic interactionists have also shown how behaviour which from one perspective would be interpreted as totally irrational, from another perspective is a rational response to circumstances. This is associated with an interest in the processes by which members of society define their own circumstances and respective identities. This is encapsulated in a dictum attributed to W.I. Thomas: 'if men define situations as real, they are real in their consequences' (Merton, 1968, p. 475). This definitional approach has had particular applications to what has come to be known as the *labelling theory of deviance*, that is, how members of society come to define and label some of its members as deviant in certain respects and interact with them in such a way that the person takes on the characteristics related to the label. In the study of ageing, labelling theory has been used to explain the way in which elderly people are forced to act out specific roles. Thus, once someone has been labelled old, say they receive a retirement pension, they are expected to act the role of elderly or retired person and not try to seek employment. A further example of labelling theory is included in Chapter 10.

For symbolic interactionists the organisation of social life arises from within society itself and out of the processes of interaction between its members. They do not accept that external factors, such as economic ones, determine the form that society takes, although such factors do exert influence. Such influences will vary, however, depending on how they are perceived and dealt with. While the organisation of social life arises from within, it does not take on any autonomous features like those attributed by structuralist sociologists. To assume that society imposes or determines the action of society's members is incompatible with an interactionist perspective. Neither do the symbolic interactionists regard the structure of society as rigidly adhering to some *basic*, almost universal structure, as Marxist theory does. Rather, society consists of a relatively loosely articulated array of heterogeneous and overlapping social groups. While the relationships between groups or sub-groups may be characterised as competitive, there is no basic theoretical reason why one group should predominate.

Typically, symbolic interactionists are concerned not with an embracing concept of *society* but with the way in which individual members of society are engaged in indicating to others who and what they take themselves to be. This is portrayed in the conventional ways in which people communicate their social status, social role and sense of self. Goffman (1971) sought to understand how people come to decide, through social interaction, who they are and he employs the metaphor of life being just like life on the stage.

Sub-culture theory of ageing Although interactionist theory underlies a number of studies of ageing and old age there are few interactionist theories specific to the study of ageing. The main contribution is the sub-culture theory of ageing (Rose, 1965b), which postulates that sub-cultures tend to form when members of any group in society, such as elderly people, interact with each other significantly more than they do with other people in society. The development of a sub-culture would be encouraged by elderly people having a positive affinity for each other and their exclusion from interactions to any great extent with other groups in society. In Britain there are a number of events which contribute to the development of a sub-culture. The influence of compulsory retirement will encourage group affinity, while the decline in family contacts, the development of retirement communities (see Chapter 8) and the explosion in day care will encourage the development of a sub-culture. The strength of some family relationships, particularly in times of ill health and disablement, the continuation in employment and an inbuilt resistance to becoming old might restrict the development of a sub-culture, not to mention structural divisions which make elderly people a heterogeneous group in society. However, changes in the structure of the family and the lack of employment opportunities for older people suggest that sub-cultures may still develop because of the processes of labelling described above.

Phenomenology and ethnomethodology

Like the interactionist perspective, the ethnomethodological perspective has been used widely in recent years as the underlying theoretical perspective in studies of ageing, but has produced no *grand theories* (Mills, 1959) of ageing. To some extent this is because of the very nature of ethnomethodology.

The basic assumptions of ethnomethodology, deriving largely from the phenomenological philosophy of Husserl, are very different from those of other sociological theories. Husserl attempts to describe the ultimate foundations of human experience by 'seeing beyond' the particulars of everyday experiences to describe the 'essences' which underpin them. Only by grasping such essences do we have a foundation for all experience which enables us to recognise and classify it in an intelligible form.

In order to grasp these essences it is necessary for the philosopher to disengage from our usual ideas about the world, to examine the stream of experiences available to us – past, present and future. Phenomenology is about perceiving phenomena in the world as objects or events which are, in essential respects, *common* – the same for others as they are for ourselves. Therefore, the foundations of social life are not within the mind and experience of an individual, but in a commonly lived world of experience. This is a social world known in common with others.

The phenomenological approach was developed in sociology by Schutz and subsequently became known as ethnomethodology (ethno = people, ethnomethodology = the study of people's methods). This approach is particularly concerned with the language used in and used to describe everyday life. The approach is concerned with the basis of common assumptions we all make in order to render comprehensible the routines and activities of our everyday lives. Such order is achieved through what Schutz (1972) has termed our *taken-for-granted assumptions*, in other words our expectations of what should happen in a normal day and how we expect others to act. The social fabric is maintained through the use of *typifications* (Schutz, 1972) – common ways of classifying objects such as tree or elderly woman, events such as buying a loaf of bread and experiences such as pain or love, but in ways which are capable of being redefined or adapted. One taken-for-granted assumption is that others, by and large, see the world as we do, something which is clearly not always borne out. These elements of everyday life are not only learned through the process of socialisation but are also identified as 'mental tools' which we carry around with us in order that we can adapt our own actions according to the situations in which we find ourselves. Thus, like interactionists, phenomenologists and ethnomethodologists are concerned with how members of a social group perceive, define and classify the ways in which they actually perform their activities, and what meanings they assign to acts occurring in the context of their everyday lives.

THEORETICAL APPROACHES TO THE STUDY OF DEMENTIA

By way of illustration we highlight dementia in old age in order to show the complementary nature of theoretical perspectives drawn from clinical medicine, psychology and sociology.

Clinical approaches to dementia

From a biological perspective the first step towards elucidating the nature of a disease is to define the problem. During the nineteenth century, accurate *clinical descriptions* of many diseases of the nervous system appeared, and in 1835 James Cowle Prichard described a syndrome which he called incoherence or senile dementia. He noted 'forgetfulness of recent impressions, while the memory retains a comparatively firm hold of ideas laid up in the recesses from times long past'. The description of the symptoms and clinical signs of a disease, and their progression ('natural history'), enables the classification of diseases and allows the distinction of one from another. 'Dementia' is a 'syndrome' of progressive, global impairment of intellectual function, not a specific disease entity in itself. For example, the dementia which may be caused by infection with syphilis has a different clinical picture and natural history from the inherited disease causing dementia known as Huntington's chorea.

Pathology is that branch of medicine which includes the study of changes in tissues and organs as a result of disease. Early in this century, Alzheimer described abnormal microscopic loops and coils seen in the brain of a patient who died with dementia; this was the first demonstration of a specific brain pathology in any form of insanity apart from that associated with syphilis, and led to the concept of a specific type of dementia known as 'Alzheimer's disease'. The study of the pathology of Alzheimer's disease and senile dementia has been increasingly refined over recent years, since it is more difficult in elderly subjects to distinguish between brain changes due to 'disease' and those due to 'normal ageing'. Similarly, techniques of clinical and *psychological* assessment have been improved in an attempt to make reliable distinctions during life between Alzheimer's disease and other causes of dementia. However, difficulties remain in clinical diagnosis of dementia during life and in pathological diagnosis, particularly among elderly people. These difficulties are more marked in early, less severe cases, where there is considerable overlap with what may be regarded as 'normal'.

The epidemiology of dementia

Epidemiology is concerned with the occurrence of disease in populations and its control or prevention. In order to establish the prevalence of dementia in a community with any precision, it is obviously important to have sound diagnostic criteria. The difficulties in diagnosis have been alluded to above, but epidemiological research can of itself improve the instruments used to detect disease or to measure change over time. Not only are epidemiological studies necessary for the planning of services and policy-making but they also enable the identification of 'risk factors', which may give clues as to the possible causes of dementia. The most striking risk factor is age, dementia being rare before the age of 60, but suffered by some one in five of those aged over 80 (Report of the Royal College of Physicians, 1981). There is some *genetic* component of risk, more cases of Alzheimer's disease than expected being found in first-degree relatives of affected subjects, and people with Down's syndrome nearly all develop Alzheimer's disease if they live long enough.

Biological explanations of the aetiology of dementia

In the last two decades or so, it has become possible to study the biochemistry of nerve cells and as a result the understanding of neuronal structure and function has increased. In the case of Parkinson's disease, it was discovered that a particular type of nerve cell was involved, which functions by releasing a particular chemical signal known as dopamine. This finding led to the development of a successful treatment using a precursor substance from which dopamine can be synthesised in surviving nerve cells. Similar efforts have been directed at Alzheimer's disease in an attempt to find out which types of nerve cells are involved, their structure and function, and how they pass chemical or electrical signals to other nerve cells. In living patients, it is normally possible to use only rather indirect means of looking at the brain, such as X-ray or similar imaging techniques (which can be used to study function as well as structure), or electrophysiological methods of recording signals such as the electroencephalogram (EEG). Animal models can be used to study normal brain function or to try to reproduce pathological conditions, but there is no very satisfactory animal model of Alzheimer's disease either occurring naturally or artificially induced in the laboratory.

Treatments for dementia

Ultimately, the hope with any disease is to find its cause and to develop means of prevention or cure. To date, research on dementia has led to greater understanding of the nature of the problem and generated further hypotheses, but as yet the cause is unknown and no pharmacological solution so far is capable of arresting or reversing the progression of the disease. It is sometimes possible to develop drug treatments for a disease without knowing the fundamental cause: Parkinson's disease is a case in point, since treatment ameliorates the symptoms over several years but the underlying death of nerve cells continues for reasons which are unknown. Even where no 'treatment' as such is available for a disease, clinicians still have a role in planning and providing services for the diagnosis and support of sufferers and their carers. Dementia is now the principal cause of admission to long-term institutional care. The practical management of dementia requires psychological and educational skills and raises questions of resource allocation, in addition to the more commonly thought of 'clinical' skills.

Psychological approaches to dementia

A major role of psychologists in the study of dementia has been in developing appropriate cognitive tests used in its detection. For example, it may be difficult to distinguish at a superficial level the reactions of an elderly person who is depressed from one who is demented. Procedures which provide a profile of an individual's mental abilities will help in making a more confident diagnosis. Psychological interest in dementia, however, has recently broadened to include the development and evaluation of different types of therapeutic intervention in addition to the improvement of assessment tools.

A much greater curiosity is also evident in regard to the sufferer's own experience of being demented. Considerable imagination is required to appreciate the impact of crumbling powers of memory and identification upon the individual's feelings of security. A life-span approach can be valuable as we try to understand an individual's behaviour and the cues to which he responds in terms of habits established earlier in life. There is also the possibility that a study of psychological factors will eventually contribute in significant ways to a total picture of the causation of dementia. If this seems implausible, one should ask oneself why psychology is relevant to understanding the origins of heart disease and cancer, but not brain disease.

Assessment
Issues concerning the correct identification of dementia remain important and will become crucial if ways are found of treating dementia effectively, whether to reverse the condition or to slow down its further progression. Presumably it will be desirable to treat as early in the onset of the condition as possible, and to measure the success of treatment. Whereas crude forms of behavioural assessment may suffice when the behavioural changes are gross, more refined methods will be needed to detect dementia in its early stages and to measure change over time. For example, the most evident early signs of dementia are impairment of memory for recent events, name-finding difficulties and slowing of responses. But even very healthy people complain sometimes of similar problems. Moreover, the increased variability between people's abilities with age makes the detection of a threshold level for early onset of dementia very difficult to achieve. There is a danger of overdiagnosing dementia in persons of limited intelligence or poor education.

There exists a number of different approaches to the assessment of cognitive deterioration. These include taking account of the individual's self-report or the evaluation of someone who knows him/her well. Although important to the total picture and especially to an understanding of the meaning of dementia to the people involved, both of these sources of information are biased by the particular and perhaps idiosyncratic concerns of the informants. Therefore more widely used methods for the detection and measurement of the severity of dementia are so-called 'objective' or 'independent' measures, including observation by a trained individual, rating scales completed by a neutral observer, and actual tests of performance. The last provide the most complete and unbiased picture, but until recently few of such measures were available which tested a broad range of tasks and had sufficient range of scores to allow use with people of varying degrees of dementia. There are now a number of such tests in operation (see Huppert and Tym, 1986), which also take account of the time to perform a task as well as accuracy. It is possible to foresee the increasing application of computerised mental testing in this field of work.

In addition, application of techniques from experimental psychology is leading to a better understanding of the nature of the various deficits, in memory, use of language and spatial function, which demented people display. One would expect there to be useful comparisons between observations of abnormal behaviour in clinical settings and studies of normal functioning in laboratory settings. Models derived from the latter should have the potential for explaining what is involved in cognitive deterioration. For example, in memory retrieval tasks it has been shown that patients with dementia of the Alzheimer type fail to benefit from more meaningful organisation of material in contrast to elderly people who are depressed. This suggests deficits in the ability to put incoming 'information' in the appropriate 'store'.

Intervention
Efficient provision of help depends upon accurate assessment of need. A hastily formulated view of a situation may lead to an unhelpful response. A consideration of dressing ability provides a simple example of the importance of good assessment. This is a common difficulty with dementing illness, but can reflect quite different problems, for example the inability to remember what to wear or the inability to work out the right movements to put the clothing on. Simple physical limitations in stretching and bending must also not be overlooked.

Assessment is also important in defining not only the weaknesses, but also the remaining strengths that can be built on. Indeed one of the major problems in caring for people with dementia is the tendency to neglect what they can do for themselves. Abilities that are not practised soon deteriorate. 'Reality orientation' represents an approach to mentally deteriorated people which deliberately tries to counteract the tendency to shun them but rather to keep them in contact with ordinary daily events, and thus to minimise 'excess' disability. It is discussed further in Chapter 6.

Understanding
It is hard to appreciate what it is like to suffer from relatively simple handicaps such as blindness and deafness, let alone a set of disabilities as complex as those resulting from dementia. What is it like to hear people talking but to be unable to make sense of what they are saying? Or to understand that someone is cross but not to be able to understand why? The lack of understanding shown by demented people and their difficulties in communicating their own needs require that those who try to help them should use their own powers of imagination and empathy to help bridge the gap in understanding. It is a proper concern of psychology not only to describe a person's behaviour patterns, but also to conceptualise the view (or lack of view) of the world which may underlie them.

It is insufficient to characterise dementia purely in terms of cognitive failure. Its impact is more global, more terrifying. The clinical psychologist Chris Gilleard has written of dementia in terms of 'loss of self'

(Gilleard, 1984). Whereas the amnesic person suffering brain trauma and the person with a mental handicap still retain a self and a grasp on reality, the onslaught the dementing person faces eventually takes away the basis for a sense of personal integrity.

Close observation and discussion with people in the early stages of dementia shows that they have some insight and awareness of what is happening to them (Froggatt, 1988). No easy help is available. Appropriate medication has not been found to favourably affect the course of the condition. Practical support services are not yet required. But it is conceivable that a better understanding of the experience could contribute to a fuller knowledge of ways of retaining and reconstructing the individual's sense of self.

This becomes a more plausible line of investigation if one accepts the possibility that psychological factors, as loss of self-esteem, are involved in the aetiology of dementia. As some authors, most recently Kitwood (1988) have stressed, there is room for a consideration of social and psychological factors. It is sometimes mistakenly assumed that levels of dementia can be explained in terms of observable pathology of the brain. But post-mortem studies show that the states of the brains of some demented people are well within the range of those of mentally well preserved individuals whereas some people become demented with comparatively little accompanying neuropathology. The roles of stress and of personal reactions to stress in the aetiology of dementia have still to be properly considered. Resistance to this view is understandable given the horrifying nature of dementia and the comfort that a technical view of dementia provides. It may seem to exclude the threatening possibility of human responsibility for such a disturbing end to a person's life. But in the long run we may be neglecting an important line of enquiry.

Even if the aetiology of dementia were to be accounted for satisfactorily without recourse to psychosocial factors, it would still be important to take into account life experience. Obtaining the right information may require some degree of detective work on the part of the professional helper by interviewing relatives, friends and neighbours to construct a picture of the important people and events in a person's life. But it is worthwhile if as a result we can find cues which will help elicit a meaningful response. Speaking about the past itself may be an enjoyable activity. The past for a demented person may be much clearer than the present and talking about familiar memories has been shown to be an ideal way of establishing contact for many people (although in our use of reminiscence we must be as sensitive to individual differences among demented people as among 'normal' elderly people – see Chapter 5).

Investigation of past life may also help explain present behaviour, pointing sometimes to mundane facts (for example, understanding that someone tends to wander in mid-afternoon because that is the time she used to take her dog for a walk), but also sometimes to more serious matters (for example, attacks of panic in circumstances similar to the scene of traumatic events in the individual's past). The work of those life-span psychologists who have tried to make links across periods of an individual's life, in explaining reactions to loss for example, is as relevant to demented people as it is to other sections of the elderly population. The tendency to treat people in this condition as a 'category apart' has to be firmly resisted.

Sociological approaches to dementia

The structuralist approach

Ever since Durkheim (1897) towards the end of the last century attributed suicide to social causes, mental health has been regarded as the appropriate subject matter of sociology. According to Durkheim the behaviour of individuals depends on their social environment and what their society influences them into doing. Therefore, while *individuals* are mentally ill, some sociologists look for reasons not in these individuals themselves but in particular aspects of the social structure in which mentally ill people live.

A structuralist approach to the study of mental health was demonstrated by Hollingshead and Redlich (1958), who sought to show that the incidence and type of mental illness varied as a consequence of position in the social class structure. Thus, while the highest social class contained 3.1 per cent of the population, only 1 per cent of people with a mental illness came from this class. Conversely, they showed that the lowest social class included 17.8 per cent of the population but contributed 36.8 per cent of people with a mental illness. Illness designated as 'neurotic' was concentrated in the higher levels of social class while 'psychotic' types of illness predominated in the lower social classes. This kind of analysis has also been used widely by social epidemiologists interested in the prevalence of dementia and other psychiatric illnesses among older people (Bond, 1987).

The interactionist approach

In contrast with structuralists, sociologists who take an *interactionist* perspective provide rather a different view of mental illness. They begin with no taken-for-granted definition of what mental illness is; they do not see it as something lying with the individual himself. Rather it is a *social status* conferred on an individual by other members of society. For interactionists, mental illness is not like some disease within the person which can be universally observed and defined. Being regarded as mentally ill depends on individuals making that definition of others, labelling them and acting towards them as if they were mentally ill. The definition of mental illness occurs in the process of social interaction. This process can be observed in many geriatric wards where aphasic and deaf elderly patients may be labelled as 'demented' by nursing staff when no formal psychiatric diagnosis has been made by medical staff.

This is in contrast to an understanding of mental illness founded on assumptions about society with a structure which exerts strong influences on individual members and how they behave. Interactionists stress individual actions and perceptions, each person taking account of the actions of others on the basis of the meanings and interpretations they give to them. It is not a case of individuals being governed by and reflecting the structure of their society. Rather, individuals, through social actions, *create* their society. Individuals have to interpret their world, make sense of it and give meaning to it. Thus 'mental illness' and 'mental patient' are not absolute conditions or objects which exist 'out there'. Interactionists concern themselves in studying the processes by which people go about classifying others as 'mentally ill'.

In social life some people occupying particular roles have more power than others when it comes to labelling people as mentally ill. Szasz (1971) has taken this approach in examining the process of a person becoming so labelled. While most of us would say that we could recognise someone who was mentally ill, it is psychiatrists who are generally accepted as experts in so doing. Psychiatrists have considerable power to declare that someone is sick, requires treatment and should receive a specific kind of institutional care. Such is that power that others are likely to accept their categorisation that someone is mentally ill and to act towards that individual accordingly. In this way the individual becomes one who is 'mentally ill' not simply on the basis of his behaviour but because he now has a particular label attached to him. If others apply the label it is less likely to stick if it is not supported by a psychiatrist's opinion. Psychiatrists are also able to decide on the label to be given to describe a particular disease entity. In recent years, particularly in North America, there has been a move away from the label 'dementia', which engenders a certain expected way of acting on the part of the patient and other actors, toward the label 'Alzheimer's disease', which engenders a different set of actions, although the actual disease has remained unchanged (Finlinson, 1985).

However, not everyone agrees with such categorisation. Studies based on interactionist assumptions have shown that disagreements occur over the interpretation and meanings given to the behaviour observed. The differentiation of the 'mentally ill' from 'normal' members of society can be contingent upon the particular circumstances of the social situation in which people find themselves. Scheff (1964) examined the psychiatric screening procedures used in a Midwestern state in America to decide whether patients should be released. Scheff found that this decision is influenced more by the financial, ideological and political position of the examining psychiatrist than by patient factors. The study demonstrated that court-appointed psychiatrists with particular ideological and political views were predisposed to assume that the person was *ill* from the outset. Within this frame of reference which pre-classifies the patient, psychiatrists then go on to interpret the patient's behaviour and records.

Scheff argues that without this prior definition of the person as mentally ill, the patient's records, behaviour and responses to the psychiatrist's tests can be interpreted differently.

On the other side of the coin, interactionists are also concerned with the individual's conception of himself. This follows from the assumption that individuals have to interpret and give meaning to their own actions as well as make sense of those of others with whom they interact. How individuals act depends on their own self-image and this is constructed largely from their interpretation of how other people react to what they say and do. This has led to studies of the effects of labelling people as mentally ill and how these individuals see themselves. Conferring the label subsequently produces abnormal behaviour because of the way others act towards the person so labelled, which in turn produces actions by him which he recognises that others expect of him.

The ethnomethodological approach

The ethnomethodological approach assumes that the social world is constantly being created by members of society which for them is unproblematic because it is regarded as the result of society's members using their own common sense. Society is created by its members using their taken-for-granted knowledge about how the world works and how they can deal with it in acceptable ways. The concern of ethnomethodologists is to study and explain how it is that society's members actually accomplish the social world which they created through commonly accepted, albeit sophisticated methods. Of major importance is language: we accomplish social encounters largely through conversation. Individuals have learned methods for doing so and ethnomethodologists are interested in how they have achieved such methods.

Ethnomethodologists would be unlikely to study mental illness as such; they would be more likely to have as their concern the society-building methods people use which may have relevance to mental illness. The assumptions of ethnomethodology are used in a study of Alzheimer's disease as 'biographical work' (Gubrium and Lynott, 1985; Gubrium, 1986). The way that friends and relatives construct diverse individual biographies of Alzheimer's disease sufferers are described. In the analysis biography is treated as a practical activity of those friends and relatives and is not so much the presentation of the facts of the sufferer's life as it is the descriptive product of retrospective and prospective biographical activity. The ethnomethodological study, by examining these biographies, highlights the social processes which have been part of the production and reproduction of the individual biographies.

In this kind of analysis Alzheimer's disease is not the focus of analysis but a means to an end. It is used as a code for rendering meaningful, chronologically and substantively, the general, age-related problems of later life. By itself, the code tells us little about the meaningful articulation of the problems of later life; it informs us only of an end product, what

the troubles recognisably become. In social support groups, 'chapels' of
The Alzheimer's Disease and Related Disorders Association, Gubrium
and Lynott found that biographical work by the friends and relatives
of sufferers revealed the pervasively social character of the disease, the
diverse nature of their related experiences and how much it brings people
together who attempt to make sense of their experiences.

Understanding dementia

This description demonstrates the different approaches to the study of
dementia used by clinicians, psychologists and sociologists. Different disciplines approach the subject from different perspectives. As a result they
use different conceptual frameworks, carry out different kinds of studies
and use different methods to collect and analyse data, which provides the
basis of their theory. None of them are more correct than any other: they
simply represent different ways of studying the same phenomenon. Thus
different biological, clinical, psychological and sociological approaches
are complementary, each area fertilising the other. They each have a
different contribution to make in the understanding of dementia.

THEORY AND METHOD IN THE STUDY OF HUMAN AGEING

There is a close relationship between theory and method in any scientific
discipline. This is no less the case in the study of human ageing. Just as
biological, psychological and sociological perspectives provide different
views of ageing, make different theoretical assumptions and ask different questions, they also use different methods. Within psychology and
sociology different perspectives are often committed to using particular
research strategies to define, generate, collect and to interpret empirical
data. Thus 'methods and theory are inescapably connected' (Smith, 1975,
p. 27) irrespective of the degree to which that theory is made explicit.
Method means here not merely the practical considerations of which
data-collection techniques to use, but fundamental considerations such
as whether to study causes or functions, whether to describe phenomena
or explain them, or whether to determine the meaning of a phenomenon
or examine the relationship between various variables. There is not space
to outline here the variety of methods used in the study of ageing, but we
will focus on a major methodological decision which faces all students of
human ageing: whether to use a cross-sectional or longitudinal design.

Cross-sectional and longitudinal studies

A major research activity of the biological sciences has been the study
of declining physiological effectiveness during ageing. Senescence brings
about changes in the structure and function of many organs including the
brain and nervous system, the heart, lungs and circulation, bone, muscle

and skin. In psychology, attention has focused on changes in intelligence and personality, while sociology has been concerned with changes in the process of retirement, among others. In order to measure change, two approaches have been used.

In cross-sectional studies, measurements are made amongst cohorts of different age groups, or subjects are asked to recall retrospectively data from the past. If we wanted to measure changes in average muscle strength, for example, we might make measurements in 20-year-olds, 40-year-olds, 60-year-olds and 80-year-olds and show a progressive diminution of strength with age. However, a limitation of this method is the influence of secular changes. For example, we know that 20-year-olds are now taller, heavier and therefore perhaps stronger than 20-year-olds at the beginning of the century. Similarly, cross-sectional studies of intelligence cannot separate influences due to 'ageing' from those due to change in education and training. A cross-sectional study of retirement would also be unable to detect changes which were the cause rather than the consequence of retirement.

An alternative approach is to use a longitudinal study, in which the same individuals are assessed at intervals over time. Thus we can show that women do lose a little height as they age, due to shrinkage of the backbone, but not nearly as much as we might have predicted had we measured and compared 80- and 20-year-olds. However, longitudinal studies are difficult to carry out. By definition we would need a lifetime to follow people throughout their lives, so we can only follow people over a limited period of time. Longitudinal studies also suffer because the tools of research, especially of biomedical research, become outmoded over time. They suffer from the impact of important historical events, like wars, which may affect the behaviour of lots of people but which could not be described as ageing changes. Selective survival is also an important factor to consider in longitudinal studies. For example, if people scoring higher than average on IQ tests live longer this will give a faulty impression of the relationship between advanced age and intelligence. A combination of cross-sectional and longitudinal studies, referred to as a cross-sequential design, in which cohorts of different ages are simultaneously followed up over time, appears to give the best chance of sorting out the relative influence of social, historical and intrinsic factors.

In biology, longitudinal studies are more easily undertaken in short-lived laboratory animals such as rodents. For this reason as well as others including economy, availability and the possibility of restricting genetic and environmental sources of variation, much biological research on ageing has used animals or even cultures of cells or tissues. There is, of course, a danger in extrapolating findings from such experiments to humans. However, research in 'model' biological systems may elucidate the basic nature and mechanism of the ageing process, and give rise to hypotheses which may be tested in humans.

UNDERSTANDING HUMAN AGEING

In this chapter we have been concerned with delineating the various approaches taken by different disciplines to the study of human ageing. We have shown how these different approaches consider the subject of dementia, highlighting the complementary nature of the different scientific enterprises. The emphasis of this book is on social gerontology and in subsequent chapters a number of theories introduced here will be discussed further.

3

BIOLOGICAL AGEING

Roger Briggs

In the previous chapter, we discussed biological theories of ageing in the context of living organisms in general (including man) and within the framework of biological concepts of evolution and natural selection. We shall now turn to the effects of ageing on humans in particular.

AGEING AND THE POPULATION

In primitive societies, or non-industrialised societies even now, death-rates are high around the time of birth and in childhood, and subsequently the risk of death remains relatively constant throughout life. A *survival curve* for such a population is represented in Figure 3.1.

Such a survival curve is known as a 'wild-type' because it is found in natural animal populations as well as in human populations living under severe conditions (for example, Europe in the middle ages, Mexico in 1930, some African countries now). It can be seen that most of the population survive for less than half the maximum lifespan, so that *average* age of death might be 30 to 40 years in such conditions, though a few individuals may live to about 100 years of age. Characteristically, these populations would have a 'pyramidal' structure, with large numbers of children and young people but comparatively few old people – perhaps one or two per cent of the population being over 65. The major concern for 'public health' in such countries is the prevention of infant and child mortality.

Modern, industrialised societies (or animals protected in an artificial environment such as a laboratory) have largely removed the problems of infant and child mortality, causing a 'rectangular' survival curve as shown in Figure 3.2.

As the survival curve of a population becomes increasingly rectangular, average lifespan approaches maximum lifespan; it should be noted that maximum lifespan is presumed to remain more or less constant. Thus, in 1900, only about a quarter of the population survived their 65th year, whereas now over two-thirds do so. This dramatic change has come about very quickly, and the major challenge to public health in industrialised societies is how to cope with the problems associated with a high proportion (15 to 25 per cent) of people over 65 in the population,

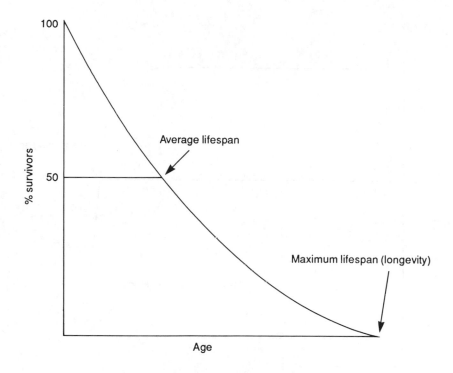

Figure 3.1 *Wild-type survival curve*

many of whom will be in their eighties and nineties (see Chapter 1).

It has optimistically been suggested, as medical and social interventions continue to promote a healthy middle age,

> that the average period of diminished physical vigour will decrease, that chronic disease will occupy a smaller proportion of the typical lifespan, and that the need for medical care in later life will decrease. (Fries, 1980, p. 130)

This view is appealing, particularly to health policy makers and fiscal planners, but it must be said that there is very little supporting evidence. In our present state of knowledge, it would be dangerous to ignore the potential for increasing levels of disability in our ageing population (Brody, 1985).

AGEING AND DISEASE

As discussed in Chapter 2, ageing is associated with a decline in physiological effectiveness which affects us all sooner or later and is an intrinsic part of growing old. Unlike the universal changes of senescence, *disease* is sporadic, a particular disease affecting only certain members of the population. However, many diseases are *age-related*. Thus strokes, which are uncommon before the age of 50, become increasingly more prevalent

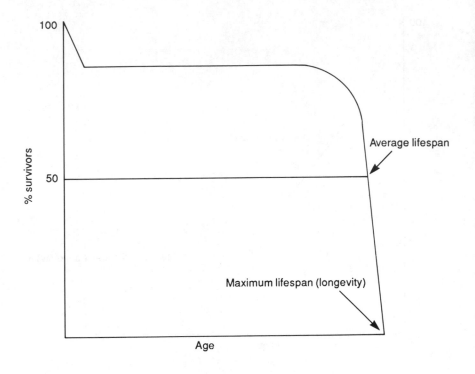

Figure 3.2   *Rectangular survival curve*

with age and are the third most common cause of death in Britain today. Another example of an interaction between ageing and *accident* is that of fractured hip, a rare injury in young people but one which affects one woman in eight by the age of 85. As people age, their bones become *thinner*, a senescent change which is more pronounced in women. A fall which might cause a younger person no serious injury may fracture the weakened hip of an old person.

Not only are old people at risk of particular age-related diseases, they may also suffer from a combination of several diseases and senescent changes. In addition to the multiple disabilities caused by the diseases themselves, complications may arise due to the complexity of drug treatment prescribed.

It is important to note that 'good health' is not synonymous with the absence of disease. Only 10 per cent of those over 75 years admit to no physical symptom; on average elderly people complain of over five medical problems each. The 'top ten' are shown in Table 3.1.

However, many such symptoms are well tolerated by the majority of elderly people, and do not interfere greatly with their lives. Thus, in a survey of 1406 over-65-year-olds interviewed in Manchester, Luker and Perkins (1987) found that 93 per cent believed their health to be

Table 3.1   *Proportion of people aged 75 or more suffering from various ailments: England 1977*

Arthritis, rheumatism	58%
Unsteady on feet	49%
Forgetfulness	44%
Poor eyesight	42%
Hard of hearing	36%
Backache	36%
Breathless after any effort	35%
Swelling of feet, legs	33%
Giddiness	31%
Indigestion, flatulence	29%

Source: Abrams (1978), Table 77, p. 55

'fair or good' and the number of those unable to perform a range of activities of daily living was relatively small. Whilst it is unjustified to 'see all older people as being frail, dependent and diseased' (Freer, 1988), it is also a mistake to see 'the elderly' as a homogenous group. It is true that most 'young elderly' are fit and active, but it has long been known that the prevalence of chronic illness and disability rises rapidly with age. Thus, defining disability as inability to exist at home without help and dependence as a further degree of impairment of self-care, the prevalence of disability increases from 12 per cent at age 65–69 to over 80 per cent above the age of 85; dependence is found in only 2 per cent below 85 years, but in 25 per cent of those older (Akhtar et al, 1973).

The remainder of this chapter describes ageing changes and diseases which commonly affect old people. However, it must be remembered that each old person is more than just a collection of isolated tissues or organs, and that the particular combination of problems or disabilities will vary from one individual to another. Finally, it should be borne in mind that diseases do not affect all old people, and that whilst ageing is universal it affects different people at different rates.

Hearing

Deafness is a common accompaniment of ageing, though not inevitable. The gradual deterioration in hearing ability associated with ageing is known as *presbyacusis*, and results from wear and tear of the cells in the inner ear which respond to sound waves. Prolonged exposure to excessive noise earlier in life, for example a noisy working environment, may predispose to hearing loss in later life. Perhaps one-third of the population over 65 years suffers from a hearing impairment (see Table 3.2) which can have unfavourable social consequences.

The hearing loss of presbyacusis is usually greater for high frequency sounds than those of low frequency. Normal conversation consists of sounds over a wide spectrum of frequencies: consonants are generally

Table 3.2   *Difficulty with hearing among elderly people*

Age:	65–69	70–74	75–79	80–84	85+	All 65+
	%	%	%	%	%	%
Wears an aid	4	8	10	14	22	8
Does not wear an aid, but has difficulty	20	22	28	31	34	24
Does not wear an aid, has no difficulty	76	70	63	56	44	68

Source: Office of Population Censuses and Surveys (1982), Table 10.11

of higher frequency than vowels. Thus, an old person has poor *speech discrimination* – he may know that someone is talking, but cannot discern what is said because some elements such as consonants are missing. Hearing loss is usually assessed clinically by means of an *audiogram*, in which the subject listens to pure tones, whose loudness can be varied, across a range of frequencies between 125 and 8000 Hertz. Normal speech generally ranges between 250 and 3000 Hertz. Poor speech discrimination is exacerbated by high levels of background noise, such as are often found in institutions, and where the deaf person cannot see the speaker (consonants are relatively easy to lip read).

In addition to poor speech discrimination, presbyacusis commonly causes *loudness recruitment*: this means that sounds become disproportionately louder to the sufferer as they increase in intensity. There may be only a small increase in intensity between a sound that is loud enough for the person to hear and one that causes discomfort or pain. Many old people who find a normal, quiet speaking voice inaudible find shouting intolerable, and for the same reason cannot wear a hearing aid with comfort. Presbyacusis also causes impaired *sound localization*, making it difficult to tell where a sound is coming from.

When an old person complains of deafness, the first step is to make sure that their ears are not stuffed with wax. The diagnosis of presbyacusis is established by an audiogram, and if hearing loss is significant a hearing aid may be helpful. Many old people find a hearing aid difficult to use, and they need adequate training and encouragement, preferably from an after care service run by a hearing therapist. Although deafness is common, it is often neglected and may be associated with significant psychiatric problems such as depressive illness (Gilhome-Herbst and Humphrey, 1980). (See Chapter 5.)

Vision

Young people are able to focus on objects at different distances from the eye because the lens is elastic and its shape can be changed by small muscles from which it is suspended. By the age of about 50, the lens invariably becomes less elastic and focusing becomes difficult: vision for

Table 3.3 *Difficulty with eyesight among elderly people*

Age:	65–69	70–74	75–79	80–84	85+	All 65+
	%	%	%	%	%	%
Wears glasses, still has difficulty	18	20	30	32	45	24
Wears glasses, then has no difficulty	78	77	68	65	51	73
Does not wear glasses	4	3	3	4	4	3

Source: Office of Population Censuses and Surveys (1982), Table 10.9

distant objects usually remains intact, but close vision (such as reading) becomes blurred. This is a usual feature of ageing known as *presbyopia*, and the majority of the population eventually requires glasses. Table 3.3 shows the prevelance of vision impairment among elderly people. Many old people just use spectacles for close vision; an alternative is bifocal lenses, in which the upper part of the spectacles is designed for distance vision and the lower part for close vision, but bifocals may cause problems of their own due to the borderline between the two lenses.

The reason that the lens in the eye becomes less elastic with age is because it is constantly growing by the addition of new layers – rather like an onion. In some old people the centre of the lens is compressed, becomes hard and opaque: this opacity is known as a *cataract*. Initially the cataract may disperse light entering the eye so that vision is affected in bright light, which is why some old people need eyeshades or peaked caps. As the cataract enlarges and 'ripens', vision becomes obscured and only surgical removal can restore vision. After removal of the cataract, an artificial lens must be implanted in the eye or the patient must wear special glasses or a contact lens. Old people with diabetes are much more likely to be affected by cataract than their peers.

Light entering the eye is focused by the lens on specialised nerve cells in the retina. The eyeball between the lens and the retina is filled with fluid, which may develop small opacities known as 'floaters' since they appear to drift across the field of vision. Floaters are usually harmless, though occasionally they herald the sudden loss of vision due to retinal detachment. Raised pressure of the fluid in the eyeball is known as *glaucoma*, and becomes more common with age. Sometimes glaucoma can come on acutely, with pain and impaired vision in the eye, but more commonly the condition is chronic with insidious loss of peripheral vision: only at a late stage is central vision affected. The most important part of our visual field is the central part, since objects we see when looking straight ahead are focused on a specialised part of the retina, the 'macula'. The most common cause of intractable blindness in elderly people is *senile macular degeneration*, in which the specialised nerve cells deteriorate. Unfortunately, the scope for treatment is very limited except in the earliest stages, though magnifying aids are helpful.

Skin, muscle and bone

The most obvious change in skin is the familiar wrinkling. This is due to degeneration of the elastic tissues in the skin, and is more severe in people who have had extensive exposure to sunlight. With ageing, skin tends to lose its pigment, as does the hair. Irregular purple patches may develop, particularly on the backs of the hands, which occur spontaneously though the old person may often attribute them to 'bruising'. Sweat glands work less efficiently with ageing and the skin surface is rougher and drier: some old people complain of intolerable itching (*pruritus*).

Increasing age is also accompanied by a decline in muscle power. Part of this decline is due to an age-related loss of nerve fibres which supply muscles, leading to degeneration of the muscle cells. However, reduced physical activity also plays a part, particularly in those retiring from active work, and there is much current interest in the role of exercise in maintaining fitness in old people.

Bones become 'thinner' from middle age onwards, this bone loss being more marked in women after the menopause. Extreme thinning of the bones is known as *osteoporosis*, and makes fractures more likely after a fall (particularly broken wrists and hips), or bones in the spine may even collapse spontaneously causing episodes of severe back pain. Treatment of osteoporosis is not very satisfactory; continued physical activity and an adequate diet including a good supply of calcium may help to minimise bone loss. Fracture of the hip is now a very common injury among elderly people and is a terminal event in a significant number.

Arthritis affects many old people. The commonest form, *osteoarthritis*, is mainly due to wear-and-tear on large, weight-bearing joints such as the spine, hips and knees. *Rheumatoid* arthritis may develop for the first time in old people and usually affects smaller joints such as the hands, wrists and ankles. The mainstay of treatment for the pain and stiffness of arthritis is with drugs, but artificial joints can be implanted surgically if symptoms are severe.

Nutrition and digestion

Malnutrition affects a surprisingly small proportion of the elderly population – obesity due to overeating is a much more common problem. When malnutrition does arise, it is often in the context of significant mental impairment or physical illness rather than for purely 'social' reasons, though isolation and poverty play their part. Most old people have an adequate intake of food in terms of protein, carbohydrate and fat to service their reduced energy requirements. However, intakes of vitamins (such as Vitamin C) or 'trace' elements (such as zinc) are sometimes borderline or inadequate, particularly among frail elderly people living alone (Panel on Nutrition of the Elderly, 1972).

Old people often have poor teeth, since regular dental treatment is a comparatively recent development. Most British people aged 65 or more have no teeth of their own, and wear dentures which may be ill-fitting. Taste sensation and salivary flow tend to deteriorate with ageing, and all these oral problems may add to loss of enjoyment of eating in addition to any limitations of the 'social' quality of meals.

In general, the absorption of food from the intestine is not significantly affected by ageing. A few old people lose the cells in the stomach which are responsible for the absorption of Vitamin B_{12}; this condition causes *pernicious anaemia*, which responds readily to regular injections of the vitamin. Ulcers in the stomach or duodenum, or lesions such as cancer of the lower bowel, may cause continued blood loss from the intestinal tract (known as occult bleeding since the amount passed in the stools is too little to be noticed by the patient). Stomach ulcers may cause pain, and bowel cancer may lead to a change in bowel habit, but often there are no specific abdominal symptoms and the only clue to intestinal disease is the finding of *iron-deficiency anaemia*. Identification of the various types of anaemia is by means of a blood test, which is often done for rather non-specific reasons such as a patient being tired or breathless, looking pale or losing weight. Although change in bowel habit may be a worrying symptom, *constipation* is often due to a general reduction in activity and mobility, coupled with a decreased dietary intake of roughage.

Kidneys and bladder

The function of the kidneys is to excrete waste products and excessive fluid in the urine. From the age of about 30 years, kidney function deteriorates so that by the age of 60–70 it is about half that found in young adults. Under normal circumstances this decline in kidney function does not cause any problems since there is a considerable 'reserve', but if an old person is stressed by illness or given drugs which are excreted by the kidney then the impaired, ageing kidney may be unable to cope.

Urine excreted by the kidney is held in the bladder until it is voided through the urethra. In women, the urethra is comparatively short and continence is partly maintained by muscles of the pelvic floor. These muscles tend to weaken after the menopause, particularly if there has been a history of difficult childbirth, so that the walls of the vagina sometimes *prolapse* and distort the urethra. Prolapse may cause *stress incontinence* in women with leakage of small amounts of urine when straining or coughing; treatment is aimed at supporting the walls of the vagina, either mechanically with an internal ring pessary or by surgery. In men, the urethra is surrounded by the prostate gland, which may become enlarged either by benign growth or due to cancer. An enlarged prostate causes difficulty in starting to pass urine with a poor stream of urine flow.

In both sexes, continence is maintained by the nervous system, which prevents contraction of the bladder muscle until it is desired to pass urine. These nervous pathways may be damaged by brain disease such as stroke or senile dementia, so that the patients are unable to control bladder function. Initially, such incontinence is often worse at night but ultimately patients may be quite unaware of their bladder, not even realising when they have been incontinent. Incontinence is a common and distressing condition, probably affecting some two million people in the United Kingdom to a greater or lesser extent. Patients often do not report incontinence to their general practitioner or nursing staff, presumably out of embarrassment. There are now several helpful books on the subject, including short, simple texts suitable for patients themselves such as that by Feneley and Blannin (1984).

Heart, lungs and circulation

The heart pumps blood through the lungs, where oxygen is taken up and carbon dioxide released, then around the body via the arteries before blood returns to the heart through veins. Ageing is accompanied by a variety of changes affecting all these elements of the circulation. Heart muscle degenerates with age, and the heart valves become less pliable. In some old people, the heart rhythm becomes abnormal, the heartbeat becoming too fast and irregular (in which case digitalis treatment may be needed) or too slow (in which case an artificial pacemaker may be required). For many old people, these changes in the heart do not cause any problem at rest, but limit the amount by which the heart can respond to exercise. Some elderly patients develop *heart failure*, when blood is not pumped effectively away from the heart so that blood returning from the venous system and lungs becomes dammed back. The ensuing lung congestion causes breathlessness, and impaired venous return leads to ankle swelling. Treatment is with diuretics ('water tablets'), which remove excessive fluid from the circulation to relieve congestion.

Ageing leads to reduced efficiency of the lungs, and weakness of the chest muscles also contributes to a loss of maximal breathing capacity on exercise. However, a normal old person should be able to walk steadily, even if they are unable to run. More severe breathlessness implies heart disease, or lung disease such as chronic bronchitis, rather than ageing alone. It is becoming increasingly apparent that old people can improve their ability to respond to physical stress by 'training', if not so dramatically as the young, and more emphasis is now being placed on the role of exercise in the maintenance of fitness among elderly people.

In industrialised societies, people's arteries tend to become 'furred up' over the years, a process known as *atherosclerosis*. Arterial disease is hastened by a number of factors, such as high blood pressure, excessive fat and salt intake, smoking and diabetes. Arteries may become so narrowed that blood flow to various organs is diminished, or an artery may even become completely blocked. Although the heart is full of blood, the muscle of the heart wall is so thick and works so hard that it needs a rich supply of blood from its own arteries, the coronary arteries. When blood flow to the heart muscle is limited, episodic chest pain may develop on exercise – *angina*. If a coronary artery becomes completely blocked (*coronary thrombosis*) an area of heart muscle may become irreversibly damaged, an event known as a *heart attack or myocardial infarction* which is a major cause of death in the western world. Atherosclerosis affects other arteries in addition to those supplying the heart; poor blood supply to the legs can result in pain on exercise, ulcers or even amputation, and blockage of arteries in the brain leads to stroke.

Hormones

In a large organism composed of many cells, tissues and organs, it is necessary for these different elements to 'communicate' with each other in order to coordinate the body's response to external stimuli and to maintain a stable internal environment. The latter function, maintenance of the internal environment, is crucial to the survival of complex organisms and is known as *homeostasis*. Examples of homeostatic mechanisms are the increase in heart rate in response to the increased oxygen demand of exercise, sweating in response to heat, or the regulation of the amounts of salt and water in the circulation. Many of the adverse consequences of ageing can be seen in terms of the breakdown of homeostasis, such as the development of *hypothermia* when an old person is unable to respond effectively to cold. 'Fast' signals from one part of the body to another are carried electrically by nerve cells; slower signals can be achieved by glands which liberate chemical messengers, known as *hormones*, carried to their target organ or tissue in the bloodstream. Thus, in response to the increase level of sugar in the blood following a meal, a normal person secretes the hormone insulin from the pancreas gland, causing the sugar to be burnt up for energy production or stored. Defective production of insulin causes the condition known as *diabetes*, in which sugar cannot be utilised properly by the body and may cause damage to the eyes, kidneys and arteries. Diagnosis is made by detecting excessive amounts of sugar in the blood or urine, and treatment comprises restriction of sugar intake, tablets which help the body to deal with the excess sugar in the blood, or if necessary (mainly in younger patients) giving additional insulin by injection. Diabetes is common, affecting one or two per cent of the population over 65 years.

The *thyroid* gland, which is situated in the neck, may also become diseased in elderly people. Thyroid disease is often an example of *auto-immune* disease, in which the body attacks its own tissues as if they were foreign invaders such as bacteria. (Another example of an autoimmune disease mentioned previously is pernicious anaemia, in which the body attacks some of its own stomach cells. At one time, an 'autoimmune theory of ageing' was fashionable by which senescent changes were thought to be due to the body turning its defence mechanisms upon itself, but this theory has not stood the test of time.) Thyroid disease can manifest as an overactive gland, hyperthyroidism or *thyrotoxicosis*, when the patient tends to be irritable, losing weight, sweating and tremulous, or an underactive gland, hypothyroidism or *myxoedema*, causing a slow, lethargic patient tending to gain weight and with a dry coarse skin and croaky voice. Although these clinical pictures seem very distinctive in theory, in practice thyroid disease may be difficult to diagnose in elderly people. Both an underactive and an overactive gland may cause apathy and depressive symptoms. Thyroid disease is best detected by blood tests measuring the amount of circulating thyroid hormone; these tests are very worthwhile for sick elderly people, since both thyrotoxicosis and myxoedema are easy to treat.

In women, after the *menopause* the female hormone oestrogen is deficient. Apart from cessation of menstruation, other symptoms such as depression, anxiety and headache may have a biological basis in women between approximately 40 and 55 years. The soft tissues of the vulva and vagina lose substance, and reduced vaginal lubrication may make sexual intercourse difficult. Men may also experience a 'climacteric' period, based on a decline in the secretion of the male hormone testosterone, some 10 to 15 years later. Erections are less frequent and less well maintained, and the force of ejaculation is diminished. In both men and women, therefore, there are physiological changes in the secretion of sex hormones with ageing which may reduce the potential for intercourse and orgasm irrespective of any additional problems posed by disease. Many sexual difficulties in later life, however, are caused by psychological problems or restricted opportunity and reinforce the need for caring, loving relationships unhindered by ignorance, insensitive relatives or uninformed professionals (Weg, 1983b).

Brain and nervous system

The nervous system consists essentially of two parts, a 'peripheral nervous system' of nerves travelling to the limbs and organs, and a 'central nervous system' in the brain and spinal cord. Nerve cells are 'fixed' in that they do not undergo cell division once they have reached maturity and have to carry out their function for the remainder of the person's life. It is not surprising that the function of nerve cells deteriorates over lifespan; a nerve supplying a muscle in the foot is nearly a yard long, originating near the base of the spine. Nerve cells cannot get rid of some of their waste products, and with age accumulate substances such as the pigment *lipofuscin*. It has been proposed that some features of ageing are due to 'waste-product accumulation', though many believe that these substances do no harm to cells in themselves but simply bear witness to the passage of the years. Nerves transmit messages by a process similar to electrical conduction throughout most of their length, except where they meet the next nerve cell with which they communicate: here they release a chemical across a tiny gap (the 'synapse'), which interacts with the next nerve cell. Chemical transmission across the synapse is similar to the action of hormones, except that the whole process of nerve signalling is much quicker. With ageing, the transmission of nerve signals to muscles or the return of messages conveying touch, pain or temperature, slows down due to deterioration of the peripheral nervous system.

With regard to the central nervous system, function also tends to deteriorate with ageing in some areas of the brain such as those concerned with learning and memory. The psychological effects of 'normal' ageing will be considered in more detail in Chapter 4, and the remainder of this section is devoted to the effects of age-related disease on the brain.

The brain is organised such that particular brain regions subserve particular functions. Thus, a lesion affecting a discrete brain region will cause a specific pattern of disability. Atherosclerosis may cause impairment of the blood supply to a part of the brain, causing a sudden loss of function known as a *stroke* either because the artery supplying that part of the brain becomes blocked or because it bleeds into the brain substance. Usually, a stroke affecting the right side of the brain causes weakness and sensory disturbance on the left side of the body and a stroke in the left side ('dominant hemisphere') of the brain causes weakness in the right arm and leg which is often associated with difficulty in speaking. Stroke is common, affecting one or two people in every thousand each year and being the third commonest cause of death in Britain; the incidence of stroke rises dramatically with age, most of those affected being over 60. Of those who survive their first stroke, roughly one-half regain functional independence, a quarter need some help with activities of daily living, and a quarter are dependent on help from a carer.

Some diseases affect areas of the brain not according to the pattern of blood supply but according to the function of that brain region or the chemical transmitter substance. The classical example is *Parkinson's disease*, affecting those nerve cells which release the transmitter dopamine. The reasons for this selective degeneration are unknown. *Senile dementia* affects perhaps two or three per cent of those aged over 65 years, rising to 20 per cent of those aged over 80. About one in five cases of senile dementia are due to diffuse atherosclerosis affecting the blood supply to the brain; the majority of cases of senile dementia are due to a degenerative condition known as Alzheimer's disease (see Chapter 2). The underlying cause of Alzheimer's disease is unknown, though there is a relatively selective degeneration of nerve cells in a brain region known as the hippocampus which is concerned with learning and memory. The clinical presentation of senile dementia is initially with gradual loss of memory for events over recent months or years, with increasing behavioural disturbance including insomnia, wandering and sometimes aggression, and finally the patient is virtually mute, incontinent and bedridden. The course of the disease is relentlessly downhill over five to ten years before death, progression being gradual in the case of Alzheimer's disease and by a series of stepwise deteriorations in the case of dementia due to a series of small strokes – 'multi-infarct dementia'. Some patients show combined features of degenerative (Alzheimer) dementia and atherosclerotic (multi-infarct) dementia.

The gradual onset of dementia over months or years must be distinguished from the sudden onset of an *acute confusional state*. The delirium of an acute confusional state supervenes over hours or days and the picture is often of a previously competent old person who rapidly becomes totally disorientated with a fluctuating level of arousal – one moment lying quiet, the next shouting and fighting. Acute confusional states are usually due to the effect of intercurrent illness such as infection or heart disease tipping the balance for an ageing brain working near the margin of its reserve. The investigation and treatment of an acute confusional state is a medical problem of some urgency, the outlook depending on the underlying illness (Briggs, 1985).

Depressive illness is the commonest mental disorder of old age, affecting some 10 to 15 per cent of people over 65 years at any one time. There is scope for argument as to how much depressive symptoms in late life are a response to life-events and losses such as bereavement, and how much 'depression' is an illness with a biological basis (Jacoby, 1981) (see also Chapter 5). Having said this, although minor depressive symptoms may be a common feature of old age, so too are 'psychotic' depressive illnesses with severe symptoms of withdrawal or delusions and an appreciable incidence of suicide. Such symptoms cause considerable distress which may be alleviated by treatment with drugs (or, in severe cases, electroconvulsive therapy), but not all cases make a good initial response and there is a significant relapse rate (Murphy, 1983). A full discussion of psychiatric illness among elderly people is beyond the scope of this chapter, but specialised psychogeriatric services have become increasingly important in Britain in the management of this large burden of misery.

CONCLUSION

This chapter has reviewed, very briefly, the effects of ageing and disease on the human body and its component parts. Most old people do not present with their symptoms falling neatly into a particular 'system': an elderly woman with 'falls' may have a combination of poor eyesight, arthritis and Parkinson's disease, whilst an old man with 'confusion and incontinence' may be suffering from a urinary tract infection, heart failure and senile dementia. Just as the 'medical' components of an old person's problems may be a complex mix of ageing and disease affecting bodily structure and function, so too will the psychological and social aspects of their situation require detailed evaluation. This summary can only give a superficial overview of the medical input to a multidisciplinary team. The rehabilitation of the sick old person requires the expert help of practitioners from many disciplines, each of whose skills and views on management are relevant and worthy of consideration.

Many of the conditions discussed above are due to the 'wearing out' of tissues and cells with ageing. However, as we saw in Chapter 2 some cells continue to reproduce by division throughout life, and this process of cell division is open to error. When 'faulty copies' of cells replicate without constraint, a malignant tumour may grow and possibly spread to sites remote from its origin. Several forms of malignant growth (*cancer*) are increasingly common with age such as cancer of the bowel, lung and certain forms of leukaemia, cancer of the breast in women and of the prostate in men.

Finally, although relatively minor consequences of ageing are virtually inescapable, such as impairment of vision and hearing, greying of the hair and wrinkling of the skin, not all is gloom. Although 20 per cent of the population over 80 suffer from mental impairment, this means that 80 per cent do not. Whilst there is no certain way of preventing the deleterious effects of ageing, there is much to be said for a good mixed diet and plenty of exercise.

FURTHER READING

Brocklehurst, J.C. (ed.) (1985) *Textbook of Geriatric Medicine and Gerontology, 3rd Edition.* Churchill Livingstone, Edinburgh, London, Melbourne and New York.

Caird, F.I., Kennedy, R.D. and Williams, B.O. (1983) *Practical Rehabilitation of the Elderly.* Pitman, London.

Hall, M.R.P., MacLennan, W.J. and Lye, M.D.W. (1986) *Medical Care of the Elderly, 2nd Edition.* Wiley, Chichester.

Pathy, M.S.J. (ed.) (1985) *Principles and Practice of Geriatric Medicine.* Wiley, Chichester.

Taylor, R.C. and Buckley, E.G. (eds) (1987) Preventive care of the elderly: a review of current developments. Occasional paper No.35, Royal College of General Practitioners, London.

Wheatley, D. (ed.) (1982) *Psychopharmacology of Old Age.* Oxford University Press, Oxford.

4

PSYCHOLOGICAL AGEING

Peter Coleman

In Chapter 2 we have described the short but complex history of psychology as a systematic study of individual human behaviour and its contribution to the study of human ageing. This chapter focuses on the major findings from the psychology of human ageing: intelligence and ability, personality change and life-span perspective.

In the area of intelligence and ability a considerable amount of research has been carried out on age differences in performance. However, this approach has been criticised for paying almost exclusive attention to the general intellectual abilities that decline with age and neglecting those special expertises that characterise the individual person which do not. The second area of investigation is that of personality change. The research work here is more slender by comparison and has produced less in the way of substantive results in regard to generalisable changes with age. Nevertheless, general developmental theories of ageing are still being proposed and deserve serious consideration for the insights that they offer.

Much is currently expected of studies which seek to understand the behaviour of older people within the context of a life-span perspective, which is the third area of investigation considered. This approach takes into account formative life experiences and differences in social circumstances in explaining changes in behaviour with age. As age by itself does not appear to be a crucial marker of psychological change whether in intellectual functioning or personality, research ceases to be aimed at establishing general age changes and becomes more the creation of a 'differential gerontology' (Thomae, 1976), defining different patterns of ageing and the factors associated with them.

AGEING AND ABILITY

Studies of intelligence in later life

Within the study of the psychology of ageing, studies on intelligence and cognitive performance have predominated. In part this is because these are relatively easy topics to study in the laboratory. However, intelligence – which can be defined as a general ability to think, solve problems and learn new tasks – is a complex phenomenon that cannot only be studied in laboratory conditions. We also need to examine the exercise of intelligence in real life. Therefore, although there is much published research on the subject of intelligence and ageing, it needs to be examined critically and set in context.

Improvement and decline in ageing

The influence of a crude 'rise and fall' model of the life course has also biased the study of intelligence to look for negative rather than positive changes in later life. But psychological ageing is not necessarily negative. It is important to avoid the error of identifying it with biological ageing which by definition implies decline and deterioration. This inevitably affects psychological ageing, and much of the research on the psychology of mental ability has focused justifiably on such deleterious changes in function. But age also carries with it the benefits of additional experience. Wisdom has been seen as a characteristic of old age in most cultures. In many situations experience enables older people to make better judgements about life decisions than younger people.

In really advanced age the negative effects of biological ageing upon psychological functioning may be more evident than the benefits of experience, but for the greater part of the life course the gains are likely to be as evident as the losses. This of course will depend very much on which activities one considers. Athletic performance declines early on in adult life after the optimal levels of biological functioning are passed, but political activity often reaches its peak in later life. The prospects of further improvement are cut short by biological decline. As George Bernard Shaw lamented, 'if only we were allowed to live longer to properly benefit from life's experience. Youth is wasted on the young!'

Conceptualisations of intelligence reflect this dual aspect of human development (Cattell, 1971; Dittmann-Kohli and Baltes, 1990). The basic mechanisms of intelligence are developed in childhood and thereafter remain well set until subjected to attack with biological decline in later life. But more relevant to behaviour in adulthood are the particular kinds of intelligence or repertoires of ability that the individual develops. Such abilities are essentially pragmatic, related to the way an individual copes with his own life situation, and can only be appropriately studied in a naturalistic way in the settings in which they occur. A number of psychologists have recently begun to stress the importance of observations on human performance in natural contexts (see for example Neisser, 1982) but most of the literature on ageing and performance is based on laboratory experiments and thus neglects this broader perspective on human abilities. Restricted focus on the decline of the basic mechanisms in advanced old age provides a very incomplete and misleading view of the relationship between age and mental ability.

It is important to stress this point at the outset of a review of the literature on intelligence and ageing, as two different types of comparison are often confounded. The first is the comparison between 'younger' and 'older' adults and the second that between adults and very old people. Studies of the former kind may vary very much in the age groups they consider – 20-year-olds with 40-year-olds, for example, or 40-year-olds with 60-year-olds. It is important to pay attention to the crucial detail of who is being compared with whom. By and large 'older' people come out well from these comparisons. But studies of the second kind choose to focus on very old people, usually those over the age of 70 and often over the age of 80, whom they compare with 'younger' people. This 'elderly' group is the one in the age spectrum most likely to reveal defects in cognitive functioning when considered collectively (although not necessarily individually).

The influence of disease and biological ageing upon mental functioning in later life

Effects of disease

In the last 30 years a clearer picture has emerged of the destructive factors acting upon older people's mental abilities. The most evident of these are the diseases that are especially prevalent in later life.

Diseases of the brain account for most cases of intellectual decline. It is now generally accepted that the mental deterioration of dementia, including memory failing and clouding of understanding, is associated with brain disease and is not typical of the fate of most old people. As a result the 'senility' stereotype of old age has begun to disappear and those afflicted with dementing illnesses treated with more understanding. However, the more general relationship between health and mental functioning in later life is less widely understood (Coleman, 1983). For example, many studies of cognitive functioning in older people still neglect adequate control of the health status of their subjects and therefore are less likely to accurately estimate the influence of factors other than disease.

This neglect is the more surprising when one considers that it is already more than 25 years since a study by the National Institute of Mental Health in America (Birren et al, 1963) showed that the presence of even a mild degree of chronic disease has a noticeable effect on a wide variety of mental functions in old age. Negative associations between mental ability and pathology indicators were evident in people who had been selected for their ostensible good health. Subsequent studies have repeated these findings for particular bodily systems such as the cardiovascular system and for sensory deficits such as hearing loss (see Woods and Britton, 1985). Studies that neglect the health status of their subjects thus tend to overestimate the influence of chronological age on cognitive functioning.

Effects which appear age-related may in reality be health-related.

Essentially the same point can be made in regard to the phenomenon of 'terminal decline', in which intellectual performance deteriorates in the period before death. This may not necessarily indicate that death is imminent but that the person is seriously ill. As Siegler concludes in her review of the subject: 'any large change in the cognitive capacity of an older person should be treated with suspicion – it may be a terminal sign, or it may indicate a potentially treatable illness' (Siegler, 1980).

Effects of biological ageing
Nevertheless some changes in cognitive performance with age do appear to be independent of physical pathology. There have been studies which have attempted to control for health status and still found some age-related differences in performance. For example, in a large multidisciplinary Dutch study on people between the ages of 65 and 90, measures of perceptual problem-solving ability were found to be related independently to age as well as to a number of health indices (including sensory functioning, lung capacity, coordination and functioning of joints) and to education and past occupation (Coleman, 1983). Although one can often question whether the health indicators in particular studies have been sensitive enough, it does seem possible to make a distinction between those cognitive changes due to health and those due to age. Health-related changes seem to be much more global, affecting performance on all types of tests, whereas age-related changes generally seem more limited to non-verbal performance tasks and especially those requiring to be performed at speed.

The distinction between intellectual abilities to do with words and language (verbal skills) and those concerned with visual and spatial aptitude (non-verbal or performance skills) is reflected in the design of intelligence (IQ) tests. People can perform quite differently on the corresponding parts of such tests. The differential response to age in fact is one of the most striking demonstrations of the value of the distinction. Its discovery led Wechsler, who devised one of the original large tests of intelligence, to formulate the terms 'hold' and 'don't hold' tests (Wechsler, 1944). Many subsequent studies have confirmed his observation that vocabulary test scores and memory for words show very little change with age, whereas certain performance skills like copying symbols or completing visual puzzles show a small but significant decline in people over the age of 40 (see for example Hooper et al, 1984).

However, it now appears that the expression 'verbal' vs 'non-verbal' misses the essence of the distinction. More to the point is the distinction made by the American theorist Raymond Cattell between 'fluid' and 'crystallised' aspects of intelligence (Cattell, 1971). Fluid ability involves the immediate adaptive ability of the individual to perceive relationships between objects and events, to reason and to abstract. Crystallised ability on the other hand reflects the aggregated experience of the individual, the acquired familiarity with materials and relationships. Whereas fluid abilities are adversely affected by the biological ageing of the individual, crystallised abilities appear to remain more stable and may even continue to develop. This view explains the findings from some studies where certain 'verbal' tests, for example involving reasoning, show decline with age whereas tests of vocabulary do not (Savage et al, 1973; Hooper et al, 1984).

It is important to bear in mind that these effects are most noticeable in advanced old age. A number of studies have shown only minimal average changes in general intelligence up to the age of 70 (Eisdorfer and Wilkie, 1973; Schaie and Strother, 1968). A major study using the type of cross-sequential design referred to in Chapter 2, in which cohorts of different ages are followed up over time, was carried out by Schaie and his colleagues in the United States. They began with a first study of this type in 1956, and repeated observations on the same people where possible in 1963 and 1970, as well as beginning second and third studies respectively at the same times. Besides demonstrating the stability of performance up to the age of 60 or even 70, their most notable finding is the large size of cohort effects. Different generations can perform quite differently at equivalent ages (Schaie and Labouvie-Vief, 1974).

Moreover, even beyond the age of 70 decline may not be inevitable. From both American and British studies it appears that a small but significant proportion of people growing old, maybe as many as 10 per cent, do not show any deteriorating change at all, except perhaps in extreme old age. This was an observation from the major longitudinal study carried out over 20 years at Duke University in the United States (Siegler and Botwinick, 1979). A large study of elderly people in Britain also identified a group of 'supernormals' who were noticeably free from physical and mental health problems, adjustment and social difficulties, and who also obtained higher IQ scores than their peers and indicated much less intellectual deterioration, as measured by the discrepancy between verbal IQ (more likely to be stable with age) and non-verbal IQ (less likely to be stable with age) (Savage et al, 1973). These kinds of people are currently the subject of investigation to find out what keeps them functioning so well.

A persistent problem in making further advances in this area is the lack of general models, beyond the fluid/crystallised distinction, of cognitive processes against which one could explain what is or is not changing with age. At this stage we can do little more than postulate associations between the slowing down that we observe in older people's reactions and the comparable age-related changes in measures of electrical activity (EEG frequency) of the brain. Both may reflect an adaptation to decreased efficiency of the brain with age. Brain cells, unlike most other cells in the body, but like the cells in some organs such as the liver and kidney, do not regenerate. It is not surprising that decline occurs as some cells die and are not renewed. It should be noted that the brain changes associated with dementia are generally considered to be of a wholly different order to that of normal ageing. However, even this point is controversial as critics have pointed to the relatively poor association between observable brain pathology (on post-mortem investigations and on brain-scan measures) and recorded mental deterioration (Kitwood, 1988).

Experimental studies
It may be that the fundamental advance required in formulating a model of the basic mechanisms of cognitive processes, which also allows for changes with age, can only be made by detailed experimental studies on cognitive processes in action. British as well as American psychologists have made a notable contribution to analysing one of the basic features assumed to underly cognitive decline with age, namely speed of information processing, firstly through the pioneering work of Miles (1931) and Welford (1958), and more recently through the work of Rabbitt (1980). Much of this research has focused on analysis of the individual's speed of response to a signal, for example pressing a button when a light appears, at various levels of complexity, both regarding the possible signals and alternative responses required.

These studies themselves have obvious practical importance. Many of the tasks analysed are similar to those required of older workers on production lines. The early studies showed that having controlled for age changes in sensory acuity and speed of limb movement, increased delay with age in reaction time must be due to slowing in the central processing mechanism. Some experimenters quantify the decrement in response as some 20 per cent between the ages of 20 and 60. In older individuals a more severe decrement may exist. Physical health status is again an important explanatory factor. Raised blood pressure, cerebrovascular and cardiovascular disorders and low levels of activity have all been related to slower reaction time (Birren et al, 1979).

More recent work has tried to find more ecologically 'natural' tasks on which to analyse differences in performance with age. It is recognised that older people may well use different strategies in tackling a task compared with younger people. For example, they may give greater relative importance to accuracy than speed, thus artificially raising their reaction times. Older people also seem less able to maintain readiness during the preparatory interval, between the warning signal and the stimulus, and if a fast rate of responding is required may be impaired because they are still involved in monitoring the previous response. With suitable encouragement and preparation their performance can be speeded up (Gottsdanker, 1982). What is required is more descriptive analysis of the way people actually do cope with growing failures in their own efficiency by devising ways of compensating for them (Rabbitt, 1982b). Such successful techniques could then be applied more generally.

What does disturb older people in particular is when other information

·competes for their attention (Talland, 1965). In tasks in which they have to divide their attention (try to do two things at once) decline with age is very marked and is already evident in those over 30. Experiments carried out by Rabbitt (1985) lead him to conclude that older people find it difficult to ignore irrelevant information. This again is a finding with practical implications. Older people may be at a particular disadvantage in group conversation. It has even been suggested that the elderly car driver may be adversely affected by roadside advertising!

Learning and memory ability

Many older persons claim to be functioning to their own satisfaction, from a cognitive perspective (Pratt and Wood, 1984). However, the deterioration that they themselves seem to notice and complain about more than anything else is memory. Because of the association with early symptoms of dementia this is often a cause for worry. However, the memory in question is usually memory of a particular kind, namely the ability to remember bare data like names and numbers. When it comes to remembering factual information like what they have read or seen on TV or heard other people saying, older people's memories are usually no worse at all (Cohen and Faulkner, 1984). We need to be much more precise about the nature and extent of the greater difficulties older people have than younger people in memory ability.

Deficits with age

A more exact analysis of the increased problems older people incur is very much dependent on our general understanding of the processes underlying memory. It is important to stress at the outset that what is being considered is a relatively small increase in limitations. To be human is to be limited in one's capacity.

This is well illustrated by experiments of 'immediate memory', the memory mechanism which registers incoming information and keeps it for a few seconds while waiting for action, for example holding a telephone number in one's head while dialling. This kind of memory is limited in duration. To remember the number accurately beyond a few seconds it would be necessary to repeat it constantly to oneself or write it down or learn it (ie consign it to one's memory store proper). Immediate memory is strictly limited also in the amount of information it can hold. Seven or eight items seem to be the limit for most people. There are strategies for holding more in one's head but this involves 'chunking' information into larger units. Older people are little different in this regard, right up to the age of 60. Even in their sixties and seventies people can still remember five or six items, so that the decline in later life is quite small (Craik, 1977).

Studies on longer-term memory in which, for example, people are asked to recall as many as possible words out of a list they have been given a few minutes earlier, show up clearer differences between older and younger people (Botwinick, 1984). Older people typically recall fewer, but appear less deficient when it comes to recognising the material with which they have been presented (eg Perlmutter and Mitchell, 1982). This suggests that the age difference is not so much in establishing memories in the first place but in 'retrieving' information from 'store'. Other studies suggest that the problem lies in the way memories are organised. Older people appear not to organise material that they are required to remember as well as younger people, for example, by grouping them into categories and so on. Techniques of presentation which encourage them to use such strategies appear to be beneficial (Twining, 1988).

More recent thinking has moved away from the idea of conceptualising memory deficits as reflecting an acquisition deficit or a storage deficit or a retrieval deficit. A simple hypothesis which underlies much contemporary research is that, as people grow older, they suffer a general decline in information-processing resources which reduces their accuracy at both recognition and recall (Craik and McDowd, 1987). The 'strength' of a memory is seen to depend on the strength of the processing carried out on it. Shallow encoding would be in terms of the item's physical characteristics; deep levels relate to the item's meaning. Elderly people seem to encode material more generally, and take in less of the specific, unique features of the item or its context (Rabinowitz and Ackerman, 1982). This deficit is reflected both in acquisition, in what people take in of the item in the first place, and in retrieval, since retrieval cues are more limited. Again, it needs to be stressed that there are large individual differences in this respect among the elderly population, some showing performance on recognition tasks and active encoding strategies comparable to younger adults (Bowles and Poon, 1982; Zacks, 1982). But some elderly people seem to lack the necessary mental 'energy' to take in more than the most obvious features of their environment.

Recent studies have also tried to examine more natural situations. For example, Rabbitt (1981) has tried to analyse elderly people's performance in group conversations. Although they remembered what had been said, they had much more difficulty in remembering who said what and to whom. This makes it easy to understand why they could become ineffective in a group, failing to distinguish between different people's points of view, while maintaining well one-to-one conversations.

Although it is commonly thought that elderly people's memories for distant events are better than for more recent events there is no experimental evidence to support this generalisation. It is difficult to devise appropriate experiments to test remote memory, but tests of memory for events and faces from the past have shown people to have similar failings as with memory for more recent events and faces (Warrington and Sanders, 1971). Of course, in cases of dementia where the ability to remember new events is greatly affected, the contrast with memories for the distant past will appear great. But it is important to distinguish abnormal from normal ageing. Normal age changes are generally small. Indeed, the literature on the subject indicates that older people's memories of past events, as well as of more recent events, are remarkably accurate (Botwinick and Storandt, 1980; Field and Honzik, 1981).

Persisting strengths with age

Many studies now have stressed the strengths that remain in elderly people's memory and learning and memory ability. Simple measures of learning show little or no decline into old age (Savage et al, 1973). Particularly if the material is fully learned initially, elderly people appear to retain information as well as younger people. They are at a disadvantage with speedy and novel (unexpected) forms of presentation, but in many situations they appear to learn as well as younger people.

Indeed, there are psychologists who argue that the differences observed in older people's test performance reflect sometimes not deficits but different ways of approaching tasks to that of younger people. For example, following a developmental model similar to that of Riegel (1973), referred to in Chapter 2, Schaie (1977–78) argues that adults develop from an acquisitive stage, through achieving, responsible and executive stages to a final, reintegrative stage. As existing intelligence tests relate only to the first two stages we fail to examine the qualitatively different ways of thinking of the latter part of the life course.

There are some studies that report evidence that people over the age of 60 can actually perform better than younger people at certain tasks. Typically, these are situations where people are required to remember personal, meaningful information as opposed to meaningless information. Older people do much worse at the latter than younger people but may do better at the former, probably because they attend to it better (Cohen and Faulkner, 1984). Other studies report that older people remember better than younger people the gist of a story that they have been read, again perhaps because they seem better able to focus on essentials (Labouvie-Vief and Blanchard-Fields, 1982).

Such findings seem to be at variance with those which report considerable muddle and forgetfulness on the part of elderly people in reporting back, for example, the content of a television news episode. However, it is worth repeating the point that we need to avoid confusing the comparisons drawn between younger and older people with those comparisons drawn between the adult population as a whole and very old people. The latter will be heterogeneous in ability, containing some people whose abilities are well preserved but also others who have been affected by both physical and mental decline. We must avoid seeing all people over a certain age, whether it be 40, 50, 60, 70 or more as a single group.

Certainly, we need more studies which report older people's abilities rather than disabilities. A very real problem in our society is that older people underestimate themselves. In one experiment in Toronto (quoted by Cohen and Faulkner, 1984) an experimenter asked old and young people to remember to telephone his laboratory at prearranged times over a period of weeks. The older members were expected because of poorer memory to do worse. In fact they did much better than the younger members, maintaining near perfect performance. What they were doing of course was relying on written reminders. They realised better than the younger people that they were liable to forget and as they were more concerned about remembering they remembered better. Younger people tend not to complain about their memories, although they may forget appointments quite as readily as older people!

Some of the most interesting studies on older people's learning are those that focus on real-life situations. For example, Harwood and Naylor in Australia (Harwood and Irvine, 1985; Naylor and Harwood, 1977) investigated a group of 80 volunteers aged 63 to 91 years in an exercise in which they were expected to learn German from scratch, a convenient choice for a naturalistic study of learning since learning to read a foreign language is not difficult to assess quantitatively. The learners were remarkably successful. After six months the majority of people had reached a level of skill in reading German which normally takes schoolchildren five years to achieve. A study by the same group on the learning of recorder playing was likewise very successful.

Experience and wisdom

Reference has already been made to a theoretical distinction between two different types of intelligence: 'fluid' intelligence which is the person's basic potential to acquire new ideas and to adapt to new situations, and 'crystallised' intelligence which reflects the person's cultural and environmental experience. The former is assessed mainly by non-verbal methods of IQ testing and is liable to decline with biological ageing. The latter is assessed mainly by verbal tests and is considered to remain stable with biological ageing, although like 'fluid' intelligence it can be affected by disease. However, more recently psychologists have begun to point out that 'crystallised' intelligence may not only remain stable with age but may also increase, and that current methods of approach to studying it are inadequate.

Researchers at the Max Planck Institute for Human Development and Education in Berlin, for instance, have argued that intelligence tests become more inadequate the longer people have lived and therefore acquired different experience from one another (Dittmann-Kohli and Baltes, 1990). Such tests are capable of measuring age decline but not age improvement. They do not do justice to the complex and socially valued activities that many people continue to develop over a long lifetime. To assess such development one would need tests attuned to the specialist activities of the people in question, whether politicians, writers, managers or therapists. There is considerable variation in the knowledge and problem-solving skills required for the position in life different people hold, and they consequently come to vary considerably in the domains of expertise they possess. This expertise can be heightened by further challenges, it can decline through lack of use, but it remains as essential a part of the individual and his adjustment to his life situation as the basic 'fluid' intelligence potential he is born with.

Older people with particular skills are likely still to impress in advanced age, if those skills are still required and maintained in use. The elder statesman – Harold Macmillan was a good example even in his nineties – can still write and deliver complex speeches. In some cases older people can make use of their experience to develop more efficient ways of doing a job. This may sometimes help counteract decline in speed of action with age. For example, it has been observed that older workers faced with difficulties on a production line can develop their own ways of altering the job to keep up the pace (Twining, 1988). It is a sign of the increased recognition that the benefits of experience may outweigh the detriments of age that insurance policies of older car drivers are less cautious than they used to be. We can expect more such recognition of the abilities of older people as advanced age becomes less associated with decrepitude. The study of the influence of experience upon cognitive ageing is now a recognised research topic (Salthouse, 1987).

While expertise can distinguish a person, it can also limit him. Indeed, some of the problems of old age may relate to overspecialisation, and inability to pursue new ways of thinking, feeling and behaviour which are required by present circumstances. Nevertheless, some people as they age succeed in acquiring a greater general expertise in dealing with life's concerns. This is the concept of wisdom, which is difficult to define but appears as a generalised form of intelligence in judging life situations that are both important and uncertain. Not all tasks of life require wisdom.

The philosophical and religious thought of many cultures associates old age with wisdom (Clayton and Birren, 1980). It is usually considered to depend on an extended period of experience, but it is not an inevitable product of a long life. Not all old people are wise. This was well recognised also by earlier writers. The Greek tragedian Sophocles for example, in his work *Oedipus at Colonus*, written in his own old age, explicitly contrasts the wisdom of the long-suffering Oedipus with that of his brother-in-law Creon who thinks he can persuade Oedipus to return to the city from which he was banished. Creon is 'old' too, but not 'wise'.

Attempts to study wisdom empirically are very recent and have begun by delineating key characteristics of wise judgements, including the situations to which they are applied (Holliday et al, 1986; Dittmann-Kohli and Baltes, 1990). They appear to rely on integration of knowledge and experience over a long period; they consist of problem definition and judgements of exceptional clarity. Their field of application comprises situations that involve important decisions that have long-term implications, and situations that are complex and perhaps also ambiguous in interpretation.

While having a personal concern for the issues he is judging or thinking about, the wise person will not let emotion distort his judgement. Crucially, therefore, wisdom does not only deal with cognition. Rather it involves the integration of cognitive, affective and reflective components of understanding and reasoning. Wise judgements are often characterised by the reconciliation of contradictory information and the recognition of factors that have been neglected. Sometimes it is the solution that is proposed which is complex, recognising alternative strategies and multiple goals. It is interesting that a number of recent authors have suggested a progress to higher levels of cognition in adulthood involving greater degrees of relativistic thinking (Kitchener, 1983; Kramer, 1983; Labouvie-Vief, 1985). Such cognition may underly the development of wisdom.

Social and environmental factors influencing cognitive performance

Intelligence does not develop or decay in a vacuum. Much greater consideration needs to be given to the environmental and social circumstances which hinder or promote the continued growth of established expertise or the development of new expertise, as well as to those which lead to atrophy of function and mental decline. As has been stressed before, old age is a particular time of inequality. This is evident in the incidence of disease, but it is also reflected in social circumstances. While many older people maintain respected roles and positions within society and within their families, many also find themselves in a marginal position.

A number of models of intellectual change with age have been proposed which take the environment into consideration. For example, Labouvie-Vief et al (1974) present an operant model in which intellectual behaviour among elderly people is seen as changing due to altered stimulus or reinforcement patterns. Lack of prompting and poor quality reinforcement lead to cognitive decline.

Probably the most well-known model of socially-induced decline in older people is the vicious cycle of 'social breakdown' described by the sociologists Kuypers and Bengtson (1973). According to this view elderly people are often actively induced into a role of social and intellectual incompetence. Role loss as a result of retirement and departure of children from the family house is accompanied by 'ambiguous normative guidance' and 'lack of a reference group'. In other words there are no guidelines on how one should spend one's time and who one can look to as exemplars. Instead, the person becomes receptive to ageist attitudes towards elderly people as incompetent. He begins to see himself as incompetent, which leads to a slow diminishing of the skills he still has. A downward spiral is created in which failure in one aspect of daily life is used to justify and excuse failure in other areas.

Central to this model of social breakdown is the idea that individuals become willing actors in their own decline by adopting society's expectations of their own behaviour. For example, when people define themselves as 'old' they will, unconsciously, conform to external beliefs about old people. They will think, feel, sound and act older. What is required is the creation of strategies for avoiding self-categorisations in terms of negatively valued stereotypes. Much can be learned from the work of psychologists studying other negatively stereotyped groups, such as black people in British society (eg Giles and Johnson, 1981).

The role of social attitudes in older people's cognitive decline is as yet a little explored subject, but will become more recognised as older people develop their own pressure groups to resist social stigmatisation, as has already happened in the United States. The most telling empirical studies so far have been experiments in American homes for elderly people where attempts have been made to reverse this spiral of decline. Competent behaviour is often undermined by the attitudes and practices of staff working within institutions. Even minor interventions can change the situation dramatically, for instance giving people more control over what is happening to them and involving them more (Rodin, 1986). Improvements in mental alertness and increased involvement in activities as well as high adjustment levels have been reported from controlled studies where residents have been encouraged to take the initiative for themselves (Langer, 1983). This is not an easy matter when people have long been used to having decisions made for them, but it is possible.

Consideration of mental function in old age therefore cannot be isolated from the broader study of adjustment in later life, issues such as motivation of interest, maintenance of morale and a sense of control over the environment in which one lives, which are the subjects of the next chapter. Disuse of functions and abilities leads to their decline, and this is true at any age. Much is now known about the psychological effect of such brain-washing treatments as isolation and sensory deprivation on younger people. Disorientation and confusion are common results. We are often slow to recognise that older people may be living in circumstances where, by any ordinary standards, they are extremely isolated and deprived of stimulation.

Rabbitt (1988) also concludes that it is necessary for cognitive psychologists of ageing to take account of social factors. He gives illustrations from his own studies, citing for example how cognitively intact but institutionalised people show patterns of recall similar to neurologically impaired individuals but dissimilar to community-resident volunteers, in that they remember relatively more from their early years and less from the recent past. He looks for an explanation in the circumstances of their lives.

The institutionalised, but cognitively alert, elderly do not have to plan the routine lives which they share with all their immediate acquaintances. In this static, communal environment rehearsal of everyday minutiae makes poor conversation. When the theatre of the mind becomes the only show in town archival memories begin to be actively explored for scripts. Remote memories are increasingly rehearsed for recreation and the pattern of memory accessibility across the life-cycle is changed. (Rabbitt, 1988, p. 503)

AGEING AND PERSONALITY

Intellectual functioning comprises only one part of human behaviour. Psychologists reserve the term 'personality' to refer to the many other characteristics which can distinguish individuals one from another in the types of behaviour they display. The question has long been posed whether individuals as they age display distinct differences in social and emotional behaviour as well as in their mental capacities (see for example Burrow, 1986), but it was not systematically researched until the latter half of this century.

Nearly all reviews of the research findings indicate considerable stability in personality with ageing (eg Woods et al, 1985). However, the use of personality inventories does indicate a shift on the introversion–extroversion dimension towards introversion. This is apparent from British as well as American studies which have asked people of varying ages to fill in questionnaires (Schaie and Marquette, 1972; Savage et al, 1977). This suggests that as people grow older they become somewhat more preoccupied with their own inner selves, their own thoughts and feelings, and less with the outside world. Recent studies comparing coping strategies in younger and older people also indicate that older people use proportionately more passive, intrapersonal, emotion-focused forms of coping (for example distancing, acceptance of responsibility, and positive reappraisal) as opposed to active, interpersonal, problem-focused forms of coping (for example confrontive coping, seeking of social support, planful problem solving) (Folkman et al, 1987).

Such age differences in attitude are evident too from responses to projective tests, where subjects are asked to describe or react to stimuli they are presented with, such as pictures of individuals and groups in unclearly defined situations. But studies using projective tests have also indicated more profound changes in personality dynamics, with striking differences between men and women – men becoming less and women more assertive (Gutmann, 1964). Many psychologists question the validity of these techniques, principally because of the lack of agreement with other measures (eg Savage et al, 1973). However, as Gutmann (1987) points out, measures of inner fantasy are not measures of current behaviour. Correlations with objective data may be revealed only over time. It is also worth pointing out that questionnaire measures of personality are essentially measures of self-concept, how the person views himself, and are open to conscious and unconscious bias. The individual may indicate a greater measure of stability in his behaviour than is evident to an outside observer.

Others, adopting a more phenomenological approach to personality change in adulthood, have shown that adults have a subjective sense of both change and stability in themselves as they age. For example, Ryff and Heincke (1983) present data supporting Erikson's notion of 'integrity' as the task of later life. Old persons rated themselves higher on this dimension (ie accepting the limitations of the life cycle and viewing their lives as inevitable, appropriate and meaningful) than they recalled being in the past. Young adults and middle-aged individuals also anticipated scoring higher on 'integrity' in old age than they saw themselves in the present. It is interesting that similarly consistent findings did not emerge in regard to 'interiority', (ie the extent to which people associated ageing with turning inwards). Ryff and Heincke conclude that there is a lack of consensus in American society regarding the inevitability or desirability of the process of turning inward in the later years.

There is then considerable disagreement on the subject of personality change with age. At the one extreme stability is indicated by a study such as that of Costa and McCrae (1978) which followed a sample of American adult males over a ten-year period using a detailed personality inventory (the Cattell 16PF). At the other extreme Gutmann argues for fundamental developmental changes in later life on the basis of many years' collection of projective and other material in various cultures in different parts of the world (Gutmann, 1987). To pursue this topic sensibly we need to pay close attention to what the different studies have investigated.

Disengagement theory

The best starting point for considering this issue is provided by the so-called 'disengagement theory' which was formulated following the first major study of ageing carried out in Kansas City in the late 1950s by a team from the University of Chicago (Cumming and Henry, 1961). The main authors were sociologists and as discussed in Chapter 2 the theory is generally regarded as a sociological theory of older people's place in society, but the research team also contained a number of psychologists who have subsequently become major contributors to the study of ageing. As a general sociological theory, in which ageing was seen as a normal and necessary process of disengagement whereby the individual withdrew from the major roles of life whilst society concomitantly ceased to depend on the individual for the performance of those roles, disengagement theory aroused immediate controversy. Opposing theories were established and research activity for more than 10 years was dominated by the attempt to prove which was the most valid perspective.

It is important to bear in mind that the original theory of disengagement itself was set up consciously as a reaction to what the authors regarded as the underlying 'theory' of ageing current in American society at the time, namely that ageing is intrinsically deteriorative and that 'successful ageing consists in being as much like a middle-aged person as possible'. The suggestion is that 'personality should ideally be immutable, that the valued outgoingness of middle-aged Americans should persist through-out life' (Cumming and Henry, 1961).

Cumming and Henry and their collaborators challenged this view of ageing. Their data dealing with 279 people between the ages of 50 and 90 years indicated older people to have lower levels both of social activity and psychological involvement in the outer world, but they did not interpret these findings negatively, rather as indicating a different standard of behaviour for older people. Far from being pathological, social disengagement in later life, they argued, was universal, inevitable and healthy. Crucially, so they interpreted their data, it did not lead to any loss of morale, well-being or satisfaction with life. There is a harmony between the individual and society. Society does not offer new roles and the individual does not seek them either. Society thus prepares itself for the older person's eventual demise, while the individual turns inward on himself becoming more self-centred and reflective.

As we saw in Chapter 2, objections to the theory have been consid-erable. It was pointed out that social disengagement is not universal. When it did occur it was not related to age as such but to various losses and stresses connected with age, such as bereavement, retirement or ill health. Most importantly, some studies indicated that those who did not disengage but remained active and socially integrated had a greater degree of life satisfaction than those who did disengage.

Certainly it is easy to imagine how 'disengagement' from one's sur-roundings can be the result not of any inherent personality change but of failings, for instance in sensory acuity and cognitive capacity. Uncertain situations, where it is not clear how one should behave, make even younger people agitated and lead to avoidance reactions. A good example of this phenomenon are older people with failing hearing who avoid conversations with others because they find them too difficult to cope with. It is not because they really want to withdraw. Such self-inflicted isolation is well documented as is its association with depression (Gilhome-Herbst, 1983).

However, disengagement theory has been widely criticised for encour-aging certain negative aspects of social policy and attitudes towards older people (eg Estes et al, 1982). It provided a scientific rationale for the new twentieth-century practice of retirement from the labour force. It justified the rocking chair lifestyle, and placement of housing schemes for older people on the periphery of towns and cities, away in the peace and quiet. It could even be seen to excuse custodial forms of treatment in institutional care. It was a peculiarly dangerous form of theory because of its potential of becoming a self-fulfilling prophecy. If we expect and demand less of people because they are old, they are likely to conform to this expectation.

It is also true that, just as with the studies on intelligence referred to earlier, the disengagement theory research suffered from the limitations of its cross-sectional design. Differences between age groups could more properly be interpreted as differences between generations. When the activities of older people are studied longitudinally, as with the later follow-up studies of the Kansas City Study of Adult Life, the activity patterns typically reported involve considerable continuity with previous styles of life.

The subject is more complex because continuity of lifestyle is easier for certain work roles than for others. The relative importance of leisure interests and family life also has to be taken into account. Some people may look forward to, while others dread, the opportunities provided by retirement. But it is worth stressing that the British literature including the large-scale studies of Hunt (1978) and Abrams (1978; 1980) have demonstrated that people continue active participation in all aspects of living well into old age. Ill health is the indicator for withdrawal from activity, not through a person's choice, but through reduced energy.

Nevertheless, although many of the criticisms voiced about disengagement theory are well made, in particular the non-interventionist policies on ageing it appeared to condone, some of the insights that emerged in the course of the research and also gave rise to the theory still remain of considerable interest. For example, it was recognised that society allows old people a degree of 'permitted deviance'. They are granted a kind of licence for eccentricity, which permits them oddities and idiosyncrasies of behaviour which would not be tolerated from younger people. For some old people this is a genuine liberation. Perhaps for the first time in their lives they feel able to express themselves freely. Disengagement thus means not only a decrease in social responsibilities but the development of self-expression that is in Cumming and Henry's words 'egocentric, cheerful and blunt'.[1]

Arguments suggesting intrinsic personality change with age

More importantly, additional data collected by the Chicago psychologists involved in this same research project came to constitute the empirical basis for the construction of a developmental psychology of ageing (Neugarten, 1979). The observed shift in coping styles is one example (Gutmann, 1964). On projective tests older men in particular reacted as if they were less oriented towards coping with stress by producing changes in the stressful situation itself, and more oriented towards

---

[1] In this consideration of disengagement theory the author would like to acknowledge his debt to an unpublished manuscript by the late Alastair Weir.

accommodating themselves to their environment. As a result adjustment appeared to be increasingly achieved through changes in perceptions of the self in relationship to the environment.

One reason for thinking that some at least of these changes are intrinsic to the individual is that they are evident already in people in mid-life, from the age of 40 onwards, before the physical and social losses associated with ageing are usually felt (Neugarten, 1964). Earlier psychodynamic theorists, notably Jung who was referred to in Chapter 2, also stressed the importance of inner changes occurring at mid-life reflecting the different goals of the second part of life. This increased focus on the self can lead to heightened self-awareness and help facilitate expression of creative impulses. At the same time, depression can result from the individual's confrontation with aspects of himself about which he feels shame. These positive and negative outcomes are central to Erikson's description of the last task of life as the achievement of 'integrity' versus 'despair' (Erikson, 1950, see Chapter 2).

A narrowing of psychic focus to the self may also be in harmony with the biological process of ageing in that 'it ensures survival by utilising remaining energy to meet one's essential needs' (Newton et al, 1986). One thesis postulates that a number of the psychological changes of old age, such as disengagement and preference for simple and familiar situations, are evidence of a basic change in the organism from a primarily arousal-seeking to a less arousal-seeking state (Dibner, 1975). This change may come about as a result of a need to conserve energy with a decline in efficiency of energy systems, reflected in basal metabolism rate, respiratory function, and cardiac output. Energy is preserved in particular to maintain the basic survival of the self.

The priority of maintaining a coherent sense of one's self in later life, particularly in stressful situations such as relocation, is the theme of much current writing on ageing (Lieberman and Tobin, 1983). Certainly it is a common observation that older people may neglect superfluous details of everyday life, but will attend carefully to information that is most personally relevant to them. For example, an elderly person with a hearing deficit may miss much of what is going on around but become surprisingly attentive when his or her children talk in hushed terms about placement in residential care.

Development in later life?

We have as yet few conceptions of psychological development in later life which are at the same time well grounded in empirical evidence. But this does not mean that the views of theorists as Jung and Erikson are not to be taken seriously. However, British psychologists have always been suspicious of including adult life under the rubric of developmental psychology. The British Society of Developmental Psychology is explicitly devoted to child development, and the result has been an unfortunate

.neglect of adult development. The basis of this exclusion, however, seems to be a rather restricted epigenetic concept of development, derived from biology, where development is understood to proceed along a certain path towards a specific end point, and for the pattern to be universal in the species.

Certainly it has become more difficult to imagine that psychological development in adulthood is determined in epigenetic ways. It is the social environment that determines which developments are feasible. Erikson himself, particularly in his more recent writings, acknowledges this point. His earlier accounts express in places what appears, to late twentieth-century eyes, a rather over-optimistic view of the influence that social environments have on human development. Moreover, in the last 20 years the rate of change in society has quickened. As a result it is conceivable that patterns of development observed in one generation may not apply to the next. In this case research into human development would become primarily of historical interest. To quote two contemporary Californian psychologists: 'it is now of importance for longitudinal researchers to begin to explore the possibility that societal upheavals and responses to them in the "generation of the sixties" may have disrupted such normative or presumed stage sequences, and that as this generation grows older may well continue to do so' (Fiske and Chiriboga, 1985, p. 185).

The implication for a notion like 'integrity' is clear. There can be no guarantee that society is organised so as to encourage older people to develop the qualities subsumed under this term. Successful ageing depends on the satisfactory resolution of issues raised earlier in life, but this internal development is itself dependent on the opportunities and encouragement provided in the person's present environment. The crucial spur to growth and resolution may be lacking. Clayton in her analysis of the theory's applicability comes to the conclusion that 'many people simply do not complete the life cycle. They die uncommitted, unresolved and frustrated, never having arrived at the stage where they could fully integrate and utilise their accumulated years of experience and knowledge' (Clayton, 1975). Erikson admits the same possibility:

> each new development must wait for the inner and outer conditions which make its full unfolding possible and necessary .... the fate of old age clearly reflects the way in which ingrown habituations and social mores can inactivate an individual's potential, even as they isolate and incarcerate him – actually and symbolically – from the beginning to the end of life. (Erikson, 1982)

It is therefore possible to argue that some 'developments' in later life are not apparent because our present society itself inhibits them. One would expect moreover that recognition and interpretation of signs of development would also be impoverished in such a society. These considerations make the approach of an anthropologist who is well acquainted with a number of different cultures particularly relevant to the study of ageing. Indeed, it seems significant that the psychologists who have had the most constructive things to say about ageing have also had a wide knowledge of other cultures. This applies to Carl Jung who travelled widely and had an almost encyclopaedic knowledge of the symbols used in different cultures, and to a lesser extent to Erik Erikson. It also applies to David Gutmann, who both studied with Erikson and worked in the original Chicago research team in Kansas City.

Gutmann has subsequently worked widely in other cultures, notably in the Middle East and Central America, and on this basis in his most recent writings sets out a well argued view of psychological development in later life (Gutmann, 1980; 1987). He claims that in modern western society we both miss the evident strengths that older people do display, such as the capacity to adjust to loss, and do not allow them to exploit their full potential. Development is easier to observe in more traditional societies because these societies provide the necessary circumstances for old age to flourish, namely a 'coherent culture with well defined traditions' (Gutmann, 1980, p. 493). Just as a maternal figure is vital to development in infancy, and a peer group is crucial to the formation of identity in adolescence, so a well-rooted culture is a necessary requirement for later life to achieve its real potential.

In traditional societies, Gutmann claims, older people come to take on new roles as 'emeritus parents' – thus echoing Erikson's developmental task of 'generativity'. While women become more assertive and powerful within the realm of the extended family, older men appear to 'disengage' from the world of pragmatic action, but in order to become tenders of the values of their cultures. Their detachment from ordinary affairs frees them to make this advance so that they represent the abstract but vital elements underlying their culture. They do this by engaging closely in the moral values and religious practices which underlie their cultures. In doing so they gain new meaning in their own eyes and in the eyes of others. 'Old men help to provide young men with the powerful meanings that they require in exchange for giving up the temptations of barbarism and random procreation in favor of civility and fatherhood' (Gutmann, 1987, p. 233).

Although comparable possibilities do exist for older people in western society – one of Gutmann's favourite examples is the courage of the old lawyers who more than their younger colleagues were determined to prosecute President Nixon because he had offended against the fundamental ideals of the American constitution – the bases of western civilisation have been diluted in the rapid social changes of the last 200 years and more. Increased pathological behaviour shown by older people, regression into self-absorption and self-pity, are for Gutmann the signs of loss of stability in a culture. Lack of shared meanings and values is shown in the decline in respect for and consequent degeneration of the older members of society. They have lost their vital role in renewing and strengthening the basis of their culture. Degeneration of these older members is the first sign of the decay of a culture. But it is followed by degeneration of the younger members of society as they lose the security and guiding presence that the older members represent.

This then is Gutmann's thesis. A shifting, changing society poses a threat to the realisation of integrity in old age. A coherent culture with well-defined traditions is the necessary context for the development of such characteristics as wisdom and self-transcendence which give old age its special meaning.

One does not necessarily have to agree with this argument and its radical implications, of the need for counter-revolution in favour of tradition, to acknowledge some of the important insights that it contains, such as the loss of traditional roles that older people have incurred in modern societies and the difficulties for them of adjusting to a fast-changing society. It is clear that technological innovation and the development of information systems have made cultural transmission much less of a role for older people. But much more significant because of its threat to a sense of continuity is value change within a society.

It is also important that Gutmann counters the damaging consequences of pitying the old by pointing out that older people by dint of experience have often acquired a much greater strength in coping with loss. But his indisputable contribution is to point to the need for a much broader cross-cultural perspective in the study of the psychology of ageing. We cannot pretend that we know what the potentials of older people are if we restrict our consideration to modern western societies.

Alternative viewpoints on behaviour in old age

It is apparent that even within the field of psychology there are many occasions where different interpretations are possible for an older person's behaviour. Thus, deterioration in cognitive performance can be seen to reflect intrinsic psychological changes, the product of biological ageing, but it can also be the result of living in circumstances which are themselves incapacitating. Likewise, social withdrawal can be interpreted as 'natural' disengagement, or the result of a depressive illness, or of the lack of stimulus to further growth. It requires careful observation and comparison of similar cases in different circumstances to reach justifiable conclusions about the merit of such conflicting views. Before we have such studies available it is better to keep an open mind on the subject of psychological change with ageing.

Take for example the subject of 'cautiousness'. It is commonly stated that people become increasingly cautious with age (Schaie and Marquette, 1972; Botwinick, 1984). Certainly older people appear more likely to 'play safe' than younger people, and this may reflect in part an adaptive response to ageing. Risk taking is less likely to be profitable when one does not have extra energy in reserve to call on.

But other factors are also implicated. Tests of cautiousness overlap considerably with tests of intellectual ability, and age differences may reflect the same generational differences in education (Edwards and Vine, 1963). The same observation applies to reported increases with age in 'rigidity', a stereotyped response to situations (Chown, 1962). Intellectual factors can force people into dealing inadequately with complex situations whatever their other characteristics may be. This illustrates the artificiality of attempting to divide intelligence from personality.

On the positive side, the longer an individual lives the more chance he has to develop expertise in the areas of life in which he has 'specialised'. This in itself will tend to guarantee a greater certainty of response in those areas. Regular as opposed to random responses may therefore indicate not cautiousness per se but expertise as the product of experience.

Added experience may also have quite a different result. There is a striking passage in the writings of the Swiss author Max Frisch (1975) which refers to the relationship between age and 'not-knowing'. Despite growth and knowledge, it is the awareness of what one does not know which increases with age, he argues, a theme which Socrates also stressed. So it may be that when an ageing person becomes cautious, it is no longer that he no longer trusts himself, but rather that the number of things he questions has become greater. He can no longer be so certain in his reactions as he was (Munnichs, 1987). It should be evident by now that 'cautiousness' itself may mean quite different things both to the actor and to an observer. It is best, therefore, to avoid hasty generalisations about its meaning.

AGEING IN A LIFE-SPAN PERSPECTIVE

In Chapter 2 it was suggested that the study of the psychology of ageing is best placed within the study of the whole lifespan. Erikson's theory of life stages is one of the forerunners of an approach to the human life course which conceptualises it in its entirety and looks for connections between earlier life experiences and later behaviour and attitudes. Lifespan developmental psychology is at last sufficiently well established in Britain to have produced its own textbook (Sugarman, 1986). Applications to the study of ageing are as yet limited but are growing (eg Munnichs et al, 1985). It should be pointed out, however, that there are those who argue that such an enterprise is too ambitious and prefer a more limited focus on the processes of ageing itself (eg Bromley, 1990).

Research on development during adulthood

One of the most publicised recent studies on adult development is the work at Harvard University on the structure of adult life conducted by Daniel Levinson (Levinson et al, 1978; Sheehy, 1976). As a result of in-depth interviewing of 40 men in different occupational groups a normative theory of the life structure was proposed which consisted of a series of alternating stable (structure-building) and transitional (structure-changing) phases.

Thus, the early adult transition (17–22 years), in which the individual distances himself from the pre-adult role within the family of origin, leads into a structure-building phase (22–28 years), in which choices are made for an occupation and also a life partner. A transitional phase follows (28–33 years) in which the first life structure may be changed, then another stable 'settling down' phase (33–40 years). The mid-life transition (40–45 years) heralds a wish to be more oneself and more self-generating in one's actions, and its successful resolution leads into another stable period (45–50 years), before yet another transition around the age of 50. Beyond the age of 50 Levinson's data fade but his expectation is that there will be a continuing sequence of structure-building and structure-changing periods.

Although there are many stimulating ideas in Levinson's theory, for example the importance of formulating a 'dream' when young of how one's life could be, the role of a 'mentor' in sustaining one's belief in oneself and in one's dream, and also his discussion of the components of the period of mid-life individuation (which have close parallels to the ideas of both Jung and Erikson), the generalisations he makes are open to criticism. His basic work was carried out on a group of subjects which was small and restricted to men – middle-aged, middle-class residents of the eastern United States. At best, Levinson's account describes the life course of such people growing up in the middle of the twentieth century, but we must be wary of generalising too far. Moreover, much of the theory rests on retrospective descriptions of an individual's life course which though of interest in their own right are not a substitute for proper longitudinal study. Memory itself is susceptible to many influences (Neisser, 1982).

One can expect in the coming years more substantial longitudinal studies on adult life which will test the applicability of models such as Levinson's. It is important that data on ageing – and childhood – are included in their design. This is the requirement of a life-span perspective. But it has to be admitted that this will only be possible in academic climates where teamwork is emphasised and working for long-term results is promoted.

Differential ageing

The value of anthropological studies such as Gutmann's is to point to the possibility that ageing may be quite a different experience in a culture which offers new roles to older people. But even within one culture, circumstances of life can vary widely. Almost all data, physiological as well as psychological, show increased variability with ageing (Palmore, 1974; Rodin, 1986). If we conceive of development as at least partly the result of learning then this is not surprising. The longer one lives the longer one's learning history will be.

When one takes into account as well the influence of changes in patterns of upbringing and social habits over time and the vital role these play in determining the characteristics of ageing people, the search for generalisations in the psychology of ageing comes to appear over-ambitious. The most maybe we can hope for is to determine 'patterns' of ageing and to define their associates and determinants.

This type of thinking was already reflected in the studies that flowed from the disengagement research. During the 'disengagement' versus 'activity' theories controversy (see also Chapter 2) both sides pointed to the fact that their respective patterns of behaviour could be associated with high levels of well-being. They could also be associated with low levels. Further differentiation therefore was required.

An important early study using the same Kansas City data attempted to define patterns of good and poor adjustment in old age in terms of the attitudes individuals expressed (Reichard et al, 1962). There were three well-adjusted groups: the 'mature', who took a constructive, considered and flexible view of life; the 'rocking-chair' type, who were relaxed, dependent on others and essentially rather disengaged; and the 'armoured', who strove to stay active and at work, avoiding retirement and especially being dependent. The two poorly-adjusted groups were the 'angry', who blamed others for their misfortunes, resented their wives and had a great fear of death, and the 'self-haters', who blamed themselves for their troubles, were depressed and welcomed the prospect of death. A somewhat more sophisticated typology was published a few years later on further re-analysis of the data (Neugarten et al, 1968).

Although crude in their groupings these accounts were a considerable advance in thinking about psychological ageing. Subsequent studies in the United States have resulted in further groupings of styles of ageing. Some of these are based on the major areas of interest and investment in life which an individual displays, such as work or family (Williams and Wirths, 1965; Maas and Kuypers, 1974). Indeed, some of the most useful studies on personality in old age are those which have shown how important it is to take into reckoning a person's lifestyle: for instance, in explaining why people react differently to changes and losses such as retirement, bereavement and living alone, or a move to a residential home.

Any research finding about old people usually has to be qualified by a reference to lifestyle. For example, one American study demonstrated the advantages to be found in grouped housing for elderly people in allowing for more contact with people of similar ages and interests. But it was careful to point out that this did not apply to those with a lifestyle exclusively orientated to family, or those who could be classified as inveterate 'outsiders' (Carp, 1966; 1968).

The most substantial contributions in recent years have come from publication of the results of large-scale longitudinal studies, notably the Bonn study in West Germany (Thomae, 1976; 1983; Lehr and Thomae,

1987) and the Berkeley and Duke studies in the USA (Munnichs et al, 1985; Busse, 1985; Siegler, 1983). The major impression from these studies is the considerable stability in people's behaviour over time spans of up to 10 years and more (Palmore, 1970; Maddox and Douglass, 1974; Thomae, 1976). Individuals continue to enjoy the same interests and activities, and display the same attitudes that characterised them earlier. Differences between individuals relate little to age, and much more to factors such as social class, education, health and environmental stimulation.

Some systematic change in patterns of coping with changing circumstances are observable (Olbrich, 1985; see also Chapter 5). But clearly distinguishable patterns of ageing have not yet emerged. The variety of patterns of consistency and change are too great. Major influences are evident but these are compensated for or reinforced by a host of other factors. The numbers involved in the studies are too small to allow for statistical analysis of the combination of variables required in a longitudinal way. In the Bonn study in particular systematic classification has eluded the researchers, and led some to wonder whether more detailed investigation of individual cases over time may not be a more profitable means of proceeding (Thomae, 1976).

Moreover, it is probably misleading to search for 'types' of individuals ageing in different ways as in the earlier American typologies, since this gives too much weight to the assumed existence of underlying stable traits of personality. A more reasonable working assumption is that patterns of ageing should be defined in multidisciplinary terms including, therefore, biological and social as well as psychological processes.

AGEING AND NEW BEGINNINGS

Although it is undoubtedly mistaken to think that old age must necessarily be a time of change, it is also probably misleading to exaggerate the degree of stability in the last period of life. One needs to bear in mind that later life not only presents threats but also offers opportunities to develop abilities and capacities that have been inhibited earlier in life. This is the perspective on the second part of life emphasised not only by Jung but also by Gutmann, Levinson and others. In the pursuit of 'wholeness' individuals may cultivate potentials in areas that they have neglected in the first half.

The often sudden changes in societal roles and family relationships that follow in later life may provide further occasions for the emergence of other aspects of the self. For example, older men who have been preoccupied with production and competition during the achievement, career-oriented period of adulthood may be confronted with previously repressed needs to nurture and desires for intimacy. Women by contrast may become more aware of previously submerged strivings to be assertive and to live out their own needs. These developments pose problems as well. Adults who cannot negotiate the necessary changes in their marriages and other areas of life may be vulnerable to developing emotional problems (Gutmann et al, 1982). Certainly, there is a growing awareness of the need for marital therapy as well as retirement preparation for older people.

These issues are also reflected in general literature. For example, Vita Sackville West's *All Passion Spent* (Sackville-West, 1931) illustrates well the emergence of a new independence and of artistic interests in a recently widowed older woman. These facets of her character have lain dormant since her marriage, and her children are disturbed by their appearance. She is led to reflect on the different course her life could have taken and to empathise with the current dilemmas of her granddaughter.

Whether ageing means change or stability, its study can only benefit from being placed within the context of the study of the whole lifespan. Childhood and old age are part of the same story. The handling of issues early in life has major repercussions for later development. This is the major insight of Freud and later psychodynamic theorists. It could now be a primary question of investigation for life-span psychology. But there is an unfortunate trend for psychologists of ageing to neglect child psychology. Gerontologists should in fact pay much more attention to concepts current in child development – concepts such as attachment, competence and commitment, which can be studied over the whole lifespan (Maas, 1985). The study of childhood too can only benefit from this broader life-span perspective.

CONCLUSION

Most early research work on the psychology of ageing concentrated on the subject of intelligence. As a result we have a rather unbalanced picture of the changes that occur with age. This is the more so because investigations on intelligence have examined the decline in basic mechanisms, but have paid little attention to the continued development of particular areas of expertise which enable individuals to excel in many fields, such as politics and art, late in life.

Cognitive decline is not usually marked before the age of 70 and is primarily determined by processes of physical disease. Decline due to biological ageing per se is more limited and mainly affects tasks which have to be performed at speed. Social and environmental factors also play an important part in encouraging or discouraging older people to maintain high levels of mental functioning. As a result there is considerable variation in capacity among people of an advanced age.

Stability in outer attitudes and interests appears to characterise most people as they grow old. There does, however, appear to be a shift towards an increasing focus on inner thoughts and feelings, already evident in mid-life, consistent with the ideas of developmental theorists such as Jung and Erikson. A culture's expectations of older people's roles within society have a vital place in encouraging or inhibiting personality change in later life.

Psychological change with age is best studied in a life-span and multidisciplinary context, thus taking account of formative experiences earlier in life as well as present biological and social circumstances. The complexity of the issues involved requires that we make careful observations, in context, of the individual's behaviour and attitudes, paying full attention to their meaning for the individual. Generalisations based on superficial recordings of behaviour are unlikely to improve our understanding of the process of ageing.

5

ADJUSTMENT IN LATER LIFE

Peter Coleman

ADJUSTMENT AND AGEING

Is old age a difficult period of life?

Adjustment, adaptation and the various expressions that are used to refer to the individual's experience of well-being, morale, life satisfaction, depression and so forth, are some of the most commonly used terms in social and psychological studies of ageing. Such is the frequency of their use in British and American gerontology that a naive observer would be likely to conclude that ageing was a particularly problematic period of life. The same impression is conveyed in other ways as well. For example, the very first British government discussion document on policy for older people, issued in 1978, was entitled *A Happier Old Age* (DHSS, 1978). That in itself suggests that old age is often not a happy period of life, certainly not as happy as younger periods of life.

Moreover, there is also evidence from British epidemiological surveys that there is a high prevalence of depression among older people, affecting one in seven of all people over the age of 65. This is not only true of Britain. Similarly high rates of depression have been recorded in the USA and in other countries (Gurland and Toner, 1982). It is then not so surprising that the study of ageing has adjustment as one of its main foci of interest.

Above all old age is associated with the experience of loss. As Lieberman and Tobin observe in one of the most notable recent books on the subject of adjustment to ageing:

> The psychology of old age is often synonymous with the study of crises that alter the elderly's social world and psychological milieu. Retirement, economic changes, widowhood, alterations in family constellation, numerous signals that the body and mind are not functioning as well as they previously did, frank physical illness, and the increasing sense of personal finitude have all been considered within a stress perspective. These conditions have become the benchmarks of the last decade or two of life; they are the filters through which investigators examine what it means to grow old, as well as what is necessary to age successfully. (Lieberman and Tobin, 1983, p. 3)

Yet it is worth stopping to reflect whether this emphasis is justified. Might this negative orientation not just be another of the ways in which we unjustly stigmatise old age? Do we give sufficient weight to the positive elements in later life? Certainly there is something to this criticism. Policy makers do tend to look at old age with blinkers which make them recognise sickness, poverty and mental deterioration, but not the pleasures and achievements. Depressive symptoms are prevalent among older people, but epidemiological studies suggest that severe depression is more common among younger groups in the population (Henderson, 1989).

It has to be acknowledged too that older people display much higher rates of expressed satisfaction with their lives than younger people. The national survey *The Elderly at Home* (Hunt, 1978) pointed out that the over-sixties age group in Britain had a greater degree of expressed life satisfaction than any other age group with all aspects of life, apart from health. The same findings have emerged from American studies (Larson, 1978; Palmore and Kivett, 1977). These findings seem paradoxical when set against the evidence on high rates of depression. They may reflect the particular characteristics of the recent generations of older people, stoical and acceptant. Or they may represent a genuine developmental change towards greater resilience in the face of difficulties (Gutmann, 1980). But they certainly suggest that we should consider more carefully the preconceptions that we may have about old age as a difficult and tragic time of life.

Every change that occurs in the life course requires adjustment. Taking up an adult role, beginning work, marriage and childbirth require particularly major adjustments, often in close proximity to each other early on in adult life. If old age has a special character in this regard it is the likelihood of *unwanted* changes occurring, sometimes also in close proximity and often unprepared for: loss of work role, loss of spouse, decreased income and increased physical frailty.

Loss is a common element in many old people's lives. Indeed, from this perspective the rates of depression observed in later life are not remarkably high but remarkably low. Older people cope well with loss. But too often gerontologists 'miss the particular resilience that the aged can show in the face of death. They forget that many older individuals are like combat veterans, who have seen "a thousand fall"' (Gutmann, 1980, p. 490). Often indeed it seems that depression occurs when the losses of old age reawaken earlier losses that have never been properly healed.

The capacity to adjust to life's changes does not appear to be diminished in later life, but rather enhanced. This appears from the observations of psychotherapists that older patients can be maintained in the community with less frequent contact with the therapist than younger people require (Gutmann, 1980), but also from more general studies on life satisfaction and living circumstances (Abrams, 1978), and such specific topics as adjustment to bereavement (Bowling and Cartwright, 1982) and to kidney dialysis (Auer, 1987). They show how well many older people do adjust to loss. But this is often not the message that is read from them. The focus tends to be on the minority who show signs of maladjustment.

Methods of investigation

The American sociologist Rosow (1977) has suggested that the emphasis on adjustment and well-being in the study of ageing reflects the applied orientation which also has been characteristic of gerontological literature, less interested in understanding the experience of ageing in its own right, more in the product and the conditions which seem to maximise 'welfare'. This applied bias has been very evident in British research on ageing which has developed considerable sophistication in evaluating types of service provision (see, for example, Goldberg and Connelly, 1982; Bond and Bond, 1987), to the neglect perhaps of more fundamental theoretical issues. Fortunately there are now signs of a greater interest in the study of normal ageing.

Rosow's view helps explain why measures of 'well-being' have become so popular, measures which allow the efficacy of services to be evaluated. They were first developed in the course of American sociological studies on older people in the 1950s, and there are now a variety in common use. The most well-known in Britain are the Chicago Life Satisfaction Index (Neugarten et al, 1961) and the Philadelphia Geriatric Center Morale Scale (Lawton, 1975), both of which have been slightly altered to suit British linguistic usage (Luker, 1982; Challis and Knapp, 1980). They contain items like: 'As I grow older, things seem better than I thought they would be'; 'My life could be happier than it is now'; 'As you get older do you feel less useful?'; 'Are you satisfied with your life today?'.

Although convenient for research purposes, there are many problems with such measures which have been well articulated in an article by Gubrium and Lynott (1983). They observe that the methods used force a frame of reference onto the respondent, for example on past/present comparisons, and do not allow for further qualification of the meaning of questions and answers. As anyone knows who has administered such a questionnaire, the comments people make while answering are often more revealing than whether they say yes or no. The measures are also excessively individualistic in that the resulting scores are attributed solely to the individual, rather than to the measurement occasion and the particular themes raised in the individual's mind by the questions.

Of course, this is perfectly understandable since the aim is to provide standardised scores with which individuals can be compared and, for example, the impact of different living circumstances or different types of service delivery can be contrasted. But these are very grave limitations and the measures have been of relatively little use in understanding ageing or adjustment. We do, therefore, need to question why in a field so underdeveloped as ageing we have so much research of this nature and so little which asks individuals to describe their actual experience.

Is adjustment always desirable?

One final query that needs to be placed against the study of 'adjustment' is the dangerous assumption that adjustment is always desirable. The notion of individual adjustment implies a harmony between an inner state and outer condition. A perfectly adjusted organism would be silent, wrote Freud. But some conditions are intolerable and deserve protest rather than acquiescence. Dylan Thomas urged his father to 'rage, rage against the dying of the light'. His own perception of his father's situation may have been faulty, but why should there not be 'angry old men' as there are 'angry young men'? The writer Graham Greene gave himself this title in an interview at the age of 86 (*The Spectator*, June 1986, pp. 9–12).

SPECIAL ASPECTS OF ADJUSTMENT IN LATER LIFE

Theories of ageing

We have little systematic knowledge about how people manage the last parts of their lives. What we do possess are certain 'pictures' or 'images', positive and negative, about how people cope with problems in this period (see Chapter 2). Stereotyped views, for example stoic acceptance of hardship on the one hand and crippling loneliness and depression on the other, play a large part in people's thinking about being old. These images affect our own everyday and working attitudes, perhaps more than we imagine, and it is good to try and bring them out into the open and examine them. As has already been mentioned in Chapter 1 there is a growing number of popular books which address the subject of attitudes to ageing and propose more positive ones to those commonly expressed.

In both the physical and social sciences, 'theories' also provide a way of thinking about the world and about human behaviour and society which satisfy the need for a model which fits our experience of reality (see Chapter 2). The study of ageing has as yet generated little theory of its own, and even less has percolated through to influence ordinary attitudes. One exception is the theory of 'disengagement', which is an interesting example both of the power and danger of theories (see Chapters 2 and 4).

Experience with the negative implications for social policy of a theory such as disengagement made gerontologists wary of embracing too eagerly any generalisation about how older people do or should behave. Indeed, American sociologists such as Rosow (1974) and Rose (1965b) have argued that an essential point to be recognised about old age in late twentieth-century western society is that there are no societal or cultural expectations about how old people should behave and live. Therefore, if there are goals or values for which they are to live they must be created by the old themselves. Although this might seem a rather depressing conclusion, it can also be seen as a liberating one. The old person is free to follow whichever path he or she chooses. This is not to deny the influence of social or physical constraints due to low income or disability for example, or the influence of events earlier in life upon the individual's attitudes and motivations, but it is to assert the uniqueness of each individual's situation and decision-making.

But lack of theory and lack of norms can be as detrimental as overemphasis on a particular theory or way of life in old age. People require some framework in which to understand their experience of life, including growing older and interpreting older people's behaviour. Absence of constructive ideas breeds the kinds of stereotypes and prejudices about the deterioration, self-absorption and rigidity of old age which are certainly as damaging as disengagement theory has been. Gutmann has recently offered a vigorous challenge to atheoretical views on ageing. He criticises in particular any confounding of the study of development 'with the study of "whatever works" or "whatever feels good" to the isolated individual ... Such "humanism" ends by making the older person particularly vulnerable to the general, cultural phobia against aging. When spokesmen for the unique and imperial self consider aging from their favored perspective, of idiosyncratic individualism, the second half of life appears as a wasteland' (Gutmann, 1987, p. 19).

Writing from the more general context of life-span developmental psychology Gergen (1980) also argues for the importance of theories.

> Theory offers a means of dissecting the flux; through theory the rough and tumble of passing experience is rendered orderly. Theory furnishes an essential inventory of what there is and ideally satisfies the individual's quest for why the units of the inventory are related as they are. In this way, theory furnishes a satisfying sense of understanding, along with terms enabling the individual to communicate this understanding to others. (Gergen, 1980, p. 50)

Moreover, Gergen stresses that there is a continual need for new theories to counter the myopia induced by established accounts of reality. A theory can outlive its usefulness, and instead of drawing our attention to phenomena we had not noticed before, become a hindrance to developing new insight.

It is striking how researchers and students learning about ageing turn to the handful of writers who do present an ideal model for growing old. In particular, the writings of Erikson (eg Erikson, 1965), whose contributions as a precursor of life-span developmental psychology have already been referred to in Chapter 2, have attracted considerable attention from those working with older people. This is not because he wrote much about ageing in itself, but because he saw ageing as an integral part of the lifespan. He also powerfully conveyed the idea that in order to understand a person in old age it is necessary to see him or her in the context of a whole life history with the problems both successfully and unsuccessfully resolved from earlier periods of life.

This is a challenge, above all to professions working with older people and Erikson's writing can be illuminating and provide new horizons precisely in those settings where work with older people often seems so dull, as in long-stay hospitals. Archer, for example, provides a telling account of how she came to find added meaning in working with mentally infirm older people on British psychogeriatric wards, through a consideration of each of Erikson's stages of development (Archer, 1982). It allowed her to recognise each person's individuality, to acknowledge the achievements and struggles different people displayed in maintaining a sense of 'trust' or 'industry' or 'identity', and striving for 'intimacy', 'generativity' and 'integrity'. The insights she gained enabled her to continue responding to the people she cared for as persons and not only as patients.

Erik Erikson's concept of integrity

The notion of 'integrity', the last stage of life, is only sketchily worked out in Erikson's early writing. Subsequent accounts have given more substance to it (Peck, 1968; Erikson et al, 1986). Essential characteristics of a state of integrity seem to include: firstly an acceptance of one's life and the way it has been lived; secondly the abandonment of a self-centred view of life and the movement to a transcendent interest in humankind; thirdly an acceptance and loss of fear of death.

Such an ideal model of ageing has been criticised for being too idealistic. As was discussed already in Chapter 2, the nature of modern society itself may make it more difficult for someone to achieve such positive qualities. Certainly, since in Erikson's account the possibility of successful resolution of each stage seems to depend on success at previous stages, the probability of failure increases exponentially throughout the life stages. Others, however, would argue with such a strict interpretation of the stage theory and suggest that there are, even in late old age, alternative roads to the state of integrity that Erikson describes (eg Sherman, 1981).

It would be foolish to pretend that Erikson offers a worked out theory of adjustment in later life. His value is that he points to key elements that have to be taken into account in any consideration of adjustment to ageing. He raises the special issues of adjustment which older people must face.

Judgements on the value of one's own past life do become inevitable in old age as new opportunities diminish. It may appear too late to start again or to make amends for wrongs done. The lack of a sense of fulfilment can be crucial to adjustment in later life, as indicated by the author Somerset Maugham: 'what makes old age hard to bear is not a failing of one's faculties mental and physical, but the burden of one's memory' (Maugham, 1959). Reminiscence has long been regarded as a characteristic behaviour of old people, but its purposes and functions were disparaged at the time that Erikson formulated his account of the lifespan. Yet he stressed that 'acceptance of one's one and only life cycle' was a key element in later-life integrity.

People should be generally concerned with what will happen to their society after they die. Ill health and the other stresses of later life may lead to self-absorption with one's own problems unless interest in the world outside can be maintained. Yet if society is to be so different from the one one has known, if it appears likely to overthrow or indeed already has overthrown the values that were so important in guiding one's own life, it can be harder to die. It needs courage and imagination to see through the different manifestations of human interests and activities and to perceive an underlying constancy. Erikson refers to 'the comradeship with the ordering ways of distant times and different pursuits ..... Although aware of the relativity of all the various life styles which have given meaning to human striving, the possessor of integrity is ready to defend the dignity of his own style against all physical and economic threats' (Erikson, 1965, p. 260). It is not to deny that there are differences. It is to be confident enough about one's own life to defend the course it has taken, yet be able at the same time to tolerate other ways as well. Self-acceptance and acceptance of others go hand in hand.

Death itself must be central to the interests of the study of old age. Yet much gerontological writing almost gives the impression that death is an avoidable rather than inevitable conclusion to old age. But those who are old know well enough that their life is nearing an end. As those researchers who have investigated attitudes to death readily acknowledge, older people do not generally share the same hesitancy and reluctance to discuss death. They talk about it openly and in personal terms (eg, Lieberman and Tobin, 1983). Coming to terms with one's 'finitude' is a key feature of adjustment to old age and one which Erikson clearly signalled. In fact, he brings his account of the life cycle full circle with the closing statement: 'it seems possible to further paraphrase the relation of adult integrity and infantile trust by saying that healthy children will not fear life if their elders have integrity enough not to fear death' (Erikson, 1965, p. 261).

Each of these three aspects of adjustment to ageing will now be considered in detail: the role of reminiscence, attitudes to present society, and death and dying. Although not peculiar to old age, together they give an idea of some of the general features of adjustment that characterise the last stage of life. Adjustment to the particular physical and social stresses and difficulties occurring in old age – which will be considered later in this chapter – is best studied against the background of the individual's understanding of the meaning of life and death.

Attitudes to Past Life and to Reminiscence

Ideas on the role of reminiscence

The role that reminiscence can have in older people's lives has only recently been affirmed. Although recognised by Aristotle as an important feature of old age, its treatment has often been unsympathetic. Even fairly recent textbooks have stressed an association with mental deterioration rather than any positive role it might have in old-age adjustment.

The formulators of 'disengagement theory' (Cumming and Henry, 1961) saw increased reminiscence as one manifestation of the process of ageing, which they understood as involving growing interiority and withdrawal from concerns with the outside world. Since their intent was to put forward disengagement as a normative process of adaptation to old age and death, reminiscence appeared in a more positive light. But the subsequent backlash against the thinking typified by disengagement theory – and in particular the research which demonstrated that the greater part of the withdrawal from involvement with the outside world shown by elderly individuals was forced upon them rather than initiated by them – tended to confirm the original negative connotations given to reminiscence.

Serious consideration first began to be given to the value of reminiscence following the publication of an article by the American psychiatrist Robert Butler: 'The life review: an interpretation of reminiscence in the aged' (Butler, 1963). Quoting his own clinical experience as well as a wide range of literary authorities, Butler made out a case for viewing reminiscence as a normal activity of old age, and the life review indeed as a process that people may have to undergo if they are to come to terms with their lives as they have lived them. Although he made no reference to Erikson's account, Butler's 'life review' can be considered a means by which a person achieves 'integrity'. Indeed, both Butler (1963) and Erikson (1978) cite Ingmar Bergman's film *Wild Strawberries*, in which an elderly egocentric professor achieves more sensitivity in helping those around him as a result of a process of life review, beginning with disturbing dreams but continuing with conscious recollections.

Butler's article was followed by a number of other important contributions to the understanding of reminiscence. For example, McMahon and Rhudick (1964) published a study of veterans of the Spanish/American War. They were struck by how well adjusted this particular group of men was, and also by the extent of reminiscing they displayed. Reminiscence, therefore, did not appear to be a negative sign, but on the contrary seemed closely related to freedom from depression. They observed that the reminiscence of these men tended to be of a story-telling nature, meant to be entertaining and/or instructive, and McMahon and Rhudick related this to anthropological studies on the role of old people in primitive societies in preserving and handing on traditions. They also noted that the 'reminiscers' tended to exaggerate the value of the past in comparison with the present, claiming 'to have seen the best'. They suggested that reminiscence could play a significant role in the face of the losses of role and function in old age, in preserving self-respect by investing in the image of oneself as one has been, and stressing its importance.

Both these perspectives on reminiscence suggest the importance to the individual of the achievement in old age of a positive view of past life. Those who feel they have lived their lives as they would have liked will be happier in the present as well. This is the concept of 'sense of fulfilment'. But the two strands of thought are also quite distinct and it is worth drawing attention to the differences.

Butler implies that the mental process of reviewing one's life is a universal experience in older persons. Often as a result of this life review, negative experiences can be better understood, lessons are drawn from them and the person gains in the process. He or she feels more 'whole', develops a sense of peace, even of wisdom. But there is also the possibility of a negative outcome, a continuing obsession with certain events and actions, the lack of any 'solution' to them, and persisting feelings of guilt and depression. It should be noted that a number of other therapists have also emphasised the importance of reflecting upon one's accumulated personal history as a task to be accomplished prior to death (for example, Frankl, 1963; Krasner, 1977; Blum and Tross, 1980).

However, it is not so much the 'life review' theory which lies behind the present trend to promote 'reminiscence therapy' with groups of older people, especially those living in institutions (Help the Aged, 1981). Rather it is 'identity maintenance' theory which claims that a greater identification with past lives and past achievements is helpful to older people in situations of deprivation and loss. The discrepancy between how one would like to live one's life and how one is actually leading it is minimised by stressing the value of the life that has already been lived, and that this in itself justifies a sense of self-worth. In addition, reminiscence therapy can also be seen as a tool, a ready means of promoting interest and engagement, provoking the traditional role of the older person as a 'story teller', a preserver of memories.

Evidence on the adaptive value of reminiscence
Subsequent studies which have followed up the work of Butler and of McMahon and Rhudick and tried to show in a rigorous way that reminiscence was related to individual adjustment, have by and large produced disappointing results. Lieberman and Falk (1971), for example, explored the function of reminiscence in three samples of older people: those who were living in their own homes; those who were waiting to enter old people's homes; and those who had been living in such institutions for some time. They found that those who were in the waiting situation were considerably more involved in reminiscence than either of

the other two samples. But when they investigated whether the degree of reminiscence was related to subsequent adaptation to the stress of moving, no relationship was found. Havighurst and Glasser (1972) did identify an associated pattern between high personal/social adjustment, positive effect of reminiscence and high frequency of reminiscence, but their study was not able to clarify causation. Taken altogether, as many studies seem to have found no evidence for the adaptive value of reminiscence as have found positive evidence (Merriam, 1980; Thornton and Brotchie, 1987).

Reminiscence therapy, therefore, cannot be said to stand on a very solid base, and recent commentators, notably Merriam (1980) and Thornton and Brotchie (1987) have been led to criticise simplistic thinking about reminiscing and its value. Talking or thinking about the past may serve various functions, and we must try to be more discerning in our observations. Reminiscence, too, may mean different things to individuals in different situations. For example, a frail disabled elderly person may learn to appreciate thinking back on past memories in a way yet inconceivable to a younger, active person. Whether a person stands to gain from reminiscence will depend on his past history as well as his present needs. More detailed analysis of individual cases therefore seems to be called for, using diverse samples of older people.

In a study (Coleman, 1986) in which 50 older people living in sheltered housing were followed over a period of up to fifteen years and also interviewed in depth about their attitudes to past life and to reminiscence, paying particular attention to any changes in attitudes, the most striking feature was the stability of people's attitudes. The largest group were those who valued their memories of the past and thought reminiscence to be helpful in adjustment. But also numerous were those who saw no point in reminiscence and preferred other modes of adjustment. This group of people seemed as well adjusted as the first group. The least well-adjusted groups were those who reminisced but were troubled by memories of regret and hardship which they could not avoid, and those who avoided reminiscence because it made them depressed to think of the contrast between the past and the present. These differences helped explain why neither the tendency to reminisce or not to reminisce is likely to be associated with morale. Both reminiscence and non-reminiscence can be expressed positively and negatively. Reminiscence can be an encouraging or comforting activity, but it can also be a worrying and disturbing process. Similarly, not reminiscing can be purposeful because there are better things to do. But it can also be avoidance of memories of a past that overshadow the present, and that heighten the experience of loss. Coleman (1986) illustrates a general point, that in understanding human adjustment we may do better to study people in their own terms rather than as large groups in which we neglect vital differences between individuals.

The function of reminiscence is likely also to vary between different circumstances in which people find themselves. In their book *The Experience of Old Age: Stress, Coping and Survival*, which presents a detailed psychological investigation of elderly people moving into homes for the aged based on many years research and reflection, Lieberman and Tobin (1983) clearly express their support for an identity maintenance or defence rather than a developmental view of the function of reminiscence. Particular data on which their perspective on reminiscence is based were taken from a longitudinal study of 85 elderly people awaiting admission to homes in the Chicago area. They demonstrated the existence of much reworking of the past among the people they interviewed, but believed that it was rarely comparable to the process of life reviewing as described by Butler.

> Like the Life Review, it involves considerable effort and re-organisation, but rather than reconciliation with one's personal past, such re-organisation is the creation of an image. It serves, we believe, to resolve a critical dilemma posed by the issues of old age and leads not to serenity but rather to stability. (Lieberman and Tobin, 1983, p. 309)

Reminiscence, they argue, thus often serves the purpose of creating a 'myth', a story that justifies a person's life and is intended to be believed. But again one must not make the mistake of overgeneralising from a study of elderly people being institutionalised in America. It is understandable that preserving a sense of identity should be so predominant in such circumstances.

Lieberman and Tobin criticise the status of the 'life review' as a normative concept, for its implicit assumption 'that humans function only at the highest level'. This is not to say that life reviewing is unimportant. More focused studies indicate that providing the opportunity for a properly structured life review is beneficial (Fry, 1983; Haight, 1988). Similarly, use of the past in storytelling may be very rewarding in the right circumstances. But we do well to bear in mind the context in which reminiscence occurs and the support the listener provides.

Attitudes to the present and to modern society

A more general loss older people face which has only begun to be given much attention is the global change in the nature of the society in which they live. Although a common perspective of ageing is on change experienced by the person, in many ways older people display great continuity between their past and present in their basic activities, interests and values. Stability of attitudes is the finding of most longitudinal studies that have followed people in later life over a number of years. Indeed, it is often the outer world that has changed most. Speaking from the context of research on cognitive functioning, Rabbitt has compared older people recently to time travellers.

> ... people now aged 80 are time travellers, exiled to a foreign country which

they now share with current twenty year olds. These groups have been fed, housed, and educated very differently, have received, or failed to receive, different medical treatment for different conditions, have been taught to prize different skills and attitudes, and have been shaped by dramatically different experiences. (Rabbitt, 1984, p. 14)

It is worth reflecting on the social changes that British people have witnessed in the twentieth century. Besides the First and Second World Wars and the dramatic dissolution of the British Empire following the last war, they have also seen dramatic political and economic change, nationalisation of industries, the creation of the welfare state, the development of new technology and the drastic reduction in working hours. Perhaps even more important have been the changes in culture and values, the rise of the so-called 'permissive society', the decline in church attendance and the growth of television and the media. Value changes can be disturbing to people brought up with very different values. Seabrook has identified such problems from his own interviews with older people.

... Many of the old grew up in a world where they had to be disciplined, frugal, stoical, self-denying, poor; and what this taught them, often in bitterness and pain, appears to be of no use to their children and grandchildren, who have been shaped for different purposes by changed circumstances .... (Seabrook, 1980, p. 118)

In a study in Southampton on older people's attitudes, McCulloch has adopted the concept of 'moral siege' to describe a set of attitudes characteristic of a large number of the people he interviewed living in sheltered housing accommodation. Such people actively compared the past with the present, emphasising differences between the generations rather than similarities, and giving a high moral estimation to old people and a low one to the young. Strongly associated too was a tendency to attribute changes in society to the upheavals of the First and Second World Wars. It appears that many of these people felt obliged to condemn modern society. Accepting the values of modern society is tantamount to denying meaning to their own lives as they have led them (Coleman and McCulloch, 1985).

Such work as that by Seabrook and McCulloch helps make much more understandable what is often seen as a fault of older people. We saw in Chapter 1 how older people are often seen to be criticising the young and present-day society. It would perhaps help if we were more sensitive to the very understandable reasons why they do so criticise.

At the same time we must be careful not to exaggerate the extent to which the experience of old age is different nowadays than it was in previous generations. It has probably always been a challenge to older people to adjust to the changes within society in their own lifetime. There is an interesting comment made by the writer of Ecclesiastes in the Old Testament: 'Never ask why the old times were better than ours: a fool's question.' (Ecclesiastes, 7.10).

Nevertheless, a fast-changing society poses particular problems. It is harder to die in a society that is so different from the one that one was brought up in, a point brought out by George Orwell in a passage written nearly 50 years ago:

> ... it's also true that people then had something that we haven't got now. What? It was simply that they didn't think of the future as something to be terrified of. It isn't that life was softer then than now. Actually, it was harsher ... and yet what was it that people had in those days? A feeling of security, even when they weren't secure. More exactly, it was a feeling of continuity. All of them knew they'd got to die ... but what they didn't know was that the order of things could change ... it's easy enough to die if the things you care about are going to survive ... individually they were finished but their way of life would continue .... (Orwell, 1939, p. 106)

The attitude of 'moral siege', therefore, is a way of coping with social change which enables individuals to remain satisfied with their own past lives. It is not entirely satisfactory, however, because the old person will always experience some social pressure to adopt more modern values. There are others indeed who are confused by change and are left in a no-man's land between their own past values and beliefs and the values of a new world, an unhappy state which Andrew McCulloch calls 'questioning'. In McCulloch's study 'questioning' was represented by an association between the failure to understand modern society and a questioning of personal religious beliefs, in particular, belief in a beneficent god. Also associated was a low level of thought about the past, which would suggest that such people found difficulty in finding solace in reminiscing. Still others managed to transcend the differences between past and present, and achieved a sense of continuity or even of progress with which they could identify their own lives. But such a state of harmony with a changing world does not appear easy to achieve.

Death and dying

Attitudes to finitude

A number of authors have kept death in perspective in theorising about adjustment in old age. Disengagement theory was explicitly formulated as a functional theory of ageing, in which older people prepare society for their eventual demise by disengaging first. Both Erikson and Butler saw the key task that they identified in old age, developing integrity and life reviewing, as being triggered by awareness of the end of life. And yet older people's attitudes to death, to the awareness that their life is coming to an end, have received comparatively little attention in their own right.

The most well-known work on the psychology of adjustment to death is the pioneer study by Kubler-Ross (1969) in which she describes five stages in the process of psychological preparation for death observed in terminally ill patients. This kind of process is not age-specific and books on death and dying make little or no reference to old age. Yet as already observed in Chapter 1, in modern western societies it is predominantly elderly people who die. This is one of the major demographic changes affecting older people this century. Perhaps for this very reason the focus of studies on adjustment to death has been on younger people who have not been brought up to expect death early in life. Death is thought to be less of a problem for the old.

Studies which have compared death attitudes of older people with those of other age groups have consistently shown that the former think and talk more about death (Kalish and Reynolds, 1976; Cameron et al, 1973). General researchers 'often comment on how readily older people speak about the subject (Munnichs, 1966; Lieberman and Tobin, 1983; Schneider, 1987). Most speak about it calmly and without anxiety. Studies which have focused on fear of death have found as expected less fear expressed in the older groups (Bengtson et al, 1977; Kalish and Reynolds, 1976).

Kalish (1985) makes a link between Kubler-Ross' observations and those of the disengagement-theory writers. Her final stage of dying, 'acceptance', is described as pertaining to a dying person who is well advanced in reducing attachments to people, groups, material possessions, and ideas. The dying person's sense of loss diminishes as attachments diminish in importance. Kalish argues that, to the extent that an elderly person has already begun a process of disengagement from worldly concerns, the additional detachments involved in the coming of death will be easier to bear, than for a young person whose disengagement has only begun in response to the dying process itself.

This view accords with common observations and also has the merit of helping explain why some older people remain fearful. Keith has developed a useful typology of four 'life–death' attitudes: 'positivists', people who have achieved the goals they have set themselves in life, and who 'reflect positively on both their present activities and death as an aspect of the future'; 'negativists', people who show the qualities of Eriksonian despair, disgusted with their lives but unable to start again; 'activists', people who have achieved much but fear death as an end to achievement and opportunity; 'pacifists', people who see death as a respite from the disappointments of life (Keith, 1979). The continued 'activity' in old age shown by the third group may be a defence mechanism which, although effective in maintaining well-being, does not prepare the individual for death. However, recent research does not support the view that acceptance of death ought to enhance feelings of well-being. High death acceptance appears to be associated with low personal well-being (Reker et al, 1987). Individuals who are satisfied with their present lives and who remain very engaged with situations around them are most likely to want to go on living and to be anxious about giving life up.

As far as religion is concerned, a general finding has been that religious belief reduces fear of death. However, this general statement must probably be qualified to take account of differing degrees and types of religious commitment. Kalish and Reynolds (1976) found that strong religious believers were rated lowest on death anxiety, but those with confused religious beliefs were rated higher than agnostics or atheists. Kalish and Reynolds also found that old people differ from other age groups in the opinions they expressed about preparation for their own death. They asked people to imagine that they had been told that they would die within 30 days, and to report what changes they thought they would make in their lives as a result. Old people were more likely to say that they would not change their lifestyle, but that they would concentrate on the inner life. They were less worried by the idea that experience and opportunity would end and that they would no longer be able to care for others. Some of those who have followed the psychoanalytic theories of Jung have stressed that the unconscious 'believes' in a life after death, and that from middle age onwards, but especially as death approaches, dreams prepare us for the hereafter, pointing to imbalances in our attitudes which need to be corrected, a concept similar to that of the life review (von Franz, 1986).

Taken together, the literature available on the subject does not support a fearful idea of death in old age. In Kastenbaum's study of the meaning of death, older people most often personified death as 'gentle, well-meaning' (Kastenbaum and Alsenberg, 1976). Yet the research to date has been dominated by American studies and we need to integrate observations from quite different cultures. British literature on the subject in particular is still very sparse. Death is very much a part of life and attitudes to it will likely be responsive to changes in other areas, in evaluation of past life and in changing patterns of value and religious belief within society, as already noted. Clinical observations suggest that some older people may have severe problems with anticipatory grieving of their own demise and separation from those that they love.

Impending death

A separate issue is the experience of impending death itself. But again comparatively little research has been done. The various stage theories of the dying process that have been proposed, including that of Kubler-Ross (1969), have not yet been subjected to the substantial empirical evaluation required, so we do not know whether it is important that people follow a particular psychological path to death. Individual differences are no doubt very important. A significant British study was a detailed investigation of 60 terminally ill cancer patients by Hinton (1975). The results suggested that those whose mood and acceptance of death were highest were those who had previously shown high coping skills, high life satisfaction and good marital relationships. This indicates that a life-span approach is also important to the subject of dying.

Age differences in dying behaviour would not be surprising since the circumstances of elderly people's deaths are likely to be different from that of younger people. They are most likely to die from chronic disease that develops over a period of time, to be of frailer physical and mental condition. They are therefore more likely than younger people to be confused or comatose during the period leading up to their deaths. Death is regarded as less tragic. But because communication can become difficult or impossible greater stress may be placed on the dying person and the relatives. The phenomenon of 'terminal drop' in which some degree of cognitive deterioration occurs prior to death has been observed in a number of studies (eg Riegel and Riegel, 1972; Savage et al, 1973). More recent studies suggest a wider area of change reflected in the person's 'sense of decreased adequacy, a sense of ego-disintegration that manifests itself in lessened cognitive abilities as well as a lessened potential for maintaining a stable and consistent self' (Lieberman and Tobin, 1983, p. 231). People cope by withdrawing from the environment around them, by emotional constriction, by simplification and also by a turning away from their inner life. A passive stance suits a world that is no longer experienced as controllable.

It is important to stress that these strategies are generally successful. Eruption of anxiety and unmanageable fears are not normal, as indicated by a recent Dutch study involving careful observations in nursing-home institutions (Bruning and Hesselink, 1986). It is when issues not related to death impinge upon the elderly person, and force him or her to come to terms with life again, that anxieties are more usually aroused. The circumstances of death are important and deserve much more public consideration. Unfortunately, we live in a society in which the discussion of death continues to be largely taboo.

COPING WITH STRESS

Stress and ageing

Coping with stress in old age is an area of investigation with two distinct traditions of research, that of research by psychiatrists into the symptoms, prevalence, causation and prognosis of affective disorders especially depressive illness, which has been particularly well represented in Britain, and research within the social sciences linked to theories of stress appraisal and coping which has flourished more in the United States and the continent of Europe. There is obviously a connection between the two types of research. But few constructive links have yet been made between them, which is a pity.

Variations in reactions to stress
It is clear from all kinds of investigation that there is considerable variation in the way people adapt to changing life events and circumstances. Although there is a clear connection between such stress and the onset

of depressive illness, 'only relatively few old people develop depressions in the wake of the kind of life experience to which practically all their peers are sooner or later exposed' (Post and Shulman, 1985, p. 125). To explain such observations connections have been made with research on lifestyles, thus categorising the event differently according to its importance for the individual's total pattern of activities. For example, a person who is exclusively dedicated to his work role will experience forced retirement from this role quite differently from someone whose work role is only a subsidiary part of his life's activities.

Connections are also tentatively being made with observations on earlier periods of life. Experiences of attachment and loss in childhood may determine to a considerable extent experiences of loss in later life (Bowlby, 1980). Furthermore, there has been an awakening of interest in a more phenomenological approach to understanding experience in old age. It is what events *mean* to people that counts, not necessarily how they appear to an outside observer. We know well enough how apparently similar events can be experienced differently by different people. To understand their significance we have to try to interpret the individual's experience (Sherman, 1981).

Types of stressful experience
There is a danger in talking of stressful life events as if they formed an easily definable category. The most commonly used concept to describe the experience of ageing is 'loss'. This is seen as a common denominator in many experiences in later life: loss of home and possessions in moving to residential care; loss of relationships, of spouse, of friends and neighbours; loss of memory in the early stages of dementia where there is still insight into what is going on. It is easy indeed to see loss as the only form of stressful life event in old age. In fact, this is not the case. There are other types of external factors which can contribute to the development of depression.

Hanley and Baikie (1984) provide a useful breakdown of stress factors in terms of four categories: 'loss', 'attack', 'restraint' and 'threat'. 'Loss' is defined as the removal of external circumstances which individuals have relied on to satisfy their needs. Bereavement of spouse would be a clear example. 'Attack' on the other hand is an external force which produces discomfort. This could be an illness or the hostile reaction of others. 'Restraint' is constituted by external restrictions on activities which have been necessary for the satisfaction of needs. Immobility and being obliged to stay indoors, or not being allowed to go to work, could be examples of 'restraint'. Finally, 'threat' is defined as any event which warns of possible future loss, attack or restraint. These distinctions can be useful in helping to understand the relative difficulty of adjusting to different life events. For example, a physical illness such as a heart attack, although it is not strictly speaking a 'loss', can be linked to all three other categories. It attacks the individual, restrains him and forebodes loss of life in the future. It is strongly linked to depression.

It should also be noted that it is not only major threatening life events such as illness and bereavement which are related to the onset of depression. Also minor events which are annoying and persistent bring about depressive reactions in some people. Basically, this is what the Americans call – and the British are learning to call – 'hassle'. 'Daily hassles' are defined by the American stress researcher Lazarus as 'irritating, frustrating, distressing demands and troubled relationships that plague us day in and day out' (Lazarus and DeLongis, 1983, p. 247). These kind of continually annoying difficulties in everyday life, for example in dealings with the neighbours, in doing the shopping or even crossing a busy road, seem to put as excessive demands on some individuals' ability to cope as do threatening life events, and remain a source of damaging stress. Indeed, there is evidence that among older people daily hassles are more strongly related to psychological distress than major life events (Holahan et al, 1984).

Depression and demoralisation

Although there appear to be two separate research traditions on old age adjustment, one focusing on the phenomenon of 'depressive illness', the other more broadly based, both groups of researchers have inevitably strayed into each other's territory. Social scientists speak loosely about 'depression' in older people and psychiatrists have now started referring to 'demoralisation' and 'senile dysphoria' as distinct from clinical depression (Post and Shulman, 1985). There are important issues of definition to be clarified.

Symptoms of clinical depression

Though persistent feelings of misery, hopelessness and inertia are the most characteristic symptoms of depressive illness, these are usually accompanied by vegetative symptoms, loss of appetite, weight loss and sleeplessness. The individual usually withdraws into himself, but may also appear very anxious and agitated.

There is strong evidence from both clinical experience and research evidence (Gurland, 1976) that older people who become depressed show more hypochondriacal symptoms than young depressed people. Concern about health and bodily states may indeed be the most persistent symptom and is difficult to handle because of the close link between depression and physical illness. It is easy to reinforce depressed older people's concern about their health. However, it is often not concern about matters that are wrong with them that preoccupy their thoughts but typical health 'bogies', cancer for example (in Britain, especially of the bowels).

It is also said that older people rarely come to the doctor saying they are depressed. Often this is because they think something else is the matter with them. It may also reflect relatively unsophisticated thinking about psychiatric illness. This is likely to change in the future as older people gain greater expectations about their lives, and awareness that depressive illness can be treated very successfully in old age becomes more widespread (eg Godber et al, 1987).

Epidemiological studies of 'depressions'
There have been a large number of recent studies on the prevalence of depressive states among older people. Results have differed according to the types of measurement instrument used (Kay et al, 1985; Bond, 1987). Using a sophisticated instrument comprising a semi-structured interview, Gurland and colleagues reported a prevalence among 800 elderly people living in the community in New York of 22 per cent as possibly depressed, but only 13 per cent with depressions, which, if known to mental health personnel might have triggered action from them (Gurland et al, 1980). In a recent study in London of 396 patients aged over 65 years in GP practices 17 per cent were diagnosed as depressed (Copeland et al, 1986).

It should be noted that not only do definitions of depression vary between psychiatric and ordinary usage, but psychiatrists vary in their usage between countries. For example, British psychiatrists favour a wider definition of depression than their American counterparts. In fact, Copeland and colleagues tried to apply American criteria to their London data and came up with a 13 per cent rather than a 17 per cent prevalence of depression, ie exactly comparable to the New York figures. Gurland himself in his review of various recent studies states that 'the rates of clinically significant depressions are in the region of 10–15 per cent of the general elderly population; 2–3 per cent would fit the criteria for major affective disorder or manic-depressive disorder' (Gurland and Toner, 1982, p. 229). Although these are clearly not insignificant figures they are also not abnormally high. Indeed, comparative studies indicate higher rates of depression in other age groups (Henderson, 1989).

Demoralisation
Many more older people are troubled by depressing thoughts and feelings than actually develop full-blown levels of clinical depression. Gurland and Toner (1982) estimate that the rates of demoralisation are at least double that of clinical depression. It is probably, however, misleading to view demoralisation in the same way as clinical depression. Mood, for example, is a continuum between high and low and most individuals experience both extremes over relatively short periods of time.

It is also necessary to differentiate among various aspects of subjective well-being in old age. It was mentioned at the beginning of this chapter that there have been a plethora of questionnaires measuring what are variously called 'life satisfaction', 'morale' and 'adjustment' formulated in the last 30 years. It can be very confusing for a researcher trying to decide what is the best method for use in a particular project. The problem is also a conceptual one, because the terms are not always used in consistent ways. 'Morale' in particular is given a variety of meanings by different authors. Some proposals to standardise usage have been made (eg George, 1981) but a consensus in this respect is far from being achieved. Different questionnaires show both large areas of overlap as well as unique features. Some, for example, do not include questions on satisfaction with past life. Others neglect attitudes to health, or direct questions on self-esteem. There seems to be no nucleus of essential concepts at the core of subjective well-being. Assessment includes a variety of criteria including attitudes to health, old age, one's environment, one's life as a whole, as well as feeling of loneliness, depression and anxiety and feelings of uselessness.

The most detailed attempt to differentiate aspects of subjective well-being has been made by Lawton, who administered a large number of questionnaires for different scales to 285 American subjects. His initial analysis produced 13 different dimensions. On a second-order analysis these divided into two broad groups. The first had 'negative affects', as a core indicator and loaded heavily also on 'self-esteem', 'subjective health', 'psycho-physiological symptoms' and 'congruence between desired and attained goals in life'. The second had 'positive affects' as a core indicator and loaded also on 'residential satisfaction', 'perceived quality of time use' and 'satisfaction with friends'. Interestingly, simple expressions of 'happiness' loaded equally highly on both factors. Lawton argued plausibly that the first set represents 'interior well-being' and the second 'exterior well-being' (Lawton, 1984).

Certainly, this distinction between psychological or inner well-being and perceived quality of life seems intuitively reasonable. Discrepancy between them also does quite often occur in the way older people speak about their lives. For example, one can think of many elderly people who are depressed within themselves, yet are quite uncomplaining about external factors and express satisfaction about their environment. They say that they are 'happy with' their circumstances in life, but do not 'feel happy'. This distinction explains the apparent paradox mentioned at the beginning of this chapter, that older people display relatively high rates of depression, but express themselves the most satisfied with the circumstances of their lives.

Determinants of depression and demoralisation

Coping and stress over the lifespan

Research in the area of stress and adaptation has outgrown its early over-simplistic phase of ranking and counting objective life events and circumstances as measures of severity of stress. It is necessary to take into account people's appraisal of stress, not only its objective severity, in explaining whether their mood changes or not (eg Lehr, 1982). People employ various methods of coping with different degrees of success in stress reduction (eg Folkman and Lazarus, 1988), and the frequencies of use of these coping responses may change over the course of life. Thus, one cannot expect much from studies which simply investigate associations between objective life circumstances and morale in old age. Lohmann (1980) has concluded that 40 years of research on the influence of five prime variables on life satisfaction in older people – marital status, retirement, health, social activity, and housing and the physical environment – has 'not resulted in any clear-cut answers with regard to the causes or correlates of satisfaction' (Lohmann, 1980, p. 35). In Larson's (1978) review of the gerontological literature, only health – and that self-reported – consistently correlated as high as 0.40 with measures of subjective well-being.

To make further advance in understanding why some individuals cope better than others we need to examine closely how they experience what happens to them, and the internal, ie intrapsychic, as well as external coping resources they have available. As mentioned already in Chapter 4, there is evidence from American studies that the use of intrapsychic methods, involving the control of emotions, becomes more common with age and problem-focused approaches decline. It has of course also to be borne in mind that sources of stress tend to change with age. Thus, Folkman et al (1987) reported that younger adults experienced significantly more hassles in the domains of finances, work, home maintenance, personal life, and family and friends than did their older counterparts. Older men and women reported proportionately more having to do with environmental and social issues, home maintenance and health. Nevertheless, the age differences in styles of coping did remain even within individual areas, which tends to support a developmental interpretation of change in coping methods with age.

One of the most substantial studies into the styles of coping shown by older people has been the Bonn longitudinal study (Thomae, 1976; 1983; 1986), which is still unfortunately little known in Britain. This has investigated stresses in the areas of health, family, housing and income, among a sample of 222 older people of 55 years and over followed up over periods of 20 years and employing in-depth interviews. The investigators developed the concept of 'hierarchies of coping responses' with which to describe their observations over time (Thomae, 1986). Considerable consistencies have been demonstrated but also changes. 'Hope for change' and 'active resistance' diminish whereas 'revision of expectancies' and 'asking for help' increase. However, differences between areas of stress in the coping methods employed remained significant. For example, 'asking for help' did not increase in regard to problems of income, perhaps because older people, of this generation at least, found it too demeaning a solution to their problems. Subsequent studies in Germany have developed further this approach to the study of coping (eg Kruse, 1989).

The American stress researcher, Lazarus, argues that researchers investigating stress and coping in old age should do more than carry out sophisticated assessments, taking account of individual differences in appraisal of stress and methods of coping. They should also recognise that any particular encounter with stress is part of the individual's 'lifelong drama', and the commitments, values, fears and hopes shown throughout that life have to be taken into account in understanding the individual's reactions (Lazarus and DeLongis, 1983). Clearly, major determinants of later-life adjustment do lie in experiences earlier in life. For example, it has been suggested that a non-normative crisis such as the death of a child can inhibit the bereaved family's ability to cope with subsequent losses (Callahan et al, 1983). We are beginning now to gain evidence on this subject from the earliest longitudinal studies of child development which began in California in the early 1930s. The then parents of young children were interviewed and data on them at that time have now been compared with data collected 40 years later when the survey parents were about 70 (Mussen, 1985). Analysis shows consistent patterns of relationship between later-life satisfaction and earlier traits reflecting a relaxed, emotionally stable personality. Good health when young also seems to be an important predictor. So too is marital adjustment, also for women who subsequently have been widowed, which indicates that the association with later-life adjustment is based on more than simple continuity of a compatible marriage.

Inconsistencies in development have also been revealed by longitudinal study. A different study on the same sample of people revealed that mothers in two lifestyle clusters who reported the highest life satisfaction in old age were not happy with their family roles as young adults, but in mid-life and later years became happily involved in occupations or social organisations. 'By contrast, among the least satisfied in old age are another cluster of mothers who were completely and very contentedly engaged as wives and mothers all through their early and middle adult years. Their lives were completely family-centred, but in old age they seem bereft' (Maas, 1985, p. 171). Longitudinal studies thus provide important lessons for thinking in a life-span way about one's own commitments and interests.

Stress and clinical depression
In recent years we have learned a good deal more about the origins of depression, biological, psychological and social. Although we appear to be a long way from a generally acceptable theory of depression, attempts at integrating information from different types of scientific research are being made (eg Willner, 1985). The role of stress in the aetiology of depression has emerged with greater clarity. It is no longer possible to view psychosocial factors only as precipitating factors of a depressive illness which would have occurred eventually without them. The most influential studies in the UK have been those carried out by Brown and

colleagues among younger women living in the London area. Employing a more sophisticated assessment of stress which involved an analysis of the subjective implications and emotions aroused by the life events, they demonstrated that events with severe long-term threatening implications – eg bereavement, news of a shattering nature – were major causes of depression (Brown and Harris, 1978).

The same methods have been employed by Murphy in a study of older people in East London. She examined 150 depressed people over the age of 65 consecutively admitted into an Area Psychiatric Service as out-patients, day-patients or hospital in-patients. As well as these she found 19 cases of depression among people in the community while selecting 168 control subjects. In comparison with the control subjects the depressed older people had experienced in the preceding year significantly more severe life events, major social difficulties, and poor physical health. In only 15 per cent of cases some independent and severe precipitating causes of depression could not be discovered (Murphy, 1982). As in a number of other studies on depression in older people, physical health problems appeared to play the major role in its onset. Because of the wide range of conditions involved Murphy argues that they have impact through their meaning – of loss, attack, restraint and threat – for the individual rather than through a direct organic effect via biological mechanisms.

In some studies, however, other forms of stressful life events, notably bereavement, have appeared more significant. For example, Linn et al (1980) found that deaths of friends and relatives as well as personal arguments were more frequent antecedents to non-clinical depression than illness or financial problems. In a national survey of recently widowed elderly persons in the UK, one-half still described themselves as depressed some five months after the death of their spouse (Bowling and Cartwright, 1982). Apart from medication received by 37 per cent of them, very little professional assistance had been given. Understanding of bereavement in Britain has been greatly influenced by the pioneering work of Parkes, much of which is summarised in the recent edition of his book (Parkes, 1986).

Another way of looking at the impact of stress is to consider the additive effect of a number of stresses. Data from Murphy's study indicate that as the types or numbers of stress present increase so does the risk of developing depression. For her community subjects the risk of developing depression was 25 per cent following one severe event, 44 per cent when a severe event occurred in the context of a marked personal health difficulty, and 50 per cent when a severe event was combined with a major social difficulty. Of those subjects with all three risk factors, 80 per cent developed depression (Murphy, 1982).

All of the losses and other problems that occur with age deserve recognition in their own right. However, some are less noticeable than others and deserve closer examination. One of the most neglected problems associated with ageing is hearing loss. In a detailed study in London using audio-metric techniques Gilhome-Herbst (1983) found well over two-thirds of her sample of over-70-year-olds to be impaired. A much smaller proportion admitted to difficulty, but this would appear to be due in part to the stigma associated with being labelled deaf. Remarkably, it seems to be the one disability that is laughed at and found annoying by others. One only has to compare common reactions to blindness to realise the degree of stigma. It therefore is not surprising that people are reluctant to admit to hearing impairment, and prefer to hide their problem by withdrawing from society – by 'disengaging' in fact. Gilhome-Herbst found people with hearing impairment to go out less and to have fewer friends than people without impairment. In such circumstances – where, for example, three-quarters of those who admitted to hearing problems said they would not admit it to anyone else – it is not surprising that the high incidence of depression is so evident (Gilhome-Herbst, 1983). Much work needs to be put into public education in this field.

Evidence on factors protecting against depression
None of what has been said so far on the relationship between stress and depression might seem surprising. The striking point is the individual variation in reaction. Many people – perhaps even the majority of people – manage to cope well with severe social losses, adverse life events and poor health, and retain or regain their balance within a short time, while others become chronically depressed. Of course, a certain degree of stress and daily hassle is to be expected in life. It is therefore essential to find ways earlier on in life of managing difficulties. While most people manage to cope, there are some who can be disturbed by what would appear to others quite minor events. The question inevitably arises why it is that some people appear better protected against depression. This is obviously a very practical area of research because if we understood better how people are normally protected against developing depression, we would have a better idea how we could intervene more effectively with those who are vulnerable.

Both Brown's and Murphy's research already mentioned demonstrate the importance of having a confidant – someone in whom one can 'confide' and speak to about one's problems and concerns. The role of a confidant – as a buffer in life's difficulties – was first stressed in the gerontological literature many years ago (Lowenthal and Haven, 1968). The issue was tackled as a central one by Brown, who showed that young women who lacked a close confiding relationship with a husband or some other person appeared to be highly vulnerable to developing depression in the face of adversity. Murphy followed up the same theme in her comparable research with older people (Murphy, 1982). It was those elderly people who reported a lack of confiding relationships who were most vulnerable to depression when they encountered poor health and adverse life events.

Although the knowledge of the value of the confidant is important, it would be even better to understand what it is about a confiding relationship that protects against depression. There are a number of possibilities. For example, is it the value of having someone to whom one can speak about one's problems that is crucial, or has it more to do with the behaviour and attitude of the confidant him or herself? Furthermore, it has to be borne in mind that some people still become depressed even though they appear to have a close confiding relationship and others do not become depressed even though they face great difficulties alone.

Certainly, the value of having a confidant does not lie in any quantitative aspect of human interaction. In Murphy's study those who reported seeing a confidant only once every two to three weeks, often a child or sibling who lived at some distance, were as protected against depression as those who had a number of intimate relationships. The key to the support gained did seem to be the feeling of reciprocal warmth, trust and – perhaps above all – a sense of being valued. There was someone who understood. Brown too in his study stressed the importance of factors in relationships which had an effect on the self-esteem of the young women he studied (Brown and Harris, 1978; Murphy, 1982). A greater understanding of the nature and development of social support networks is likely to become a major field of study within the social sciences (see for example Pilisuk and Parks, 1986).

One contemporary view on adjustment that has received much support emphasises the importance of a view of oneself as a good person, both lovable and respected. But one cannot gain such a perception of oneself without reference to the external world. We are dependent on others, especially those closest to us, those in whom we can confide. There are extreme variants on both sides. Some people's self-esteem is more vulnerable than others, perhaps as a result of childhood experiences. Some people on the contrary appear to have almost an inviolable sense of their own worth. Research, again with younger women, has confirmed that the former are liable to become depressed even without major stressful life experiences and despite the presence of a confidant, whereas the latter appear to survive severe stress and with relatively low social support (Parry and Brewin, 1988). The former tend to attribute responsibility to themselves for negative outcomes, and to others for positive outcomes, while the latter do the opposite.

As a result of their recent research, Brown and colleagues have suggested that low self-esteem is the final common pathway of factors causing vulnerability to depression (Brown et al, 1986). They make a distinction between core support and resource support, the former provided by individuals who are especially close to the person in question, the latter provided by others with whom the respondent feels less close. The former are likely to involve longstanding relationships with a high degree of reciprocity. The latter may not and as a result individuals may actually experience a loss of self-esteem if they seek support from this type of relationship. Studies on older people also suggest that effective social support helps to reduce the deleterious effect of stress upon depression primarily by boosting self-esteem (Krause, 1987).

Thus we are led once more to recognise the importance of subjective experience in understanding human adjustment. It is with a review of contemporary approaches to this subject that the chapter continues.

ADJUSTMENT AND INDIVIDUAL MEANING

The role of subjective variables in human experience

Advances in our understanding of individual differences in coping responses will come from research in a variety of fields, biological, psychological and social. In the social sciences investigation into relationships between early-life and later-life experience have only just begun and will hopefully provide many rich insights in the years to come. Also crucial to further progress are improvements in our methods of collecting and analysing data on subjective experience.

Wherever one turns in the field of ageing, one is struck not by any commonality of reaction as the stereotypes about ageing people would have us believe, but by the diversity of personality and responses to similar life situations and events. On examination these differences so often relate to differences in perception. Take, for example, two older women both living in residential-care homes. Both are visited once a month by their only daughter who lives 20 miles away. For one this is a source of strength and joy, but the other is saddened, by what on a standard questionnaire ('How often are you visited by members of your family?') would appear the same circumstances. The reason for this difference lies in the interpretation. The first woman is buoyed by the thought that her daughter, in the midst of her busy life, finds the time to visit her mother regularly. The other interprets the frequency of visits to mean that her child does not love her enough, not as much as other daughters love their parents. She might even go further and interpret her child's actions as a judgement on how good a parent she has been, with depressing consequences.

The approach of phenomenology

The 'phenomenological' tradition of research in psychology requires that we take the individual's point of view and try to discover the meaning he or she gives to experience. If the theories (described in Chapter 4) which emphasise the salience of 'inner life' in middle and old age are correct, and development becomes more concerned with self-knowledge and self-awareness than external achievement, then a phenomenological approach may be particularly appropriate to the study of ageing. Neugarten, for one, emphasises the need for research employing self-reports:

In general, in studying the relations between personality, adaptation, and major life transitions, psychologists will probably gain enormously by focusing more attention on the issues that are of major concern to the individual – what the person selects as important in his past and his present, what he hopes to do in the future, what he predicts will occur, what strategies he elects, and what meanings he attaches to time, life and death. In short, psychologists would do well to make greater use of the person himself as the reporting and predicting agent, and by gathering systematic and repeated self-reports along with other types of data, to combine the phenomenological with the 'objective perspectives'. (Neugarten, 1977, pp. 639–640)

Thus, rather than in the positivist tradition of looking for causal or mechanistic explanations of 'observed' behaviour, the researcher is encouraged to seek a fuller description and understanding of behaviour and consciousness by elaborating the meaning that it has for the individual. Typically, this method of research requires an involved interviewer rather than a detached 'scientist'. It also requires 'open-ended' procedures employing spontaneous reports and personal narratives. However, the recognition of the danger of biasing one's accounts towards the experience of the most articulate and expressive of people has led some researchers to prefer a more structured approach to interviewing. In such interviews a greater number of standard probes are used, despite the inevitable loss of naturalness. Of course, there are some experiences which are difficult for most people to put into words. They may require the skills of a great writer or someone who has spent time pondering their meaning. In such circumstances the formulations of others can be used as probes. Phenomenological research would therefore seem to benefit from a variety of methods, some emphasising the recording of natural personal descriptions as they occur in context, others following a more guided form of questioning. For a well-informed review of phenomenological methods in relation to the study of adult development, see Ryff (1984).

Anthropological approaches
Recent anthropological studies on adjustment to ageing have also served to illustrate the greater interpretative power achieved by the attempt to see things 'from the inside'. Thus, Hazan (1980), in his study of a Jewish day centre in north-east London, discovered that the centre offered a radically different way of coping with life, which was acceptable to most attenders. Certain norms of behaviour and interpretations of events were enforced. Most features of the individual's past were eliminated, except those to do with shared experiences (eg anti-Fascist demonstrations in the 1930s) which did not single out individuals. The role of luck and chance in events was emphasised. Thus, any relationship was denied between investment in children or good health and the return on such behaviour. Talk on death was also taboo, even any public display of grief and mourning. The centre thus became an alternative reality, a timeless and changeless sanctuary. Hazan describes how this reality was 'defended', against those who contravened the norms, through joking,

ostracism and other means. People who could not conform eventually left the centre.

It is important to stress that it was Hazan's patient, attentive and sensitive approach to relationships and interactions within the home that allowed him to come to these penetrating and rather shocking conclusions. It is highly unlikely that the same results could be achieved by more superficial methods of research.

Another good example of the importance for personal adjustment of the interpretation people make of their life situation is provided by the work of another anthropologist. Francis (1984) looked at two communities of Eastern European Jewish origin, one in Cornell, USA and one in Leeds, England. In both cases the children provided relatively similar services for their aged parents. They assisted in illness, gave financial help, telephoned and visited regularly, and demonstrated concern. But the differences in attitude to these same children could hardly have been greater.

> Cornell parents seem uncertain and ambivalent. They want to be with their children, yet they are uncomfortable when they are. They feel that their children are too busy for them, too involved with business or their own families. Leeds informants, in contrast, seem genuinely to want to do things on their own, out of a sense of independence rather than a fear that they might be a burden. Leeds parents continue to give emotional support to their children; Cornell informants want to receive such support ....'. (Francis, 1984, p. 75)

Of the many explanations offered for these differences, the most convincing is in the life histories of the people concerned. The Cornell elderly informants were mainly Russian-born Jews who emigrated to America in their teens, but failed to adopt new modes of intergenerational relationships. The Leeds elderly informants by contrast were English born and had a similar understanding of family ties to that of their children.

The area of gerontological work with some of the best recorded material on the impact of subjective interpretation is in the study of the influence of health on morale. Although there is an association between subjectively perceived health and objectively (medically) determined health, morale and health-related activities are much more closely related to subjective health than to objective health (eg Maddox and Douglass, 1973; Palmore and Luikart, 1972; Tissue, 1972; Olbrich and Thomae, 1978). The point was illustrated in research in the Netherlands on older people who applied for places in residential-care homes. Those who were refused admission on the grounds that they were not disabled enough were found on analysis to have felt if anything worse about their health than those who were accepted. Presumably this explained in part why they wanted to enter care (Coleman, 1983). Also from the same research it was evident that although indices of disability and pathology were higher in the older members of the sample, subjective estimates of health were not associated with age. This was despite the fact that there was in general an association between objective and subjective indicators.

The most natural explanation has to do with expectations. People may expect to be somewhat disabled as they grow older and become unable to do all the things they used to. In fact, they will adapt better to infirmity in old age if they do have such expectations. On the other hand, if they remain fit and healthy, they will feel fortunate.

Perception of salience of an issue (for example, as a result of mass-media coverage of rising crime rates) and expectations (for example, of poorer health with advanced age) are important subjective factors in later-life adjustment. It is important that older people are given the opportunity to discuss the matters that concern them. Lack of contact with others can intensify anxieties and inhibit activities. For example, people may not feel able to go out because of exaggerated fears of being mugged or false notions of what is good for their health. In discussion with others they are more likely to achieve realistic attitudes to life.

Experience of the self

Central to the analysis of subjective experience are individuals' perceptions and feelings about their own self and their place in relationship to others. Self-perception is in a very real sense fundamental because so many perceptions relate directly or indirectly to the self, from the woman who interprets the frequency of her daughter's visits as a judgement on her own value, to the contribution of health and vigour to a person's self-concept, and even the position of being old in a society where crimes appear to be increasingly perpetrated on older people. The American gerontologist Schwartz has called self-esteem – the affective component of the self-concept, what people *feel* about themselves – 'the linch pin of quality of life in old age' (Schwartz, 1975). This conveys the centrality of self-perceptions.

Sources of self-esteem

We have seen that the notion of 'vulnerable self-esteem' is a helpful one indicating why some people appear to become depressed more easily than others. But virtually all people are vulnerable to a degree. We rely on sources in the world around us, in our contacts with others, our roles and activities, to maintain our sense of who we are. The challenge often in later life is to maintain a strong sense of self-identity when so many of these contacts, roles and activities are lost. Maintaining a sense of continuity of self and of self-esteem can become an overriding motivation, representing the psychological survival of the person.

In their study of old people moving into residential-care homes in the USA, Lieberman and Tobin (1983) point to the analogies between maintenance of sense of self and of physical survival. It can be a desperate matter. Many people find it difficult to acknowledge change. For example, changing appearance can be hard for a woman to bear who has always prided herself on her appearance. The same applies to a man who has always emphasised his physical strength which he now sees declining. Evidence of change, whether from mirrors, photographs, individual comparisons, is resisted. Sometimes extreme strategies are used to maintain the old sense of self, which can appear strange and illogical to observers. Often these involve myths – which exaggerate and dramatise certain personal qualities – myths of being in control of circumstances when really one is not, myths of self-constancy which deny change, and the blurring of the boundaries between past and present. People may reiterate behaviour which points to their own importance, for example writing to one's MP to complain about ordinary daily hassles!

Reminiscence, as already mentioned, is very important in the maintenance of a sense of identity, but we have to recognise that this too will sometimes be of a myth-making character – less often serving the higher order purposes of resolving conflicts and putting one's life in order according to the 'life review' theory, rather preserving an enduring sense of self. Sometimes the distortion of past or present reality will become too extreme, too bizarre, and diminish the possibility of successful adaptation, but generally a great deal of bending of reality is acceptable, and indeed in certain difficult circumstances may seem almost essential to survival.

This is not to deny that there are many even very old people whose sense of self-esteem is genuinely grounded on relationships within their family or particular activities and interests and social responsibilities. From research conducted on older people living in their own homes in the community, as well as in residential homes and sheltered housing, it is evident that most people can point to sources for a positive view of themselves. However, if we are to help those who are vulnerable because they have lost significant sources of self-esteem, we need better techniques for assessing both self-esteem and the sources people rely on than we have at present (Coleman, 1984b).

Sense of control
One important form of self-perception is the perception of being in control of events. It is clear from recent studies that this is both a crucial component of adjustment to life in an institutional setting and that it can be influenced (Langer, 1983; Rodin, 1986). Loss of perceived control is damaging both to morale and eventually to physical health. A number of experiments have shown that it is possible for people to regain a greater sense of personal responsibility. For example, in one investigation in a residential-home setting (Langer, 1983) a group of residents was addressed with speeches from the home administrator which emphasised their responsibility for their own lives. A control group received speeches from the same person which emphasised rather the staff's responsibility for them. Of the latter group, 71 per cent were rated as becoming more debilitated over a period of time as short as three weeks. In contrast with this group, 93 per cent of the people who were

encouraged to make decisions for themselves, given decisions to make, and given responsibility for something outside of themselves actually showed overall improvement. Based on their own judgements and by the judgements of the nurses with whom they interacted on a daily basis, they became more active and felt happier. Perhaps more important was the judged improvement in their mental alertness and increased behavioural involvement in many different kinds of activities.

What is particularly striking about these studies is the demonstration

> that the belief that one can affect outcomes relevant to one's own life is of paramount importance to psychological and perhaps even physical health. Interestingly, this has been shown to be true regardless of whether or not such belief in fact reflects the reality of control. (Langer, 1983, p. 280)

They emphasise the gains to be expected from shifting people from a passive state of mindlessness to an active state of mindfulness, reversing the process of social breakdown (Kuypers and Bengtson, 1973).

Perception of meaning

Self-evaluation and self-worth

Self-esteem is a broad concept which is worth differentiating further. Sometimes self-esteem is used to mean simply the ascription of positive qualities to oneself, implicitly by comparison with others or at least by reference to some standard that indicates that one is intelligent, beautiful and so forth. But there is more to self-esteem than this. The Swedish psychologist Freden makes a distinction between 'self-evaluation', which is self-esteem in this sense of 'measuring up to', and 'self-worth', which is less involved in measurement and assessment and more concerned with the perception of absolute value. People have self-worth if they value themselves and see their life as meaningful (Freden, 1982).

This distinction is important for the study of old-age adjustment. For we may be mistaken to overemphasise the self-evaluation component of self-esteem, as in feelings of being useful and capable for example, and neglecting the cultivation of perceptions and feelings of self-worth, such as perceiving and feeling there is meaning to one's life, having a sense of purpose, and having hope. These are different matters from self-evaluatory ascriptions but are no less important. I remember well a man I interviewed some years back, in his late eighties, living in sheltered housing, very frail and totally dependent on others for his survival. Someone got him up in the morning, someone brought him his meals and others helped him throughout the day. He answered my questions on self-esteem calmly. Yes, he said, he felt useless, but in his condition and at his age he was entitled to feel useless, he did not struggle with the thought at all, he accepted it with equanimity. It was quite a revealing experience to me; because of the way he said what he did, he took away the negative connotation from the term 'useless' as it applied to his situation. What was more important was that he still saw meaning in his life.

Meaning is not an abstruse issue. It is a very interesting question whether people find meaning in their lives and how they do it (Antonovsky, 1979). Some find it in the course of their ordinary everyday pursuits, whereas others do not. Some lose it with their partner, with their job or with their health. In old age the issue of meaning often becomes more acute because previously given meanings disappear, contained for example in the tasks that society requires of one in growing up, working, raising a family, and so on. It is probably no accident that many great writers have chosen old age as their theme when it comes to raising issues of the meaning of existence. Loss of meaning is the ultimate loss, the feeling of emptiness and disgust conveyed by Shakespeare's Macbeth when he hears that his wife has committed suicide and as he begins to realise the collapse of his ambitions: 'A tale told by an idiot ... full of sound and fury ... signifying nothing'. Researchers have recently begun to address the question of how older people find acceptable meanings in situations where their abilities and resources may be seriously impaired (see for example Nies and Munnichs, 1986; Reker and Wong, 1988; Dittmann-Kohli, 1988).

As meanings are constructed and continue over a period of time, negative and positive reactions are to a certain extent predictable. For example, recent Dutch longitudinal studies have highlighted attitudes to dependency as the major predictor of changes in self-esteem in older people being relocated to institutional settings. Those who previously had negative feelings about being taken care of by others suffered the most damage to their sense of self once they had moved (Mertens and Wimmers, 1987).

Religion, values and psychophilosophy

Religion is one of the great providers of meaning to life, and it is a great shame that the mutual antipathies between many psychologists and religious ministers have meant that we have very little understanding of the role of religion in human development generally. Fortunately that situation is now changing (see for example Leech, 1977; Bergin, 1983). From recent research it is clear that religious faith and sentiment play an important part in older Americans' lives. For example, religious thinking constitutes one of the most prominent and successful ways older people control their emotional responses in difficult situations (Koenig et al, 1988). Although religious attitudes to life appear to be less common in Britain than in America, it is surprising that their study has been so neglected by gerontologists (see Coleman, 1990).

A religious faith is not the only provider of meaning in people's lives. Many philosophies do the same, whether the stoicism of the classical world or the existentialism of the twentieth century. The American writer on counselling older people, Sherman, has pointed to the special

importance in old age of what he calls 'psychophilosophy', ie a philosophy which has the power to change a person's psychology, their way of
feeling as well as thinking about themselves (Sherman, 1981). He argues
that older people need a way of thinking and feeling that allows them
to be compassionate with themselves, and indeed in the last analysis to
transcend concern with themselves. This is a lifetime's task, of course,
but one which receives its culmination in later life. We should provide
opportunities for older people to talk and discuss issues relating to their
perception of life, its values and meanings, and the things which concern
them. It is an advantage if they have the opportunity to clarify their
thoughts and feelings together with people who have the same concerns.

A fundamental issue for the present generation of older people is
that often they are caught between two sets of values, which is one
of the problems they may need to clarify for themselves. The so-called
'functional worth ethic' has been dominant for most of their lives, and
works against them in later life where lack of occupation seems akin
to idleness. But now we are approaching a period in human history
where leisure time pursuits, voluntary community work and creative
expression are becoming more important and paid work less. Older
people, therefore, should feel entitled to make good use of the free time
they have available. They should be able – if they have the resources – to
fully partake in this new pattern of life.

Meaning and case-study analysis
The study of meaning, of what makes life worth living, is less susceptible
to recognised forms of scientific investigation than other areas of enquiry.
This is part of the reason for its neglect. If what we are concerned with
is people's own understanding of their situation, standard tests and
questionnaires on which individuals can be scored and generalisations
made are less applicable. Such perceptions are by their very nature subtle.
More detailed acquaintance and investigation of the individual subject
are required, which place particular observations of a person's attitudes
in the context of his or her daily life. The person in context becomes the
focus of investigation.

Bromley has recently argued in favour of the development of systematic case-study methods, particularly in the field of the study of
adjustment. He demonstrates that judicial and natural-history methods
are capable of dealing rationally with empirical data and are respectable
scientific procedures (Bromley, 1978; 1986).

> The essential feature of a psychological case study is that it focuses upon
> the 'person in a situation'; it does not attempt to study the personality as
> a whole (an impossibility) but to study this or that specific problem of
> personal adjustment. The case study method, in other words, is a way of
> solving problems – human problems. (Bromley, 1978, p. 35)

If data were collected systematically a body of 'case law' could be built up
based on comparisons and contrasts between individual cases. Such 'case

law' already exists, mostly informally and unsystematically, in many areas of professional work such as psychogeriatrics. It is a pity that not more advantage is made of opportunities for more systematic studies. We must not, of course, only look at examples of maladjustment in later life. A proper consideration of examples of well-adjusted older people could in the long run be of much greater benefit in indicating the conditions conducive to optimal living in later life.

UNDERSTANDING ADJUSTMENT IN LATER LIFE

This chapter began by pointing out that the focus on adjustment to old age in so many studies of ageing may conceal an ageist bias. It is only more recently that investigators have pointed out just how well older people do cope with life. In fact, theorists who have seen old age positively provide the most useful models of adjustment. Thus, Erikson's ideal of 'integrity' as the goal of life was drawn on to focus interest on the special tasks that confront people in advanced age: coming to terms with life as it has been lived, making sense of a changing society, and facing the reality of death.

Stress in old age has been the object of study of psychiatrists as well as social scientists. The former have highlighted the depressing effects of poor physical health in particular and the importance of the presence of a confidant. Social science research has demonstrated age differences both in frequency of types of stress encountered and styles of coping employed. However, individual differences remain large and improved understanding of the ways people cope with difficulties requires intensive study, preferably both multidisciplinary and longitudinal.

Above all, we need to understand better the way in which individuals interpret experience. This requires the introduction of different research methods to the standard scientific paradigms, for example approaching social situations in a more holistic anthropological way, employing phenomenological means of data collection, and carrying out detailed case-study analyses of individual adjustment. Successful ageing seems to involve not only maintenance of self-esteem, but also perception of continuing meaning in life. Detailed investigation of the latter has only just begun.

6

ENVIRONMENT AND BEHAVIOUR:
A CLINICAL PERSPECTIVE

Jeffrey Garland

Defining 'behaviour' as a function of personality interacting with a range of environmental situations, and encompassing what people do, say, think and feel, we adopt in this chapter a perspective from clinical psychology, reviewing the main factors believed to influence the psychological well-being of old people and their carers. For a detailed development of this standpoint, the reader is referred to Woods and Britton (1985), or to Woods (1987) for an overview.

Our concern here is with factors both external (physical surroundings and the behaviour of others) and internal (health status and personality). An individual's personality is of particular interest as determining the appraisal of, and reaction to, environmental demands.

As already outlined in Chapters 2 and 4 a promising context for understanding human ageing is provided by life-span development theory (Sugarman, 1986). As Bromley (1986) explains in his presentation of case study methods of research, clinicians are prime examples of investigators who need to consider both current events and life history in their accounts of individual cases.

Inevitably, the perspective of clinical practice with older people is grounded most firmly in the study of processes of abnormal ageing and failure to cope with normal ageing. Lack of integration of this material with information concerning environmental influences on normal individuals coping relatively well with normal ageing must be acknowledged (see also Chapter 5).

Theory and technology for understanding and influencing the behaviour of older people and carers is developing rapidly, and professional practice is in a state of ferment. Complicating factors include: heterogeneity of population; conflicting aims; a history of piecemeal and uncoordinated research; narrowness of approach by specialists neglecting approaches that have been shown to benefit younger subjects; and lack of resources for early detection of problematic behaviour.

This chapter attempts to define 'environment' and lists major factors contributing to psychological well-being. The clinical significance of stress as a major mismatch between environmental demands and an individual's perceived ability to cope is examined, and scope for increasing knowledge of the ways in which older people shape their own environments is recognised. Requirements for institutional living and the establishment of guidelines for practice in residential care are outlined. Key issues concerning the management of psychological problems of individuals and of the systems with which each person is involved are discussed, with illustrations of clinical principles and method. Finally, some difficulties in measuring quality of life and in assessing change in psychological functioning of older people are explored, with suggestions for their partial resolution.

It is argued that clinical understanding of environment in relation to behaviour is advancing unevenly. It is proposed that further exploration is particularly needed in the following areas: the identification and fostering of inherent coping skills in older people and their carers; the development of a programme of shared setting of priorities and engagement in projects, to bring social and clinical perspectives closer to each other.

THE ROLE OF THE ENVIRONMENT

'Environment' is a complex term embracing internal and external factors, and incorporating physical, psychological and social features. Effects of the environment cannot be understood in isolation from characteristics of the older person, and of interaction between the individual's predisposition to respond, environmental stimuli, the person's response, and its consequences for that individual. Understandably, faced with such complexity, theories of human ecology strive to simplify, although at the cost of verging on caricature.

With ageing there is loss of adaptability, as homeostatic mechanisms that underpin adaptive responding to challenges from the environment lose sensitivity and accuracy. The ultimate manifestation of such change is of course death as a result of demands that can no longer be met. Reduced tolerance may interact with increased pressure: for example, as the general standard of home insulation and heating for older people is poorer than that enjoyed by younger adults, risk of exposure of the most frail to hypothermia is increased (Wilcock et al, 1982).

Those individuals most impaired by ageing can be expected to show increased 'environmental docility' (Lawton, 1982), with greater dependence on external environmental cues to trigger responses, and reduced likelihood of purposeful 'spontaneous' internally cued responses. As an individual's competence decreases, the proportion of behaviour directly attributable to external influence appears to increase.

Three current models for understanding environmental influences on older people are reviewed by Scheidt and Windley (1985). The first of these, the adaptation theory proposed by Lawton and Nahemow (1973) assumes that the individual consistently works to maintain a steady state between two factors: awareness of environmental press (challenge from stimuli that activate behaviour); and consciousness of competence (the sum of physical and psychological coping resources). It is proposed that a relatively close match is optimal for maintaining adaptive behaviour.

This resembles the congruence model of Kahana (1982), which relates environmental press and individual needs, and views adaptive behaviour as a balancing mechanism by which the person can regulate external stimulation or review priority of needs to achieve or maintain optimal congruence. It is suggested that complete congruence can have a negative impact, and that the more competent older person can be expected to seek out environmental challenge, stretching adaptive capacity.

Taking account of older people's increased vulnerability to environmental risk, Schooler (1982) adopts a cognitive theory of stress and coping influenced by Lazarus et al (1974). The individual is assumed to scan environmental challenges (primary appraisal), and when threat is perceived, to review choice of reactions to remove potential harm (secondary appraisal). This perspective has allowed, for example, evaluation of whether the presence of a social support network has a positive effect on primary or secondary appraisal.

The global concept of 'environment' needs to be broken down into component factors if it is to be understood more clearly. Scheidt and Windley (1985) list the following 10 factors:

1. sensory stimulation;
2. comfort, with adequate temperature and lighting, compensating for increased sensitivity to glare, and for slowness in dark/light adaptation;
3. aesthetic attractiveness for the occupant;
4. privacy and security, supporting maintenance of self-esteem, with a feeling of attachment and belonging;
5. clearness and consistency of lay-out, with relatively stable organisation and structure;
6. flexibility if remodelling is required to suit the old person's needs;
7. a feeling of control by the occupier, so that territory is free from trespass;
8. opportunity for social contacts as required;
9. accessibility for the occupier, so that any part of the surroundings can be reached as needed; and,
10. whether the density of population is variable, rather than space being consistently empty or always crowded.

It should be noted here that detailed evidence on which to assess the relative significance of such factors can be difficult to find. For example, Zeisel et al (1977) reported the opinions of a group of eight experts (psychologists, sociologists, architects and interior designers), who advise on the design of accommodation for old people. They were asked to rate the importance of each of 123 design features, on the basis of availability of research evidence. Only eight features were known by at least three experts to be the subject of systematic data to support a judgement, and only 32 were known by at least two experts to have such evidence. It might be hoped that if this study were to be replicated now there would be a substantial improvement in knowledge, but it cannot be asserted with confidence that this would be the case.

Nearly all the research into environmental influences on behaviour of old people has focused on institutional settings. However, as Rowles (1980) and Lawton (1980) explain, an older person's own home and locality, territory which is familiar and secure, is wherever possible the most desirable of all prosthetic environments in facilitating adaptation. This consideration can be expected to prompt sustained growth in investigation of the interaction of older people with their domestic and community settings. A notable example is offered by Sixsmith (1986), who has investigated the 'amalgam of subjective feelings and physical opportunities and constraints' that appears to represent meanings and experiences of home for a group of people over 65 living in their own home, either rented or owned, in two working-class areas of Newcastle upon Tyne.

EFFECTS OF STRESS ON INDIVIDUAL FUNCTIONING

The role of accumulated consequences of acute and chronic stress over the lifespan on mental or physical health problems in old age is an extremely complex issue which is largely unresolved. A generally accepted model (Lazarus, 1966; Lazarus et al, 1974), is that 'stress' represents demands from within or without that tax or exceed available resources of the individual or social system. Key components in stress reaction include both psychological mechanisms (cognitive appraisal of the significance of stress stimuli, preferred coping strategies, and repertoire of behavioural responses) and physiological mechanisms (internal stimuli and body changes, emotional states, and physiological responses). Feedback loops connect these components and their elements, and there are pronounced individual differences in the expression of response to stress.

For example, Mr Burns, an 83-year-old patient in a community hospital who will remain unfit to return home, refuses to agree to apply for a place in an old people's home. He is obdurate, becomes increasingly difficult to nurse, and is referred to a clinical psychologist for assessment. Mr Burns explains that he feels 'bothered' and 'distressed' by his situation. He views the local home as 'a place where they sit around in bunches, wanting to die'. He construes the repeated invitations by carers to sign his application papers as tantamount to the invitation 'dilly, dilly, come and be killed'.

During such sessions he feels tightness in his chest, difficulty in breathing, and increased awareness of his arthritic stiffness, as though he's becoming 'just like a corpse'. These physical sensations feed back into a state of 'panic', and he shouts at the carers because 'I just want them to clear out and leave me alone'. In emotional arousal, he frequently finds himself thinking of a grandson who, he claims, owes him several thousand pounds. Mr Burns considers that while he is in the hospital he is 'free' to pursue (or at least to feel that he could pursue) his claim against the young man. Once in the home, he considers, he would become a powerless 'inmate' and the grandson would be confirmed as 'having won'.

He acknowledges that he alternately bullies his carers ('because I can't abide being so helpless'), and cajoles them ('because I know I need them for every blessed thing'). He contrasts his working life as a lime burner ('16 hours a day, 7 days a week') with his present existence ('not being able to do a damn thing'), and recognises that being demanding with carers, and rehearsing endless details of projected litigation is his way of coping with the stress of prolonged inactivity.

Not all stress is necessarily experienced as negative. Studies of younger adults frequently divided 'stress' in terms of: 'normal' stress, produced by disturbing events or changes, either positive or negative, which evoke emergency reactions; 'distress', chronic normal stress associated with frustration and conflict, often accompanied by a feeling of helplessness, and capable if prolonged of depressing the immune system and increasing liability to infection and illness; and 'eustress', in which an individual feels positively challenged to energetic achievement (Selye, 1976).

Such distinctions are not usually made in studies of older people and it may indeed be the case that with ageing stress tends to be experienced in a less differentiated way, and hence many individuals have a less flexible range of responses and, with lower adaptive capacity, are more likely to show disorganised responses. Disturbed bowel functioning, with cycles of chronic constipation, or diarrhoea, can be produced by chronic stress, and preoccupation with bowel functioning characterises many old people receiving treatment for psychological stress.

Stress and caring

Stress is also experienced by family and friends of more disturbed old people (Gilhooly, 1987) and the appraisal of such burdens (objective problems) and strain (subjective reaction) is one of the best developed areas in the British literature (Gilleard, 1984). The rapidly developing body of investigation into carer support should assist in understanding the gross discrepancies between burden and strain that are sometimes observed.

The model of family-oriented community care for elderly people who are mentally infirm proposed by Gilleard is becoming increasingly influential in British practice. His analysis of the situation of both sufferer and carer is worth quoting:

> Dementia is fundamentally the erosion of self, whose management requires
> an increasingly supervisory and supportive agency to take responsibility for
> the dementing person's behaviour as their intending and adapting self fades.
> The difficulties and limitations of family carers that are evinced in this
> process are sufficiently stressful for the majority of carers to require some
> form of professional intervention, but one based upon developing a shared
> commitment to the supervisory and supportive aspects of caring at a rate
> which permits the principal carer to maintain their caring role as they have
> the desire and resources to do so (Gilleard, 1984, pp. 119–120).

The most noxious product of stress is abuse of old people by carers or of
carers by old people. Kosberg (1983) offers a comprehensive review of this
emotive issue. Definition of what constitutes physical or psychological
'abuse' remains a vexed question, as Eastman (1985) recognises, in a brief
text that has raised the awareness of British professionals. There are no
easy answers. For example, it may be observed, as Gilleard has argued,
that emphasis on community care may involve 'care' that is vestigial, or
ill-conceived, bordering on abuse.

One example, from the experience of a clinical psychologist, involved
a referral from a home-care assistant of a client couple. The devoted,
but frail and increasingly forgetful, wife was the principal supporter
of her physically disabled husband, and had developed a detailed care
routine. This began each morning with giving him a blanket bath. On
the carer's more harassed mornings this could seem interminable for the
long-suffering husband, as she not infrequently forgot where she'd got to,
and 'went back to the top to start again, just to be on the safe side'. The
care assistant remonstrated gently with the wife, but was told bluntly
that this was her way of caring, and 'if you know so much, take him into
hospital and they'll do it properly there'.

The extent to which home-care practice, excellent in principle, colludes
in practice with such borderline procedure appears to be relatively
undocumented, and this topic merits research.

OLDER PEOPLE SHAPING THEIR ENVIRONMENT

In considering environmental influences on behaviour, it is important
to recognise a principle of reciprocity. Older people are not necessarily
passive recipients of influence, but can shape the responses of the relatively young who may have set out to influence them. This fascinating
phenomenon of reverse behaviour change ('the biter bit'), in which
carers find their own activity being altered by a resistant target, has
been described (Rebok and Hoyer, 1977) but has not yet received the
attention it deserves.

A related consideration, also unduly neglected, is that even apparently
maladaptive acts in late life can represent attempts to maintain relatively
intact functioning, or at least a semblance of it, by a damaged old person
trying to make sense of a confusing world.

For example, a new resident at an old people's home scandalises the

Head when, asked how he is settling in, he replies: 'It's not too bad – down here on the pig farm!'. This is interpreted as unequivocal evidence of 'confusion', until it is ascertained that the resident had as a teenager worked unhappily on the family pig farm at his father's insistence until the business went bankrupt, releasing him to do what he really wanted, but leaving him with a continuing tendency to label any situation in which he felt under duress as 'just like the pig farm'.

Five basic coping styles have been outlined by Kahana and Kahana (1983), based on longitudinal study of older people in institutional care. They list these as: instrumental (to recognise a problem and deal with it directly); intrapsychic (to avoid conflict by changing one's attitude); affective (to release tension by expressing feelings); escapist (to turn to alternative activities); and resigned helplessness. As they illustrate, a resident in an old people's home, finding lack of privacy stressful, may, to establish 'private' territory, come to accept 'it doesn't really matter'; express resentment of the situation; keep on the move to avoid contact; or just give up trying.

A further mode of responding to pressure to be observed in some older people, which has suffered relative neglect in the literature, is the so-called 'Goldwyn syndrome', named after the Hollywood producer who is reputed to have cultivated a reputation for naive uncultured sayings ('Goldwynisms'), to disarm business rivals and win publicity. Essentially, a victim of negative stereotyping turns this to advantage by consciously acting down to low expectations, exploiting the leeway others allow.

Thus, a 'confused' day-hospital attender sought by an officious Sister only a few feet away shouting 'Mr Harris! Where's Mr Harris?' carols back, 'He's on the roof! He's on the roof!', meets Sister's alarmed recognition calmly, and as she turns away deflated, winks broadly at a companion.

OLDER PEOPLE DETERMINING THEIR HEALTH

While much has been made of the influence on public and professional attitudes of 'ageism' (see Chapter 12) we should recognise that older people can be 'ageist' too in their health beliefs and behaviour. The origins of these health attitudes need to be carefully considered. An increasingly cost-conscious National Health Service in Britain is directing more attention towards health promotion, with old people as a priority target. This prospect should stimulate professionals' interest in influencing health-related behaviour.

Johnson (1986) forecasts that this interest will be spurred on by the demands from within the retired population of a rising number of people who

> will have experienced relative prosperity, support of the welfare state, and the rise of consumerism. A new and more aggressive climate of expectation can be expected to replace the polite acquiescence and minimal expectations to which

researchers and practitioners are currently accustomed. (Johnson, 1986, p. 24)

Commenting that surprisingly few studies of health beliefs deal with old people, in spite of the high visibility of elderly people as a high demand group, Ford (1986) points out that the low explanatory power of a health beliefs model in predicting illness behaviour is hardly surprising in view of the complex structure of such behaviour. He suggests:

> The decision to seek medical aid is only one possible outcome in a complex process of assessment and decision-making which is shaped by culture, attitudes, folk medical knowledge, personal biography, influence from social networks, present goals and perceptions of the costs and benefits of entering the 'sick role', as well as by the inherent ambiguity of most symptoms themselves. (Ford, 1986, p. 130)

Although the literature is limited, Ford comments, a few stereotypes can be effectively challenged. For example, old people in general are not heavy users of the health service, but this impression is given by the fact that a relatively small proportion of elderly people use a great deal of health care.

Reviewing the use of medicines by older people, Anderson and Cartwright (1986) find that general practitioners tend to lack knowledge about medicines (both prescribed and otherwise) being taken by their elderly patients. They acknowledge that, until regular review and audit of medicines is universal, not all compliance by patients can be regarded as necessary. These authors see:

> Wide scope for research in this field, documenting first who uses what medicines when, and including the use of non-prescribed medicines, and secondly considering the role of some factors, other than the demographic, as influences upon the use of medicines, particularly, perhaps, the meaning and significance of medicine use from the patient's perspective. There is a need to establish the frequency of drug problems in the elderly and to identify the medicines with which these problems are associated: from study of side effects and difficulties in using medicines, to identification of medicines which are not used when they could be helpful, and of other medicines which continue to be used when they are no longer helpful and may be hazardous. (Anderson and Cartwright, 1986, p. 195)

ENVIRONMENTAL REQUIREMENTS FOR INSTITUTIONAL LIVING

Ideally, residential care would cater for individual needs, and promote residents' sense of being in control, remaining as independent as possible, and being approached as individual persons rather than under the collective identity of residents.

In practice it is inevitable that residential living enforces a degree of conformity, in that an individual's rights and responsibilities have to be weighed against those of the group, and the process of looking after residents can involve limits on liberty. Norman's *Rights and Risk* (1980) has been particularly influential in shaping attitudes of staff towards support of relative independence for residents, while recognising that this can entail risk for the more physically frail.

Physical environment

Physical and social factors interrelate frequently. For example, following Sommer and Ross (1958) many papers on environmental issues have underlined the value of changing chair arrangements from round-the-walls rows to clusters to promote social interaction, and perhaps because of its intuitive appeal this finding probably has been applied more widely than any other in this field. An illustration of the increasing precision that can be noted in recent environmental research is provided by Finlay et al (1983), examining chair design features in relation to maintenance of mobility by elderly occupants.

It must be accepted that containment is a major priority in residential care, particularly for those residents deemed to be at risk because of their disorientation should they 'wander' out of the care setting. The environment may maintain such residents through various means, including: locked doors, double-handled doors, a photo-electric circuit with bell or buzzer; discouragement and distraction by staff; dressing residents in night clothes by day for ease of recognition should they leave; physical restraint, for example in a geriatric chair locked in with a tray; a 'chemical straightjacket' of medication; behaviour modification programmes; activity, exercise and structured day design which features areas of protected space where residents may move in safety; confident, positive staff attitudes, through which 'wandering' is perceived as understandable and tolerable.

The residential-care setting need not exclude the outside world. Rowles (1981) points out that an important source of stimulation for residents comes through the provision of viewing areas looking out onto foyers, courtyards or entrances, to watch the parade of life around a home. However, requirements of keeping building costs down and of maintaining residents' safety can conflict with the need to offer a rewarding environment, and compromise is inevitable, since it must be recognised that an extreme emphasis on secure custodial care interferes with expression of residents' individual needs (Willcocks et al, 1987).

Social environment

Goldberg and Connelly (1982), in their review of British literature on social care, find little consensus on this topic, but offer a list of positive aspects:

1. flexibility of management practices;
2. individualisation and autonomy for residents;
3. opportunities for privacy;
4. opportunities for social stimulation;

5. communication and interaction with the outside world;
6. social interaction between staff and residents (in addition to instrumental communication);
7. maximum delegation of decision-making to care staff and to residents;
8. good communication channels between staff;
9. a minimum degree of specialisation of rules and tasks among staff. (Goldberg and Connelly, 1982, pp. 272–273).

Dick (1985) has challenged nurses 'in ward or residential home' to consider whether some of these features exist, indicating the relevance of similar indices for both settings.

Attempts to conceptualise and measure different care environments derive from different purposes, focus on different features and assess them in different ways. Notable research has been carried out in North America by, for example, Moos (Moos et al, 1979), who has developed a number of indices to measure social environment. Lemke and Moos (1986) report on the developments of eight of these: comfort, security, staffing levels, staff richness, services, autonomy, control, and rapport. These are only moderately interrelated, suggesting that the social environment is multi-dimensional and that staffing levels are relatively independent of the other indices. Pincus (Pincus and Wood, 1970) has also developed assessment of social environments, through residents' descriptions of such characteristics as physical features, the kinds of rules, regulations and programmes and staff behaviour with residents.

An important recent British investigation is by Booth (1985), who offers a detailed review of resident dependency and outcome of care in relation to institutional regime and caring routines in 175 homes for elderly people. He describes the development of an Institutional Regimes Questionnaire, in a study intended to enhance the influence of social service authorities in adopting

> a much firmer and more consistent stand on the management of residential homes by spelling out the kind of principles and policies that should underpin the care they give and determine every home's practices. (Booth, 1985, pp. 139–140).

However, Booth admits:

> The findings of this study make rather depressing reading. On the one hand, real differences in what happens to residents have been found: in some homes they die sooner and deteriorate faster than in others. On the other hand, success or failure in this respect appears to have nothing to do with how the homes are run, with the caring routines and practices followed by staff. The diversity of outcomes among homes occurred despite and not because of any differences in the character of their regimes.
> This conclusion has led us to reject the comforting idea that most of the damaging consequences of institutional living could be avoided by improved methods of care and better training for staff, and seriously to question the rationale that informs current notions of good practice in residential work. The effects on individual residents of living in old people's homes seem to be very much a matter of pot-luck. (Booth, 1985, p. 205)

One way of reducing institutional pressures in residential care is through group living schemes, breaking down a home of, say, 40 or 50 places into living units of between eight and 10 residents. Each unit has its own living space, group tasks, and domestic activities, maintaining normal living as far as possible. Rothwell, Britton and Woods (1983) found residents in group living more engaged (in constructive activity) and happier, and noted that staff attitudes and expectations became much more positive.

Among those to advocate group living units have been Lipman and Slater (1977), who suggested that such units needed to be shielded from care staff by physical barriers (stairs, lobby areas), to reduce excessive staff contact which could erode residents' independence. However, Booth and Phillips (1987), in a comparative study of outcomes of care for residents in traditional regimes and in group living, find only modest differences, not all of which favour the latter, and conclude that group living arrangements have been 'oversold' and promise more than they can deliver.

Establishing guidelines for practice

Guidelines for residential care such as *Home Life* (Centre for Policy on Ageing, 1984), and the recent report of the independent review *Residential Care: A Positive Choice* (National Institute for Social Work, 1988), and formulations of good practice in services for people with dementia such as that produced by the King Edward's Hospital Fund for London (King's Fund Centre, 1986), are invaluable aids to structuring thinking in regard to environmental requirements.

Home Life: a Code of Practice for Residential Care is a report of a working party sponsored by the Department of Health and Social Security and convened by the Centre for Policy on Ageing under the chairmanship of Lady Avebury. A wide range of client groups including old people are featured, and among 218 recommendations are five based on research findings (Goldberg and Connelly, 1982), referring specifically to old people: the right of elderly residents to autonomy and choice should always be recognised; the layout, decor and furnishing of the home should be designed to minimise confusion; staff should be trained to understand the needs of mentally and physically frail old people; community support and treatment services should be consulted in the care of mentally ill elderly people; and physical restraint and control by sedation should not be used.

The King's Fund project paper *Living Well into Old Age* sets out principles of good practices for services for older people with psychiatric disorders, with particular attention to dementia, and relating to support services in the community as well as institutional settings. As the paper recognises,

> the principles of our existing services are very muddled. They are a mixture of government statements, the traditions of the past and day-to-day solutions

to problems drawn up by staff. Much of the policy is unwritten. (King's Fund
Centre, 1986, p. 7)

Five key principles are spelled out: people with dementia have the same
human value as anyone else irrespective of their degree of disability or
dependence; people with dementia have the same varied human needs as
anyone else; people with dementia have the same rights as other citizens;
every person with dementia is an individual; people with dementia
have the right to forms of support which do not exploit family and
friends. In each case the paper proceeds to examine: what this means
for the individual; the implications for frontline staff and services; how
to establish the effectiveness of a service in relation to the principles; and
implications for managers and planners in the strategic tasks of service
development.

How may such guidelines be translated into practice? Barrowclough
and Fleming (1986) suggest goal planning for meeting residents' individual needs, based on the principles spelled out by Houts and Scott (1976):

1. involve the resident from the beginning;
2. use the resident's strengths to set goals which help with his needs;
3. set reasonable goals;
4. spell out the steps necessary to reach each goal; and
5. state clearly what the resident will do, what the staff will do and when
   you hope to reach each goal.

As Houts and Scott comment, such principles seem obvious, but are often
forgotten because residents tend to be seen as passive recipients of care
and professional carers are apt to focus on problems which take up so
much of their energy that goal-setting is relatively neglected.

Among notable examples of the many training packs which bid to
promote more positive attitudes in residential care staff are *In Our
Care* (Crosby and Traynor, 1985), and 'Over the Hill and Far Away'
(Murphy, 1986). Such initiatives proliferate (Garland, 1985), although
their evaluation is cursory as yet.

DISTURBED BEHAVIOUR

A generally agreed taxonomy of disturbed behaviour in late life is lacking.
Regarding mental health, Woods (1987) indicates the two major problems
as dementia (progressive and irreversible intellectual impairment, accompanied by adverse personality change) and depression.

Reality orientation

Psychological management of the dementias focuses on improving quality of life for sufferers and their carers, with care programmes encouraging as much independence, socialising, and activity as possible. Reality
orientation (RO), which is used more generally in residential care than

in the community, as a means to these ends, is described by Holden and Woods (1988). The term covers a range of environmental features designed to orient sufferers verbally and behaviourally, so they can be more aware of what is happening around them and use this information in their daily lives. Informal or 24-hour RO is used throughout the day in staff–patient interactions, and patients are encouraged to use memory aids, signs, and notices for orientation. The advantages of such cues are demonstrated by Hanley (1981). In so-called 'classroom RO' small groups of about four to six patients engage in supervised structured activities and discussion with cues, prompts, reinforcement of approximations to improved orientation, and withdrawal of attention from confused behaviour.

Reality orientation prescribes distinct staff attitudes to be adopted for different types of patient: active friendliness for the apathetic; passive friendliness for the frightened or suspicious; matter-of-fact for the manipulative or maladjusted; kind and firm for the depressed; and no-demand (other than to stay, not to harm others, and to take medication) for the angry. Many researchers have pointed out that RO's main recommendation could be that it is a philosophy of care which gives staff encouragement to communicate with patients and a rationale for doing so. In view of the aversive nature of many demented patients (Bromley, 1978), such an incentive is particularly important.

Recently, other approaches to interacting with demented people have been recommended, including 'reminiscence', which makes use of the fact that a confused person's memory for the past is often relatively well preserved (Norris, 1987), and 'validation therapy' which encourages the worker to recognise the validity of the emotions the person is expressing (Robb et al, 1986).

Approaching behaviour problems

Apart from intellectual impairment, a wide variety of behavioural problems may also be observed in sufferers, both in residential care and in the community where the majority are to be found. Some of the most oppressive for carers to cope with (Gilleard, 1984) are: nocturnal disturbance; incontinence; immobility; absence of purposeful behaviour; following carer or asking the same question, continually.

Disorientation can be a factor in 'apparent incontinence', ie incontinence which does not necessarily have as its primary cause impaired bladder or bowel functioning. Among many other possible causes can be unfamiliarity with location of toilets in new surroundings, impaired mobility, or failure of carers to prompt appropriately. An excellent review of factors affecting the maintenance of continence is provided by Smith and Smith (1987).

To assist with understanding and management of such problems, there is a growing number of guides for carers, for example by the Health

Education Council (1986), and a series of short texts on specific problems begun by Stokes (1986, a,b,c,d). For professionals, Wattis and Church (1986) offer a valuable introduction to these problems and other issues in the psychiatry of old age.

Depression

For psychological understanding and management of depression in older people, Hanley and Baikie (1984) offer an analysis leaning heavily on practice and research in cognitive therapy (see also Williams, 1984), in which the patient is helped to identify and distinguish characteristic patterns of thinking which are productive and to separate these from destructive patterns. He or she is then supported in developing patterns of thought related to positive coping, and in trying out environmental changes and modes of behaviour consistent with positive thinking.

Depression is frequently allied to sensitivity to pain and physical discomfort in older people (Wattis and Church, 1986), reduced sexual functioning (Baikie, 1984), and bereavement (Woods and Britton, 1985). It needs to be seen in the context of the general study of adjustment to ageing. For a review of the evidence on causative and preventive factors see Chapter 5.

Anxiety

The use of 'anxiety management', a package of self-control procedures (for example, relaxation training), taught by a therapist and practised by the client under supervision has been extended to older people, as Woods and Britton (1985) illustrate.

As Hussian (1981) suggests:

> Age-related anxiety-producing stimuli ... may include changes in residence, fears of losing control, financial problems, death and dying, being alone, stairways, steps, going outdoors alone, being too far away from a bathroom, inability to remember recent or remote events with any clarity, spending holidays alone, fear of post-holiday depression, losing one's sensory acuity, losing one's mind, choking, being robbed or accosted, being laughed at, various modes of transportation, going shopping, physical examinations, and minor surgery. (Hussian, 1981, p. 102)

All of these situations may pose serious threats to an elderly, slightly incapacitated person for very good reasons. A recent survey in London has highlighted a high prevalence of phobic disorders (10 per cent) among people aged 65 years and over living at home (Lindesay et al, 1989).

A systematic approach

Although an individual old person generally is presented as sole cause and origin of untoward behaviour, the involvement of the system with which the old person is engaged, whether family or a wider network of neighbours, volunteers and professional carers, is often found to be crucial.

Increasingly, clinical psychologists and allied professionals working with support networks find themselves adopting a systematic approach in which the network itself is the major target of influence. Thus, an intervention which begins with a focus on 'disturbed' behaviour in an elderly woman, apparently in reaction to recently introduced day care, switches to family therapy when an initial interview with husband and unmarried daughter with whom she lives reveals high evidence (no less than 14 fault-finding topics in one hour) of critical comment by them in relation to the 'designated' patient, fuelling her longstanding feelings of rejection which introduction of day care had exacerbated rather than triggered.

Issues and techniques in family work with older people are illustrated by Pottle (1984) and Ratna and Davis (1984), and with increasing emphasis on community care such literature is expanding rapidly.

A summary of the systems approach as applied to the promotion of change in residential care of old people is offered by Jeffery (1986). He considers, as essential for success:

1. a time scale of years rather than months;
2. support for change agents from those in positions of power;
3. keeping freedom to manoeuvre by maintaining a distance from the system while at the same time working within it;
4. knowing the system – its rules, politics, hierarchies and boundaries;
5. an appreciation of the complexity of organisational change;
6. a planned strategy and tactics for implementation of change which allow for flexibility; and
7. skilled observation, analysis, interaction and persistence.
   (Jeffery, 1986, p. 146)

Groupwork

Groupwork with older people in which a number of individual patients are seen together by a therapist or therapists, to take advantage of opportunities for learning from peers and using the positive pressures that group commitment can exert, is growing in popularity beyond familiar reality orientation functions, to encompass problem-solving, memory training (Wilson and Moffat, 1984), anxiety management, and other therapeutic topics. A useful introduction is provided by Bender and Norris (1987).

Clinical psychology in practice

For intervention to influence disturbed behaviour in older people, whether the focus is on a network, a therapeutic group, or the individual alone, guiding principles can be distinguished from a consideration of the relevant literature (Garland, 1987):

1. emphasize early action, producing minimal disruption;
2. maintain client's independence as far as possible;
3. consult fully with designated client, principal carers and supporters;
4. establish the client's needs and what incentives will help meet those needs;
5. reflect on the advisability and nature of a proposed intervention before starting;
6. accept that often it is more economical of effort and in the client's interests to work through carers rather than solely one-to-one with the client;
7. model and encourage objective assessment throughout the intervention;
8. set out action in small, specific steps which are clearly understood;
9. review progress regularly with participants; and
10. evaluate outcome and follow up where necessary.

It is rare for an intervention dealing with disturbed behaviour involving an old person to rely on a single axiomatic technique. Even if behaviour management theory and technology were to evolve substantially, it would still remain the case that most problem behaviours would appear to be multiply determined, and that intervention should be geared to the complex and idiosyncratic needs of the system concerned.

'Menu' selection

Therefore, the consultant on a problem behaviour usually needs to make available a 'menu' of advice and procedures from which selections may be made. This is illustrated by the following (condensed) example (Garland, 1987) of guidelines in general use for carers seeking to understand and manage excess noise-making by older people.

1. Noise that is made because of delirium and/or terminal illness is unlikely to respond to behaviour management. However, if noise-making is clearly affected by events in the client's surroundings, behaviour management can be applied. Share awareness of problem with the client. Attempt to get her views. Begin taping and/or charting frequency and/or duration of noise, having consulted client.
2. Check possible rewards for noise: self-stimulation; tension release; feeling of control over others; feeling of security when attention comes; satisfaction from stimulation attention brings; route to being sedated with relief from distress.
3. Find immediate causes, e.g. physical discomfort, worry about toileting need. Correct. Look for underlying causes, e.g. concern about results of disability, fear of death.

4. If noise-making persists, tell client that changes in routine will be made, 'because it's our job to see you get what you need without having to shout for it'. Repeat message at intervals.
5. Tape noise and play it back to client. Playback may need to be done several times. Be prepared for possibility that she will disown the sounds, denying responsibility.
6. Often the noise-maker is isolated by sensory impairment. This can be compounded if client is kept to own room to buffer others from the noise. Make the immediate environment more stimulating. Gradually reintroduce contact.
7. Approach the client if she is quiet and awake for a while; and praise her for coping. Identify valued events (a sweet, a cigarette, a drink, a newspaper, a back-rub) and present with your approach.
8. Do not respond to noise (unless an emergency). If approaching during noise, use minimum standard response.
9. Prompt client's listening to radio/tape recorder with headphones. Use tapes known to be of individual appeal.
10. If client is being placed in seclusion at intervals to discourage noise-making, this should be done with a brief explanation and no further comment. Return her when quieter, and use seclusion for brief set intervals.
11. Routine may be adjusted if it appears that such adjustment reduces noise.
12. Assess effectiveness by monitoring.

Behaviour management

Central to much psychological intervention with disturbed behaviour of old people is behaviour management. A key concept is that much of our behaviour operates on our environment to produce consequences. A great deal of what we do is operant behaviour shaped by these consequences. If an action is followed by consequences we value, these are reinforcers (making it more likely that we will act that way again). Consequences we do not value, do not act as reinforcers. Thus, in regard to a client's disturbed behaviour, if carers systematically change the consequences for the client, it may become possible progressively to increase desirable behaviour and decrease undesirable behaviour. A very clear introduction to this topic, for generic social workers, is offered by Hudson and Macdonald (1986), while the most compelling presentation of behavioural principles in geriatric psychology is by Hussian (1981).

While this approach is of proven worth with some categories of disturbed behaviour (Woods and Britton, 1985; Woods, 1987), even its most ardent supporters admit that its range of convenience is limited, and that much of the problem behaviour of old people can be contained or even ameliorated, but cannot be 'cured' by behaviour management. Furthermore, as Davies (1982) illustrates in her discussion of long-term care settings, environmental constraints such as pressure on staff resources can blunt the impact even of thoroughly practical and relevant interventions.

MEASURING QUALITY OF LIFE

This multi-dimensional concept involves both relatively objective variables such as health and socio-economic status, and relatively subjective ones such as life satisfaction and self-esteem. Davies and Knapp (1981) review the status of both kinds of assessment in the field of care of elderly people.

In recognition of the complexity of successfully identifying a single global index of quality of life, researchers are seeking improved definition and measurement of component variables, and their inter-correlations, as Fillenbaum (1984) demonstrates. However, as Booth (1985) comments, not only do many of the instruments which purport to measure subjective well-being need further development, but the effects of apathy and undue compliance related to institutionalisation undermine residents' reports.

Attempts to take a more objective approach, by measuring outcomes such as morbidity or dependency which may be held to relate to subjective well-being have run into difficulty because of the complexity of diagnosis and behaviour rating, and the elastic nature of the concept of 'dependency'. Walker (1982b) reminds us that this is used in at least four different ways: life-cycle dependency, physical and psychological dependency, political dependency and economic and financial dependency (see also Chapter 10). Woods and Britton (1985) view measuring quality of life in residential care as an increasingly sophisticated process, involving not just discussions with staff, but also gathering of residents' views, careful observation of day-to-day happenings, and analysis of discrepancies between values enshrined in official policy and those expressed in actual procedures.

While a high level of engagement of residents in activity that is apparently purposeful has been said to characterise a good quality residential setting (Jenkins et al, 1977), Woods and Britton would seek evidence of a high level of activity meaningful to the resident concerned, and see little to choose between enforced inactivity and enforced activity. Their review concludes that because methodologies for assessing engagement vary considerably, for the great majority of studies direct comparisons cannot be made. However, one common factor does appear clearly: 'Doing nothing appears to be the norm, whether in terms of proportion of total time, or of observations, or of residents present' (Woods and Britton, 1985, p. 260). They report that the average old person in residential care, 'has less than eight minutes per hour social contact, mostly with other residents. Contact with nursing staff will be largely related to physical care' (Woods and Britton, 1985, p. 263).

However, quality of life may be enhanced, even in such unpromising settings. Baltes and Baltes (1986) offer a series of useful perspectives on increasing older people's feeling of being in control of what happens to them, through, for example, encouraging residents to exercise choice over events of daily life. As already stressed in Chapter 5, maintaining a sense of control over one's life appears to be an important feature of adjustment to ageing.

As Willcocks et al (1987) report, in a research-based critique of life in local authority old people's homes, positive advocacy of 'normalisation' as a philosophy of care is required.

> The aim would be to devise a form of care that old people and their carers might choose on the basis of the particular balance of security and freedoms that can be achieved in a residential setting. This involves three sets of assumptions: first, that responsible authorities will have a view to the heterogeneity of the population they are serving and develop, accordingly, services that are different in kind but equivalent in status for different needs and different aspirations; second, that sufficient information will be provided to clients in a manner that enables them to negotiate the optimum package of care for their personal requirements after weighing up the 'gains' and 'losses' inherent in the various options; and third, that old people will be encouraged and assisted to work their way through this gains and losses equation so that they are in a position to exercise real consumer choice. (Willcocks et al, 1987, p. 144)

Measuring change

The effectiveness of any attempt to influence behaviour needs to be demonstrated by a reliable and valid assessment procedure which samples behaviour either directly or by reasonable inference, and is supported where necessary by appropriate experimental design for single case study (Barlow and Hersen, 1984), or group comparison as required.

A wide range of tests, techniques and systems of interview and observation have been applied with this population, and many of these have been devised for use with old people, standardised for them. Automated computer-interactive programs for specialised cognitive assessment of old people are now available. There is no lack of painstaking effort to develop measures of change which are more sensitive to altered functioning, and which possess a substantial degree of ecological validity, being credible for elderly subjects in appearing to tap aspects of behaviour that they recognise as relevant for their everyday performance. The issue of 'ecological validity' is discussed by Kendrick (1982) and Rabbitt (1982a). As Kendrick points out, a major justification for developing more sensitive measures of intellectual change with ageing is in the investigation of Alzheimer's disease in its early stages. He envisages as a long-term possibility the introduction of general cognitive screening – an intellectual M.O.T. test – in later life.

Nevertheless, there are substantial difficulties in the interpretation of such measures. Older subjects can have a variety of health problems which can appear in a fluctuating way to affect results; they can be exposed to a variety of simultaneous interventions to deal with these, so that it may be well-nigh impossible to determine the effectiveness of an individual component in influencing behaviour; barriers to communications tend to be experienced more frequently in older subjects; and the 'old' old in their eighties are not well served, having few procedures which take their seniority into account in estimating expected performances.

As Rabbitt (1982a) argues, the research of experimental psychologists into cognitive functioning has given relatively little attention to the understanding and measurement of change in intellectual status over time, so that the measurement of such change by applied psychologists has lacked secure foundation. A comprehensive examination of measurement issues is presented by Woods and Britton (1985, pp. 129–188).

CONCLUSIONS

While the topic of environment and behaviour is indeed a vast one, and has suffered as much as any other subject of psychology from the discipline's tendency to piecemeal and uncoordinated research, six objectives may be selected on the basis of their emerging salience as likely targets for investigation:

1. study of specific aspects of older people's experience of community environments;
2. analysis of coping styles and health care beliefs;
3. appraisal of the evidence 'experts' have for making design recommendations;
4. more thorough investigation of family process in distressed families with one or more older members;
5. development of more refined means of measuring care systems, and more considered means of intervening to promote 'normalisation' in such systems; and
6. for the older person whose behaviour is disturbed to extend a range of psychological prescriptions from which reasoned selection can be made according to individual needs.

While practice is indeed in a state of ferment, controlled fermentation is a healthy process, and within the supportive framework of the national British special interest group for the application of clinical psychology to work with older people (which is about to celebrate its tenth anniversary) sustained progress on at least some of the above targets is assured within the next ten years.

SUMMARY

While models (based largely on the study of residential care) for understanding the interaction between older people and their physical and social environment have been developed, a more detailed understanding of the influence of environmental factors is required. Understanding of the effects of stress on individual older people and their carers is relatively well advanced.

Progress is being made in establishing how older people shape their own surroundings and view the maintenance of their own health. Research into staff and resident perception of institutional life has identified positive options for living in residential care, and has encouraged development of guidelines for practice, goal planning, and staff training.

Reality orientation, cognitive therapy, anxiety management, systematic intervention, groupwork, and behaviour management offering a 'menu' for individualised care are among psychological interventions available to those working with older people whose behaviour is disturbed.

While 'quality of life' is difficult to evaluate, interest is being maintained in developing 'normalisation' and enhancing experience of residential care by, for example, encouraging residents to exercise greater choice. Awareness of need for more sensitive measurement of change in functioning in late life is increasing.

FURTHER READING

Gearing, B., Johnson, M. and Heller, T. (eds) (1988) *Mental Health Problems in Old Age.* Wiley, Chichester.

Hanley, I. and Gilhooly, M. (eds) (1986) *Psychological Therapies for the Elderly.* Croom Helm, London.

7

THE SOCIOLOGY OF RETIREMENT

Chris Phillipson

Retirement has, in the post-war period, been a major focus for research and debate in social gerontology. Its significance has been acknowledged in a variety of senses: as a mechanism for assisting the individual's withdrawal from social life (Cumming and Henry, 1961); as an institution helping to redistribute work from older to younger people (Phillipson, 1982; Graebner, 1980); as part of a movement to a 'leisured society' (Hochschild, 1973); and, from a critical perspective, as a contributory element in the creation of dependency in old age (Walker, 1981; Townsend, 1986).

These differing interpretations complicate any assessment or discussion of the issue of retirement. An additional element is that our understanding of this social institution is closely tied to and affected by dominant cultural values. Thus, in a culture which values work, retirement is seen as a 'problem' and a source of tension for the individual. Moreover, we all know – or claim to know – people who have suffered stress after compulsory retirement. Worse still, we can point to cases of people who have died in the ensuing months or first two years: proof, it would seem, of the harmful consequences which loss of a lifetime's work brings. Reflecting this pessimism we find very few social scientists ready to defend the present retirement system. As Stearns (a historian) writes:

> A cultural history of gerontological literature would note that its authors are often work enthusiasts themselves who find it difficult to imagine a satisfactory life divorced from employment. This is not to say that their judgement is wrong, however, and in individual cases empirical results on the problems posed by retirement have been impressive. There is a tendency, however, to assume a capacity for continued work that is not in turn empirically tested, rather reversing, but not necessarily improving upon, the exaggerated sense of elderly decay that dominated the literature of the nineteenth century. (King and Stearns, 1981, p. 595)

As a generalisation, it might be argued that there is a powerful mythology which affects our thinking about retirement. The purpose of this chapter is to analyse, from a critical perspective, the present status of this important institution. We shall also examine, using a sociological perspective, its impact upon individuals and groups. In doing so, we shall highlight the contradictory feelings often expressed about leaving work and the variety of meanings attached to retirement. Finally, in a concluding section, the future of retirement will be assessed along with some key issues for social policy.

RETIREMENT AND OLD AGE IN HISTORY

Historical perspectives on old age have recently begun to challenge orthodox views about the position of older people in past society.[1] In particular, there has been a questioning of the view that industrialisation and urbanisation necessarily weakened the status of elderly people, in comparison to their position in rural and peasant communities. In pre-industrial society, for those elderly people without property, growing old could be a desperate and humiliating experience (Hufton, 1974; Thomas, 1976). According to Thomas:

> for most manual workers old age meant, first, a move to lighter (and lower-paid) work, then a decline to abject dependence. Every contemporary list of paupers contains a proportion described as 'ancient and decrepit', 'aged and past work', 'old and her work done'. For miners, tailors, and metalworkers, this stage could come very quickly. Almshouses did not take those capable of working, yet the minimum age of admission was sometimes as low as forty. For literary commentators fifty was usually the point when old age began: 'at fifty', said Bishop Babington, 'we go down the hill again and every day grow weaker and weaker'. When old age pensions were first proposed, by Defoe in the 1690s, and by Dowdeswell in 1772, fifty was the age at which they were to be payable. On this point Burke agreed with Paine: from the age of fifty a workman's decline became 'every year more sensible'. (Thomas, 1976, p. 240)

With only limited accommodation available in almshouses and with retirement pensions virtually non-existent before the nineteenth century, there was a genuine fear of old age amongst working people. Most, as Thomas (1976) observes, had little choice but to struggle on as best they could:

> At Norwich in 1570 there were octogenarian women still spinning, while in 1679 Oliver Heywood was pleased to hear that a man of 94 and his wife of 104 had been seen carding in front of their house. Ralph Thoresby cited the equally inspiring example of Lawrence Benson of Leeds, who one afternoon reaped half an acre of wheat, ground it at the mill, made a cake with the flour, and ate it for his supper, all at the age of ninety-one. (Thomas, 1976, p. 240)

The research by Thomas and other historians has also been helpful in explaining some of the contradictions and doubts expressed about retirement. Modern retirement policy is a product of the late nineteenth century as large private companies and branches of the civil service

[1] In Britain, some of the most influential work has been produced by the Cambridge Group for the History of Population and Social Structure, led by Laslett (see, for example, Laslett, 1977 and the special issue of *Ageing and Society* on History and Ageing, Vol.4, part 4, 1984). For important American research see Achenbaum (1978a), Graebner (1980) and Haber (1983). Thomas' (1976) study of young and old in early modern England remains one of the most exciting examples of historical scholarship on old age.

adopted pension policies. Subsequently, at key periods in the twentieth century (usually in periods of economic slump or through the impetus of war), pension coverage has been extended to cover virtually all sections of the population (Hannah, 1986).

Behind this development in social policy can be traced some important industrial, economic and political influences. Thus, as a number of studies have shown, retirement and the spread of pensions was stimulated by demands for greater efficiency and productivity in the work place (Graebner, 1980; Phillipson, 1982; Thane, 1978). For factory workers, retirement may also have been hastened by workmen's compensation legislation, introduced in 1897. This required employers to insure against accidents at work and may have increased their tendency to lay off older and possibly accident-prone employees. According to Thane: 'Employers both introduced occupational pensions and pressed for a state scheme as this would let them lay-off older workers with clear consciences' (Thane, 1978, p. 236).

Fischer (1977) suggests that the growth of the factory system accelerated the process of retirement, with the development of assembly-line production hastening the displacement of older workers. However, as Quadango (1982) and others note, the issue is not simply one of technological change creating the right climate for the emergence of retirement. First, older people probably entered the new industries at a slower rate than younger workers. The reverse side of this is that they tended to be clustered in industries subject to economic decline. Secondly, retirement has to be seen in more global terms. For industrial capitalism, according to Graebner (1980), retirement provided a means of challenging security of tenure or jobs for life. It was a reaction against the persistence of personal modes of behaviour and provided a mechanism for discharging loyal workers. As an added bonus, it also assisted the stabilisation of corporate hierarchies, creating a permanent flow of employees and guaranteeing promotion through the ranks.

Thirdly, as Graebner (1980) and Phillipson (1982) suggest, retirement has played an important role in periods of mass unemployment. The idea of older workers being surplus to labour requirements has been crucial to the development of pensions both in Britain (the 1925 pensions legislation) and America (the Social Security Act of 1935). Similarly, the growth of unemployment in the 1970s and 1980s stimulated early retirement policies in a number of countries (Laczko and Walker, 1985).

An additional perspective introduced by historians concerns the differential impact of retirement on working-class and middle-class life. Stearns argues that retirement created considerable difficulties for working-class people:

> First, of course, inadequate material preparation, so that retirement was a time of immense physical hardship. But second, the lack of any active concept of what retirement should be: it represented stopping something, work, but did it represent starting or continuing anything of interest? Without pretending

to fathom the fate of retirees as a whole, for even in old age, and perhaps particularly then, individuals' variations are immense, we can suggest that a rapidly changing behaviour pattern found no correspondence in public policy or collective activities. (Stearns, 1977, pp. 65–66)

Despite these difficulties, retirement has, in the twentieth century, become a mass experience. In Britain in 1881 73 per cent of the male population 65 and over were economically active; by 1981 this had shrunk to less than 11 per cent, and by the late 1980s to below 10 per cent (Dex and Phillipson, 1986). But this revolution in work patterns has created much uncertainty. In the late 1940s and early 1950s there was widespread concern about the burden of an ageing society and, in particular, the economic threat imposed by increased numbers of retired people (Political and Economic Planning, 1948; Royal Commission on Population, 1949). Similar views have been expressed in the 1980s, with politicians suggesting that the increasing cost of pensions will create tensions between generations (Bornat, Phillipson and Ward, 1985). In fact, as we shall see, these views have had a significant impact both on the attitudes of older workers and on the conduct of research on retirement.

ATTITUDES TO RETIREMENT

Historians and sociologists have argued that the 'triumph of retirement' only took place after the Second World War (Graebner, 1980; Phillipson, 1982; Freter et al, 1987). In the period from 1950 to 1980, retirement grew in three particular ways: first, in terms of the proportion of people reaching retirement age; secondly, in terms of the decreasing significance of paid work after retirement; thirdly, as regards the number of people who receive state and occupational pensions.[2]

Yet the idea of triumph suggests that retirement was viewed as a positive development both in policy terms and amongst middle-aged people. Both these suggestions have, however, been heavily contested in the literature. In policy terms, as we have already noted, retirement was viewed with some hostility in a climate of post-war austerity and manpower shortages (Morgan, 1984; Phillipson, 1982; Blaikie and MacNicol, 1989). At the same time, and especially in Britain (in part because of the economic problems), there was particular emphasis on loss of work representing a 'crisis' for the individual. In the 1950s, retirement was seen as causing 'problems' less because of its financial implications, rather more because of its social and psychological impact, for example the loss of work-based friendships and the reduction in status and self-esteem. This perspective was explored in a range of studies undertaken in Britain, America and elsewhere and was supported by structural functionalism (see Chapter 2); the main theoretical orientation used in sociological studies. For a more

[2] The number of state pensions paid in Britain grew from 2.5 million in 1936 to 8.9 million in 1979. In the same period, the number of occupational pensions paid grew from 0.2 to 3.7 million (Hannah, 1986).

detailed analysis see Fennel, Phillipson and Evers (1988), Ch.3.

The view of retirement representing a social and individual problem was a powerful theme in early gerontological writings. Stieglitz, for example, one of the founders of gerontology argued, in his handbook on old age, published in Great Britain in 1949, that:

> Abrupt and obligatory retirement even if anticipated and accepted intellectually, almost invariably induces severe emotional stress. Its consequences are often drastic. There is an old saying among clinicians that to order the retirement of a businessman is tantamount to signing his death certificate within the year. (Stieglitz, 1949, p. 251)

In similar vein, Gumpert (1950), in a study entitled *You are Younger Than You Think*, suggested that:

> Most physicians agree that the essence of any treatment of the aged is to keep them at work. Idleness is the greatest enemy of the aged and presents them with their ticket to death. Financial premiums on retirement, which become automatically effective at a certain date, confer none of the blessings of real security and are not only socially unsound but detrimental to the health of the individual. (Gumpert, 1950, p. 128; see also Wermal and Gelbaum, 1945; Todd, 1946)

Retirement and health

These general statements were reinforced by numerous socio-medical studies, of varying quality, which appeared to show both that retirement *was* detrimental to health and that it was actively disliked by *most* retirees. This was the view of pioneer geriatricians such as Sheldon (in his study in the 1940s of older people in Wolverhampton) and sociologists such as Townsend (in his research in the 1950s on family life in Bethnal Green).

The connection between retirement and poor health was explored in numerous medical studies in the 1950s (see, in particular, those by Anderson and Cowan, 1956; Batchelor and Napier, 1953; Logan, 1953; Johnson, 1958). The sociological studies were fewer but followed the same theme in equating retirement with a deterioration in mental well-being (see, for example, Townsend, 1955; Tunstall, 1966). Comprehensive reviews of the health effects of retirement are provided by Minkler (1981) and McGoldrick (1989).

Some of the negative findings can be attributed to methodological problems in much of the above research. For example, medical research tended to include those who had a physical or mental problem *before* retirement, thus raising the question of whether ill health might not have been a cause rather than a consequence of leaving work (see below). But leaving this point aside, we should also note those studies in the 1950s and 1960s which gave a different interpretation to the experience of retirement. Some examples here are Richardson's (1956) work in Scotland in the 1950s; Emerson's (1959) research on the transition to retirement, also in the 1950s; national surveys (for example by the Ministry of Pensions and National Insurance, 1954); studies on the future of work and leisure (see, especially, Le Gros Clark, 1966); research in the field of industrial and occupational psychology (Welford, 1958; 1976) and finally the longitudinal research by Crawford in the 1960s, of couples facing the transition to retirement (Crawford, 1971; 1972a).

These different research projects were significant in that they indicated a more complex view of the reasons which people gave for leaving work and the impact retirement had on their lives. Early research, for example, tended to assume that compulsory retirement forced people to leave work against their will and, moreover, that most retirees were only too willing to return to paid employment. In contrast, both the small-scale study by Richardson (1956) and the national survey by the Ministry of Pensions and National Insurance (1954) suggested that ill health was a major factor people gave for leaving (or wanting to leave) work and an important reason as well in preventing many from returning to a paid occupation. Similar findings were reported in America in this period (see Corson and McConnell, 1956) and in British research some 20 years later (Parker, 1980).

The work of the various research units on ageing, at the Universities of London, Bristol and Liverpool, highlighted the difficulties facing older workers in the labour market. These included occupational downgrading and loss of pay (Heron and Chown, 1967); the pressure of assembly-line work (Brown, 1957); and inadequate retirement preparation (Heron, 1962; 1963; see also Phillipson and Strang, 1983).

Some of the research also questioned views which necessarily linked retirement with a period of anxiety and disorientation (Townsend, 1955). Emerson (1959), for example, in a study of 125 65-year-olds, whilst confirming that retirement had some initial impact in increasing tensions and anxieties, found that psychological problems were usually resolved after the transitional period. Moreover, his research suggested that even during the first year of leaving work, retirement *per se* had little effect on physical or mental health. The findings in Richardson's study of 244 men came to a similar conclusion:

> The extremes of complete contentment and bitter dissatisfaction with retirement were easily discerned but the majority of statements revealed mixed feelings; attitude to retirement was the product of a number of variables – state of health, the meaning of former jobs, length of retirement, use made of retirement, the relationship with family and wider social groups – all of these in varying degrees and diverse ways affected the replies. (Richardson, 1956, p. 385)

Some ten years later, Crawford's research on the way couples anticipated retirement, the rituals associated with it and its effect on lifestyles and relationships, confirmed the influence of the variables identified by Richardson. Moreover, her research, although indicating that some couples did indeed perceive retirement in crisis terms, found no evidence that this was expressed in the form of psychosomatic illnesses (Crawford, 1972b).

The challenge to the view of retirement as necessarily creating problems and tensions was also apparent in American social gerontology (see, especially, the work of Streib and his colleagues at Cornell University). The Cornell research is summarised in Streib and Schneider (1971). In line with this, it is interesting to find the following argument in Cumming and Henry's controversial study of the process of disengagement (see Chapters 2 and 4):

> If health care and economic independence are guaranteed, those few retired men who cannot reintegrate with a membership group and cannot shift their skills are probably the only true 'problem' group among old people in society. Generally speaking, our findings support those [who argue] that retirement in itself does not appear to be a problem for most men; it is the lack of horizontal ties and of a suitable way of relating, which retirement may carry with it, that seem to make trouble. (Cumming and Henry, 1961, pp. 153–154)

THEORETICAL AND METHODOLOGICAL DEBATES

As the number of research studies increased, so there was a shift towards viewing retirement as less problematic for men and, correspondingly, more difficult for some groups of women (see below). At the same time, this empirical observation was reinforced by (and in some cases arose out of) new theoretical arguments about the nature of retirement. In the 1940s and 1950s, the dominance of role theory led to a virtual consensus in gerontology that loss of a primary role such as work deprived the individual – men especially – of status and identity (Cavan et al, 1949; Parsons, 1942; Tibbitts, 1954). This argument was modified with the arrival of the disengagement hypothesis, although the assumption that retirement was entirely non-problematic for women remained (Cumming and Henry, 1961).

By the 1970s, other theoretical models were beginning to challenge the assumptions of role theory and the discredited disengagement hypothesis (Hochschild, 1975). For example, the political economy perspective (see also Chapter 2) focused on the way in which retirement was shaped by the social structure and by the social and economic factors which affect the individual's place in that structure (Stone and Minkler, 1984). This approach focused on the impact of class, gender and race in influencing the experience of retirement. In short, retirement came to be seen as 'socially constructed', varying according to lifelong social status and prevailing state policies and ideologies (Phillipson and Walker, 1986).

This theoretical argument, along with others, was important in shifting the focus of investigation from asking how individuals have adjusted to retirement to examining the socio-political factors which influence and control retirement outcomes (Estes, 1979; 1986).

In addition, the 1970s also witnessed important methodological debates about the conduct of research and the interpretation of results. In particular, there was growing appreciation of the limitations of cross-sectional studies and concern with the restricted nature of many samples, for example, the under-representation of women and many ethnic groups. In Britain, the majority of retirement studies have employed a cross-sectional design (see, for example, Parker 1980). With this method, however, as noted in Chapter 2, it is virtually impossible to distinguish between the causes and consequences of retirement. Thus, as we noted above, many studies in the 1950s and 1960s reported increased rates of sickness as a consequence of retiring from work. Unfortunately, on closer inspection of the design of these studies, it is impossible to say whether this sickness is caused by the poor health which people bring into retirement or whether it is an outcome of leaving work. One solution to this problem is the longitudinal design which follows people's lives prospectively from an earlier point in the life cycle. These designs are, however, expensive as well as taking a long time to complete. Fortunately, the findings from American surveys of this kind are now available and they have added considerably to our own understanding of the retirement period (see, for example, Palmore et al, 1985).

There is, though, a second issue that has to be confronted in studies of retirement. When people are asked about how they feel about leaving work, we have to remember that their replies are framed within a social context. In the 1950s, when people were urged to remain at work and when retired people were seen as a 'burden', it was hardly surprising to find negative views expressed about retirement. In the late 1980s, when there is pressure on people to leave work (to create jobs for the young), positive views about retirement are perhaps more likely to be expressed. This may appear a somewhat jaundiced view, suggesting that older people don't have views and feelings of their own. Clearly, they do have strong beliefs: however, these are subject (as with any individual or group) to manipulation within a given social and political climate. Moreover, this is particularly likely given a historical context in which retirement is a relatively weak and unpopular institution (Blaikie and MacNicol, 1989)

We must be careful, therefore, about how we interpret research findings: do they take account of the limitations of their own research designs? Do they acknowledge the powerful effect of social and cultural forces in downgrading retirement? These points need to be borne in mind when reading the next section of this chapter, which reviews research in the 1970s and 1980s on the experience of retirement.

THE EXPERIENCE OF RETIREMENT

It was suggested at the beginning of this chapter that retirement has often been seen as disruptive and disturbing to the individual. How far does contemporary research show this to be the case? What are the attitudes and views of retired people themselves?

In the years or months leading to retirement important changes and developments may be experienced. The loss of a job in middle age can cause great hardship and distress, with an extended period of unemployment and consequent loss of income (Walker et al, 1985). For those remaining at work, there may be social pressures arising from redundancy or early retirement programmes, technological changes in the work place, and adjustments due to the impact of health problems (Dex and Phillipson, 1986). A minority may feel and express concern about their future retirement. Parker's (1980) British survey found 35 per cent of women workers under pension age were expecting that they would find it difficult to settle down when they retired; the figure for men was 27 per cent. Both groups anticipated similar types of problems, financial difficulties being uppermost. Overall in Parker's survey, two-fifths of older workers were looking forward to retirement, one in eight were definitely unhappy about the prospect, and the rest had mixed feelings.

Studies have shown that the availability and size of (occupational) pensions influence individuals' retirement decision in Britain and in the US; most of the studies have been done in the US (see, for example, Shaw, 1984) but one British econometric study has been done on Parker's OPCS data (Zabalza et al, 1980). The availability of an occupational pension is related to whether a job is full- or part-time. Since many women are in part-time jobs, or have spent some proportion of their working life in part-time work, their eligibility for occupational pensions will be limited. Statistics on occupational pensions confirm that this is the case, and that women are distinguishable from men in this respect. The lack of an occupational pension is likely to act as a disincentive for women to retire, and certainly to retire early (Dex and Phillipson, 1986).

Early retirement may also create difficulties. Here we must distinguish between, on the one hand, a minority of people who choose to retire early (because they have sufficient income) and who usually report satisfaction with the decision (McGoldrick and Cooper, 1980). On the other hand, there are a much larger number who retire early because of health problems. This group appears more likely to report uncertainty about the future and to experience problems of adjustment (Cribier, 1981; Parker, 1980).

Early retirement may lead to some tensions, even where resources are relatively secure and there are no health problems. Bytheway (1986), in a study of Welsh steelworkers, found dissatisfaction being expressed with men feeling that their skills were being wasted. Walker, Noble and Westergaard's (1985) research on the impact of redundancy amongst steelworkers in Sheffield, found those who had taken the early retirement option to be evenly divided between those relieved to be leaving work and those expressing regret.

Guillemard (1986) relates the problem of the early retired to ambiguities in their social position. She sees such people as neither really unemployed nor actually retired. Very few accept the label 'senior citizen'; yet society has no category or role in between that of worker or pensioner.

Guillemard, along with Walker (1982a), highlights the way in which, during a period of economic recession, old age is being redefined to incorporate people from middle age onwards. The similarity between this argument and the historical perspective outlined earlier is clear: retirement – as an economic and social policy – is an area over which very few individuals (particularly women or those from the working class) have direct control. People cannot, in most cases, choose their retirement; nor can they (unless they have a scarce skill) carry out the option of remaining at work. It is for these reasons that many researchers continue to view retirement in negative terms. Townsend, for example, argues that:

> Those reaching retirement age do not welcome retirement as warmly as they thought they would or others suppose. Many who have retired deeply regret their inactivity or loss of status, and as time goes on many regret the restrictions on their activities imposed by a greatly reduced income. The satisfaction often expressed by many retired people turns out on closer examination to be more an assertion of hope, or what they think is expected of them, than a true representation of what they feel. As in most human situations of change, there are profound reservations and regrets as well as advantages or at least mild compensations. (Townsend, 1986, p. 25)

This argument is reflected in research findings which show a substantial minority of male and female pre-retirees who have no idea about what to do in their retirement. This was indicated in Crawford's research in Bristol in the 1960s; it also received some confirmation in Phillipson and Strang's (1983) study of pre-retirement education. In this research in an interview two weeks before their pre-retirement course, nearly 40 per cent of those interviewed (n = 217) professed not to have a clear idea of what to do with their retirement; a similar percentage expressed doubts about their ability to keep occupied. The same study also confirmed earlier British and American research by Heron (1963) and Kerckhoff (1964) regarding the lack of planning for retirement. On the specific question of financial planning, Ritchie and Barrowclough's survey (1983) found that one-quarter of men and one-third of women aged 50 plus had given no thought to the income they would have once retired.

However, if the lead-up to retirement appears stressful, it is less clear that the same can be said for retirement itself.[3] Indeed, the general conclusions from research points in a more optimistic direction. Atchley, for example, conducted a series of studies in America throughout the 1960s and 1970s, all of which pointed to the impact of reduced income and the change in lifestyle associated with it as the major factor in producing negative retirement attitudes. From his research Atchley found little evidence for those with moderate incomes and above actually 'missing

[3] For reviews of research, dating from the 1950s to the 1980s, on the topic of adjustment to retirement, see Nadelson (1969), Friedmann and Orbach (1974), George (1980) and Braithwaite and Gibson (1987). For a sociological interpretation of retirement, Maddox's (1966) essay, 'Retirement as a social event', is outstanding.

work' to any great extent. From a sociological perspective he put forward the view that:

> Each person generally has several roles that he stakes his identity on. Work may be at or near the top, but not necessarily so. There simply is not the kind of homogeneous consensus of the value of work that would keep it at the top for everyone. In fact, the many systems of competing values in a complex society ensure that there will be a wide variety of self-values. Thus, the probability that retirement will lead to a complete identity breakdown is slight, and there may be just as many people who rely on leisure pursuits for self-respect as there are who rely on work, particularly among those with unsatisfying jobs. (Atchley, 1971, p. 16)

Palmore et al's analysis of a number of American longitudinal data sets concluded that:

1. Retirement at the normal age has little or no adverse effects on health for the average retiree. Some have health declines, but these are balanced by those who enjoy health improvement.
2. Retirement at the normal age has few substantial effects on activities, except for the obvious reduction in work and some compensating increase in solitary activities.
3. Retirement at the normal age has little or no effect on most attitudes for the average retiree. Some become more dissatisfied, but these are balanced by those who become more satisfied. (Palmore et al, 1985, p. 167)

Cribier's French study confirmed both a 'marked increase in the proportion of people who view retirement as a desirable goal, and early retirement as particularly desirable' (1981, p. 66). The retirees in Parker's (1980) British study, whilst more cautious in their views, had still, in the majority of cases, 'settled down' some 12 months after leaving work (see, also, Phillipson and Strang, 1983; Long, 1987).

Beyond these general findings, however, some qualifications must be expressed. What research also tells us is that biographies and work histories remain important in influencing retirement outcomes (Long, 1987). We can see this in very obvious ways: people in retirement are survivors and this in itself is class determined (if you are in social class five you are two and a half times more likely to die before reaching retirement than if in social class one). Working-class people are also more likely to enter retirement with a chronic health problem and, in consequence, to have some limitation placed on their retirement activities (Shephard, 1978; Townsend et al, 1987).

Research also points to other consequences of given class and occupational positions. Guillemard's French study suggested that social withdrawal was a typical mode of response for working-class retirees, because their exploited position presented them with few resources to consume and convert into meaningful leisure (see also Phillipson, 1987).

Such relationships have also been indicated in the American longitudinal research. Parnes and Less, for example, found that amongst white men, both family income and occupational level had independent effects on the amount of time spent on leisure activity in retirement. They concluded from this that:

> ... the kind of work that men do influences leisure activities not only through the income that it generates, but also by conditioning or reflecting their interests. If participation in leisure activities contributes to satisfaction, one might therefore expect men who had retired from high level jobs to manifest above average satisfaction with retirement even when such factors as income and health are held constant. (Parnes and Less, 1983, pp. 90–91; see also Simpson and McKinney, 1966)

WOMEN IN RETIREMENT

Another area of differentiation concerns the question of women in retirement. Women's experience of retirement is affected both by their position in the labour market and by ideologies regarding their role as carers. In the case of the former, there has been a substantial growth in the number of women employees. Women's participation rates display, in fact, a bimodal pattern, with the first peak occurring between the ages of 20–24 and the second 45–50 (Dex, 1985).

Early research argued that entering retirement was less stressful for women, partly because work had been a less important element in their lives, and partly because of the maintenance of the role of housewife (Donahue et al, 1960; Tibbitts, 1954). However, Dex (1985) suggests that the later research literature indicates strong similarities in the attitudes of men and women towards work. Women, she notes, have been found to be more economistic or instrumental than was thought to be the case (and men less so), and both experience life-cycle variations in orientations to work. Martin and Robert's (1984) analysis of the *Women and Employment Survey* found that the majority of working women had a high financial dependence upon working and enjoyed working.

Loss of work may, therefore, have profound implications for women. At the same time, the type of work carried out by women workers also raises difficulties for their retirement. Various researchers (see, for example, O'Rand and Henretta, 1982; Stone and Minkler, 1984) point to the clustering of women in low-paid jobs with limited or non-existent pensions. In Britain in 1983 the ratio of women's to men's earnings for manual workers was 63 per cent and in the USA it was 58 per cent. The rate for non-manual workers was 60 per cent. Part-time women workers are at a particular disadvantage when it comes to occupational pension schemes. In the survey by Ritchie and Barrowclough (1983), 14 per cent had access to a scheme although had not become members, while 69 per cent had no company pension scheme available (see, also, McGoldrick, 1984).

The discontinuous nature of women's working lives may also be significant, producing both a greater decrease in retirement income (in comparison with men) and a feeling that occupational goals have not been achieved (Atchley, 1976).

Gender differences in adjustment to retirement have been reported by a number of researchers. Jacobson's British study in the early 1970s found women *less* likely than men to be positively orientated to retirement (Jacobson, 1974). Streib and Schneider (1971) found women to be more apprehensive than men about the effects of retirement. Atchley (1976) found women taking longer than men to adapt to the retirement transition, a finding confirmed in Fox's research on the adaptation of women workers to retirement (Fox, 1976).

In general, however, research on women's experience of retirement is limited in quantity and quality. Palmore et al's analysis of longitudinal research is typical of the gender bias in this area, admitting that:

> The theoretical models and variables used in [our] analysis were largely orientated toward retirement among men. As a consequence, major factors that explain individual differences in retirement among women were not included. (Palmore et al, 1985, p. 170)

However, research has also been deficient in its failure to acknowledge the important role of the sexual division of labour in affecting women's retirement experience (Stone and Minkler, 1984). The unequal nature of social care has been highlighted by numerous research studies (Peace, 1986). Retirement may, in some cases, be caused by an increase in responsibilities in the area of informal care – either for a sick husband, relative or both (Parker, 1980). Alternatively, the retirement experience may itself be structured around a range of caring activities.

The experience of retirement: continuity or discontinuity?

What conclusions can we draw from the extensive literature on retirement in the 1970s and 1980s? Perhaps the most important theme concerns the relationship between retirement and other phases in the life course. Here we have seen an important shift from the 1960s, where retirement was seen as entailing a dislocation 'whose effects would be common to everyone' (Stone and Minkler, 1984, p. 226). The impact of 20 years of research has been to focus, instead, on variations in the experience of retirement, reflecting lifelong inequalities and differences produced by class, gender and ethnicity.

The implication of this argument is that retirement is shaped at least as much by *continuities* as discontinuities in life experiences. Indeed, as has been argued elsewhere, the transition to retirement is not a movement from an old to a completely new life (as the disengagement and role theories would suggest); rather it is the final resolution of the advantages and disadvantages attached to given social and class positions. A resolution in the sense that once the advantages accruing from a particular position are consolidated they are likely to be sustained even into very old age.

Similarly, where there are disadvantages, retirement and old age may simply add to the individual's sense of powerlessness and loss of control (Phillipson, 1987).

Such arguments still leave many problems unresolved. For example, taking the above orientation, we would emphasise the importance of classifying the retired by their previous occupation or social class. This, it might be argued, would be the surest indicator of the material advantages or disadvantages of the older person. But continuity in terms of class, whilst satisfactory as an objective indicator of resources, may be less satisfactory as a subjective indicator of attitudes. Retired people may, in fact, feel that their class location is contradictory. Separated from the routine of wage labour, they may respond and have their attitudes shaped by different priorities and circumstances. At the same time, they tend not to form a common interest group in old age. The reasons for this have been analysed by Alan Walker as follows:

> ... as an analysis of the political economy of old age shows, elderly people are just as deeply divided along class and other structural lines as younger adults. While both functionalist and pluralist analyses suggest a common interest among elderly people, with age acting as a leveller of class and status differentials, a political economy perspective shows that the social construction of old age is a function of *two* separate sets of relations. On the one hand, older people carry into retirement inequalities created and legitimated at an earlier phase of the life cycle, particularly though not exclusively through the labour market. On the other hand, the process of retirement imposes a reduced social and economic status on a large proportion of older people in comparison with younger economically active adults. Social gerontology and especially political gerontology has put too much emphasis on the latter and too little on the former. (Walker, 1986, pp. 37–38)

A future task for research is to explore how these conflicting pressures influence behaviour in retirement. As this indicates, we have moved considerably beyond a view which sees the individual adjusting to retirement in isolation from his or her own life history and the wider social structure. Both are now taken to be crucial variables in understanding behaviour and attitudes. The next few years should see a clarification of how the contradictory forces affecting older people influence both patterns of adjustment and the shape of retirement as a social institution.

THE FUTURE OF RETIREMENT

The question that remains to be asked is whether the 1990s and beyond will see the final triumph of retirement as a social and economic institution. In some respects, of course, this has already happened. In the 1970s and 1980s older people withdrew from the labour force in increasing numbers and at earlier ages. The key factors which consolidated the drift of older workers from employment were: (1) the decline in semi- and unskilled jobs; (2) the entry or re-entry into the labour market of women workers; (3) the growth – through occupational pension schemes – of

Table 7.1   *Male economic activity rates, Britain: 1971–1991*

| Age | Percentage of each age group economically active | | | | | | | | | | |
| | Estimates | | | | | | | | | | |
	1971	1972	1973	1974	1975	1976	1977	1978	1979	1980	1981
45–54	97.6	95.8	96.0	96.1	96.2	96.1	96.0	95.7	95.4	95.1	94.8
55–59	95.3	93.0	93.0	93.0	93.0	92.4	91.8	91.3	90.8	90.1	89.4
60–64	86.6	82.7	82.6	82.4	82.3	80.4	78.5	75.8	73.0	71.2	69.3
65–69	30.6	29.3	28.2	27.0	25.9	23.9	22.0	19.4	16.8	16.6	16.3
70+	11.0	10.3	9.6	9.0	8.3	8.0	7.6	6.8	6.1	6.3	6.5
	Estimates					Projections					
	1982	1983	1984	1985	1986	1987	1988	1989	1990	1991	
45–54	94.0	93.1	92.6	92.3	91.7	91.6	91.6	91.7	91.7	9.17	
55–59	86.8	84.1	82.1	82.0	80.3	80.1	80.1	80.1	80.1	80.1	
60–64	64.3	59.4	56.7	54.4	53.4	53.2	52.6	52.0	51.4	50.8	
65–69	14.8	13.3	13.6	13.9	12.5	11.8	11.1	10.5	9.9	9.3	
70+	5.9	5.3	5.5	5.2	4.7	4.5	4.3	4.0	3.8	3.6	

Source: Employment Gazette, May 1987

financial provision for early retirement on the grounds of ill health; and (4) the growing number (albeit a minority) who choose early retirement as a positive and valued alternative to full-time work.

Table 7.1 examines the changes in the position of older men during the 1970s and 1980s. This confirms the steep fall in economic activity for men aged 60–64, especially in the 10 years from 1976–1986 (a drop of 27 percentage points). The change for men aged 55–59 was also highly significant, showing a decline of 12 percentage points. By the end of the 1980s, only around 50 per cent of men aged 60–64 would be counted as economically active.

Table 7.2   *Female economic activity rates, Britain: 1971–1991*

| Age | Percentage of each age group economically active | | | | | | | | | | |
| | Estimates | | | | | | | | | | |
	1971	1972	1973	1974	1975	1976	1977	1978	1979	1980	1981
45-54	60.6	63.2	64.8	66.0	66.3	66.5	66.7	66.9	67.0	67.6	66.0
55–59	51.1	51.1	51.4	51.9	52.4	54.3	56.1	55.0	53.8	53.6	53.4
60–64	28.2	28.8	28.7	28.7	28.6	26.9	25.2	23.3	21.5	22.4	23.3
65+	6.4	6.0	5.6	5.3	4.9	4.7	4.4	3.9	3.4	3.6	3.7
	Estimates					Projections					
	1982	1983	1984	1985	1986	1987	1988	1989	1990	1991	
45–54	68.1	68.1	69.2	69.4	70.2	70.8	71.3	71.5	71.7	71.8	
55–59	52.0	50.6	51.1	51.8	51.7	51.7	51.7	51.7	51.7	51.7	
60–64	21.9	20.5	21.3	18.6	18.8	18.5	18.2	18.0	17.7	17.4	
65+	3.5	3.2	3.0	3.0	2.7	2.7	2.6	2.5	2.5	2.4	

Source: Employment Gazette, May 1987

The trends amongst older women are more complex to assess because of inadequacies in manpower statistics: in particular, the failure of many women to register as unemployed or the omission of part-time workers (the majority of whom are women) from some labour statistics (Dex and Phillipson, 1986). The official statistics (see Table 7.2) for the 1970s and 1980s indicate a marked decline in the percentage of women 60 plus who are defined as economically active. In contrast, the rates for women aged 55–59 are estimated or projected to fluctuate between 51 per cent and 56 per cent throughout this period and for women aged 45–54 there is a gradual rise in economic activity.

Taking both men and women, the evidence suggests that the marginalisation of older employees gathered pace in the 1970s. This arose through: first, their concentration, in many cases, in contracting industries; secondly, the operation of particular schemes to promote worker redeployment (eg the Redundancy Payments Act) or replacement (the Job Release Scheme); thirdly, the pressure of mass unemployment; and fourthly, changing attitudes amongst government, business, trades unions and older people themselves, in respect of the older workers' right to employment in relation to other, younger age groups (Bytheway, 1986).

What is the likely outcome of these trends? At one level, they confirm the importance of retirement as a social institution, one which is now a predictable (and increasingly accepted) part of the life course (Markides and Cooper, 1987). On the other hand, we are likely to see increased stratification within retirement, with social divisions based upon unequal access to occupational pensions and considerable variation in the amount and quality of the pension received by different groups (Walker, 1986). This fact, together with the likely emphasis of governments on the 'burden of old age', will place major constraints on the development of retirement. Undoubtedly, there will be many retired people (from the middle classes especially), who will develop a leisure-orientated lifestyle, built around the expanding consumer market aimed at the over-50s: specialist holiday companies; second homes; retirement communities (most notably in America); and private sheltered housing schemes (an area of rapid expansion in Britain in the 1980s).

These are the trends for those privileged to continue their middle-aged lifestyle into retirement. But whilst some retired people will enjoy access to a second home, we must also remember the 41 per cent of elderly owners living in 'poor' or 'unsatisfactory' houses (unfit or needing more than £2,500 of repairs) and nearly half a million elderly people aged 75 or over who live in private rented accommodation (see also Chapter 8). And whilst there has been an improvement in the financial circumstances of some groups of pensioners, the majority still face – at some point in retirement – considerable poverty: some 4.8 million elderly people have incomes equal to or just above the poverty line and a further 1.1 million live below it (see also Chapter 11).

These material realities will continue to cloud the future of retirement. But of equal importance to the lives of older and retired workers will be social and political attitudes towards retirement itself. Here the evidence suggests the start of a new phase, in the early 1990s, in the fluctuating fortunes of older workers. In the decade from 1979 to 1989 there was active government support for early retirement. In the 1990s, however, we are witnessing a reversal of this trend, with a major political debate about the 'burden' of retirement and the high level of income being distributed from younger to older people (Johnson et al, 1989). At a governmental level, the debate is shifting towards encouraging a 'decade of retirement' with pressure to abolish mandatory retirement before the age of 70 (on a par with legislation in the US). The agenda here is to encourage upward flexibility in retirement ages (from 60 for women and from 65 for men) within a context of fewer younger people entering the labour market (a drop of 30 per cent by 1995).

One effect of this policy change may be a consolidation in the high level of financial and social insecurity experienced by many older workers in the 1980s. On the one hand, few governments in the future are likely to be interested in making retirement attractive: the economic 'costs' will be viewed as too substantial. On the other hand, very few initiatives are being developed – in Britain at least – to give older people greater security in the labour market. In fact, although older people are still clearly targeted as a reserve of labour, it is married women who are seen as the key group for meeting shortages in labour supply (women are projected to take 80 per cent of the 900,000 new jobs on offer in the period up to 1995). Older people are more likely to be used for low-paid jobs, particularly in the new service industries.

But an increase in part-time working may not greatly reduce the degree of insecurity experienced by older workers. They may still face above average unemployment; at the same time, financial support from the state may become more limited and targeted at particular groups. In short, in Britain at least, the social institution of retirement, whilst continuing to develop in new and important ways, will still to be regarded with some ambivalence at the level of the state. In consequence, the tension between the aspirations of retired people and the legitimacy accorded them in the 1990s will remain a crucial issue for researchers to address.

8

LIVING ARRANGEMENTS OF ELDERLY PEOPLE

John Bond

One of the most influential factors on all our lives is the environment in which we live. For older people this may be particularly so since they may spend more time in their own home than many other groups in society. In this chapter we will look at both the geographical location of older people, especially the phenomenon known colloquially as *costa geriatrica*, and the type of living accommodation experienced by older people. Although only about 5 per cent of people aged 65 or over are resident in an institution of some kind we will give relatively more space than this to the experiences of older people living in institutions.

There have probably been a number of favoured locations to which older people have retired in the past although these were probably restricted to a wealthy group of people. However, with the increasing numbers of relatively well-off retired people these favoured locations have become more popular. In addition, the depopulation of rural areas by younger people, particularly in the hundred years prior to 1950, has resulted in an ageing rural population. These trends although significant should not mask the fact that the majority of older people do not move away from their lifelong associations with a particular area.

Most older people live in normal housing. Yet generally in everyday life we associate old age with specialist housing. It has been estimated that only just under 400,000 people lived in sheltered housing in 1981 (Butler et al, 1983). Thus, when considering housing for elderly people we will be reviewing not only the specialist housing needs of older people but the role of the general housing stock in the living arrangements of older people.

The variety of housing accommodation available to elderly people is matched by the variety of institutional care used by very frail elderly people. Elderly people are resident in NHS hospitals, local authority, private and voluntary residential homes and in NHS, private and voluntary nursing homes. Although only a small number of older people live in institutions at any one time, a significant proportion will experience institutional living at some time during their later life, particularly those people who attain at least 80 years of age.

Residential location

Following retirement most elderly people continue to live in the district in which they have lived during their working lives. Retirement migration is still a minority activity which has been estimated to affect about 10 per cent of elderly people (Law and Warnes, 1982). The geographical distribution of elderly people in 1981 can be contrasted with that of 1921. In 1921 the pattern was characterised by above-average concentrations of elderly people in an axial belt across the centre of the country from the south-west to Norfolk, and two additional clusters of concentration in mid-Wales and Sussex. The axial belt reaching from the north-west through the midlands to London and the home counties supported below-average proportions of elderly people (Allon-Smith, 1982). Table 8.1 shows that in 1981 the regions with the highest proportions of elderly people were the South West, East Anglia and Wales, while the West Midlands, East Midlands and Scotland had the lowest. Analysis of the populations of the counties indicates a more varied pattern.

Table 8.2 ranks the top 20 and the bottom 20 county districts according to pensionable population. The counties with the highest proportions of elderly population were found along the south coast (except for Hampshire), in non-industrial Wales, East Anglia, Lancashire, North Yorkshire, and the Borders and Tayside in Scotland. The counties with the lowest proportion of elderly people included most of Midland England, the northern and western home counties, Cleveland and West Central Scotland. The metropolitan counties were just below average in the

Table 8.1   *Regional distribution of pensionable population in Britain in 1981*

Area	Pensionable population (000s)	Percentage of total population
South West	879	20.7
East Anglia	344	18.7
Wales	504	18.4
South East	2939	17.8
Yorkshire and Humberside	848	17.6
North West	1115	17.6
North	522	17.0
Scotland	848	16.9
East Midlands	637	16.8
West Midlands	823	16.1
Great Britain	9459	17.7

Source: Office of Populations, Censuses and Surveys and Registrar General Scotland (1983), Tables 1 and 2.

Table 8.2   *County districts with the largest and smallest proportions of the pensionable population in Britain in 1981*

Rank	Areas with highest and lowest proportion of elderly people	Percentage of total population
1	Rother, East Sussex	35.3
2	Worthing, West Sussex	34.9
3	Eastbourne, East Sussex	33.5
4	Christchurch, Dorset	32.3
5	Arun, West Sussex	32.0
6	Hove, East Sussex	31.0
7	East Devon	30.7
8	West Somerset	30.2
9	Tendering, Essex	30.2
10	Bournemouth, Dorset	30.1
11	Torbay, Devon	29.2
12	Colwyn, Clwyd	29.1
13	South Wight	29.1
14	Thanet, Kent	28.2
15	Hastings, East Sussex	27.0
16	Aberconwy, Gwynedd	26.9
17	Rhuddlan, Clwyd	26.8
18	Teignbridge, Devon	26.6
19	Wealden, East Sussex	26.5
20	North Norfolk	26.5
440	South Staffordshire	12.2
441	Knowsley, Merseyside	12.0
442	Crawley, West Sussex	12.0
443	Rushmoor, Hampshire	11.9
444	Strathkelvin, Strathclyde	11.9
445	Corby, Northamptonshire	11.8
446	South Bedfordshire	11.8
447	West Lothian	11.7
448	Wokingham, Berkshire	11.5
449	Basildon, Essex	11.5
450	Surrey Heath	11.2
451	Stevenage, Hertfordshire	11.2
452	Hart, Hampshire	11.2
453	Bracknell, Berkshire	11.0
454	Chiltern, Buckinghamshire	10.8
455	East Kilbride, Strathclyde	10.7
456	Redditch, Hereford and Worcestershire	10.6
457	Harlow, Essex	10.0
458	Tamworth, Staffordshire	9.8
459	Cumbernauld and Kilsyth	9.2

Source: Warnes and Law (1985), Table 2.

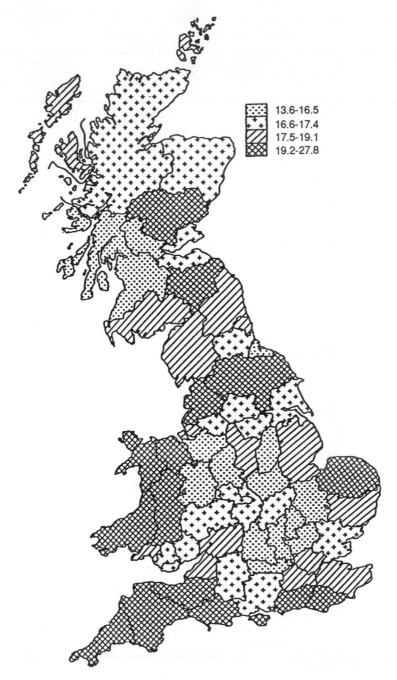

▓	13.6-16.5
▓	16.6-17.4
▓	17.5-19.1
▓	19.2-27.8

Figure 8.1 *The distribution by counties of the elderly population of Great Britain in 1981*

Source: Warnes and Law (1985), Figure 1.

proportion of elderly people resident. The distribution of these county districts is shown in Figure 8.1.

These simple statistical data, which show the high concentrations of elderly people in particular areas, are often seen as supporting the predominant societal view that old age is a problem. Concentrations of other social groups are usually viewed as social problems. Thus, we are regularly confronted with the 'problems' associated with concentrations of people from ethnic minorities or unemployed people. To national and local planners such variations make the task of planning more difficult and challenging. Similar difficulties will be faced by planners concerned with the estimation of services for elderly people or school and other education services, for example, in areas where there exists a relatively high or low population of these groups. The underlying problem may be society's inability to respond to these kinds of data irrespective of social group, in terms of a more equitable distribution of resources to match the needs of a local community.

Meeting the needs of a population with a high proportion of older people is not a short-term challenge. Unlike other age groups, there is little evidence of pronounced fluctuations in the numbers or the proportion of elderly people living in an area. Allon-Smith (1982) has shown that the current patterns of residential location of elderly people reflect historical patterns which may have been evident for over 50 years. His detailed examination of retirement areas reveals that not only favoured regions and counties but also individual retirement areas within counties were marked out as early as 1921. Like many contemporary social patterns the development of retirement areas is not a post-war phenomenon.

Migration in later life

In reviewing patterns of residential location of elderly people much attention has focused on migration between areas of the country. However, a distinction should be made between trends which reflect natural changes in the population structure and in the migration of different groups in society.

Urban sociology, the study of patterns of urban life, provides a useful framework in which to consider the way that changes in the population structure in a locality affects the lifestyles of older people. Urban life is distinctively patterned. Specific districts of our cities, towns and counties have acquired their own distinctive characteristics and social styles. Although clearly identified by early sociographers it was the Chicago school of sociologists who set about systematically to document changes in social life caused by population change and to develop models which have general application. Burgess (1925) proposed a simple ecological model derived from his knowledge of Chicago which described cities as having a series of concentric zones of distinctive social and physical characteristics (see Figure 8.2). Geographical features like major rivers,

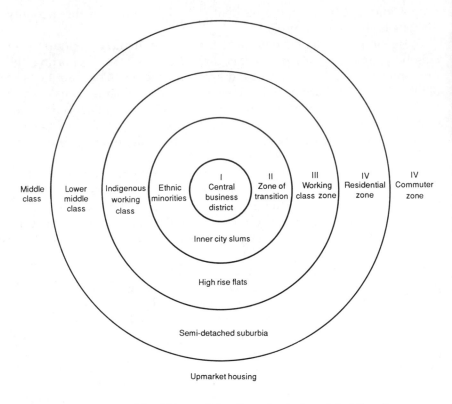

Figure 8.2   *The Chicago School's ecological model of the city*

hills and transport systems disrupt the simplicity of the model which has
been used by Young and Willmott (1973) in their analysis of family life
in London and by Rex and Moore (1967) in their study of race relations
in Birmingham.

Central to the ecological model is the idea that through the social
Darwinian concepts of competition and invasion and succession, small
'natural areas' form a mosaic of segregated social worlds reinforced
by physical environments. Individuals are selected for different areas
according to their ability to control resources and in particular physical
and social space. Those in the most dominant positions control the most
valuable part of the city: the central business district (zone I). Next to
this is the zone of transition (zone II) which is characterised in modern
British cities by the decaying inner city areas containing high proportions
of Asian and black families living in overcrowded multi-occupied large
Victorian houses vacated by the middle classes after the Second World
War. The economically and upwardly mobile families within the zone of
transition migrate outwards through zone III where semi- and unskilled
workers live in the smaller Victorian houses vacated by the lower-middle
classes or in post-war council flats. Zone IV is characterised by the
predominance of skilled workers living in their semi-detached houses,

both owner-occupiers and council tenants. Zone V (the commuter zone) which nowadays with the development of modern transportation systems may include a large rural area around towns and cities, is characterised by the middle classes seeking space and privacy. The demand for cheap land and space, coupled with the inevitable decay of older properties, creates a pattern of central decline and peripheral expansion, which continues until the core is renewed, such as is happening in the London docklands.

The complexity of the British housing market and rapid changes in the structure of modern urban areas accentuated by continuing high levels of unemployment and the collapse of the industrial substructure in many British towns and cities in the last decade makes the original model less appropriate. Contemporary urban sociologists while accepting the descriptive value of the model reject the substantial ecological framework upon which it is based (Robson, 1975; Pahl et al, 1983).

Elderly people come from all social groups and classes in society. Residential location will be to a greater part determined by their position in the urban structure prior to old age. Thus, the older members of ethnic minorities will tend to remain close to their relatives and kin in the zone of transition or in areas to which they migrated earlier in their lives. A lack of resources as well as family and kinship ties will prevent the migration of many ethnic elderly people. A lack of resources will also be prohibitive to many working-class and lower-middle-class elderly people. Thus, we might predict that migration in later life is a predominantly middle-class activity (Law and Warnes, 1982; Grundy, 1987).

The characteristics of migrants in later life

Migration in later life is increasing in France and the United States (Cribier, 1975; Barsby and Cox, 1975; Graff and Wiseman, 1978) as well as in Britain (Law and Warnes, 1975; 1980), although a fall in migration rates between 1970–71 and 1980–81 in the retirement age groups has been reported (Grundy, 1987). It is estimated that at present about 10 per cent of retired people move 40 km away from their previous residential location (Law and Warnes, 1980). The majority of such moves take place around retirement age. Karn (1977), in her study about retirement to the seaside, found that just under half moved in the year of their retirement and Law and Warnes (1980) found that about two-thirds moved within two years of retirement. This is of course a period in the later stage of the life cycle when people are most healthy and have the resources to undertake such moves. When they are older their incomes decline and their health deteriorates (Townsend, 1986) and this increasing dependence tends to restrict mobility. However, the majority of older people do not desire to move or are unable to move.

A number of factors have been suggested as influencing migration. First, individuals must have the ability to move. Thus, migrants in later life tend to be from the middle or upper income groups and from the professional social classes. Usually this means that they are owner-occupiers who are able to realise capital assets in order to make the move. Local authority or private tenants are unlikely to have the necessary resources, even if they desire to migrate. Local authority tenants also have an additional obstacle to migration because of the difficulty of exchanging tenancies.

Second, potential migrants must have the desire to move. Karn (1977) found that people moved because they were attracted to the area of their new home, were dissatisfied with their old home or moved to be nearer families and friends. Similarly, Law and Warnes (1973) found that the proximity of friends and relatives and the attractiveness of the new area were important influences on migrants' decisions to move. However, they did not find that dissatisfaction with their former residence or area of residence was a major influence for many of the people studied.

Third, social networks play an important role in the decision to migrate, not only in influencing people to move to an area but in influencing people to stay put in the family home. Law and Warnes (1980) report that people who were experienced migrants during their working lives were more likely to move in retirement while those living close to their children, as measured by frequency of contact, were more likely to stay put.

The French and British experience of migration in later life supports the view that older people who are relatively affluent will increasingly seek retirement homes away from the major urban conurbations. This pattern will be influenced by the increasing experience of lifetime migration; greater home ownership; earlier retirement and the more widespread location of a smaller number of children. Experience from the United States suggests that the majority of moves in later life will be relatively local (less than 40 km) (Golant, 1977). However, the majority of older people are likely to stay put partly because of the lack of the necessary resources.

THE HOMES OF ELDERLY PEOPLE

In Britain over 95 per cent of people of pensionable age live in private households (OPCS and Registrar General Scotland, 1983), although as people age they are likely to experience living in some kind of institution. Of older people living in private households about 5 per cent will live in some form of sheltered accommodation with a warden (Butler et al, 1983).

Since the introduction of the welfare state there has been a rapid increase in owner-occupation and until 1979 an equally rapid increase in local authority housing at the expense of the privately rented sector (Boleat, 1986), although there are substantial regional variations. These trends have been reflected in the experiences of older people (Hunt, 1978; OPCS, 1982). Just under two-fifths of elderly people who live alone and

Table 8.3   *Tenure and type of housing of older people's homes*

| | Elderly person households | | | |
	One adult 60 or over	Elderly couples	Other elderly households	Households with no elderly people
Tenure:	%	%	%	%
Owner-occupied	37	54	52	56
Local authority	47	36	38	33
Private rented	15	10	9	11
N=100%	1502	1214	744	8109
Type of housing:	%	%	%	%
House or bungalow	64	84	88	82
Ground or first floor flat	30	12	10	13
Other flat	6	4	2	6
N=100%	1502	1214	744	8109

Source: Office of Population, Censuses and Surveys (1982), Table 10.4.

just over half of elderly couples are home-owners (see Table 8.3). Most of these older people own their homes outright, and this proportion is increasing, both as younger generations with higher levels of ownership reach retirement, and as growing numbers of local authority tenants, particularly the older ones, buy their own council houses.

Around 10 per cent of the population now live in privately rented accommodation. However, older people, particularly those aged 70 or over and those who live alone, are more likely to rent accommodation privately. Older people living alone are also more likely to live in purpose-built flats or maisonettes (see Table 8.3).

Elderly people are more likely to live in older housing (see Table 8.4), which is likely to be in poorer condition, lacking in amenities and with sub-standard heating. Privately rented accommodation is particularly subject to these deficiencies (Wheeler, 1986). Elderly owner-occupiers are also increasingly likely to be living in older housing stock than younger householders (Department of Environment, 1983) and they are also likely to experience poorer housing conditions.

One method of estimating general housing conditions is the general state of properties. The 1981 *English House Condition Survey* (DOE, 1983) found that households in unsatisfactory housing were likely to be headed by an elderly person; 43 per cent of unfit dwellings were occupied by households headed by somebody of pensionable age. The survey found that many older people were not motivated to undertake repairs. The growing repair problem for elderly owner-occupiers is likely to increase as a growing number of older people own their homes unless financial support and counselling is provided to this group of owner-occupiers (Rose, 1982).

Table 8.4   *Age of accommodation and amenities of older people's homes*

	Elderly person households			
	One adult 60 or over	Elderly couples	Other elderly householdholds	Households with no elderly people
Age of accommodation:	%	%	%	%
Pre-1919	28	24	29	23
1919–1944	27	30	35	24
1945–1964	23	29	25	27
1965 or later	23	17	11	26
N=100%	1486	1216	747	8089
Amenities:	%	%	%	%
Lacking own indoor WC	8	5	6	3
Lacking bath or shower	4	3	3	1
Lacking central heating	55	49	54	39
N=100%	1500	1220	750	8200

Source: Office of Population, Censuses and Surveys (1982), Table 10.4.

For many years the importance of adequate heating in elderly-person households has been a neglected area of social policy, but with the increasing concern about hypothermia (Wicks, 1978) and the effect of poor housing conditions on people's health (Byrne et al, 1986) concern about heating is firmly on the policy agenda. Only about half of the elderly-person households surveyed in the 1980 *General Household Survey* had central heating (see Table 8.4) compared to about two-thirds of younger-person households. In addition, Hunt (1978) showed from her survey of elderly people living in the community in England that a small but significant proportion of respondents were not warm enough in bed (8 per cent), in their own living room (8 per cent), or the kitchen (12 per cent). Many of those who reported being cold blamed it on inadequate heating facilities often arising from financial stringency.

Specialist housing for elderly people

Inadequate housing conditions are particularly problematic for older people who are impaired, handicapped or disabled. A lack of adequate housing has been blamed for the unnecessary admission of older dependent people into residential care (Townsend, 1962; Townsend and Wedderburn, 1965). The development of special housing for elderly people was seen as the most appropriate solution. With the emphasis on providing support in the community successive governments have encouraged local authorities to build warden-controlled sheltered housing and it continues to be an attractive way of maintaining dependent elderly people in their own homes (Wirz, 1982).

Studies of sheltered housing have recently questioned whether it is the most appropriate policy. Butler et al (1983) concluded that sheltered housing created an elite whose housing needs were not different from those of the elderly population as a whole. Not surprisingly successive studies have shown that actual and potential tenants of sheltered housing are strongly in favour of them (Abrams, 1978; Rose, 1978; Goldberg and Connelly, 1982; Wirz, 1982; Butler et al, 1983; Butler and Tinker, 1983; Thompson and West, 1984; Fleiss, 1985); as is evident by the long waiting lists. However, a number of writers have continued to doubt the philosophy of such schemes. The most frequently cited disadvantages refer to the desirability of old people moving (Lawton and Yaffe, 1970); the desirability of segregating old people from the rest of the population (Bytheway and James, 1978; Butler and Tinker, 1983); the expense of providing a resident warden and the appropriateness of tenants' disabilities (Goldberg and Connelly, 1982); the over-provision of services (Robson, 1980); and the appropriateness of the warden's role (Boldy, 1976). Despite these concerns sheltered housing still remains the panacea for the housing problems of elderly people (Thompson and West, 1984).

A growing concern with the perceived demographic implication of continuing expansion in the provision of sheltered housing has led to alternative policies being promoted. Since 1979 central government policy has severely curtailed local authority expenditure on both ordinary council housing and specialist housing for elderly people (Kilroy, 1982; Murie, 1983; Wheeler, 1986). This reduction in the provision of public-sector housing has been matched by a marked increase in the provision of sheltered housing funded by the private and voluntary sectors (Sharp, 1988; Williams, 1988). By 1986 it has been estimated that the private sector had provided some 21,000 units (Walker, 1986).

One policy response to the severe reduction in public expenditure on housing has been the idea of 'staying put'. This policy aims at helping elderly people remain in their own homes more satisfactorily (Wheeler, 1982). 'Staying put', which presents a flexible approach to addressing the housing needs of elderly people, has come about through the activities of voluntary organisations, building societies and local authorities, rather than central government. Tinker (1984) reviews a number of these innovatory services provided by local authorities as alternatives to both residential care and sheltered housing. From the evidence presented it would appear that the majority of elderly people living in the innovatory schemes studied were satisfied with the service provided and desired to remain in their own homes. An important element of this study, given the emphasis of central government on value for money and public expenditure reduction, was an estimation of the relative costs of different schemes. There was a wide variation in the basic costs of the innovatory schemes and the associated statutory services elderly people received. Overall the services costs, including income and housing costs, were lower for the 'staying put' schemes than for residential homes or

Table 8.5   *Household structure of elderly people in 1945, 1962, 1976 and 1980*

| | 1945* | 1962 | 1976 | 1980 |
	%	%	%	%
Living alone	10	22	30	34
Living with spouse only	30	33	44	45
Living with others	60	44	27	22

* These data are not nationally representative. See source for details.
Source: Dale et al (1987), Table 1.

sheltered housing. However, if the cost of informal care was added, as a cost attributable to people in their own homes, both for sheltered houses and the 'staying put' schemes, overall costs might rise above the costs of residential care.

Household structure

Demographic, economic and social factors have all combined to change the pattern of living arrangements of elderly people. Table 8.5 illustrates the dramatic nature of these changes, highlighting the decline in the proportion of elderly people living with others. Among a number of factors which have influenced this decline are the reduction in the average number of children and their earlier and more frequent marriage for the current cohort of elderly people, greater geographical mobility, the increase in employment opportunities for women over the last 20 years and the improvement in the availability of housing for younger families since the war. The opportunity to express a general preference to live alone has been enabled by increasing personal resources, particularly among middle-class people. Data from the 1980 *General Household Survey* show that the majority of elderly people live with a spouse, or after widowhood, alone (see Table 8.6). The greater longevity of women than men means that they are more likely to be widowed and therefore live alone.

In their analysis of the 1980 *General Household Survey* Dale et al (1987) show that about 95 per cent of elderly people retain their own households, only a small minority moving into households of younger generations. This analysis found that adult sons are more likely to remain in the parental home than adult daughters, except where the elderly person is moderately or severely disabled. Elderly people are more likely to join their daughters' households than those of their sons. Among widowed elderly people, their greater age was shown to be more important in determining their household structure than either their level of disability or gender. Figure 8.3 summarises Dale et al's analysis showing the household structure of elderly people in 1980 and the likely directions of change.

Table 8.6 *Household structure of elderly people by age*

	Under 75 %	75 or over %	Total %
Lone elderly woman	22	38	27
Lone elderly man	6	9	7
Living with spouse only	52	28	45
Livingwithotherelderlypeopleonly	4	6	4
Living with younger people	17	19	18
Total	100	100	100
(Base number)	*3170*	*1383*	*4553*

Sources: Office of Population, Censuses and Surveys (1982), Table 10.2; Dale, Evandrou, and Arber (1987), Table 2.

INSTITUTIONAL LIVING

Throughout history a small proportion of all age groups have lived in an institution of some kind. At the 1981 Census in Britain some 325,000 persons of pensionable age were usually resident in a non-private household excluding persons in places of detention or defence establishments (OPCS and Registrar General Scotland, 1983). In addition, some 130,000 were present on census night but were not usually resident. Thus, at any one time, between 4 and 5 per cent of people of pensionable age are living either temporarily or permanently in an institution. Institutional living is something we are all likely to experience in our lives. As mental or physical frailty increases, so an elderly person is increasingly likely to experience institutional living. At the 1981 Census, 9.6 per cent of people aged 75 or over and 21.6 per cent of people aged 85 or over were resident in an institution on census night. This is in stark contrast to other European countries, particularly the Netherlands where three times the proportion of people aged 75 or over live in nursing homes or so-called 'caring homes' (Coleman, 1984a).

Since 1948 the care of frail elderly people has been provided by the families of elderly people and by the private, statutory and voluntary sectors. Families continue to provide the majority of care (Wicks and Rossiter, 1982; Parker, 1985) but where family care has not been available frail elderly people have always been cared for in a variety of institutions (Thomson, 1983). Institutional care for elderly people currently includes local authority, private and voluntary residential homes, NHS and private nursing homes, and acute, geriatric and psychiatric NHS hospital wards.

The United Kingdom was one of the first industrialised countries to provide a specialist service for the medical care of elderly people (Brocklehurst, 1975; Hall, 1988). However, throughout the UK this service takes on a variety of forms (Williamson, 1979). In general, all departments of geriatric medicine set out to provide a service for a defined population

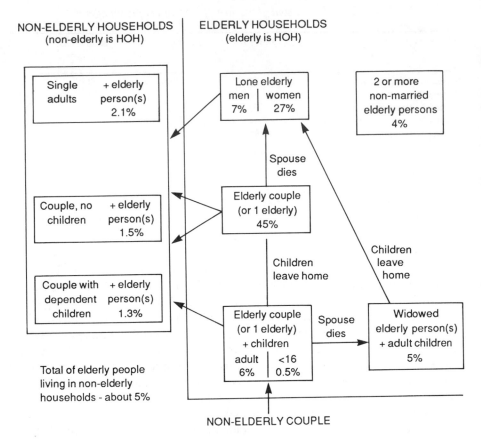

Figure 8.3 *Flow diagram to illustrate the household structure of elderly people showing the likely direction of change at different stages of the lifestyle in later life*

Source: Dale et al (1987), Figure 1.
Note: These data are based on the *General Household Survey*, 1980 and some simplifications and approximations have been necessary. (N = 4553)

and provide a comprehensive range of facilities. However, the type of person cared for varies from those who are acutely ill to those who are chronically ill.

Under the terms of the 1948 National Assistance Act local authorities are required to provide residential care for frail people. Since 1948 there has been a change in the condition of old people's homes. More residential homes are now purpose-built for the care of disabled people. With the increasing numbers of mentally impaired elderly people entering residential homes some authorities have developed separate facilities for the elderly mentally infirm in the form of either separate units within existing homes or separate homes (Willcocks et al, 1987).

Of increasing importance in recent years has been the development of a

Table 8.7   *Estimated provision of places for elderly people in England, 1984*

Type of provision		Estimated places		
	Number	Per 1000 Popl. 65+	Per 1000 Popl. 75+	Per 1000 Popl. 85+
Geriatric beds	53,262	7.6	17.8	95.4
Private nursing home places	28,413	4.0	9.5	50.9
Local authority home places	109,915	15.6	36.8	196.9
Voluntary home places	30,651	4.3	10.3	54.9
Private rest home places	59,993	8.5	20.1	107.5
Total public provision	163,177	23.2	54.6	292.3
Total private provision	119,057	16.9	39.9	213.2
Total provision	282,234	40.1	94.5	505.5

Source: Larder et al (1986), Table 2.

flourishing private sector, which expanded by 27.5 per cent between 1982 and 1984 (Larder et al, 1986). Between mid-1987 and mid-1988 private residential care expanded by 11.6 per cent and the provision of private nursing homes by 32.1 per cent (Laing, 1988). In some areas, particularly in the coastal retirement areas, throughout this century, there has always been a flourishing private sector. Until recently almost all residents of private residential and nursing homes were self-financed. Following the 1979 supplementary benefit regulations, residents in private nursing and rest homes became eligible for supplementary benefit. Until 1983 there were varying interpretations of the Act so that local DHSS officers set different levels of benefit. Variations in the provision of private homes reflected differences in benefit payments. Health and local authorities also responded in different ways to the availability of private homes and thus in some areas there has been more encouragement to develop private residential facilities for elderly people. In addition, consumer demand for private homes has been greater in some areas than others. Thus, across the country there exist considerable variations in the provision of places in the private sector, but generally with a higher provision in the south than the north of the country (Larder et al, 1986).

These developments in the provision of institutional care for frail elderly people appear to be leading towards a major change in the type of institutional care provided. As geriatric medicine increasingly focuses on acute care and rehabilitation there is pressure to remove all long-stay beds from geriatric hospitals and provide nursing-home care for elderly people. Since 1979 the majority of nursing homes have been developed by the private and voluntary sector and the majority of this provision has been provided by small businesses rather than the larger health care organisations although these are increasingly likely to develop nursing home type facilities while the political climate continues to support the private sector. Within the NHS, the DHSS has promoted the concept of

NHS nursing homes (DHSS, 1983b) and these are being established in a number of health authorities.

The most recent estimate (1986–87) of the provision of places in institutions for elderly people is shown in Table 8.7. If the increase in private provision continues at the rapid rate already experienced then the number of places provided in the private sector will shortly exceed the level of provision in the public sector. However, away from the traditional retirement areas and the affluent areas within cities institutional care will probably continue to be provided predominantly by the public sector (Larder et al, 1986).

Characteristics of institutional living

A number of studies have highlighted the similarity of the characteristics of frail elderly people who live in these different types of institutions (Townsend and Wedderburn, 1965; Wilkin et al, 1978; Gilleard et al, 1980; Bond and Carstairs, 1982; Wade et al, 1983; Atkinson et al, 1986; Lowrey and Briggs, 1988; Bond et al, 1989a). The findings from these studies show the overlap in clientele. For example, Atkinson et al (1986) found that although there were similarities in demographic and behavioural characteristics it was the NHS hospitals and nursing homes which contained the highest proportion of severely frail persons and the private residential homes which contained the lowest proportions. However, there were important differences between health authorities surveyed, particularly in terms of the behavioural characteristics of residents in the private homes. In addition, there is considerable overlap between the characteristics of elderly people living in private households, sheltered housing and in institutions (Townsend and Wedderburn, 1965; Bond and Carstairs, 1982).

Research continues to show that in NHS hospitals many general medical beds are perceived as 'blocked' by elderly people requiring long-term residential accommodation or are 'misplaced' in the care system, implying that there is a scarcity of this facility (Kidd, 1962; McKeown and Cross, 1969; Langley and Simpson, 1970; Carstairs and Morison, 1971; Evans et al, 1971; Gelding and Newell, 1972; Hodkinson et al, 1972; McKechnie, 1972; Brocklehurst, 1975; Copeland et al, 1975; McArdle et al, 1975; Rubin and Davies, 1975; Plank, 1977; Brocklehurst et al, 1978; Roe and Guillem, 1978; Currie et al, 1979; Covell and Angus, 1980; Coid and Crome, 1986). As a result of this perceived scarcity admission to NHS hospital beds and local authority residential care appears to be mainly 'crisis based' (Barnes, 1980). It has also been confirmed that for every severely physically incapacitated elderly person living in an institution there are four living in private households either alone or with other elderly people or in other types of households (Townsend and Wedderburn, 1965; Bond and Carstairs, 1982). However, for every one elderly person with a diagnosis of moderate or severe dementia or confusion living at home there are three in institutions (Bond, 1987). There would also appear to be considerable numbers of elderly people living in private households whom professionals deem to be in need of services, but for whom no service is provided (Townsend, 1957; Townsend, 1962; Williamson et al, 1964; Townsend and Wedderburn, 1965; Harris, 1968; Hunt, 1970; Andrews et al, 1971; Cartwright et al, 1973; Townsend, 1973; Powell and Crombie, 1974; Marks, 1975; Gardiner, 1975; Gruer, 1975; Isaacs and Neville, 1975; Foster et al, 1976; Bond and Carstairs, 1982).

It has been recognised for a number of years that many institutions, whatever their clientele, exhibit the characteristics of what Goffman (1961) has termed the total institution. The essential feature of the total institution, which distinguishes it from other forms of organisation is that, unlike life outside, there is no separation between the three central spheres of life: work, leisure and the family. All aspects of life are conducted within the boundaries of the institution and under the control of a single authority. Each phase of daily activities is shared with a large number of other people, all of whom are treated alike and are required to do the same things together. These activities normally follow a strict routine imposed from above by a system of explicit formal rulings and a body of officials. The routine of daily activities comprises a single rational plan which has been designed to fulfil the official aims of the institution.

Detailed British studies of residential homes for the elderly (Townsend, 1962), of residential homes for the physically disabled and young chronic sick (Miller and Gwynne, 1972), and of long-stay geriatric hospital wards (Baker, 1978; Evers, 1981) exemplify Goffman's model, although these studies also show that the concept is not relevant to all institutions. As a result of these and other studies there have been various efforts to overcome the effects of institutionalisation through the process of normalisation: the principle that people living in institutions should be able to follow a lifestyle similar to the patterns they would experience living in private households (Wolfensberger, 1972).

Attempts at providing a normal environment for frail people in institutions have been constrained by the historical legacies of institutions and the ubiquitous scarcity of resources. Townsend's early studies of residential care poignantly highlight the legacy of the Victorian workhouse. Many public-sector institutions currently used for the care of frail elderly people by local authorities and local health authorities were originally workhouses. Most will have been modernised and upgraded, but the physical memory of the workhouse continues to dominate local communities and remind residents and the local population of the social heritage of these buildings. In addition, many health authorities have inherited large isolation hospitals used before the discovery of antibiotics for the care of TB patients and other patients with infectious diseases. In a study of institutional facilities for the long-term care of elderly people in six health authorities Bond et al (1989a) found that in each study area there was at least one former workhouse and one former isolation hospital and only one health authority had a hospital ward which had been purposely built for the care of long-stay elderly patients. With the current policy of closing psychiatric hospitals and the continuing scarcity of resources for health authority managers it is increasingly likely that these facilities might also become appropriated for the institutional care of elderly people.

It is not only the former uses and locations of facilities which have hindered the development of policies of normalisation but also the institutional attitudes of staff and residents alike. The preservation of individuals' dignities and the provision of privacy has been difficult to achieve. In the health service the acute model of care dominates the training of all health care workers so that the hierarchical structure socialises staff to think and work in ways which contradict normalisation and reinforces the social environment of the total institution. Within local authority homes the presence of a large number of untrained workers who remain in the same setting for a number of years makes innovation difficult. Although staff are highly motivated there have been few examples of good continuing inservice training which would have enabled the principles of normalisation to be widely implemented. There has also been a paucity of social work literature about the care of elderly people (Willcocks et al, 1987).

There has been little research into the quality of care provided in private and voluntary homes in Britain. Those who promote private care argue that it cannot be worse than that provided in the public sector and that a mixture of public and private provision promotes a more efficient and equitable system (Judge et al, 1983). Others have expressed concern based on the American and Australian experience that some proprietors of private homes might seek to exploit vulnerable elderly people (Mendelson, 1974). Weaver et al (1985) highlight the difficulties faced by British proprietors in pursuing the dual goals of profit and care. Willcocks et al (1987) suggest that even the development of an advisory code of practice (Centre for Policy on Ageing, 1984) and the introduction of new legislation introduced in the Registered Homes Act of 1984 will not necessarily ensure good practice.

THE LIVING ARRANGEMENTS OF ELDERLY AND FRAIL ELDERLY PEOPLE

Old age has for many years been seen as a social problem (MacIntyre, 1977) and this perspective has helped perpetuate ageism. As a result, in any discussion of living arrangements there has usually been more emphasis on the needs of frail elderly people than on elderly people in general. The majority of older people are not mentally or physically frail, although it has been estimated that of those aged 85 or over one in five might suffer from moderate or severe dementia (Report of the Royal College of Physicians, 1981; Bond, 1987) and three in five a limiting longstanding illness (Office of Populations, Censuses and Surveys, 1982). In other words, four in five of those aged 85 or over are not mentally frail and two in five are not physically frail.

In this chapter we have indicated that the living arrangements of older people are strongly influenced by their structural position in society at earlier stages of the life cycle. Owner-occupiers tend to remain owner-occupiers, council tenants tend to remain council tenants, and private tenants tend to remain private tenants, but some transitions in tenure do occur as a result of bereavement or the onset of frailty. Thus, the political economy perspective outlined in Chapter 2 has shown that our lives in later life are strongly marked out by our access to resources and social goods throughout our lives. Housing tenure remains one of the most sensitive indicators of an individual's access to resources, although as we have seen in this chapter many elderly people lack the resources to keep their own property in good repair. However, as owner-occupiers become older and frailer they have a disposable asset for the securing of a smaller or more appropriate dwelling than council or private tenants. In the event of requiring institutional care owner-occupiers could also use these resources to fund institutional care of their choice. However, as we keep emphasising, most elderly people are not likely to require long-term institutional care and the majority remain in their own homes for much of their old age.

Admission to institutional care is often regarded as an inevitable consequence of frailty in later life. However, frailty alone is not a good predictor of institutional care. Townsend (1965) in an earlier analysis of reasons for admission to an institution found that family composition, structure and organisation strongly influenced admission to a residential home. Functional capacity, homelessness, and lack of economic resources were found to be less influential. More recent studies have indicated the importance of the availability of family and social support (Isaacs et al, 1972; Berkeley, 1976; Farrow et al, 1976; Bond and Carstairs, 1982; Graham and Livesley, 1983; Booth, 1985). In a study to evaluate continuing-care accommodation for elderly people Bond et al (1989b) have found that nursing staff give lack of social support as a common reason for old people remaining in NHS hospitals and nursing homes.

Townsend (1986) has argued persuasively that many people living in institutions, particularly local authority residential homes, could be readily cared for in the community if an adequate level of resources, particularly special housing, were made available for services for elderly people. From a political economy perspective he argues that this unnecessary institutionalisation is due to the wider functions that residential homes undertake for society. While accommodating only a tiny percentage of the elderly population they symbolise the dependence of elderly people and legitimate their lack of access to equality of status. This conclusion is supported by the evidence that many residents have the capacities to live in private households and the evidence of social restrictions and authoritarian styles of management in many homes.

This chapter has described the considerable data that support the view that the current living arrangements for many elderly people are inappropriate and that new social policies must be conceived which remove long-term institutionalisation. Townsend (1986) argues that the three kinds of public sector institutional provision should be merged. Residential homes should be abolished and the small minority of NHS long-stay geriatric and psychogeriatric patients should be cared for in NHS nursing homes. Sheltered housing provided in the public sector and day care provision should be expanded to care for the substantial minority of less severely incapacitated elderly people. This radical solution takes little account of the current explosion in the supply and demand of private residential and nursing homes or the realities of the difficulties of establishing an egalitarian method of allocating sheltered housing.

Tinker (1987) has advocated a more flexible approach to the use of housing for frail elderly people, arguing that since most elderly people wish to remain in their own homes a variety of options should be made available. These include ordinary housing, living with a family, granny annexes, sheltered housing with a warden, extra care housing, continuing care communities and residential care. Willcocks et al (1987) have proposed that the residential flatlet should replace the traditional residential home. Such a proposal would combine the advantages of independent living with the security and support essential for a frail population by attempting to capture the essence of what an old person would call home. The Department of Health set up three experimental NHS nursing homes in an attempt to provide a more homelike environment for severely frail elderly people (DHSS, 1983b) which have been evaluated (Bond et al, 1989c). A number of local authorities and local health authorities are also experimenting with different forms of care for very frail elderly people. However, experience of similar developments for the care of people with learning difficulties suggests that attempts to abolish all institutions may be unsuccessful even with the necessary political will. Small residential units, including flatlets, built for use by people with learning difficulties have suggested limited gains when compared with conventional institutions (Renshaw et al, 1988). Similarly, the building of modern residential homes with the exclusive provision of single rooms has not changed the fundamental nature of residential care for elderly people. Changes in physical design may be a necessary but not sufficient condition for independent living. Without changes in the social attitudes toward elderly people their living arrangements are unlikely to meet their needs or their desires.

9

INTIMATE RELATIONSHIPS

Dorothy Jerrome

Intimate relationships are characterised by emotional intensity, self-disclosure, and a high degree of personal involvement. In the psychological literature on ageing, intimacy tends to be discussed in connection with mental health. We need to 'exist in the thought and affection of another' to be emotionally secure, well adjusted and have high morale. The importance of an intimate, confiding relationship has been noted in studies of depression in earlier years (Brown and Harris, 1978) and in studies of the ability to cope with age-related losses in later years (Lowenthal and Haven, 1968).

In sociological accounts of ageing, intimate relationships are seen as synonymous with primary group ties (Creech and Babchuk, 1985). Small group size, frequency of interaction and a long history of association are conditions in which primary relations develop. Primary relationships are informal, personal and subject to negotiation. They meet a number of needs: for personal support, for sociability, for physical and emotional intimacy, and for stimulation.

In our society value is attached to caring, to sociability and to social success. Loneliness is a stigma. The capacity to make, maintain or replace intimate relationships is important. In the literature of social gerontology it is commonly assumed that sources of intimacy become attenuated through the lifespan, to the detriment of the ageing individual's health, capacity for social involvement, and general well-being. In the rest of this chapter we shall examine in detail a range of intimate relationships in later life asking whether their significance changes through the lifespan.

THE FAMILY: IDEALS AND REALITIES

An obvious starting point for a discussion of intimate relationships, given the pattern of emotional investments of most people in British society, is the family. Viewed from a structuralist sociological perspective (see Chapter 2), the family has a crucial role in social reproduction – the transmission of values and existing social arrangements from one generation to the next. It is the main institutional setting for childhood, and is one of the two realms of experience which give form and meaning to adult life (the other is work). In modern industrial society and in our own welfare state the family is a most useful institution. Its members, particularly the adult female ones, are the primary caregivers for dependants – generally speaking, the very old and the very young. It meets people's needs for intimacy and companionship. It is the main unit of consumption in a consumer-oriented society. It is the supplier of a reserve labour force (unemployed women) and it services those active in the work force. It produces future workers and generally educates the young in the ways of their particular communities.

This range of functions explains the official and popular concern shown periodically for the well-being of the family, and the regularity of state intervention.

> As a general election approaches, the family is once again unwrapped, patched up and worshipped to assure the electorate that politicians are in favour of all things good. (*New Society*, Editorial, 14 October 1982)

It has been suggested that concern with the family is growing. On the one hand, changing family patterns became visible in the 1970s, with the increase in rates of divorce and single-parent families, illegitimacy, and cohabitation before marriage suggesting to some that the family is under threat. On the other hand, there has been evidence that the demands on families are growing. The changing age structure of the population (see Chapter 1) has meant a growth in the number of very elderly people who make disproportionate demands on health and personal social services and for whom the family has traditionally been the major source of support. At the same time there have been constraints on public expenditure, with social welfare expenditure figuring prominently in the cuts. A further factor causing concern has been the increasing evidence about family poverty, which was rediscovered in the 1960s, largely through the efforts of the Child Poverty Action Group.

There is strong ideological emphasis on the family. One is expected to be a member of a couple, and a family, and exclusion from either type of relationship is viewed as a misfortune, if not a personal failing. The couple- and family-orientation of social life and the value attached to sociability make the family – or lack of it – a main reference point in the ageing process. Ageing needs to be understood in the context of the family.

Three contrasting views are discernible in recent public discussions about the family. Which view one adopts depends on fundamental values about society and the place of the family within it. We can call them the traditionalist, socialist and feminist perspectives following Craven et al (1982). Within these perspectives the family is seen as an agent for stability or change, conservation or social progress, depending on one's ideological position.

> The traditionalists, viewing the family as the key unit in society, will often view change and signs of family breakdown with suspicion. Feminists and other radicals will view the *traditional* family with suspicion, regarding it as an

oppressive unit, a barrier to individual experience and fulfilment and radical advance. They will focus attention on what happens *within* the family and the distribution therein of income, responsibility, work and power. Socialists and others on the left, while working for changes within the family, will also seek more state support for families with responsibility for children and other dependents. (Craven et al, 1982, pp. 23–24)

In all three, a critical area for debate is the way in which the dependency needs of older and younger family members are met. Within the traditionalist perspective the emphasis is on duties and obligations rather than on individual rights. The duty to care for elderly dependent relatives would take the precedence over the rights of other members, especially the right of younger female relatives to work. Within feminist thought, women are oppressed by the pattern of gender roles and responsibilities in the traditional family. Domestic labour performed mainly by women is idealised as care, love and protection. It includes caring for the old and sick, at little cost to the state. Within the socialist perspective, the highest values of family life – caring, non-competitiveness, cooperation and the non-contingent love of others – are threatened by hardship and poverty.

Conflicting views and objectives produce conflicting social policies. Over a period of time we might expect to find social policies designed in terms of one perspective to be imposed on a family shaped by a different pattern of intervention. Political intervention in family life clearly reflects an ideological position. Politicians, policy makers, churchmen and other public figures pronounce on the family on the basis of a commitment to a particular set of values. These values – 'community', 'authority', 'equality', 'individual freedom' – have powerful prescriptive force which blinds people to objective facts about family life. Assumptions are made, evidence is used selectively and ideologically 'sound' material is adopted uncritically in support of a particular viewpoint. The supposed inadequacies of the contemporary family are commonly placed in historical perspective to strengthen the case for intervention. Reference is made to earlier times when social arrangements were more satisfactory: children respected their parents, relationships were more caring, and so on.

For a different account of family life we can usefully turn to the literature of social science. Social scientists are not primarily concerned to change existing social arrangements, though their interest in particular social phenomena often arises from a personal concern with social problems. We have to remember that they, like politicians, are inclined to make apparently objective statements based on a set of implicit values. But ideally their value premises are consciously held and articulated.

THE FAMILY AND SOCIAL CHANGE

Social scientists have tended to share the concern of policy makers with the fate of the family as an institution. Indeed, much of the sociological literature in the 1940s and 1950s considered the possibility that the process of industrialisation had undermined the family, stripped it of its functions and reduced it to a small, isolated, highly specialised unit which only met its adult members' needs for intimacy and provided role models and socialisation for its younger members. This transformation was seen as part of a larger social trend involving community relations in general (Fischer, 1977). In terms of the quality of family life, the shift was thought to be from the large, multifunctional extended family to the small and inward-looking 'nuclear' family consisting of parents and their dependent biological offspring, highly mobile in response to the demands of the industrialising society, putting their own interests above those of more distant relatives and in particular neglecting the hitherto sacrosanct heads of a respected older generation. The 'classical myth of western nostalgia' (Fletcher, 1962) has since been repudiated. Writers of the 1960s, in the course of investigating the decline-of-community thesis, found the extended family alive and well, particularly in long-established working-class areas like East London (Wilmott and Young, 1962; Tunstall, 1966). Others declared that it survived in modified form; family ties were activated in time of need (Rosser and Harris, 1965).

Historians added a new dimension with a suggestion which challenged the assumption of the before-and-after school of thought: the extended, multifunctional family unit had indeed never been typical in pre-industrial English society (Laslett, 1977; Anderson, 1971). It was only in the new industrial areas, cramped and impoverished, that the family members had created networks of mutual support and co-residence. This refutation of the classical myth has come fairly recently to social gerontology. As late as the mid-1970s social gerontologists were still seeking to demonstrate the strength of ties in the extended family and the persistence of this particular structure, albeit in modified form, 'even in today's industrialised, urbanised, migratory world' (Troll and Smith, 1976). In gerontology during the 1960s and early 1970s, much intellectual energy was spent in opposing the widespread assumption of the death of the extended family. The belief that older people are alienated from their families was widespread in the media, in research and among older people themselves. In America, the work of many social scientists helped to counteract what Shanas (1979) called the myth of family neglect.

They showed that there was little evidence to support the belief in alienation. Their findings were that a significant proportion of old people and their children lived in close physical proximity; that they interacted frequently; and that families were still important to the care of old people. This optimistic view has been most recently supported by data from the longitudinal study at the University of California (Bengston, 1986). The facts of family life which emerge from the study contradict popular notions of decline and also the pessimistic views advanced by some academics. Despite evidence of structural change created by changes in marital status over the last 15 years in almost all the families in the study, intergenerational bonds are close, and viable. If anything, there is now more solidarity and interaction than when the study began, with almost 60 per cent of the youngest generation reporting an improvement in relationships (Bengtson, 1986).

However, changes *have* taken place, of a dramatic nature, over the last 100 years. These need to be taken into account in understanding the family experiences of people born in different decades, bringing with them expectations shared with others in the same cohort. Much of the contemporary American literature employs a static, ahistorical approach which conveys nothing of the meaning of dependency or the expectations of autonomy and support brought to the situation by elderly people whose own experiences of family lifespan many decades of change in family structure and processes. The result of ignoring the historical dimension and hence the perception of older people themselves, is a curiously one-sided analysis which does not tell us much about the realities of family life in old age.

To understand relationships in the later-life family – those families who are beyond the child-rearing years and have begun to launch their children (Brubaker, 1983) – we have to see them in the context of various changes which have affected the family in Britain over the last 100 years. Five areas of change can be identified.

Demographic   In the last 100 years we have seen falling rates of fertility and mortality, a reduction in family size, age at marriage and the number of children born to each family. These trends – particularly the falling age of marriage – have produced a narrowing of the distance between the generations, and a change in age distribution within the family.

Technological   The structure of employment has changed, with increasing numbers of women joining the work force. A general increase in mid-life options has had implications for women's family roles.

Legal   New legislation regulating marriage, divorce and homosexuality have affected the structure and composition of the family. It has increased the proportion of families which are divided, reconstituted and otherwise unconventional in structure.

Ideological   Within social policy there has been a growing emphasis over the last 15 years on community care, legitimated by a conservative model of the family, as opposed to care within institutions. In popular culture, changing ideologies of marriage and parenthood have introduced new value conflicts into family life.

Economic   Rising levels of affluence and the introduction of state welfare provision have allowed the operation of choice in family relationships. Ties between elderly parents and their adult children are increasingly governed by sentiment rather than obligation.

Changes in the structure of the family

The top-heavy family
Over the last 80 years the time span between the generations has been reduced. An increase of vertical ties and narrowing of lateral ties has

produced a family shaped like an inverted triangle, top heavy. It is now possible to belong to a five-generation family, or six if you are a black woman in Los Angeles (Burton and Bengtson, 1985). You can have grandparents and grandchildren simultaneously. For the first time in history, adults can have more parents than children.

The condition of top-heaviness is caricatured by the scene from the children's film, *Willy Wonka and the Chocolate Factory*, based on the book by Roald Dahl, in which the young widow, who is Charlie's mother, tends to Charlie's four grandparents as they pass their lives at opposite ends of the same large bed. An excess of parents over children is a condition exacerbated in British society by divorce and remarriage, as illustrated by the following case study:

Judy is a mature student of 52, married to Michael, a retired airline pilot, whose earlier marriage to Jean had broken up. Jean had also remarried. Michael and Jean had had two children. One of them, Christopher, had married a girl called Nicki whose parents had also divorced and remarried. At the young people's wedding there were four parents and four step-parents.

The marriage of Nicki and Chris got into difficulties, as passionate, romantic attachments are inclined to do. Under the strain of two children (now eight and six) it broke up. Nicki went home to her mother, Jane and her step-father, Peter. Jane was somewhat put out at the arrival of her daughter and grandchildren and called upon her daughter's ex-father-in-law Michael to shoulder the financial burden of the grandchildren's school fees. Feeling that the grandchildren now belonged more to their mother's side than to his, he refused to do so, claiming that his 'own' grandchildren (ie through his second marriage) would have more right to his resources. Chris' mother Jean was not going to help either. She had never really liked Nicki and had moved away from the area

A solution to the problem emerged in the form of Steven. Steven is Nicki's step-brother, the son of Jane's second husband Peter by his first marriage. Steven had also been married before but had no children. The young people – Steven and Nicki – were not passionately in love but in the circumstances 'everyone' (ie the many parents and step-parents) agreed that their relationship was a good idea. Jane was pleased because her step-son Steven would take care of her daughter, and take responsibility for her daughter's children by marrying their mother. Nicki's step-father would become her father-in-law. Steven's step-mother would become his mother-in-law. (See Figure 9.1.)

Structural complications

The kinship complications introduced here by divided and reblended families replaces earlier complications caused by family size. In the earlier, larger families with more children born to a single set of parents, a single generation – in the sense of position in the family line –

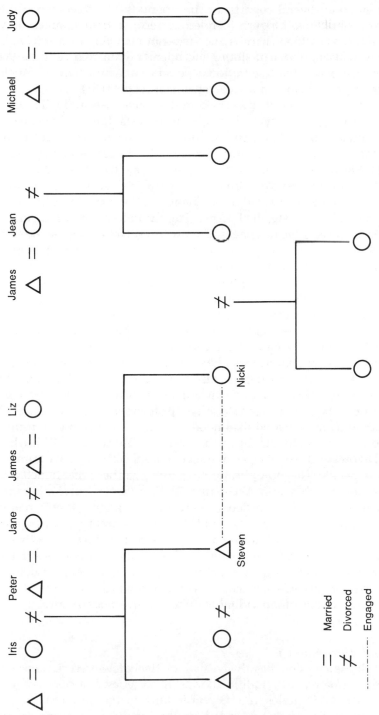

Figure 9.1   *Case study of a 'top-heavy' family*

might span several cohorts, or time periods. One cohort might include two generations. Modern blended or reconstituted families have these complications too. There is the step-mother who is close in age to her step-children, and half-siblings frequently span two cohorts. We often tend to forget that generational position does not tell us much about either age or cohort, and vice versa (Hagestad, 1985).

The group of people described in the above case study, linked by birth and marriage, is untypical in several respects. Its members are wealthy, and relationships between the formerly married are more cordial than is the case following many divorces. But in terms of the structure of relationships it might be more typical than we think. Divorce is now a major social trend in Britain. Between 1971 and 1982 the number of annual divorces granted in England and Wales doubled, one of the highest divorce rates in Europe (Family Policy Studies Centre, 1984b). One in three *new* marriages is now expected to end in divorce. It is thus increasingly likely that elderly people will be members of families disrupted by divorce (Timaeus, 1986).

There is also a growing minority of retired people who are themselves divorced. In 1981, 1.6 per cent of elderly men were divorced and this is expected to rise to 3.6 per cent by 2019. For women the proportions are higher: 2.2 per cent in 1981 rising to 7.2 per cent (Henwood and Wicks, 1985). In America it is estimated that by 2005 over half of those reaching retirement age will have been divorced at least once. In Britain, as in America, remarriage is also more frequent, at all stages of the life cycle. Currently one in every three marriages involves remarriage for one partner. The remarriage rate is higher for men than women at all ages, leading to an increased likelihood of women being alone in future years. We shall return to this aspect later on in a discussion of widowhood.

Divorce and remarriage have several implications for the family lives of older people. The multiplication of parents has been mentioned already. If the rate of birth does not keep up with the rate of divorce and remarriage, on whom will the burden of care for the many elderly parents and step-parents fall? How far will the eight parents at the wedding of Nicki and Chris look to them for support in old age? Another issue is access to grandchildren in divorce. Both of these problems – that of roles and responsibilities in reconstituted families and behaviour in families divided by divorce – reflect the confusion which exists about the rights and obligations of individual members in the modern family.

Normative confusion

Our kinship system has always had relatively few prescriptions for behaviour compared with traditional kinship societies. Priorities are undefined (Rosow, 1975). Roles and responsibilities in the new multigenerational family, and the new reblended family, are vague and undefined. It has been argued that with the introduction of state benefits and rising levels of affluence, obligation has given way to sentiment as a basis for family relationships (Eversley, 1982). Whether or not obligations are recognised is a matter for personal discretion. There is scope for this in any case in a bilateral kinship system such as ours. In the illustration given earlier, Michael, for his own convenience, defined his grandchildren by his first marriage as belonging less to him than to their maternal grandmother; as more distant from him than the grandchildren of his second marriage. In biological terms their relationships were identical.

In the novel situation of remarriage and the top-heavy family, pre-scriptions for behaviour are lacking. Some caring roles, such as those involving children, are expected in adulthood and have been learnt from older family members. By contrast, caring for an elderly relative is not generally expected, and no role models are available. Today the caregiver is herself likely to be ageing and possibly unequal to the task of caring. If she is younger, she is likely to be involved in paid employment and forced to make choices with no normative guidelines. In either case the role of caregiver to a very frail old person is not a natural developmental stage of life for the adult child (Brody, 1979).

Historically, society has relied primarily on the family to meet the 'normal' dependency needs of the main dependent population group: children (see Chapter 10). Faced with the emergence of a new population group with substantial needs – ie elderly people – society has continued to rely on the family. But what constitutes 'healthy' family functioning and 'normal' behaviour has yet to be decided. In the absence of established cultural patterns and prescriptions for behaviour, there is often anxiety, resentment and guilt when people find themselves having to give help. On the other side, too, there may be resentment at having to ask for help which might have been offered. However, the evidence is that people do not ask often (Michaud, 1986). There may be guilt at imposing on a busy daughter-in-law; and frustration at one's helplessness in a culture which values independence and mastery of the environment (Clark, 1972).

Several events or crises in the career of the ageing family threaten its well-being (Kuypers and Bengtson, 1983). These include the independence of adult children; the retirement from a job; serious illness and death or divorce, which radically alter the structure of the domestic group. The difficulty in handling these events is caused by what Kuypers and Bengtson call the historical baggage carried in each case. Each family inherits a legacy of ways of managing conflict and dealing with issues like autonomy.

In all families these crises create conflicts of loyalty, for we are governed by cultural assumptions that as families age the intensity of family involvement will diminish: that primary loyalties will transfer from parents and the family of origin to spouse and children in the new family, and that parents care for children, not the other way round. Children faced with the likelihood of a reversal of these expectations resist it. They tend to minimise the importance of impending change in the situation of an older member, denying its implications.

The main problem for the older family, in trying to function competently, is 'in coming to terms with change against a background of powerful forces promoting continuity' (Kuypers and Bengtson, 1983, p. 211). Family traditions and identities, norms and values transmitted from one generation to the next, and the culturally defined age-status positions of mother and child promote continuity. The need to accept and handle impending change is not helped by the negative cultural stereotypes of ageing, and the withdrawal of social and institutional support which tends to accompany ageing in our society.

For the participants in the intimate dramas of family life, all trying to achieve personal continuity in the face of change, issues like family traditions and 'our way of doing things' can become the focus of intense emotion and personal conflict. We shall return to this shortly.

Children's departures from family tradition can be a source of acute frustration for elderly parents. Equally frustrating is the lack of easy access to younger kin and shortage of conversation time with them. Daughters are often inaccessible on account of their physical distance and involvement in the labour force. Attitudes towards children's achievements are marked by ambivalence.

I met a woman at a bus stop recently who was proud of her daughter's good job. 'But', she said bitterly, 'she's too busy to talk to me'. In some ways this woman disapproves of her daughter's determination to work, which involves her mother in large amounts of childminding. She is glad to see more of her grandchildren and takes them to school occasionally. But it is a poor bargain, for she lives several miles away and gets relatively little out of the arrangement. She is fortunate to be able to do things for her grandchildren, albeit on their mother's terms. Other elderly people are separated from their grandchildren by the generation in between.

Grandparenthood

Grandparenthood in our culture is contingent on the actions of children, who produce the grandchildren and control access to them. The role of grandparent has been neglected in British gerontology. To date only one piece of research has focused exclusively upon it (Cunningham-Burley, 1984) though others have written about it (Adam, 1967; Stevenson, 1980; Rapoport and Rapoport, 1977). We have evidence from earlier work about rates of contact between grandparents and grandchildren in Britain (Abrams, 1980b) and the relationship has been put usefully into cross-cultural perspective as part of an extensive survey of older women's lives around the world (Peace, 1981).

The American system of grandparenthood and presumably the British, too, is distinguished by several factors. First, there is a structural separation between two generations, which results in more autonomy and privacy in the conjugal family and more remote status for the grandparents. Second, our system is not regulated by explicit rights and obligations. The grandparent–grandchild dyad, like others in the family, is voluntary and rests on personal initiative. Third, our value system encourages independence and personal freedom. In any conflict of interest the conjugal family would tend to have priority over the interests of the grandparents and others in the extended family (Johnson, 1985; Cherlin and Furstenberg, 1985).

The change in timing of life events, described earlier – earlier marriage, earlier and more closely-spaced children – have made grandparenthood a more youthful role and given it a new cultural image. The strongest feature of modern grandparenting is its diversity. Talking of role expectations, Hagestad has pointed out that 'in a society where grandparents range in age from 30 to 110, and grandchildren range from newborn to retirees, we should not be surprised to find a variety of grandparenting styles and few behavioural expectations regarding grandparenting' (Hagestad, 1985, p. 36).

Now that long life is the rule rather than the exception, and marriage more popular than ever (the propensity to marry has gradually increased to the point where marriage is now an almost universal experience in our society – in America 95 per cent of the over 65s have been married at least once) and infertility reduced by modern reproductive technology, more people become grandparents than ever before. In Britain too, the proportion of older people without descendants has declined and is likely to shrink even more rapidly as the century wears on (Timaeus, 1986). It is estimated that three-quarters of Americans over the age of 65 are grandparents (Shanas, 1979, 1980). The corresponding figure for Britons is 60 per cent (Abrams, 1980). A growing number of women may be for a time both grandmothers and granddaughters, a situation which is historically unique (Hareven, 1977).

The ambiguities surrounding normal grandparenting roles are exacerbated by divorce and remarriage. There are no models for behaviour with ex-daughters-in-law or step-grandchildren. Custody of children in divorce still goes to the mother in the majority of cases, which means that paternal grandparents are more likely to have problems with access to their grandchildren. Men seem particularly anxious about losing touch with their grandchildren. Women, it seems, are more likely to retain some contact with the divorced daughter-in-law as 'the mother of my grandchildren'. Women are in any case the kinkeepers in our family system. It is they who keep relationships alive. Even so, contact is generally lower on the 'non-custodial' side. The most vulnerable relationship is that between a grandfather and his son's son (Hagestad, 1985). Attention has recently been drawn to the legal right of grandparents in Britain too. Access following the death of a parent is upheld in the Domestic Proceedings and Magistrates' Courts Act 1978.

But in any case, the majority of modern grandparents do not wish for close relationships, according to an American sociologist (Kornhaber, 1985). They regard the tie with grandchildren as irrelevant. This role abdication rests on a philosophy of individualism and narcissism which threatens modern society. Kornhaber uses children's drawings to show that close contact is important and that children who enjoy it grow up with positive attitudes to ageing. Children who have little or no contact with grandparents view the old stereotypically, and are culturally and emotionally impoverished.

Other students of grandparenthood see it as vitally important in a time of rapid social change. The grandparent generation provides continuity with the past. Within the family, grandparents have an interpretive function. They reconstruct the family autobiography connecting its past to its present in a way that gives hope for the future. Grandparents are seen as stabilisers. In their wisdom and diplomacy they carefully manage interaction between the generations to minimise conflicts of value. Certain subjects are avoided as topics of conversation.

This optimistic view rests partly on research such as that of Bengtson and colleagues in Southern California (Bengtson et al, 1976). It rests partly on an idealised view of the modern family and the reciprocal needs of its members, a view which emerges particularly from some of the American research on grandparenthood. No equivalent body of literature exists in Britain. We do not know the extent of lineage solidarity (Bengston et al, 1976) or even how to measure it.

ISSUES IN INTERGENERATIONAL RELATIONS

In spite of the growing interest in grandparenthood in the USA we still tend in Britain to think of intergenerational family ties in terms of ageing parents and adult children. Within that parent–child dyad, we think first of the kinds of exchanges which go on – of help in domestic and personal tasks in return for childminding, for instance – and the amount of affection or sense of obligation which accompanies them. In British gerontology our thinking is limited to these two dimensions, largely as a reflection of the preoccupation with dependency in later life.

But there are other dimensions, as the study of grandparents reminds us. Bengtson et al (1976) offer a conceptual framework for the analysis of intergenerational relations in terms of three variables: association, affection and consensus. Association, the behavioural dimension, is measured by the amount and type of interaction between family members. Affection, the emotional dimension, includes feelings of warmth and liking between family members. Consensus, finally, is the cognitive or intellectual component, consisting of the extent of agreement or disagreement in attitudes and expectations. Although we lack equal amounts of evidence on these three dimensions of intergenerational relations in Britain, it is worth thinking for a moment in those terms. We will ask, first, how much interaction takes place between the generations, and how far these are ties of affection and intimacy.

Relating to kin Enough research has been conducted in Britain over the last ten years for us to be able to refer with some certainty to the availability to old people of kin, the amount of contact with them, levels of satisfaction with the relationships, and the role played by relatives in older people's lives. Urban and regional, gender and class differences have been explored in a number of major studies (Hunt, 1978; Abrams, 1978; Wenger, 1984) and attention has been drawn to the influence of other variables such as ethnic origin.

Availability In terms of availability we know that, contrary to popular assumptions, two-thirds of retired people with children have at least one of them living within a few miles. Proximity increases with age and with widowhood. Old people who move house do so in the direction of kin, and younger people, similarly, are likely to move in the direction of ageing parents (Warnes et al, 1985). (See also Chapter 8.) As we shall see in a discussion of social contact, working-class families tend to live closer together while physically-dispersed families still communicate. However, a significant number of older people have never married or had children. In 1981, among people aged 65 or over, the never married amounted to 8 per cent of men and 11.2 per cent of women (though we have seen that these percentages are likely to decrease). A study in 1978 found that 30 per cent of those aged 75 and over had never had children and 7.5 per cent had outlived them (Abrams, 1980b). There are, indeed, some people who are outside the family system altogether. According to Hunt (1978) 5 per cent of people of retirement age have no living relatives outside the household and a further 5 per cent have lost contact with their relatives. But the vast majority of elderly people – 97 per cent – do have relatives they describe as 'close'. The unattached in Wenger's sample include a concentration of women, single, divorced or separated. People with children tend to be closer to them than to any other relatives. Siblings, and after them a sibling's children, are important, particularly for the never-married or childless widowed person.

Contact A similar picture emerges in relation to social contacts. For the childless, siblings, followed by nieces, nephews and cousins, are most important. Older people with adult children see them regularly. In general, the amount of contact between elderly people and their relatives again contradicts the widely held view of isolation and neglect. They both visit regularly and are visited, the latter more frequently than the former, especially among the oldest age groups. More than 70 per cent of elderly people see a relative at least once a week. Almost half see one (especially the spouse) every day of their lives. Frequency of contacts diminishes from 65 to 86 years after which it increases again with more than half of very elderly people being in daily contact. The sharpest drop in daily contact is between 65 and 70 as aged parents die and adult children leave home. The pattern is similar in rural and urban areas, though in the former, retirement migrants are a group with significantly less contact with relatives. Christmas Day, a time which epitomises the loneliness of old age, in the media at least, is invariably spent in the company of relatives or, if single, with friends. Only one in 10 of Wenger's sample spent the day alone, often by choice, though the proportion rose sharply in the oldest groups. Four times as many over-80-year-olds spent Christmas Day alone and lonely. They were likely to be single or widowed, and living alone.

The majority of people were satisfied with the amount of contact they had with children, though more people were unsatisfied in urban areas – two-fifths – than in rural. Even more – a quarter – would have liked to see more of their grandchildren. Significantly, old people most likely to agree with the statement 'children don't care about their parents except for what they can get out of them' are persons who have no children.

Obviously, these generalisations based on statistical evidence obscure a wide range in types of family interaction. Relations in later-life families vary enormously, from those where family contact is vital, to those where it matters little, by mutual consent. In the former it is a time- and energy-consuming activity, a rewarding series of transactions among people who spend as much time with their families as they can and prefer being with them to doing anything else (a family-centred lifestyle, in Taylor and Ford's [1983] analysis). The opposite situation corresponds to the image of grandparenting offered by Kornhaber, in which the older generations pursue solitary, work-oriented or other lifestyles. It might, as some have suggested, be a bitter acknowledgement of their children's lack of interest which makes some elderly parents report satisfaction with little contact. Issues like this which have been debated in the American literature for many years underline the inadequacy of research designs which ignore the subjective experience of ageing in the family. Rates of face-to-face contact do not tell us much about the quality of relationships and their personal significance. Physical distance might not itself preclude close and meaningful ties, a fact recognised in the concept of intimacy-at-a-distance. This has been described as a euphemism; others argue, pessimistically, that what really exists is pseudo-intimacy, a state of concern based on a sense of obligation on account of children's earlier dependence. Family solidarity no longer exists but elderly people cannot bear to admit their marginality in their children's lives (Blau, 1973).

Roles

Methodological problems of the same order exist in the study of the roles played by relatives in the lives of elderly people. We know from the literature that younger relatives provide help of various kinds and that they are approached before people in other categories such as friends and neighbours, particularly when the crisis requires long-term support

(Litwak and Szelenyi, 1969). For intimate personal tasks female relatives are called upon, for normative constraints of modesty and propriety suggest that outside the marital relationship it is quite inappropriate for adult men to tend adult women whatever the relationship (Wenger, 1987a). Some constraint exists on daughters tending fathers and sons tending mothers, but children in these categories will be chosen in the absence of a carer in the appropriate category. This means that daughters are the main carers, since far more elderly mothers require care. The mother–daughter relationship is, in any case one of our culture's two significant dyads (the other is the husband–wife dyad), the basis of significant mutual exchanges throughout the younger woman's lifetime.

This is a rather different way of looking at the female caring role from the usual one in which women care because caring is unpaid, unrewarding work. It emphasises the importance of seeing caring as one more (perhaps the ultimate) act in a series based on reciprocity. Wenger (1987b) argues that the principle of reciprocity is fundamental in the caring role. Wenger points out that, contrary to popular belief, moving in with children does not appear to be triggered by the need for care. It is, indeed, difficult to make a long-term case for the dependency of any one member of the family on another. Taking a life-span approach helps us to appreciate the personal significance of family transactions and reminds us of something we often forget: that the act of caring means caring *about* as well as caring *for* (Wenger, 1987c). This approach also puts the concept of filial maturity – the coming to terms with a parent's dependence – into perspective. It is not to deny, however, that very occasionally caring for takes place in the absence of caring about. We are reminded by a growing literature on the abuse of elderly people by their families that negative feelings may dominate a care relationship with harmful consequences (Eastman, 1982).

The general significance of family ties varies through the lifespan. In some respects it might be greater for the younger woman than the older. Young women with only distant ties or none at all report that the arrival of their own children brings an acute sense of being without relatives. They need them for practical reasons, for advice and guidance, but also for a sense of social and historical location. Older women do not need their children to provide them with this sense of being in the flow of time; departed relatives are more significant in meeting that need.

The evidence reviewed so far indicates solidarity on two of the three fronts identified by Bengtson. In terms of interaction and sentiment there is little sign of a generation gap but given the methodological and conceptual problems involved, this cannot be said with certainty. Even in terms of attitudes and expectations it would appear that the generation gap is illusory, a figment of popular imagination. But the situation is complicated by a discrepancy between research findings on family expectations, and what is said by elderly people to each other outside the context of the family.

Cognitive solidarity

Over the lifetime of elderly people the former values governing sexual morality, duty, the importance of work, patriotism and authority have been challenged. There have been broad changes in the definition of family roles. Ideologies of marriage and parenthood, and notions of sexuality, have changed in ways older people often find unacceptable. Women's roles, in particular, have changed. The demographic trends mentioned earlier – earlier marriage and fewer children – have lengthened the period of adult life not devoted to active parenthood. This has paved the way for another trend: the entry of married women into the labour market.

The rise in women's participation in the labour force is, like the ageing society, a worldwide phenomenon. In Britain it is a product of technological changes creating employment opportunities in three areas: public administration; education, health and social services; and in the distribution of goods and personal services, itself a consequence of rising income and consumption (Eversley, 1982). Women have entered the work force in increasing numbers since the Second World War, albeit in areas of low-paid, part-time work. A recent survey showed that 78 per cent of all women aged 40 to 44 are in work, declining to 58 per cent in the 55 to 59 age group (Martin and Roberts, 1984). Even the mothers of young children are more likely to be in employment than they were 40 years ago. Today, 35 per cent of mothers with dependent children are in part-time work and 14 per cent work full-time.

Hand in hand with these trends in women's roles has been a shift in our ideology of motherhood. In the period after the Second World War, when the current generation of young-old people were having their children, the philosophy of child-centredness reached a peak (Rapoport and Rapoport, 1977). Parents of the 1940s and 1950s, themselves products of a much stricter and more repressive era, were beginning to treat children with a new sensitivity and respect, though still establishing firm guidelines for behaviour (Newson and Newson, 1965). The mothers of the 1940s were likely to see motherhood as a full-time job and as their main occupation in life. The needs of their children were of paramount importance. Today, children are less likely to be the pivot on which family life turns. It is recognised that parents have developmental needs too, and that a woman's need for fulfilment (as well as the family's need for an adequate income) might be met by paid employment. At the same time the trend to respect children's autonomy has developed. Modern parents, particularly in middle-class families, are more likely to negotiate with their children than dictate to them.

Older people often disagree strongly with current childrearing methods. They object to a supposed lack of constraint, an abundance of television, too much spending money, tolerance of answering back and sexual permissiveness in adolescence. But the ambiguous role of grand-parents, as we have seen, offers little scope for intervention.

In conversation with their peers older people deplore these practices. At every opportunity, invidious distinctions are drawn between themselves and younger people. The affluence and selfishness of sons and daughters, the food fads of visiting grandchildren, are popular topics of conversation. In gatherings at pensioners' clubs old people express their feelings of being apart from younger people. Their belief in the cultural and moral superiority of their own generation is confirmed in conversation, song, and prayer.

PEER RELATIONSHIPS

Peers are vitally important in the ageing process. Members of the same cohort have much in common. They provide continuity with the past, and socialisation to a variety of roles at a time of life when norma-tive prescriptions are vague, social supports have been withdrawn, and cultural stereotypes are negative. Many writers have defined the early years of retirement as an undefined stage (Dono et al, 1979; Keith, 1982), even roleless (Rosow, 1967), a time when the basis of interaction shifts fundamentally. While still in the work force, men and women are judged on the basis of universalistic criteria such as performance and achieve-ment. After retirement, the ascribed status of 'old person' takes over, the particularistic criteria of age and gender being fundamental. One could argue that old women have experienced this all their lives, but possibly age and gender together produce a distinctive status overriding social class and other achieved statuses in later life. Writers have seen parallels between adolescence and early retirement in the relative importance of peers (see Jerrome, 1984 for summary of literature). It is described as a liminal phase (Keith, 1982) between two relatively fixed statuses, when peers and peer-groupings, both formal and informal, are more important than relationships which cross age lines. Peer-grouping may be a product of identification with elderly peers and voluntary association with them, as in the case of working-class women in Britain (Harris, 1983). It is sometimes, however, a product of necessity rather than choice, in the face of abandonment by younger people. For elderly Jews in East London and in California a sense of rejection by their younger kin produces powerful ties with each other (Hazan, 1980; Myerhoff, 1978).

It is the community of interest among old people in relation to the young that is striking in meetings of the elderly peer group. At the club, among friends, elderly people are in good company. Pensioners' clubs in Britain are largely societies of widows (Harris, 1983; Jerrome, 1986). The typical member is an elderly working-class widow living alone. These women (and a few men) provide each other with moral and practical sup-port, with companionship and with help in navigating socially uncharted

.waters. The literature on social processes in the elderly peer group is extensive and will be discussed shortly in the context of friendship. For the present discussion of conflict in intergenerational relations it is worth noting that these ties of friendship in the club do not compete with family ties but rather strengthen them. Through conversation with friends the elderly mother, mother-in-law or grandmother is able to achieve a balance of dependence and independence within the family. The confused old woman whose son seems to be taking over her affairs is advised to go to the citizens' advice bureau to find out about her legal rights; friends commiserate with the mother whose adult daughter takes her help for granted. Discussions about family problems help to put them into perspective and provide an outlet for strain and tension (Jerrome, 1984; Johnson and Aries, 1983; Jones, 1980). Elderly parents renegotiate their roles through exchanges with other older parents, as well as with their adult children (Francis, 1981).

For married women as for single, recounting and comparing the intimate details of family life with friends is helpful, satisfying and role supportive. This is the case even when marriages are longstanding and stable. Married women are more likely than their husbands to have a confidant outside the marriage. When asked who their confidants are, elderly men are likely to say their wives; elderly women are just as likely to name an adult child or same-sex friend (Lowenthal and Haven, 1968). The marital relationship in later life is potentially the greatest source of affection and companionship, given our ideology of companionate marriage. Like the mother–daughter relationship, it is a significant dyad. Although in America only 3 per cent of all marriages attain the golden wedding anniversary (on account of rates of divorce and age at widowhood) it is in many cases the lengthiest and most meaningful peer relationship.

Marriage

Hess and Soldo, comparing married people with those without partners, describe married couples as living longer, staying healthier and feeling better, though in each case the relative advantage to men is greater than to women (Hess and Soldo, 1985). In our society, men are likely to be married until they die, and women to become widows. The majority of couples who stay married can expect to live alone together in the community for a significant period, from the departure of the youngest child until the death or, much rarer, the institutionalisation, of one partner. (See Chapter 8.) We would expect the quality of this relationship to have an important bearing on morale and life satisfaction, which is, indeed, the case. People who are happy with their marriages tend to be satisfied with life in general. However, it appears that intervening variables such as health or poverty might be responsible for this. Studies of marital satisfaction see it varying through the lifespan (Ade-Ridder and

Brubaker, 1983), though the shape of the curve – the position of peaks and troughs, highs and lows – varies from study to study. Three patterns emerge. In the first, marital satisfaction increases again in the later stages, after a drop in the childrearing phase, but it never attains the high level of the initial, pre-child phase. The second pattern is a gradual decline in satisfaction, a phenomenon described by some writers as disenchantment, as romance, love and companionship become eroded by separate tasks and development. The third pattern of findings suggests that the quality of the marriage in the middle years remains unchanged after retirement.

The major difficulty with studies of marital satisfaction through the lifespan is methodological. Most are cross-sectional in design, involving a selection of couples, at different stages of development. Differences in satisfaction are possibly a product of differing expectations, given changing attitudes to marriage and gender roles. Another factor which makes interpretation of these findings difficult is the marital status itself of the older couple. These are couples who, by definition, have remained married when others in their cohort will have experienced separation and divorce. The findings could, therefore, be interpreted to suggest that those people whose marriages have survived 30 years enjoy a high level of satisfaction. An alternative explanation might be, however, that such couples have remained married because their expectations have been scaled down to fit existing possibilities. The longer the relationship, the more salient it is to self-identity and the harder to disengage from or admit failure (Hess and Soldo, 1985). Evidence of long-term marriages – golden-wedding couples – does suggest though, a special quality of intimacy and satisfaction (Brubaker, 1985). But to relate present experiences to earlier phases of a marriage requires a research design which charts the development of particular marriages over time.

Looking at the later-life couple it is clear that the way in which the crises of retirement, ill health and other changes are accommodated depends on the pattern of coping built up over the years, and the degree of mutuality in the relationship. The same is true, according to the American literature, of the eventual division of labour achieved within the household. Couples vary from the traditional arrangement with gender-specific tasks to that in which roles are interchangeable or tasks undertaken jointly. This merging of roles is the social acknowledgement of the psychological phenomenon identified as the normal androgeny of later life. However, not all the arrangements negotiated by elderly husband and wife are equally acceptable to both spouses. In a theoretical essay, Hess and Soldo (1985) offer four possibilities, two of them based on a consensus of view about appropriate conjugal roles, the others involving a husband frustrated by his wife's unwillingness to let him join in her activities, and a wife angered by her husband's refusal to do so.

Marital arrangements are obviously determined to some extent by the health and physical capacity of the partners. Performing intimate personal tasks in addition to all the household maintenance tasks might eventually fall to one partner. When one of the partners needs care the spouse is the first person to supply it. This is so even in the case of frail elderly wives or husbands with adult children near at hand. Interestingly, in Wenger's small, intensive sample of very elderly people, the men commented on the physical strain of nursing, lifting and keeping house, while women found the social and emotional needs of caring most difficult. This finding adds to the evidence of gender differences in sources of emotional support. Similarly, the fact that men find widowhood more stressful seems to confirm the suggestion that old men rely primarily on their wives to meet expressive and instrumental needs while elderly wives turn for emotional support to people outside the marriage (Lipman and Longino, 1981). Women expect to outlive their husbands, and the common stereotype of the caring wife helps them to accept the caring role. Men expect to predecease their wives, rather than care for them. But researchers have been struck by the unquestionable devotion with which both wives and husbands accept the caring role for their spouse.

This devotion is the product of half a lifetime's affection and mutuality. Marriage creates a world of shared meaning and experience from which it is difficult to disengage. As Comfort (1977) puts it when talking of bereavement in later life, the elderly married couple resemble two beams propped together; if one is removed, the other falls down. A satisfactory marriage in our society provides a number of benefits such as material support and caregiving. Perhaps the most obvious, though, is stable companionship. The permanent presence of the spouse which might evoke negative as much as positive affect, is nonetheless vital in creating a secure and predictable environment. The couple in George Simenon's novel, *The Cat* (1976), live in a state of habituated conflict but when one dies the other cannot survive. This may not be typical of long-term marriages though as Cuber and Haroff (1963) have pointed out, the majority of stable and apparently happy marriages are far from the vital and fulfilling ideal fostered by our romantic ideology. Nevertheless, many long-term relationships will be important sources of affection, approval, and sexual gratification.

Sexuality

Studies of sexuality in later life, like those of marital satisfaction, are beset by methodological problems. The topic is a sensitive one, particularly for generations unaccustomed to self-disclosure about such matters. But there is a growing literature including some useful cross-cultural material (Weg, 1983a).

Contrary to popular assumption, old people are sexual beings. Sexual interest and activity are sustained throughout life, though the volume of activity might diminish, and sexual expression take different forms. As with other aspects of marriage, the rate of sexual activity in married couples is largely determined by earlier patterns. In some cases it ceases altogether, but this is often the culmination of an unsatisfactory relation-ship. It may be the wife who feels with the arrival of menopause that she can legitimately cease to engage in an unrewarding activity. More often, the husband is responsible for the termination of sexual activity, through ill health or impotence induced by temporary disability or fear of failure. Social attitudes and expectations seem to play an important part in sexual performance for men and women (Hendricks and Hendricks, 1977). The views of one's partner in particular are vital in restoring (or taking away) self-confidence and a belief in one's sexual attractiveness. From an earlier interest in rates of intercourse and comparison between youthful and older performance (the youthful being considered the norm) writers have gone on to consider psychosexual issues. Some note the importance of sexual expression for self-esteem, self-acceptance, and general well-being at all ages but particularly later on when other sources of support might be reduced (Burnside, 1975). Thus, sexual expression affirms the older woman's sense of herself as feminine, a sense undermined by the media and popular stereotypes (Huyck, 1977). For the older woman without a sexual partner this confirmation is missing, and Huyck, noting the impor-tance of orgasmic sexual expression goes on to stress the acceptability of self-pleasuring (masturbation) and homosexual contact in the absence of a heterosexual relationship.

Widowhood

Many older women regard marriage as the only legitimate context for sexual activity, and the loss of the husband signals the end of an active sexual life and all that that involves. This loss is compounded by others: companionship; material support; a partner in a world which is couple-oriented; someone to negotiate on her behalf in a male-dominated society where women often do not acquire the skills necessary to promote their own interests; in short, all the advantages conferred by marriage. There are, of course, compensations in the form of personal freedom, the ability to develop personal resources, the opportunity to build up peer relationships outside marriage especially when friends are women widowed themselves. But not all widows are equipped to exploit these advantages. For widowers the potential loss is even greater, as we have seen. But given the tendency for men to marry younger women, and women's greater life expectancy, there are far fewer widowers than widows.

The ageing society described in earlier chapters contains increasing numbers of older women, a large proportion of them without partners. A significant proportion are widowed, rising to approximately two-thirds of those over 80. Increasing numbers of divorced women also swell the ranks of unattached elderly people. Some widows remarry but the majority do not. The remarriage rate is higher for men than women at all ages, leading to the increased likelihood of women being alone in future years.

Responses to widowhood vary. Most new widows and widowers experience pain: pain over being deserted, of losing a love object or at least a significant other, of grief and loneliness (Lopata, 1980). Their suffering is compounded by the difficulty others have in handling death and accepting the needs of the bereaved for essential grief work. The degree of initial disorganisation depends partly on the extent to which the spouses were involved in each other's lives. Beyond that, the personal and interpersonal resources of the survivor come into play (Lopata, 1980). For women the new independence is made bearable by their early training in the denial of dependency needs (Clark and Anderson, 1967). Some widowed people remain desolate. Others adopt a variety of strategies, ranging from mummification – the preservation of the deceased spouse's possessions and physical space within the house as it was – to remarriage; from deliberate self-isolation to the intensification of existing ties or the establishment of new ones; from a determination to remain in the past to the vigorous development of a new lifestyle. This new lifestyle does not generally include aspirations to remarry. In Lopata's study, over 75 per cent of older widows said they would not want to remarry, for a number of reasons. These included losing their independence and taking on the role of wife again; a shortage of men of the appropriate age; having to care for another sick man; unhappiness in the first marriage; fear of fortune hunters; the possibility of conflict between a new husband and adult children; and idealisation of the former husband.

To these one might add the problems of proceeding from acquaintance-ship to marriage in a society where courtship is geared to youth. Relations with members of the opposite sex are problematic. Both men and women report being sexually propositioned. Widowers seem frightened by the abundance of female attention, though widows, even when they feel sexually deprived, frequently react to overtures with anger.

Remarriage

Despite social constraints, however, the remarriage rate is increasing partly as a result of the increase in numbers of older people, and partly for normative reasons, in particular the growing acceptability of new sexual liaisons in old age. Although the amount and nature of one's need for intimacy varies across the life course and between men and women there is no reason to suppose that it disappears with old age.

In the literature on primary relationships the assumption has some-times been made of 'functional interchangeability' within the primary group. In the hierarchical compensatory model of relationships, referred to by Dono et al (1979), same-sex friendships and kinship networks might offer adequate outlets for intimate attachments in later life following the loss of the partner. Indeed, evidence of renewed ties with siblings, adult children and friends through co-residence or intensified social contact and service-exchange following bereavement might be taken to support that thesis. But evidence presented by Hochschild (1973), Litwak and Szelenyi (1969) and Dono et al (1979) indicates that the different primary group ties are not interchangeable with respect to the satisfaction of personal needs. This, the task-specific model of relationships, helps us to account for the dating patterns of older Americans described by Bulcroft and Bulcroft (1985).

The literature on primary groups and support networks tends to assume emotional and physical dependency in old age. But dependency is only one need met by close ties. Intimate relationships meet a number of needs, and involve a number of interpersonal exchanges. They have a variety of functions: personal support of a practical nature, such as in ill health, poverty and adverse circumstances; sociability, companionship and entertainment; intimacy, both emotional and physical, which provides validation of the self, a sense of self-worth and of having personal history; and challenge, in which the stimulation of intimate involvement lends purpose to existence, and gives life added meaning.

Different relationships meet different needs. The first, personal support, is largely a function of close kinship, particularly spouse and adult children. The spouse or other sexual partner is the primary source of intimacy, too. Emotional intimacy, sociability and challenge are provided by other members of the peer group – by siblings and same-sex friends. In the rest of the chapter we examine these two remaining peer relationships – with siblings and friends.

Siblings

Some brothers and sisters, like some spouses, meet all one's personal needs (apart from sexual gratification) and the loss of such siblings can be devastating. It has been suggested that elderly siblings grow closer as they age (Jerrome, 1981; Abrams, 1980b) though British evidence of sibling contact is slender. Abrams (1980b) suggests that siblings get closer in later life with the loss of friends and need for physical security. But although 69 per cent of people over 75 in his 1978 study had living siblings, face-to-face contact was comparatively rare. Only one-third of the group saw each other as often as once a month. Presumably other ways of making contact become important with increasing frailty.

In a study of women's friendship in 1980, several women who declared themselves close to no one and seemed, indeed, to have no intense same-sex relationships turned out to be very close to siblings, cousins and in some cases nieces. They described them as best friends and it was clear that the intensity was a product of the recent past. The relationships had been cultivated both as expedient, given the likelihood (as they saw it) of failing powers, and as emotionally rewarding (Jerrome, 1981). Other studies report the same closeness and absence of rivalry between siblings, though it is not clear whether this is a product of mellowing or simply diminished contact. It could also reflect a positive value attached to

·'family', or vulnerability when one is confined at close quarters with a sibling caretaker. In such cases a *modus vivendi* is rapidly reached, though ambivalence is apparent in public.

In terms of practical support, siblings are 'standing ready' (Cicirelli, 1985), third in line after spouses and adult children. More is known about elderly sisters than elderly brothers, possibly because there are more of them. Old women provide their brothers with security and draw their sisters into social activities and networks. Sisters tend to be closer than brothers, though the intensity of childhood relationships is not normally achieved after marriage unless they are co-resident. Sisters are especially important for never-married women. For the childless widow, too, sisters can often move into first place as potential caretakers, companions and co-habitees.

Friendship

From Abram's survey of retired people in 1978 it emerged that good friends and neighbours are thought to be more important than family for a satisfying life. Other writers have confirmed the importance of friendships (Wenger, 1987b). Friends, especially longstanding ones, provide continuity (Francis, 1984). Belonging to the same cohort, they have similar values based on common life experiences. Operating within a shared frame of reference they can help each other with age-related transitions in a way younger relatives cannot (Rosow, 1975; Jerrome, 1981, 1984). The process of socialisation within the peer group can be witnessed in the formal setting of clubs and associations and adult education classes, and in informal friend relationships. At the psychosocial level, friends provide confirmation of existence as a person worth knowing.

Friendship has received little attention in gerontology and in the social sciences generally (Chown, 1981). Its private, informal and ephemeral nature makes it both difficult and unattractive as a subject for study. But interest has been growing, partly in an attempt to assess the significance of the different components of primary groups – kin, friends and neighbours. Friendships are distinguished by their basis in free choice and mutual attraction (Dono et al, 1979; Heinemann, 1985; Allan, 1986). Friendship needs change through the lifespan, and there are striking gender differences (Hess, 1979; Pleck, 1975; Seiden and Bart, 1975). Men's friendships tend to be sociable rather than intimate, and focused on shared activity. Women's friendships are characterised by emotional intensity and self-disclosure. Conversation is, indeed, one of the main activities of female friendship, from early childhood onwards. Letter-writing may take over as the sole means of communication of elderly friends who cannot meet. Gender differences persist into old age, with women's relationships continuing to be more extensive and meaningful.

Some writers suggest that women's capacity to involve themselves in intense relationships and their greater openness and responsiveness to others, may make them more vulnerable in old age. Huyck (1977) and Bernard (1976) argue that this capacity may involve considerable stress as the people in whom they have invested die or in other ways become inaccessible. Contrary to this view, the evidence that women retain a capacity for making new relationships throughout life prompts the view that they are slightly better off (Heinemann, 1985; Jerrome, 1981; Bankoff, 1981). Men are less likely to replace lost friends, and, relying on their wives for intimacy, experience great disruption after widowhood. Men, in any case, are at a psychological disadvantage as Myerhoff (1978) concludes from her remarkable study of a Jewish senior citizens' centre in California. One of the main benefits enjoyed by older women is the opportunity to use the skills for which they have been trained since birth. Girls are encouraged to direct their energies towards cultivating and sustaining relationships. The different bases for status and self-esteem in men and women give the latter an advantage in retirement when people rather than things, and the maintenance of relationships, become the focus of activity. This is a time of life when expressive activities – 'women's work' – are valued. Retirement offers little scope for the pursuit of instrumental goals and the use of conventional masculine skills.

Several writers have commented on class and educational influences on the meaning and expression of friendship (Lopata, 1979) and indeed on the shape of social networks generally (Taylor and Ford, 1983). Middle-class men and women tend to have extensive and active extra-familial ties through membership of age-mixed associations, voluntary work and other aspects of public life. Friendship dyads and groups are sustained through shared activities and reciprocal visits (Jerrome, 1981, 1984, 1986). Working-class men, similarly, have a tradition of group membership. Working-class women's closest ties tend to be with female kin though following retirement or bereavement there is a tendency to join age-specific clubs (Harris, 1983; Abrams, 1978). Old people's clubs are attractive to working-class people for reasons already given. Attendance is an activity of friendship and for the few who attend (less than 13 per cent of the over 75s, with wide regional variations according to Abrams, 1978), club-going is the main social activity. It is in the clubs that the expressive orientation of old age is most evident: the commitment to being rather than doing; and rituals of social acceptance and approval (Jerrome, 1986; Creech and Babchuk, 1985). But the club is also a forum for competitive strivings in a status conscious society. Status attributes in this community of working-class widows include the achievements of children and grandchildren, and their demonstrations of concern.

In fact, family ties have first priority. Family commitments are a legiti-mate cause for absence, despite the serious obligations involved in club membership. Despite vigorous participation and the obvious enjoyment of club activities, membership is acknowledged to be a fall-back position: a solution to loneliness and inactivity, better than staying at home.

THE BALANCE OF ATTACHMENTS

Research suggests that embeddedness in a social network is vital for general well-being. The image of the convoy has been used in longitudinal studies to suggest the movement through time of a person flanked by supportive relationships (Abrams, 1980b). The convoy concept helps us understand responses to current loss and change in terms of earlier life experiences. Involvement in a social network has emerged as the single most powerful predictor of survival (Berkman and Syme, 1979), its absence a predictor of early death (Abrams, not dated). Within the network, the presence of one or more confidant relationships has been seen to protect older people from loneliness and the damaging psychological effects of various age-related losses.

Certain social groups are more vulnerable to loneliness than others. In respect of elderly people we tend to think of widows, childless people and the never-married and those who live alone, as at risk. In fact, the never-married tend to be less vulnerable, having well-developed strategies for establishing and maintaining social contacts (Gubrium, 1975; Jerrome, 1981). Increasing numbers of older people live alone, a trend which has increased sharply since 1945 (see Chapter 8). In 1961 less than 19 per cent of all elderly persons lived alone and in 1971 just over 25 per cent did. Among women single occupancy is even more likely. Over half of all women over 85 live alone (Henwood and Wicks, 1985; Wenger, 1984).

Being alone has implications for loneliness. But one can be lonely within marriage, too. Studies of loneliness in old age suggest that the most lonely are as likely to be married as unattached (Wenger, 1984). Married women have fewer social ties outside marriage than men or unattached women (Altergott, 1985). Our ideology of marriage encourages us to underestimate the social needs of married men and women. The evidence of loneliness in marriage and the inevitability of widowhood suggest that we overinvest in the marital relationship. Acute loneliness is often a feature of the lives of women who have concentrated most of their emotional resources in marriage and find themselves in widowhood with neither friends nor the social skills to make them (Jerrome, 1983).

Another very lonely group are those living with adult children. Unfortunately, women in our culture are encouraged to see family roles as their main source of fulfilment. But people who have concentrated on family relationships at the expense of others are more vulnerable to loss in old age. In emotional terms, today's sensible behaviour might be tomorrow's risk factor.

It is generally assumed that family relations influence the well-being of older family members for the better. But despite our cultural bias towards family life there is surprisingly little explicit evidence that older people without supportive families are at a psychological disadvantage.

The evidence, indeed, warns us against the view 'that 'more family is necessarily better, or that closer is happier' (Bengtson and Kuypers, 1985, p. 26).

We should not go so far as to deny the importance of kinship, however. If we ask about the effect of being without any relatives at all we find indications of loneliness and a sense of deprivation which is hardly surprising given prevailing values and social arrangements. The ideological emphasis on the family means stigma and lost privileges for those outside the couple and family framework.

In terms of practical support being alone is to be disadvantaged. For families tend to be called upon before friends and neighbours (Litwak and Szelenyi, 1969); they feel they have a right to intervene and that neighbours should keep their distance, and having made a commitment to help they find it harder to withdraw (Wenger, 1986). This reflects the idea of family ties as primordial, and non-contingent, expressed in the popular saying 'blood is thicker than water'. Against this is the view which stresses the growing basis of family ties in sentiment, and the discretionary element in the recognition of kinship obligations.

In structural terms there are, today, two typical situations in old age. One is to be almost totally alone; the other is to be at the pinnacle of a three- or four-generation family. Variations are caused by sexual orientation, family stability, and ethnic group membership. It is much harder to generalise about the meaning of family ties or the shape of the family network. Family members negotiate over the inclusion or exclusion of particular units. Irregular units such as widows tend to be 'unhooked' by their in-laws. The death of the 'kin-keeper' might precipitate the break-up of the family. In some families there is a reservoir of barely differentiated female kin – daughter, sister's daughter, daughter's daughter, sister – existing to support the old person. A relationship between a childless person and her sibling can be inherited by the nieces and nephews (Troll and Smith, 1976; Wenger, 1984). Each family constellation has unique elements. As far as the general spread of attachments is concerned, some generalisation is possible. Wenger (1987a) has identified six types of network, on a continuum from family-oriented to detached. In the *family-oriented* network the old person lives near kin on whom she is dependent, other ties being unimportant. Next there is the *fully-integrated* network in which the old person, long-term resident in the area and with a local family, has an active network even if housebound. The third type, described as *community-integrated* is more likely among middle-class or single people, among migrants and among the rich. The family is local, but uninvolved. As a variation on this another type of community-integrated network exists in which the family is geographically distant, though supportive. Ties are, again, stronger with community than family. Fifth is the *attenuated* network in which kin are again distant and supportive. But the retired married couples, often migrants, in this category have little local contact. Finally, there is·the *detached* network characterised by very few ties of any kind, and dependence on public services. This type accounts for very few indeed of Wenger's sample of old people in rural Wales.

The eventual pattern of ties is a product of a host of factors ranging from health and income to values and expectations. Whatever the situation, we should accede to the older person the major part in determining the balance of attachments.

SUMMARY

A major premise of this chapter has been that family relationships, particularly between the generations, are problematic in view of changes in the culture, technology and demographic composition of British society that have transformed the family in the lifetime of the present generation of old people. The task of older people, and indeed of the whole family, is to come to terms with these changes. Family members must learn new ways of relating to each other in what is essentially a normative vacuum. The establishment of appropriate ways of behaving in the modern family, and socialisation to new family roles, is achieved through discussion and monitoring within the family itself and with members of the peer group. The role of elderly peers as helpers in the process of adjustment is generally underestimated.

10

DEPENDENCY AND INTERDEPENDENCY

Malcolm Johnson

Dependency is one of the words closely associated in the public mind with old age. The image of older people becoming like children – dependent on able-bodied adults – and the loss of mental faculties, are other stereotypes which have wide currency. Even my own children, long schooled in the rejection of ageism, like to remind me of the epigram 'Old professors never die, they only lose their faculties'.

In this chapter it is my objective to examine the validity of these distilled, negative notions of old age. To do this it will be necessary to give some consideration to what the two key words of the title mean. With greater conceptual clarity, it will be necessary to examine research literature to see how far the realities of later life reflect the images and beliefs. In asking the question 'what is done to assist elderly people?', an attempt will be made to analyse current policy and practice.

Before proceeding to the analysis, it is worth pausing to listen to the voice of the commentators of life, on the subject of old age. Poets have acted as the mouthpiece of inarticulate society for thousands of years. What do they tell us about ageing and old age?

In compiling an anthology of poems of ageing Barbara Gray and I found ourselves deeply depressed by classical and 'high' poetry (Gray and Johnson). From Shakespeare onwards and particularly amongst the nineteenth-century romantic English poets, old age brings out a melancholy for lost youth. Its corollary is a revulsion from old age. The very language of their writings has helped to shape Victorian and hence contemporary usage.

Longfellow writes 'O give me back the days when loose and free to my blind passion were the curb and rein ... In an old man though can'st not wake desire ...?' His inheritors in this century offer equally bleak images. The cheerful face of Betjeman becomes a gargoyle when he looks at old age. His poem 'Late Flowering Lust' is a grotesque mourning of the loss of carefree independence and youthful beauty. In the middle of the poem he writes more moderately: 'I cling to you inflamed with fear, as now you cling to me, I feel how frail you are my dear and wonder what will be!' And his contemporary Philip Larkin, never a romantic, brings a similar deathly pallor in his 'The Old Fools': 'What do they think has happened, the old fools, to make them like this? Do they somehow suppose it's more grown up when your mouth hangs open and drools ...'.

Not all of poetry is ageist and revolted by age. Many writers adopt a more hopeful posture, but usually based on a celebration of life in general rather than the fruits of longevity. A few adopt a fulsomely positive view. Robert Browning's lines 'Grow old along with me, the best is yet to be' are rightly famous. So too are Jenny Joseph's contemporary words of defiant warning in her poem which begins 'When I am an old woman, I shall wear purple' and goes on to say 'I shall go out in slippers in the rain, and pick the flowers in other people's gardens, and learn to spit'.

Another modern poet, Adrian Mitchell, sums up the theme of this chapter. In his 'Old Age Report' he condemns the way society rewards retired people with poverty and symbolic gestures. He rails against a retirement which is a soulless ghetto at the end of the line of life. Here is a sample:

When a man's too ill or old to work
We punish him
Half his income is taken away
Or all of it vanishes and he gets pocket money.
We should reward these tough old humans for surviving
Not with a manager's soggy handshake
Or a medal shaped like an alarm clock –
No, make them a bit rich.
Give the freedom they always heard about
When the bloody chips were down
And the blitz or the desert
Swallowed up their friends.

What Mitchell observes are the twin dependency creating agencies of illness and inadequate income, which much research has shown are intimately linked together. Those who enter retirement after a lifetime of professional work and with a solid income face the prospect of a much more comfortable, varied and trouble-free time than a former bus conductor, mill worker or coalminer. Life experience is a significant indicator of the quality of life in old age. Money cannot (usually) buy good health, but it can buy freedom from many of the limitations which accompany retirement in most countries of the developed world. In this respect it is also a device which can be used to avoid some of the dependencies which come with old age.

WHAT IS DEPENDENCY?

The implication of the term is that there is a minority of people who lead independent lives and another minority who do not and those in the latter group are in need of help. But is this a realistic set of assumptions? Who is independent in modern society? Whose lifestyle would remain unchanged if those who support them withdrew?

The Dutch psychologist, Munnichs has highlighted the fallacy of the strict dichotomy between dependence and independence. He writes:

> Dependency is always placed in contradiction to independency as if they exclude each other. In the opinion of many Western policy makers these concepts are even used to denote the object of policy aims and the means by which existing measures are tested. When these measures promote independency it is all right, if not, dependency is the root of the problem and then measures need to be changed. (Munnichs, 1976, p. 4)

Clark (1972) has distinguished a range of socio-psychological and individual-psychological forms of dependency which immediately take us into a much more analytic frame of mind. She has identified (i) dependency of crisis (the loss of spouse or similar trauma), (ii) neurotic dependency (where individuals develop a pathological reliance on others), (iii) development or transititional dependency (arising from puberty, menopause, retirement, etc), as afflictions which arise out of individuals. In further elaboration Clark even begins to rank these conditions, nominating neurotic dependency as the worst form because

> ... it persists throughout life as a dominant technique of adjustment and especially in stressful situations. The dependency is expressed in such attributes as self-effacement, dread of loneliness, ingratiation and indecision. (Clark, 1972)

The psychological conditions to which Clark draws attention would certainly reduce any individual's ability to manage their personal lives well. But so, too, would many other influences. Being grossly overweight or drinking too much alcohol would also inhibit social performance; so too would the absence of educational qualifications or the inability to form worthwhile relationships. All of the elements would act as inhibitions to the achievement of personal potential. They can be seen as limits to our progress. Equally they can be viewed as handicaps or disabilities for these terms are often used loosely as synonyms for dependency. Yet there is a curious circumscription of the usage of these words, which confines their general application to particular categories of people. Wheelchair users who cannot do their own washing and ironing are 'handicapped' and 'dependent', but middle-aged bank managers who cannot do their own laundry are considered to be neither. Women who cannot change electrical fuses and men who cannot cook are fundamentally dependent on others, but the term is never used.

From these everyday examples it is evident that we live in an interdependent world. There is no-one who in any proper sense is independent. In simpler societies than ours, individuals and families may be largely self-sufficient in food, clothing and shelter. Apart from hermits and recluses who choose to live outside of them, there is interdependence for all who exist in human societies. Indeed, the very notion of society, as a social system in which human beings live in community with each other, presupposes an agreed system of social rules and conventions which regulate our behaviour and recognise the different contributions of others to the common good. These fundamental principles of social life require certain components to be present. Salient amongst these are mutual trust, a workable system of social exchange (of goods and services) and a willingness to involve every member of society in a way that provides them with recognised social roles and consequent livelihood.

In complex societies the extent of interdependence is greatly increased. We are all totally dependent on many strangers (who produce food, power, clothing etc) as well as on those with whom we live, work and have other personal relations. These forms of universal dependence are acknowledged, but not encompassed in the usage of the word. The logic for this appears to be that we are all contributors as well as receivers and thus equal partners in a social contract. It is those who for some reason are unable to contribute, or are disbarred from contributing, in economically recognised ways, who are prone to being labelled dependent. Thus, it is children, unemployed people, those who have physical and mental handicaps, the retired and the old, who fall into the category.

Inclusion in the groupings of dependent people involves a process of *social* definition. Yet public and private reactions to those who have special need of the support of others to maintain their existence, tends to be on an *individual* basis. Whilst there is some recognition that illness is 'not their own fault', there remains a strong tendency to treat people who are handicapped in the performance of routine activities, as personally responsible for their plight. Such victimisation is not peculiar to any particular group of people, but is most strongly expressed in cases where incompetence can be observed, but the causes cannot. Deaf people and those suffering from mental illness are, in general, subject to less sympathetic and more controlling actions by others, than wheelchair users or frail elderly people (Gilhome-Herbst, 1976).

It is clear then that interdependency is a real phenomenon which is an integral component of citizenship. A special subset of this interdependency has been isolated and identified as dependency in modern societies. It is applied in the following circumstances:

(i)   Where individuals, congenitally or by acquisition, are incapable, temporarily or permanently, of performing a range of actions which are assumed to be within the competence of full citizens of a given society.

(ii) In particular, where there is an inability to carry out essential tasks related to personal maintenance, physical mobility, sensory functioning, mental stability, and communication (verbal or written).

(iii) Where society by its laws, conventions and social institutions places individuals in a dependent role or situation, eg children, those who are unemployed, sick, financially insolvent or otherwise deemed incompetent to live an independent and unsupervised life.

The interaction of personal factors and social mechanisms varies according to the characteristics of the person and the nature of the disability. For example, Cypriot or Pakistani women who come to Britain as non-English-speaking people are dependent and limited in their social participation in a similar way to a pre-lingually deaf person (Mays, 1983; AFFOR, 1981; Blakemore, 1983). An unemployed person shares the same dependence on government agencies and the same restriction in consumer behaviour as an elderly person on supplementary pension.

It will be necessary to look in more detail at the processes and circumstances which create dependent situations. However, it remains an inescapable fact that a significant minority of the population falls into this category. Millions of people in Britain can only function as human beings if others wash them, launder their clothes, clean their homes, cook their food, transport them etc. Elderly people constitute the largest group within this pool. The majority of sufferers from deafness, visual handicap, mental illness and mobility restriction are beyond the retirement ages. It is inevitable, therefore, that gerontologists have long been interested in the causes, consequences and relief of dependency.

We have already encountered a set of definitional problems which need to be clarified if the notion of dependency is to be useful. More importantly if ways are to be found of reducing the incidence, it is essential that causation is understood. So, before examining the more practical problems which arise, some attention can usefully be given to a selection of key concepts which underpin both discourse and policy.

Reciprocity and altruism

It is in the nature of dependency relationships that a person in profound need of help is given assistance, by one or more other people. They may do this as part of their paid occupation and are therefore rewarded for the service they provide. But it is now well established that the overwhelming bulk of what is called caring is done by relatives, friends and neighbours (Equal Opportunities Commission, 1982; Family Policy Studies Centre, 1984a). For them the help is given without direct payment. It is a gift. It may be a gift in return for gifts received in the past (children returning parental care) or in expectation of some return in the future (perhaps an inheritance). Equally there may be no expectation of a reciprocal gift from the dependent person. The giver may give in the belief that if and when she needs help someone will be to hand. Or the aid may be provided with no expectation or hope of reward or exchange benefit – altruistic giving.

Since Mauss in his classic essay *The Gift* (1925) and the anthropologist Malinowski in his study of the Trobriand islanders (1922), formulated general propositions about the nature of social exchange, there has been much debate about its role in modern societies. These early studies postulated a set of powerfully stated social obligations to give to others both known and unknown. Accompanying sanctions reinforced the system which ensured that there was a proper balance of reciprocity both direct and indirect. Not only is courtesy returned by courtesy and favours by favours between people who know each other, but gifts are given to strangers in the expectation that yet other strangers will give to them.

Blau (1964) writing 40 years later supported the notion of generalised exchange relationships, but drew attention to the highly developed sense of expected and observable reward which was generated by market transactions. Economic relations are fundamentally reciprocal exchanges, where all the parties involved are both givers and receivers. They involve trust – those who provide goods must trust that promises of payment will be honoured. Blau also observed another distinct set of social exchanges characterised by unseeking generosity. In his important book *The Gift Relationship* (1970), Titmuss explored this quality of altruism through a study of blood donors. He believed that two forms of value have taken a grip of contemporary society – those of the market place and those of bureaucracy where every action demanded a matching, measured and inflexible response. His socialist conviction led him to conclude that a third and more moral force was essential to act as a counterbalance; that of gift values.

As a challenge to the rising view that altruism had no place in industrial societies, Titmuss set out to demonstrate that it was alive and well in such systems as blood donorship. Moreover, he argued that social exchanges which made people ask not 'who is my neighbour?' but 'who is my stranger?' were normally superior to market exchanges and should be fostered by governments.

Subsequent empirical studies have provided less optimistic conclusions. The economist Hirsch (1977) came to the view that the trend was for individuals to choose actions which were most likely to be to their personal benefit. Abrams' research on informal care and neighbouring was also broadly consistent with this view (Bulmer, 1986). He found that much neighbouring activity was short lived and highly instrumental. The mobile middle classes were seen to engage in neighbourly activities as a way of gaining access to local social systems.

In Britain an estimated 1.25 million people are the primary, unpaid carers of dependent – mostly elderly – people. In addition, unmeasured millions provide regular assistance to the older population. The motives and pressures which generate that help are still imperfectly understood. Yet governments in the western world are engaged in what is known as the interweaving of statutory services with informal care. Experiments like those in Thanet (Davies and Knapp, 1987) and North Wales (Wenger, 1984) are consciously manipulating the willingness to give assistance by modest payments to family and other carers. So far the indications are that financial inducements and sensitive organisation can increase the quantity, quality and cost-effectiveness of care. But it could prove to be a further set of involvements to make informal care yet another saleable commodity.

It is frequently assumed that older people are the beneficiaries of giving relationships. For people who are very old, sick or frail, there is certainly a marked shift in the balance, which would justify this view. However, as

I show in detail later in this chapter, only about one in four of the retired population is placed in this 'dependent' situation. Such people often require round-the-clock attention which is very demanding indeed. But in considering their transfer into the receiver group, some countervailing factors need to be taken into account.

Intergenerational giving   People who have lived to become old and sick have by definition lived through all the earlier stages of life in which they have been contributors to the social good – as workers, parents, friends, neighbours, supporters of their own elderly relatives and contributors to wartime effort. They have usually given to the stock of social benefits more than they have received. It is by design that we ask the younger and more able bodied to provide for their contemporaries who have neither of these characteristics, in return for similar aid when they too are in need. Old age is the classic example of the giver receiving back reciprocal gifts, presented and received over time.

Old age pensions are the most obvious example. To receive assistance in old age is an earned right, based upon an age-old social contract. When politicians and commentators speak of the 'burden of the aged', they exhibit a lack of moral responsibility, a cynical disregard of time-honoured arrangements or membership of that self-serving group which wants the well-to-do middle aged to further maximise their privileges and benefits. In the United States this last set of motives has given rise to a movement which calls itself Americans for Generational Equity (AGE).

To argue that reciprocity between generations and over time is a necessary arrangement is not to say that any particular pattern or level of support is equally right. As the numbers of elders in need of help grow, it will be necessary to constantly reassess what is equitable and deliverable. AGE and bodies like it will have a part in that debate. What would be regrettable and damaging is the substitution of accountancy and rationing solutions for ones based on the historical contributions of one generation to the welfare of its successors and its reasonable expectations of reciprocity in the later stages of life. It should be remembered that the state assumed responsibility at the turn of the century for the support of elderly people, when other arrangements failed (Gunn, 1986).

Gift giving in old age   Another erroneous assumption is that retired people, because they are out of the remunerated work force, no longer make contributions to society. Once stated, this proposition becomes self-evidently inaccurate. The linkage between 'work' and social value is an unreliable one. Whilst the main weight of family caring falls on women aged 45–59 (Allen, 1983), Enid Levin and her colleagues (1988) found that the average age of the supporters of confused old people was 61 and that 30 per cent were over 70. This trend for the 'young old' to care for the 'old old' is projected to increase. At the same time this group is known to provide financial and social support to their children and grandchildren. More specifically, as more women become economically active the caring tasks they leave unfulfilled fall to the older generation.

There is also an observable rise in the involvement of the 'young-old' in voluntary bodies, self-help groups and community activities. Within the older population itself there is a great deal of mutual aid. Keith (1977) describes this graphically in *Old People, New Lives*. Her research in a new retirement community provides documentary accounts.

> Friends and neighbours check on each other daily; curtains not open by mid morning are a cue for a visit to make sure nothing is wrong. Meals are prepared, shopping done, and laundry washed and ironed for one blind resident. (Keith, 1977, p. 186)

Reciprocity and receiving　　The next part of the paragraph in Keith's book continues as follows:

> A look inside Merrill Court refrigerators also reveals an exchange network of food specialities. Except for the most extreme cases, such as the blind person, the exchanges are reciprocal. Of course, in a less tangible way, the blind man did offer a great deal in return to his caretakers. They enjoyed being the givers and carers, and they missed him bitterly when he died. (Keith, 1977, p. 186)

Gift receiving need not be an ungracious act of taking what is offered. Qureshi's (1986) study of carers in Sheffield indicates the wide variety of relationships which can exist. Some have always been one sided. Others are based on mutual regard and long experience of mutual help. The following selection of quotations represents the range:

> I think she helps me more than I help her at the moment (Daughter).

> Anytime I needed her she'd come at the drop of a hat, so I feel I owe it back, see, if she needs it. It works both ways doesn't it? (Daughter).

> She's never been a mother as mothers should be. She was out every day of her life and she didn't want anyone ... to upset her routine .... (Son-in-law).

> He's never lifted a finger for anyone in his family (Daughter).

Wright's (1986) study of lone family carers confined itself to the debilitating effects of the caring task. It would be wrong to give the impression that the full-time care of sick elderly people is anything other than immensely demanding and exhausting. But it should be equally improper to presume that it is always unrewarding. The gift relationship which Titmuss drew to our attention is an integral and durable part of intergenerational relations even when one of the parties did most of his or her giving in the past. The grateful and the thoughtful receiver is still a giver.

LABELLING AND DEVIANCE

To carry the label 'dependent' is to carry the burden of being a deviant – someone who no longer enjoys a place in the mainstream of society and whose behaviour is 'abnormal'. Others who share this status suffer a range of indignities and punishments which reinforce the deviance. Being excluded from social recognition and having no role in social relations is hurtful and damaging. Perhaps more importantly, it carries with it a set of attitudes, sanctions and prohibitions which have the effect of dehumanising the individual and engenders depression and reduction of self-esteem.

Social scientists have written extensively about the impact of labelling and the cluster of consequences which customarily accompany it. The literature encompasses criminals (Matza, 1969), drug users (Becker, 1963), those who are deemed mentally ill (Scheff, 1974; Skultans, 1979) and anyone – especially elderly people – who becomes reliant on the services of others for their everyday existence.

What characterises those who are subject to the labelling process is that the attribution of deviance results in negative stereotyping. Old age remains a deviant state in a society which celebrates youth and has not yet accustomed itself to the demographic revolution. But it is the disabilities that accompany old age which attract the penalties. It is a response to perceptions of the abnormal, to the threatening and the unexpected. Such reactions are socially conditioned categories of action, rather than reflections on the individual.

Becker summarised the construction of deviance when he wrote:

> Deviance is not a quality of the act the person commits but rather a consequence of the application by others of rules and sanctions to 'an offender'. The deviant is one to whom the label has been successfully applied; deviant behaviour is behaviour that people so label. (Becker, 1963, p. 9)

The existence of differences between older people and those of younger generations are well known, but exaggerated. There are, for example, no medical conditions exclusive to 'old age', so in that sense they are sick in common with all ages. It is the association – often misinformed or simply wrong – between ageing and decline which provides the foundation for stereotypical treatment. Sadly, elderly people themselves and those who seek to represent their welfare frequently provide fuel for such misconceptions. Repetition of 'oh dear; it's my age ...' by elderly people or 'what can you expect at your age?' by doctors only add to the conspiracy of ignorance against truth in the matter of ageing. Even organisations which set out to promote the well-being of elderly people and know the scientific evidence will amplify the negative features of later life in order to raise funds or make political points.

It would not be proper, however, to make too much of the notion of old age as deviance, for it has too many flaws to be a worthwhile theory. What is valuable about the analysis of old age as a labelling phenomenon, is that it draws attention to the negative circumstances which the visible maladies attract.

MEASURING DEPENDENCY

With the definitional problems which remain unsolved, it is inevitable that statistical information about the nature and extent of dependency creating disability and illness is subject to the same uncertainties. On the one hand there are many research studies and population surveys which allow quantitative description of the retired population. On the other hand much dispute exists about what these data mean. Before looking at the incidence of these conditions, we will look briefly at the technical definitions of dependency used by demographers, planners and economists, who see old people as an economic 'burden'.

Dependency ratios

Economic analyses of population structure and change are preoccupied with the relative sizes of the economically active (ie in paid employment) segment of the population and those who are designated as dependent (all those not in paid employment, including children and retired people). The United Nations publication *The World Ageing Situation: Strategies and Policies* (1985) summarises the position well.

> As the proportion of the population of working age increases, total dependency ratios (defined for the purposes of the present report as the number of young people, aged 0–14, plus the aging, aged 60 and over, divided by the population of working age, aged 15–59) concurrently become lower. The total dependency ratio is often used as an indicator of economic potential, the principal argument being that a low dependency ratio implies relatively more workers and the need to divert fewer resources to dependent populations. (United Nations, 1985, p. 46)

As the total dependency ratio includes young and old the two can be separated and their independent impact assessed and compared. Falkingham (1987) has studied the UK figures which are used to measure the cost to the economy. She points out that as dependency is defined by age, the 'gerontic' (old age) ratio will inevitably rise as the population ages. It has increased during this century from 12 old people (60/65+) per 100 in the working age ranges to 34 in 1981 and this figure is projected to reach 38 by 2021. During the same period, the child dependency (neontic) ratio (aged 0–19) has fallen from 83 to 54. Projections indicate it will fall further by 2021, to 48. Figure 10.1 presents these trends graphically.

It is widely assumed that this shift in the balance of population is in itself bad and likely to damage the economy. As older people consume higher proportions of the national budget for health, social services and social security this has a somewhat self-evident aspect. Data such as that produced by Clark and Spengler (1980) serve to encourage that view. For the USA, they estimate that the *per capita* costs for elderly persons are approximately three times those incurred by youth. Comparable figures for the developing world indicate that economic progress brings increased 'dependency' costs. In Africa and East Asia, the costs of elderly people are only 1.5 times higher than for young people (United Nations, 1985).

The assumptions about relative costs and their damaging economic

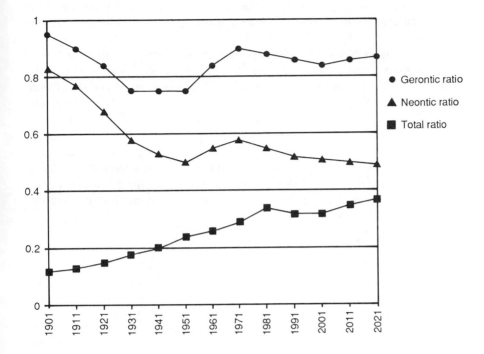

Figure 10.1   *Dependency ratios Great Britain 1901–2021*

Source: Falkingham (1987)

effects have recently come under attack from two separate quarters. Firstly, from those who have adopted a political economy view of ageing which sees old age as a period of dependency created by modern society (see Chapter 2). The other reaction comes from the ranks of demographers, economists and historians, who have looked more closely at the real (as opposed to assumed) economic worth as well as the costs of old age. Falkingham (1987) argues it is not necessarily the case that a change in the age structure will lead to a greater dependency cost. Demographic factors alone do not determine the ratio of workers to non-workers. In addition, shifts in labour-force participation involving many more women make dependency assumptions based on age and gender very suspect.

Thane (1987) sets out to quell the panic, first by drawing attention to the stability of the total dependency ratio throughout the twentieth century and the fact that this is scheduled to continue into the next. Within this framework she envisages a fall in *per capita* health and social services costs, as the increased healthiness of younger cohorts is transmitted into old age. This is a case also promoted by Bosanquet (1978) and more recently using American data by Pifer and Bronte (1986). In a similar essay on the implications of greater activity in old age Johnson (1982) associated these arguments with evidence of considerable increases in the income and wealth of a portion of the elderly cohorts of the next century, who will constitute not an economic burden but a much sought-after market.

In some ways more fundamental than these technical arguments is an ethical point about what counts as economically and socially worthwhile activity. Calculations are based on all income-generating activity which is recorded in the public domain. But is all of it worthy to count in the calculus of human welfare? Is the making and selling of hard drugs, pornography or 'stink bombs' to count equally with the production of wholesome food and nursing skill? And what about the work which is done and valued but not paid for (like informal care and domestic labour)? Not only are the dependency ratio calculations simplistic and inaccurate, they embody a set of values which leave much to be desired.

DISABILITY AND DEPENDENCE

The universal association of disability, both physical and mental, with increasing age is also present in the UK. There is some evidence to support Fries and Crapo's (1981) claim that morbidity is being compressed into the later years of life, but there is no denying that incapacity increases significantly beyond the age of 70. Distinctions between those with different levels of impairment are therefore of importance, for both the self-perceptions and the reality experienced by most elderly people is that they are fit and able to lead their own lives (Johnson, 1972).

No national register of disability or disabled persons in Britain exists, despite the intentions laid down in the Disabled Persons Act 1971. As a consequence there is no census-based inventory from which reliable data can be drawn. The best available national survey remains Hunt's study *The Elderly at Home* (1978) conducted in 1976 and Martin et al's (1988) survey of disability in Britain. Hunt found 0.3 per cent of those over 65 were bedfast and 4.2 per cent housebound. Wicks and Henwood (1988) calculate that 1.1 million over-65s are severely disabled, constituting one in eight of the total age group. A further two million are estimated by Walker and Phillipson (1986) to be moderately disabled. Within these global figures Victor (1987) has taken data from the *General Household Survey* and reconstructed it to produce a clearer breakdown by age, gender and severity (see Table 10.1).

Victor (1987) also draws attention to the social class differentials which show a consistent gradient of disability at all ages. Sixty per cent of classes 1 and 2 have no disablement compared with 45 per cent in classes 4 and 5. Five per cent of the higher social class category are severely affected compared with 8 per cent of manual workers. Thus, the trend in recent years has been for the total population to be marginally more healthy than in previous generations, but for there to be a marked increase in those with moderate disability (Bebbington, 1979).

Elderly people form a large proportion of the total population of

Table 10.1   *Disability classification of people over 65 (Great Britain)*

	65–69		70–74		75–79		80+	
	M	F	M	F	M	F	M	F
	%	%	%	%	%	%	%	%
None	72	59	60	47	44	30	34	17
Mild	18	26	24	28	31	34	24	24
Moderate	7	12	11	19	19	28	24	34
Severe	3	4	6	6	6	8	17	25

Source: *General Household Survey* unpublished data. Reproduced from Victor, 1987, p. 253.

disabled people. Two-thirds of all mentally and physically handicapped people are over 65. They constitute the largest group of those with severe visual handicap. Gilhome-Herbst (1976) estimates that 25–30 per cent of over 65s have some kind of hearing impairment. These conditions along with other physical disabilities, mental frailty, incontinence and the limitations of poor housing represent the range of handicap for older people.

Bond and Carstairs (1982) in their survey of elderly people in Scotland identified heart conditions (15 per cent), arthritis and related conditions affecting the back (10–15 per cent), joints (15–35 per cent) and sight defects (2–21 per cent) as the most widely reported illnesses which restrict functional capacity. These in turn have consequences for the performance of activities of daily living (ADLs) where bending and stooping are ingredients in the process.

The Audit Commission (a government efficiency unit) concluded from its (1985) study '... about 50 per cent of the elderly population have no specific physical disability and are able to live independent of any support; and that a further 35 per cent have relatively little disability but are unable to perform heavy household cleaning. However, at least 15 per cent of the elderly population are likely to be dependent on others for the performance of at least some tasks which they would previously have

Table 10.2   *The effects of disability (England and Wales)*

	65–74		75–84		85+	
	M	F	M	F	M	F
	%	%	%	%	%	%
Walking	17	14	26	17	39	24
Bending	7	10	10	13	13	13
Mobility	6	9	10	8	13	16
House Care	1	8	2	11	4	8
Stairs	2	5	3	7	2	6
Lifting	4	4	5	3	2	2
Gardening	3	2	5	1	6	1
Self Care	1	2	2	2	0	2

Source: Hunt (1978), Table 10.6.1

performed independently'. This latter group is highly likely to contain the 1 in 250 over 65s who suffer strokes, and frequently the seven per cent of males and 18 per cent of females over 70 whom Vetter (1981) reports as suffering from regular urinary incontinence.

Mental illness is prevalent at all ages, but there is a cumulative effect which manifests itself in higher levels within post retirement populations. It is usual to separate organic syndromes (those with a physical cause) from affective disorders. Distinctions between the two are very difficult to sustain with the result that both practical diagnosis and research leaves large areas of doubt. Within the organic syndromes, dementia in its various forms and that of the Alzheimer's type in particular are both very disabling and relatively common in later life, according to current research. Unfortunately, it is virtually impossible to be sure of a diagnosis of Alzheimer's in a living patient. Moreover, as sufferers are at high risk of institutionalisation, community studies suffer from a number of well-known deficiencies both of sampling and methodology. Nonetheless, it is commonly accepted as Brayne and Ames (1988) report that dementia occurs in about five per cent of the population aged over 65 and up to 20 per cent of those over 80. 'The rate of new cases is about one per cent per annum in the over 65s, rising with increasing age.'

Of the functional mental illnesses for which no definite organic cause is yet established (which includes symptoms such as delusions and hallucinations), depression is the most prevalent. It is the commonest psychiatric condition encountered in epidemiological studies and routine medical practice alike. Depression *is* the epidemic condition of old age. Again, because of the problems of definition as well as study methodology, research findings vary. Brayne and Ames' tabulation of the most important British studies (Table 10.3) depicts a range from six per cent to 26 per cent of over 65s which is at least an order of magnitude greater then the much discussed forms of dementia.

It is essential to restate that the majority of elderly people in the UK lead lives as independent of the assistance of others as people in younger age groups. Media reports and even governmental statements about the 'burden of dependency' serve only to reinforce unwarranted images.

CARING SERVICES

It has already been established that family and informal carers provide the major part of the support given to dependent people. Nonetheless, the system of statutory and voluntary services – both health and personal social services – is an indispensable professional complement. Historically they have grown up in five unrelated organisational patterns (i) local health authorities which provide hospital treatment, containing specialist geriatric provision, (ii) primary health care providing general practitioner home nursing and health visitor services, (iii) local authority social services departments offering a range of residential, day and

Table 10.3 *Depression in UK community samples*

Study	Location and Age	n	Instrument	Findings
Kay et al 1964	Newcastle 65+	505	Psychiatrist interview	26% affective illness and neurosis (inc. 1.3% endogenous affective illness)
Parsons 1965	Swansea 65+	228	Psychiatrist interview	0.9% endogenous depression (lifetime prevalence ED 6%)
Hare and Shaw 1965	London 65+	211	Interview	11% depressive symptoms
Gurland et al 1983	London 63+	396	Interview (CARE)	12.4% pervasive depression (inc. 1.3% manic depressive illness)
Maule et al 1984	Edinburgh 62+	487	Psychiatrist interview	5.1% depression
Copeland et al 1987	Liverpool 65+	1070	Interview (GMSA/AGECAT)	11.3% depression (inc. 3.0% depressive psychosis)
Morgan et al 1987	Nottingham 65+	1042	Interview (SAD)	9.8% depression (4.9% met stricter clinical criteria)

Source: Brayne and Ames (1988), p. 20.

domiciliary forms of care, (iv) voluntary bodies, some of which offer residential accommodation and other community services including meals on wheels and day centres, and (v) private-sector residential and nursing homes.

The diversity of these services and their administrations has long been a weakness leading to wasteful duplication and lack of coordination. As a consequence many elderly people in need receive only some parts of the assistance they need, for no individual professional worker is authorised to bring together the full complement.

Residential and nursing homes inevitably provide for the most dependent people – though many who are equally needful of care and support are maintained in community settings. About 5 per cent of the retired population are resident in long-term care (see Chapter 8). Unlike in North America, Australia and some other parts of Europe, in Britain this provision is predominantly on the social care model. Nursing homes contribute only 57,000 beds to the total of 426,800 beds – just over one in 10 – the remainder being residential (sometimes known as Part III homes). Residents are by definition very old and almost always dependent on others for their daily existence. The average age of entry is now over 80. A decade ago it would have been a little over 70. One in five people in the 80+ age group is in one of these forms of care. (See Chapter 8.)

Significant change has occurred in the past decade in long-term care provision. Prior to this period, statutory agencies – the NHS and local authorities – were the largest suppliers of these services. Demographical shifts, increased wealth amongst middle-class elderly people and the availability of social security funding for elderly people on supplementary pension, have fuelled private-sector expansion. In Laing's (1987) analysis of the 1986 position, the NHS had 74,600 long-stay geriatric beds, local authorities 136,900 residential home places, the voluntary sector 47,700 beds (of which 8,000 are in nursing homes) whilst the private sector offered 57,000 nursing home beds and 110,600 residential home places.

Long-stay care in geriatric hospitals on wards of general hospitals has become far less common than in the early 1980s and before when old people were often described as 'bed blockers'. Extension of private provision has provided a ready discharge route for the chronically sick patient, leaving beds free for more acute care and rehabilitation. Despite this change hospital geriatrics remains a low-status and medically under-regarded service. Evans (1981) has reported that whereas consultants in general medicine had an average of 30 beds in their care, geriatricians had about 180, plus commitments to outpatients, day hospitals and domiciliary visits. Even against these odds the length of hospital stay by elderly people has declined since 1970. Victor (1987) reports that the mean length of stay for males 65–74 in 1974 was 18 days, but had fallen to 13 days by 1983.

For those who are sick at home or discharged from hospital a variety of domiciliary services are supplied by the NHS and by local authority social services departments. Supplemented by home-based voluntary services, these inputs build upon family and other informal care. Linkages between hospital and community services are notoriously poor and the system's ability to coordinate services so that an elderly person returning home from hospital care gets home help, home nursing or meals on wheels at the point of discharge is very limited. The Continuing Care Project's survey (Amos, 1980) showed that 14 days after discharge about half of all elderly patients could not cope with domestic tasks or personal care, of whom more than a quarter had no one to help them. Of these two categories together, 84 per cent either had a caring person who could not cope, or had no caring person at all. By 28 days after discharge 39 per cent of the principal caring persons were themselves found to be frail and at risk. Home visits from general practitioners (family doctors) are also delayed. The same survey showed that 63 per cent of patients had not received a call by 14 days after discharge.

An increasingly impressive range of services exists for elderly people at home, but there is great geographical diversity in the extent and availability of them. Table 10.4 summarises the domiciliary services available for elderly people in the United Kingdom. However, there are considerable variations in quantity and quality of these services across the country.

Up-to-date and reliable data on the delivery of these services are difficult to find; but *Health and Personal Social Services Statistics 1985* (DHSS,

Table 10.4   *Domiciliary services for elderly people*

Service	Provider
Primary health care teams	NHS
Clubs	Local authority/voluntary
Day centres	Local authority/voluntary
Meals on wheels	Local authority/voluntary
Luncheon clubs	Local authority/voluntary
Health visitors	NHS
Domiciliary physiotherapy	NHS
District nursing	NHS
Nursing auxiliaries	NHS
Aids for daily living/house adaptation	Local authority
Nail cutting service	Voluntary
Library service for housebound	Local authority/voluntary
Night sitting	Local authority/voluntary
Sheltered housing	Local authority/voluntary/private
Incontinence laundry	Local authority/NHS
Community psychiatric nurse	NHS
Social worker	Local authority
Respite care	Local authority/NHS
Geriatric day hospital	NHS

1985e) reported findings for a one-year period in 1982. It was found that of those aged 65 or over, 605,462 were seen by a health visitor, 1,632,881 were visited by a home nurse, 1,732,452 received NHS chiropody services and 765,754 received the services of a home help. Such global figures tell only of relative magnitudes and nothing of the effectiveness, match with needs, regularity or duration. In general research evidence indicates a shortfall of provision on all these principal services, inadequacies in design to meet the needs of consumers and failure to coordinate care packages for individuals. (Johnson et al, 1981; Midwinter, 1987; Means, 1984; Clarke, 1984).

STRUCTURED DEPENDENCY

Reference has already been made to the proposition that dependency amongst elderly people is amplified, if not created, by the manner in which modern societies are structured and organised (see Chapter 2). Such notions are not new, for it has been evident for some time that mandatory retirement which removes older people from the work force also reduces their income and social esteem. Similarly, it is well documented that the shortage of support services and the regimes in residential-care establishments have created a reliance on others. Yet it was only in Townsend's article in *Ageing and Society* (1981) that the concept of structured dependency was articulated. He draws upon his own extensive research, especially of residential care (Townsend, 1957) to argue that the present degree of dependency experienced by old people is unnecessary. He writes:

> I am arguing, then, that society creates the framework of institutions and rules within which the general problems of the elderly emerge and are indeed manufactured. Decisions are being taken every day in the management of the economy and in the maintenance and development of social institutions which govern the position which elderly people occupy in national life, and these also contribute powerfully to the public consciousness of different meanings of ageing and old age. (Townsend, 1981, p. 9)

The argument proceeds through a series of claims about the ways in which retired people are excluded from socially valued activities and statuses. Governments find it convenient to reduce unemployment figures by enforced retirement, whilst new technology makes their skills redundant or undervalued. Townsend adds:

> Less consideration tends to be given in sickness and disability at older than younger ages and, indeed, retirement is cavalierly associated with failing health and incapacity. Thus, the combined effects of industrial, economic and educational reorganisation are leading to more rigid stratification of the population by age. (Townsend, 1981, p. 11)

This influential paper rapidly gave rise to a body of writings in the political economy of ageing. Prior to its publication the American gerontologist Estes (1979) had produced her book *The Aging Enterprise* which gave a critical edge to previous writings about old age and the state, by entering into a class analysis. Concurrently Walker (1980, 1981) was producing material which developed the same themes by examination of income and wealth in later life. His contention was:

> ... that poverty in old age is primarily a function of low economic and social status prior to retirement and the depressed social status of the retired, and secondarily, of the relatively low level of state benefits. (Walker, 1981, p. 73; see also Chapter 11)

Gaullier (1982) analysing post-war policies for retired people in France asserts that the government converted the positive aspects of the Third Age movement to create a new social ghetto. A similar process was described by Kohli et al (1983) based on their studies of prematurely retired tobacco workers in Germany. By the mid-1980s volumes of collected papers began to emerge (Guillemard, 1983; Minkler and Estes, 1984) to supplement monographs like Phillipson's (1982) which located the modern formula of retirement as a repressed social category, in the development of western capitalism.

For half a decade the Townsend thesis had such a self-evident quality to it that no serious challenge was offered. But in very recent times a number of criticisms have appeared. Johnson complains that the economic position of elderly people has been extensively examined by social policy analysts, but virtually ignored by economists. In beginning to correct the imbalance he contends that:

theories of 'structured dependency' rest on the explicit or implicit argument that elderly people have experienced a constriction of economic liberty because of ... the development of welfare and employment policies ... [but] much of the detailed research that has made use of the concept of structured dependency has focused on the relatively small and exceptional group of elderly people living in institutions, for whom the concept of dependency seems more immediately relevant. (Johnson, 1987, p. i)

Moreover, he suggests that the existence of old age pensions has given both a security of income and a range of choice which sometimes exceeds what is available to younger people in employment.

Dant (1988) takes issue even with the strongest part of the case as it relates to people in residential care. He points out that 'some may even prefer the 'hotel' qualities of residential life, of not being bothered with cleaning and cooking'. Townsend is further taken to task by claims that 'He seems to regard both elderly people and all other people in society who do not have a functional role in the running of the state as 'cultural dopes' devoid of autonomy and self-determination'. In a more oblique way Wilkin (1987) also offers a critical refinement, by returning our attention to the detailed assessment of disability as a dependency creating attribute. More sophisticated measures which place physical and mental impairments in the context of relationships and environment will produce the capacity to release elderly people from excessive dependence on others. His call for more focus on 'dependency relationships' draws the discussion back to individuals and their settings rather than the macro economic structure.

The structured dependency debate has a long way to go before it is concluded. What it has provided so far is a strongly presented alternative to the view that elderly people are not only the victims of old age, they are the unconscious perpetrators of its deprivations. Similarly, it has stimulated a more constructive view of the definitions, causes and measurements of dependency. Whatever the outcome, it is inevitable that the political economy view of old age will have established itself as a permanent and proper vantage point for viewing problems in a more politically comprehensive way.

CONCLUSION

The seemingly simple notion of the dependency older people have on other people has proved to be both conceptually complex and methodologically difficult to measure. Earlier attempts to encapsulate the everyday requirements of people who have lost capacities to maintain themselves, by the use of check lists and rating scales now appear inadequate – if still widely used. Exclusive attention to the shortcomings of the person in being able to carry out 'activities of everyday living' is demonstrably incomplete, even if the measures are valid. If dependency is to gain a useful meaning – rather than being another negative label – it must be considered within both the local and national contexts. Much more attention is now being given to the specific identification of conditions which inhibit independent functioning and their matching with tested and effective social, medical and financial support. Developments of this sort which individualise assessment and responses to it, whilst removing the individualisation of the causes of pathology, appear to be fruitful lines of progress.

11

POVERTY AND INEQUALITY IN OLD AGE

Alan Walker

The purpose of this chapter is to analyse the distribution of income and wealth both among elderly people and between elderly people and younger age groups. It does so, firstly, by outlining the financial status of elderly people in contemporary Britain; secondly, the sources of income in old age are discussed, with particular reference to the main source of income: the state retirement pension; and, thirdly, the causes of poverty and inequality in old age are examined. (For accounts of the development of the approach to the analysis of poverty and inequality in old age adopted here see Walker, 1980; 1981.)

FINANCIAL STATUS OF ELDERLY PEOPLE

Poverty and low incomes

The observation that poverty and deprivation are concentrated on a substantial proportion of elderly people has been a recurring theme of research on ageing in all industrial societies. In Britain, elderly people have been shown to be the largest group in the population living in poverty ever since such statistics were collected systematically (Booth, 1892; 1894). Subsequent research has confirmed, over and over again, the deep-seated nature of poverty in old age (see for example, Cole and Utting, 1962; Townsend and Wedderburn, 1965; Townsend, 1979). A report from the then Ministry of Pensions and National Insurance (1966) was particularly important in establishing officially the acceptance by government of both widespread poverty among elderly people and also the large proportion eligible for but not drawing supplementary benefit. The Royal Commission on the Distribution of Income and Wealth (1978, p. 234) reported that one in every three elderly families had incomes on or below the poverty line in 1975 and that nearly three in every four lived in or on the margins of poverty.

Today, despite the significant political commitment given to pensions in the 1970s – culminating in the introduction of the New Pension

Table 11.1   *Numbers and percentages of people of different ages living on low incomes (Britain, 1975–1985)*

Family income in relation to supplementary benefit standard	Thousands				
	1975	1977	1981	1983	1985
Adults over pension age					
Below	740	2760	1120	1080	960
Receiving SB	1930	1970	1960	1880	1880
On margins	2870	2860	2810	2750	2730
All on low income	5540	5590	5890	5710	5570
Per cent of all pensioners	66.3	65.4	66.8	63.7	61.3
Adults under pension age					
Below	690	760	1130	1310	1080
Receiving SB	970	1170	1720	2620	3190
On margins	2170	2240	2600	2860	2050
All on low income	3830	4170	5540	6790	6320
Per cent of adults	12.6	13.7	17.3	21.1	19.6
All under pension age					
Below	1100	1140	1690	1700	1460
Receiving SB	1780	2150	2880	4250	5080
On margins	4120	4110	4540	4720	3320
All on low income	7000	7400	9110	10670	9860
Per cent of all adults and children	15.8	16.7	20.4	23.8	21.9

Sources: DHSS (1983), Tables 1–6; DHSS (1988), Tables 1–6.

Scheme in 1975 and the series of pledges to uprate pensions in line with earnings or prices, whichever was the greater – which resulted in some improvements in the relative position of elderly people in the income distribution (see below), poverty is still the principal financial problem faced by elderly people. This is one extreme aspect of the substantial inequalities in income and other resources between the majority of those under and those over retirement age.

While just under one in five (17 per cent) of all persons in Great Britain are over pension age they comprise one in three of those living on incomes on or below the supplementary benefit level, the official, or socially agreed, standard of poverty. As Table 11.1 shows, the risk of experiencing poverty is three times greater for adults over retirement age than it is for adults below retirement age. The most recent information made available by the government showed that just under one-third of elderly people in 1985 were living on incomes at or below the poverty line compared with one-tenth of those under pension age. In all nearly two-thirds of elderly people, 5.5 million people, live in or on the margins of poverty (ie within incomes of up to 140 per cent of the appropriate supplementary benefit rates) compared with one-quarter of non-elderly people (DHSS, 1988).

Not only does poverty affect a substantial proportion of older people, but when it does, it is likely to be an enduring experience. Thus, elderly people predominate among both claimants of supplementary benefit (income support from April 1988) and long-term claimants. The national survey of supplementary benefit claimants, carried out by the Policy Studies Institute in 1982, found a large proportion of long-term claimants among pensioners. Also, pensioners were much more likely than other claimants to have been living on unsupplemented social security pensions *before* claiming supplementary benefit, that is, below the poverty line (Berthoud, 1984, p. A5). Thus, as Table 11.1 shows, there are just under one million people living on incomes *below* the supplementary benefit poverty line. For several reasons, but primarily because of the stigma associated with claiming (Townsend, 1979; Walker, 1986a) some 800,000 pensioners who are eligible for supplementary benefit do not claim it. So the take-up rate of supplementary pensions is 67 per cent compared with 83 per cent for under pension age supplementary allowances (Central Statistical Office, 1988).

In addition to the problem of poverty, elderly people are likely to experience low incomes compared with younger adults, particularly those in paid employment.

The independent national survey of household resources and standards of living, conducted by Townsend (1979) found a striking difference in the proportion of elderly and non-elderly people living in poverty and on low incomes:

> Twenty per cent, compared with seven per cent, were living in poverty; another 44 per cent, compared with 19 per cent, were living on the margins of poverty. At the other end of the income scale, more than twice as many of the non-elderly than of the elderly were living comfortably above the (supplementary benefit) standard .... Although the elderly comprised one-third of those in poverty, and nearly one-third on the margins of poverty. (Townsend, 1979, p. 788)

Expenditure provides an alternative to income as a measure of living standards. A study carried out by the DHSS, using the data from the 1975 *Family Expenditure Survey*, showed that the expenditure of pensioner households was about one-quarter of the median for households not receiving supplementary benefit. In fact, the total expenditure of pensioner households living on supplementary benefit was less than half that of pensioner households not receiving SB but designated as poor (ie in the bottom quintile of the income distribution) (Baldwin and Cooke, 1984, p. 44). Some two-thirds of the budgets of pensioner households receiving supplementary benefit are consumed by food, fuel and clothing. This suggests that at 1988–89 benefit levels a single pensioner would spend about £29.07 out of the income support allowance and *pensioner (60–74) premium* of £44.05 on these items, leaving £14.98 per week to be spent on so-called 'non-essentials'. By comparison median income level households spend less than half of their budget, which is nearly four times as large, on 'essential' items (Baldwin and Cooke,

1984, p. 45). Moreover, some elderly people have lower expectations and aspirations than younger adults and, therefore, are more likely to choose to go without or consume less than they need of basic necessities. The *Breadline Britain* survey found that 73 per cent of pensioners on low incomes 'chose' to go without at least one necessity compared with 57 per cent of non-pensioners, while 24 per cent of the former 'chose' to go without three or more necessities compared with 9 per cent of the latter (Mack and Lansley, 1985, p. 97).

A special analysis of data from the 1982 *Family Expenditure Survey*, by the DHSS Economic Advisers' Office, found that despite improvement in the general financial position of pensioners over the last 30 years, many pensioners still have relatively low incomes. On the one hand, few elderly people are among the very well off: only one in 10 has an income above the average for working families. On the other hand, few of those in paid employment have incomes as low as most pensioners; only a fifth of working families have incomes below the average pensioner income (DHSS, 1984).

The high incidence of poverty and low incomes among elderly people is reflected in other measures of deprivation. For example, they are less likely than non-elderly people to own consumer durables, such as television sets and refrigerators; they are less likely to eat fresh meat most days a week; they are less likely to have a summer holiday and to take part in social activities requiring money (Townsend, 1979). Elderly people are more likely than younger age groups to live in council housing and unfurnished private rented accommodation (Central Statistical Office, 1988). When they are owner-occupiers, pensioners are more likely than younger adults to own older houses which lack one or more basic amenities (Butcher and Crosbie, 1978).

Official underestimation of poverty in old age
A considerable body of data could be adduced to show further that there is a significant difference between the incomes and other resources and expenditure of elderly and non-elderly people and that a very large group of old people live in poverty or on its margins (Walker, 1980). Moreover, the problem of poverty in old age is not peculiar to Britain, it is endemic among both western and eastern advanced industrial societies as well as Third World countries (Hendricks and Hendricks, 1977; Maeda, 1978; Neysmith and Edwardh, 1984). Yet in recent years the argument has been gaining ground in official circles, and some academic ones, that poverty in old age is no longer a serious problem. The ministerial foreword to the Green Paper on elderly people issued by the last Labour government implied that the problem had been solved (DHSS, 1978). It was not mentioned at all in the White Paper issued by the Conservative government (DHSS, 1981). This official forbearance turned to antagonism in the mid-1980s when the government and some independent commentators began to question openly the extent of the financial needs among elderly

people and, either directly or by implication, the level of social security expenditure on them. The four reviews of social security initiated in 1983 by the Secretary of State for Social Services – particularly the Inquiry into the Provision for Retirement – were the forums in which the arguments against further increases in pensions were most trenchantly expressed (DHSS, 1985a). There is not space here to examine the reasons for this sea-change in official attitudes (see Walker, 1986b) which has resulted in reductions in state pensions. However, these cuts have been legitimated by the argument that pensioners are relatively well off – which has led to the proposition that Britain may actually be overproviding for old age – and, therefore, it is important to assess the factors underlying this apparent paradox.

Official reports and some independent social scientists have started recently to point to relative improvements in the position of elderly people in the income distribution. The most important of these commentaries was prepared by the DHSS Economic Advisers' Office as a background paper to the Inquiry into Provision for Retirement (DHSS, 1984). This showed that between 1951 and 1984–85 pensioners' share of total disposable income (total income from earnings, savings, investment, pensions and other social security benefits) increased from 7 per cent to 15 per cent (DHSS, 1984). The reasons given for this improvement include both the growth in numbers of pensioners and their rising incomes. While the former is relatively straightforward the improvement in the disposable income of pensioners relative to non-pensioners rests on two factors. On the one hand, there has been a slowing down in the growth of real disposable income among those below pension age, caused mainly by the reduction of the numbers in full-time employment and, on the other, the value of the basic pensions has risen in relation to average earnings (see below). (The main advance in the value of pensions took place in the mid-1970s.)

This official analysis of rising incomes among pensioners was supported by other independent assessments. For example, one recent examination of changes in the distribution of income over the life cycle showed that whereas 45 per cent of married pensioners were in the bottom quintile of net income in 1971, this had fallen to 28 per cent in 1982. For single pensioners the proportions were 43 per cent in 1971 and 22 per cent in 1982 (Bradshaw and O'Higgins, 1984). However, while analyses such as this correctly highlight recent improvements in the relative incomes of pensioners, they have mistakenly been translated into the myth that elderly people are now affluent, a myth that has legitimated policy proposals which redistribute income from elderly people to other groups in poverty. Three factors should be considered.

First, the relative 'improvement' in the value of the basic pension has been modest: from 19 per cent of gross average male manual earnings for a single pensioner in 1948 to 23 per cent in 1986. For a married couple the proportions are 31 per cent in 1948 and 36 per cent in 1986 (DHSS,

1986). Moreover, since the de-coupling of increases in pensions from average earnings, in 1980, the maintenance of the value of the pension established in the mid-1970s has relied on the relatively small growth in average manual earnings. It is likely that this modest improvement will be seriously undermined by the recent fast rise in average earnings.

Second, the validity of any assessment of relative poverty depends on the group with which comparisons are made. The previous discussion of poverty and low incomes in old age rested on a comparison between elderly and non-elderly people, particularly those in employment. This was the relative framework implicitly accepted by Parliament, in 1977, when it linked pensions' upratings to earnings (or prices, whichever rose faster) and so gave pensioners a share in rising national prosperity. This link was broken in 1981 and subsequent comparisons have not been between elderly people and those in employment, but between elderly people and other groups in poverty. So a major plank in the official case against increasing pensions relative to earnings, as well as against the State Earnings Related Pension, has been the recent relative improvement in the incomes of pensioners in comparison with other groups living in poverty (DHSS, 1985a). Incidentally, this argument also entails the denial of the relative nature of poverty, so that policy makers have chosen to concentrate their attention on the relative position of various poor groups rather than looking at the relationship between poverty and affluence.

While state pensions have not increased significantly in value compared with average earnings, they have increased against other social security benefits, particularly unemployment benefit. In 1972–73 unemployment benefit and retirement pension were paid at the same rates (and had been for most of the period since 1948); by 1984–85 the latter was worth 26 per cent more than the former, as it is in 1988–89. However, this increase had as much to do with recent cuts in the value of unemployment benefits as rises in the value of pensions and, therefore, it is partly artificial. Moreover, the decoupling of pensions from earnings had an immediate impact on the relative value of the retirement pension, which fell from a high of 132 per cent of the level of the unemployment benefit in 1981 to 126 per cent in 1984 (DHSS, 1985b). Thus, the 'advantageous' position of pensioners among the poor has been manufactured, to a large extent, by government policies largely outside of the pensions field: the creation of mass unemployment, the abolition of earnings-related supplement, cuts in unemployment benefit, failure to maintain the value of child benefit and encouragement of low wages (Walker and Walker, 1987). The outcome of these policies is that there has been an increase in people, particularly single people below pension age and families with children, falling into the bottom fifth of the income distribution and, because unemployment benefit is set at a lower rate than the pension the average income of the lowest income group has declined as their numbers have swollen. This change is reflected in the composition of the lowest quintile group of the income distribution: in 1971 pensioners comprised 52 per cent of the lowest fifth, single people of working age 19 per cent and working-age couples with children 17 per cent. By 1985 the picture had changed considerably: pensioners made up 27 per cent of the bottom quintile, single adults under pension age 34 per cent and couples with children 22 per cent (Central Statistical Office, 1988). As the Central Statistical Office notes, this shift 'does not necessarily indicate an improvement in the living standards for pensioners', but the increase in unemployment (Central Statistical Office, 1988, p. 96).

The answer, of course, would be to reverse recent policies and improve the incomes of the unemployed and families with children. However, the recent reviews of social security did not propose any improvement in the social security status of the unemployed. The Green Paper (DHSS, 1985a) and the ensuing White Paper (DHSS, 1985d) and Social Security Act 1986, did propose increases in benefits for families with children (some of whom have unemployed heads), but because of the nil-cost constraint imposed on this reform of social security, elderly people were viewed as the *source* of finance for these improvements. Thus, when the changes in the Social Security Act 1986, were introduced in April 1988 it was officially estimated that some 2.1 million pensioners would be worse off as a result (DHSS, 1985c).

Third, as was shown earlier, the majority of elderly people still live in poverty – in terms of both the official poverty line and average living standards – in spite of recent improvements in the value of pensions. In so far as elderly people have shifted, or, more correctly, have been shunted, out of the bottom fifth of the income distribution they have been moved predominantly into the adjacent quintile. 64 per cent of single pensioners were to be found in the bottom two-fifths of the income distribution in 1982 compared with 74 per cent in 1971 (Bradshaw and O'Higgins, 1984).

Inequalities between elderly people

Like all good myths, the myth of affluence in old age has some basis in reality. While there has only been a slight relative improvement in the incomes of the majority of pensioners, for some the increase has been substantial. The 'two-nations' in old age, forewarned by Titmuss (1963) 25 years ago are now firmly entrenched. Differences based on class, age, gender, race and marital status are reflected in income inequalities and, at the extremes are younger (60–74) middle-class males and married couples, and older (75+) working-class families.

Inequalities in old age are primarily a function of access to resources over the earlier stages of the life cycle. Occupational status in earlier life determines salary or wage levels and, therefore, the opportunities to save and invest in property and other possessions. Access to occupational pensions also rests on employment status. In addition to inequalities based on occupational class, certain groups, such as women, ethnic minorities, people with disabilities and older workers, experience discrimination in the labour market and are, therefore, less likely to gain access to secure well-paid employment. Finally, retirement itself superimposes reduced social status and lowered incomes on pensioners and resources tend to diminish the longer an individual survives in retirement.

Townsend (1979) found that a markedly larger proportion of manual than non-manual elderly people were living in poverty or on its margins. Higher proportions lacked basic consumer durables and were less likely than non-manual groups to own their homes outright. In addition, there were significant inequalities in income between elderly women and men and a close relationship between diminishing resources and advancing age. For example, the proportion of women aged 65–69 with incomes on or below the poverty line was 63 per cent compared with 48 per cent of men in the same age group. The percentage of women aged 80 and over living in poverty was nearly double that of women aged 60–64: 86 per cent and 46 per cent respectively (Townsend, 1979).

The incidence of poverty among elderly women, particularly lone women, is significantly higher than among men (Walker, 1987). If the data in Table 11.1 is reanalysed according to the gender of the elderly person we find that nearly two in every five elderly women (38 per cent) were living on incomes on or below the poverty line, as defined by SB levels, compared with 24 per cent of elderly men. Just under half of lone elderly women compared with just over one-third of single elderly men had incomes on or below the poverty line (Walker, 1987). Since a much higher proportion of women than men survive into advanced old age they increasingly dominate the poverty profile of successively older age groups. For example, among single people, in 1983 the ratio of women to men living on SB increased from 6:1 in the 65–69 age group, to 7:1 in the 70–79 age group, to 8:1 for those aged 80 and over. The explanation for these ratios is not simply that there are more women in older age groups, but that elderly lone women, especially widows, are more likely than lone men and married couples to have to rely on SB (DHSS, 1984). Further evidence of the disadvantaged position of elderly women in relation to men can be gained from information on the distribution of income. Elderly women in the bottom fifth of the income distribution have slightly lower incomes than men in the same quintile and elderly men in the top fifth have much higher incomes than women. Thus, in 1982 the spread of disposable income for lone women ranged from £32 per week to £77 per week compared with £34 to £91 per week for lone men. Average disposable income varied from £88 per week for married couples, to £55 for lone men and £49 for lone women (DHSS, 1984).

The important combined influence of class, gender and age in determining the structure of inequality was confirmed by a recent survey of elderly people living in private households in Aberdeen. None of the sample of younger (60–74) middle-class men had a household income of less than £30 per week and more than half had incomes over £60; whereas more than three-fifths of older (75+) working-class women had incomes of less than £30 per week and none had more than £60 (Taylor and Ford, 1983). The authors of this study concluded that:

> most personal resources do diminish with age, men tend to have more than women and those from middle-class backgrounds tend to have more than those from working-class backgrounds. (Taylor and Ford, 1983, p. 200)

Wealth and other assets

Poverty and inequality are not solely dependent on the incomes available to individuals and families. The position of different groups of elderly people in the class structure depends on their command over other resources such as savings, interest on capital, housing, employment benefits and social services. There is, usually, a close association between income and assets, particularly readily realisable ones and inequalities in wealth between elderly people of different classes has the effect of widening inequalities based on incomes.

In the mid-1970s Hunt (1978) found that only 27 per cent of couples and 15 per cent of lone elderly people had assets over £2,500. Thus, for the majority of pensioners the readily realisable savings of a lifetime are extremely small. Those with the lowest incomes had the smallest savings to draw on. Of married couples with net incomes of less than £1,500 per annum, only 16 per cent had assets worth more than £2,500, whereas of couples with net incomes of £3,000 and over, 76 per cent had assets worth more than £2,500 (Hunt, 1978).

Similar inequalities in savings were found in the 1980 Aberdeen survey. Only 4 per cent of younger middle-class men, the groups with the highest income, had savings of less than £2,500 whereas 42 per cent of the poorest group, older working-class women, had savings under £2,500 (Taylor and Ford, 1983). Not surprisingly, those with the lowest savings anticipated most difficulty in obtaining emergency cash and those with the most savings anticipated least difficulty.

These disparities in the ownership of assets are exaggerated when the lifelong social status of elderly people is taken into account. Thus, in Townsend's (1979) survey a quarter of elderly people from non-manual occupations whose fathers had also held non-manual occupations had net assets of £10,000 or more, with one-half holding £5,000 or more, compared with zero per cent and 2 per cent of those who like their fathers had held semi-skilled or unskilled jobs. If the annuity value of assets (ie potential income) was added to net disposable incomes two-thirds of the non-manual compared with only 6 per cent of the semi-skilled/unskilled group had resources of three or more times the SB poverty line.

The most significant physical asset is owner-occupied housing. Although poor elderly people are more likely than poor younger adults to own their own homes, the average home ownership for pensioners is well below that for younger age groups: 50 per cent compared with 73 per cent among those aged 30–44 and 65 per cent among those aged 45–59 (Central Statistical Office, 1988). There has been a substantial increase in home ownership among younger age groups over the last 10 years whereas the proportion of elderly owner-occupiers has remained virtually static. The main factor here is that most of the local authority tenants who bought their houses under the 'right to buy' scheme have been under 60. Pensioners are much more likely than younger adults to own older houses which lack one or more basic amenities (see Chapter 8).

The most important income-generating asset held by many elderly people is an occupational pension. But it may be that the incomes of elderly owner-occupiers will be increasingly augmented by schemes intended to annuitise some of the capital value of their home. Of course, this will further emphasise the existing inequalities in income and wealth between different groups of elderly people.

Poverty and inequality in international context

Is Britain unique in having a high incidence of poverty in old age? Are the incomes of elderly and non-elderly people more or less equal in Britain compared with other countries? Answers to questions such as these have been notoriously difficult to find, largely because of the lack of reliability in comparing published statistics from different countries. However, a special study of the economic position of families in various age groups in seven western industrial countries was conducted in 1980 and, since this was based on common methodology, it provides some reliable answers (Hedström and Ringen, 1987). The seven countries surveyed are shown in Table 11.2 along with some of the main results.

As the table shows, income differences (adjusted for family size) between elderly people and average income levels are greatest in the UK and least pronounced in Canada, Israel and the USA. Thus, the income of the UK's 65–74 and 75 and over age groups, at 76 per cent and 67 per cent respectively of the national mean, compares with an average for the other six nations of 94 per cent and 82 per cent. Moreover, since this study was carried out in 1980 the position of elderly people in Britain is likely to have worsened in relation to average incomes, primarily as a result of the de-indexation of pensions from earnings. Income is more equally distributed among elderly people in the UK than in the USA, Israel and West Germany, but less so than in Sweden and Norway. The extent of relative poverty is greater in the 65–74 and 75 and over age groups in UK compared with Sweden, Norway, West Germany and Canada, but less than in Israel and the USA. However, there are different explanations for the roughly similar poverty rates in the UK and USA: in the former case the high poverty rate among elderly people derives from the low level of income of elderly people as a whole, whereas in the case of the latter a similar poverty rate is due mainly to the unequal distribution of income among elderly people.

Table 11.2   *National differences in disposable income, inequality and poverty*

| Country | Income, inequality and poverty according to age | | | | | | | | |
| | Disposable income in relation to national mean[a] | | | Inequality[b] | | | Poverty rates[c] | | |
	65–74	75+	All Ages	65–74	75+	All Ages	65–74	75+	All Ages
Canada	0.94	0.81	1.00	0.309	0.291	0.299	11.2	12.1	12.1
W. Germany	0.84	0.77	1.00	0.298	0.340	0.355	12.2	15.2	7.2
Israel	0.92	0.96	1.00	0.360	0.429	0.333	22.6	27.1	14.5
Norway	1.01	0.79	1.00	0.250	0.229	0.243	2.7	7.3	4.8
Sweden	0.96	0.78	1.00	0.143	0.126	0.205	0.0	0.0	5.0
UK	0.76	0.67	1.00	0.266	0.240	0.273	16.2	22.0	8.8
USA	0.99	0.84	1.00	0.342	0.355	0.326	17.8	25.5	16.9
Mean	0.92	0.80	-	0.281	0.287	0.291	11.9	15.6	9.9
SD	0.08	0.08	-	0.067	0.092	0.050	7.5	9.2	4.4

Notes:

[a] Disposable income (adjusted for family size) as a proportion of the national mean for the total population.

[b] Gini coefficients for distribution of adjusted disposable income within age groups and for total population.

[c] Poverty rate defined as percentage of persons in families with adjusted disposable income below half of the median for all families in the population.

Source: Hedström and Ringen (1987), Tables 4, 5 and 6.

Overall, the Nordic, collectivist welfare states appear to achieve lower levels of inequality and poverty – both between different groups of elderly people and between elderly people and the rest of society – than the residual welfare state and dominant private sector in the USA, with the liberal mixed economies such as West Germany and Canada in between. Unfortunately, Britain appears to be in the worst position: it has a longstanding infrastructure of welfare state provision for elderly people but it has not managed to protect elderly people from poverty as well as other welfare states. As the authors of this comparative study conclude 'with the exception of Britain, the standard of living of elderly families is not far behind the national average' (Hedström and Ringen, 1987, p. 238). It is to an explanation of this paradox that the second half of this chapter is now devoted.

SOURCES OF INCOME IN OLD AGE

A description of the main sources of the income of Britain's elderly people is the first step in explaining the continuance of poverty in old age and the existence of marked inequalities in income and wealth between elderly people.

There have been important changes in the sources of elderly people's income over the last 30 years. In 1951 the proportion of total gross income

Table 11.3 *Comparison of the sources of pensioners' income and total UK household income (percentage)*

Income	Pensioners' income 1984–85		Total household income 1985
Wages and salaries[a]	9		69
Investment and rent	9		7
Private pensions, annuities	22		7
NI retirement pension	49	}	16
Other social security[b]	11		
Total	100		100

Notes:
[a] includes self-employment.
[b] mainly supplementary benefit and housing benefit.
Sources: Central Statistical Office (1988), 84; DHSS (1984), p.16.

derived from earnings was three times the current level (27 per cent), while the proportion received from occupational pensions was 15 per cent. The contribution of social security was two-thirds of the current level (42 per cent of total income) largely due to the significant role of earnings (DHSS, 1984). These gross income figures hide major inequalities between different groups of pensioners.

Employment

The main distinguishing feature of the incomes of elderly people, compared with younger adults, is the low proportion deriving from wages and salaries. Low labour-force participation is the primary source of inequality between elderly and non-elderly people and, in turn, it proves an important source of inequality between elderly people. Those who continue working after retirement age are less likely than the retired to experience poverty: in 1976 only 7 per cent of elderly families whose head was in paid employment had incomes on or below the poverty line, compared with 40 per cent of those whose head was not in employment (Royal Commission on the Distribution of Income and Wealth, 1978). Thus, there is a close relationship between employment and income level in old age. This can be illustrated among both single-person and two-person elderly households. Taking single-person households first, among men aged 65–73, 30 per cent of those in work had net weekly incomes under £30 compared with 82 per cent of the retired; for women aged 60–73 the figures were 53 per cent and 85 per cent. In two-person households, among men aged 65–73, 3 per cent of those in work had net weekly incomes of less than £30 compared with 26 per cent of the retired; the figures for women aged 60–73 were 5 per cent and 28 per cent respectively (Parker, 1980).

Labour-force participation among elderly people is dependent on a large number of factors, including socio-economic status, health, pension rules and custom, the most important of which are discussed later. Although the proportion over retirement age in full- or part-time employment is small – 7 per cent of men aged 65 and over and 6 per cent of women aged 60 and over – there are marked differences based on age and marital status. Younger elderly people, married men and single women are more likely to be employed than older elderly people, single men and married women.

Retirement pension

The national insurance (NI) retirement pension provides the largest proportion of total pensioners' income, but its significance for different groups varies according to the extent of their access to other income. The NI pension is the main source of income in single person pensioner households with gross weekly incomes of less than £80 (in 1982). In fact, the lower the incomes of this group, the greater the proportion provided by the retirement pension: one-half for those with incomes between £50 and £80 and seven-tenths for those on incomes under £50. The proportions of incomes contributed by occupational pensions were 18 per cent and 5 per cent respectively (Central Statistical Office, 1985). Among single-pensioner households with weekly incomes of £80 or more only one-quarter was derived from the retirement pension and well over two-fifths from occupational pensions. For two-person households the proportion of income derived from the NI pension nearly halves between those with incomes under £80 and those with £80 or more per week (71 per cent compared with 37 per cent), while the proportion received from occupational pensions increases by nearly five times (7.5 per cent compared with 35 per cent).

For the majority of pensioners in Britain the amount of the state retirement pension has an important influence on their living standards and the level of their incomes compared with younger adults. For low-income elderly people the retirement pension, together with supplementation by income support (previously SB), effectively determines whether they will live in poverty or not, a point we return to later.

Occupational pensions

Access to private welfare in the form of occupational pensions is of fundamental importance in determining the inequalities in income between different groups of elderly people outlined earlier and marks the main boundary between the two economic nations among Britain's elderly people. There are two main sources of inequality based on occupational pensions. On the one hand, there is unequal access to occupational and other private pensions, based primarily on socio-economic group and employment status and, on the other, there is inequality between generations of elderly people arising from changes in pension conditions and levels.

The coverage of occupational pensions increased from 2.6 million employees in the 1930s to a peak of 12.2 million in 1967, since then it has declined slightly and stabilised at just over 11 million (Government Actuary, 1986). However, in 1983 some 10 million employees were excluded from such pensions schemes because there was no scheme provided by their employer (six million), the scheme did not cover part-time or manual employees (three million) or because they were too young or their service with the employer was too short (one million). Women working part-time are particularly prone to exclusion from occupational pension schemes (Government Actuary, 1986). The majority of those excluded from their employer's scheme are manual employees. Thus, in 1983, 71 per cent of full-time non-manual employees were members of an occupational pension scheme, compared with 54 per cent of manual employees (OPCS, 1984a). The contrast was greatest between professional employees (83 per cent membership) and unskilled employees (48 per cent). Moreover, if they do have access to a pension scheme it is likely to be on less favourable terms than non-manual employees and the final pension paid is much lower. Thus, occupational pensions are an important mechanism for preserving in retirement income and status differentials forged in employment. Of course, occupational pensions are of little or no benefit to those, such as the long-term unemployed, people with disabilities, and single parents, who are excluded from the labour market.

Turning to the second form of inequality arising from occupational pensions; as successive cohorts of elderly people have become eligible for pensions on more favourable terms, previous generations of beneficiaries have become relatively worse off by comparison. Thus, in 1975, the median level occupational pension for men under 65 was £15 compared with £6 for men aged 70 and over (Government Actuary, 1978). In 1980 some 15 per cent of the total pre-tax income of those aged 65–74 was derived from occupational pensions, whereas for those aged 75 and over the proportion was 10 per cent (Hedström and Ringen, 1987).

Income packages in different countries
Is the mix of different sources of income received by pensioners, shown in Table 11.3, typical of other western industrial societies? Compared with the other countries listed in Table 11.2 the proportion of 65–74-year-old pensioners' income derived from earnings in Britain was lower than every country except Sweden, which has encouraged widespread early retirement (Laczko and Walker, 1985). The proportion of income from social security and other transfers was much lower, in 1980, than in Sweden and West Germany and greater than in the USA and Israel. The proportion of total income provided by occupational pensions in Britain was much larger than in Sweden and Norway, but roughly similar to the position in the other countries, except Israel. The percentage of pensioner income

derived from capital income was highest in Canada, USA and Israel and lowest in West Germany and Norway, followed by Sweden and the UK. Again, there is a clear division in the constituents of pensioner income packages between the Nordic welfare states, with their heavy reliance on transfer income, and the more mixed economies of North America and Israel, which have a greater dependence on other sources of income, particularly capital and earnings. In between, West Germany's pensioner income package is closer to the former, while Britain's is closer to the latter (Hedström and Ringen, 1987). These differences are particularly profound in the case of those aged 75 and over who are more likely than younger elderly people to be economically dependent. The fact that the Nordic welfare states have the lowest poverty rates among elderly people and inequalities between elderly people and other groups has already been reported.

THE SOCIAL CREATION OF POVERTY IN OLD AGE

The observation that elderly people are the largest group among the poor has sometimes resulted in the mistaken conclusion that old age is a *cause* of poverty. In fact, poverty in old age may be seen as one form – usually the most extreme one – of multi-faceted dependent status that most elderly people occupy (Walker, 1980; 1981; 1983). The inadequacies of explanations of this economic dependency couched in individual terms such as 'disengagement', 'frailty' or 'failing abilities' has been exposed previously (see Walker, 1981, and Chapters 2 and 10 in this volume). Rather than old age itself, it is various social policies which have combined to create, enhance or maintain economic dependency and poverty in old age. Thus, poverty in old age is primarily a function of low economic and social status *prior* to retirement and the depressed social status of the retired and secondarily, of the relatively low level of state benefits. The main elements of this structurally created dependency may be outlined (see also Chapters 2 and 10). Policies in the fields of employment and social security have been particularly influential in the production of poverty in old age.

Retirement policies

The growth of retirement and subsequently, early retirement, has ensured that an increasing proportion of elderly workers have been excluded from the labour force over the course of this century. This social process of exclusion has denied older people access to earnings and other economic, social and psychological benefits of the work place. This major social change has progressed rapidly and continues to do so. Between 1931 and 1971 the proportion of men aged 65 and over who were retired increased from under one-half to more than three-quarters and by 1986 the figure was around 94 per cent. Thus, in a relatively short space of time, 'old age' has come to be socially defined as beginning at retirement age and, whether by institutional rule or customary practice, the age at which older workers have to leave the labour force (Parker, 1980).

The operation of this social process of exclusion has been closely related to the organisation of production and the demand for labour. Accounts of the emergence of retirement and early retirement suggest that older people have, in fact, been used as a reserve army of labour, to be tapped when labour is in short supply, and to be shed when demand falls (Phillipson, 1982; Graebner, 1980; Walker, 1985). It is not that retirement has grown alongside industrialisation – large numbers of older people were economically active in all industrial societies during the first half of this century – but that changes in industrial processes and in the organisation of employment, particularly the employment of women, have been developed and managed in ways intended to exclude older workers. Work processes have been reorganised, the division of labour has increased and the labour process has been rationalised (Braverman, 1974). Various factors have combined to ensure that older workers were the most likely to be affected by these changes. For example, the influential scientific management school of thought in the USA argued that efficiency in the labour process depended on the removal of those with low levels of marginal productivity, which was crudely related to age; the historical tendency of capital to reduce its necessary labour to the minimum; the process of technological innovation and the high birth rate of the early 1960s all provided some impetus for the displacement of older workers and, where necessary, their replacement with younger ones (Walker, 1983). Finally, the advent of large-scale unemployment in the 1930s was crucial in the institutionalisation of retirement, and its return in the early 1980s has resulted in the growth of early retirement.

These main factors in the twentieth-century development of British society have combined to reduce the demand for older workers. At the same time, on the supply side, as retirement and early retirement have been encouraged by employers and the state they have been accepted as customary and have become part of trade union bargaining for improved labour conditions. Moreover, many of the changes in production processes, such as the spread of assembly-line production, have reduced the attachment of workers to employment and, together with the failure of employers and the state to improve the working conditions of many, have contributed to a desire to leave work.

This indicates that, like the experience of employment, attitudes towards retirement and the experience of retirement itself are socially divided. There are those, mainly salaried workers, who are able to choose whether to leave work at the retirement age or to leave prematurely or perhaps to work on. The proportion of self-employed people working beyond retirement age is double that of those employed by others (Walker, 1983). Then there are those, predominantly manual workers, who are effectively coerced into retirement, and sometimes early retirement, by poor working conditions, ill health, redundancy and unemployment (Palmore, 1978; Olsen and Hansen, 1981; Walker, 1985). Thus, for large numbers of older workers, poverty is created *prior* to retirement. In fact, sickness and unemployment account for nearly two-thirds of men and one-quarter of women who retire prematurely (Parker, 1980). A recent study of 'voluntary' early retirers found that two important factors were health and dissatisfaction with their job (McGoldrick and Cooper, 1980). So, for a significant proportion of older workers the retirement age is effectively lowered by unemployment, sickness or injury. As with unemployment itself, semi-skilled and unskilled workers are over-represented among the early retired (Parker, 1980). The policy of disengaging older workers prematurely from the labour force was formalised in Britain in 1977 by the introduction of the Job Release Scheme, which was 'designed to create vacancies for unemployed people by encouraging older workers to leave their jobs' (Department of Employment, 1980). Similar policies have been introduced in other countries, including France and Sweden (Laczko and Walker, 1985).

Pension policies

The corollary to this social process of exclusion from the labour force is that elderly people are heavily dependent on the state for financial support – around 90 per cent of them receive some form of social security benefit. Elderly people are, in effect, trapped in poverty by their reliance on state benefits, which have already been shown to be inadequate.

The implicit rationale, or social policy, underlying the income differential between those in employment and those dependent on state benefits is the assumption that social benefits are intended to maintain monetary incentives and the work, or rather employment, ethic. Thus, paradoxically, even those elderly people who have worked for a full term are not entitled to non-dependent status, nor, freedom from reliance on minimum subsistence income support unless it has been earned through contributions paid to a private or occupational pension while in employment. We have seen that retirement has a differential impact on elderly people – depending primarily on prior socio-economic status and the access it grants to resources which might be carried into retirement – but, in addition, because of the social limitation on the level of state pensions and other benefits for those outside the labour force, retirement imposes a lowered social status on the vast majority of elderly people in relation to younger adults in the labour market (Walker, 1980). Hence the substantial inequalities both among elderly people and between elderly people and the rest of society, which were outlined earlier.

Present pension policies have their foundations in the Beveridge report. Beveridge built on the insurance principles established by the National Insurance Act, 1911, and the Widows, Orphans and Old Age Contributory Pensions Act, 1925, rather than the non-contributory, means-tested model

provided by the 1908 Old Age Pensions Act or another more radical
alternative. This meant that pensions were not regarded as a right
but were contingent on the establishment of eligibility through the
labour market, or 'work-testing' (Shragge, 1984). Moreover, pensions
and other social security benefits were to provide only the minimum
subsistence floor specifically in order to encourage additional private
welfare provision (Beveridge, 1942). These fundamental principles, which
have guided the construction and subsequent operation of the post-war
welfare state, are enshrined in the following passage:

> Social security must be achieved by co-operation between the State and the
> individual. The State should offer security for service and contribution.
> The State in organising security should not stifle incentive, opportunity,
> responsibility; in establishing a national minimum it should leave room and
> encouragement for voluntary action by each individual to provide more than
> the minimum for himself and his family. (Beveridge, 1942, pp. 6–7)

As well as the contribution condition a second important condition
was proposed by Beveridge and institutionalised by the introduction
of the National Insurance pension in 1948; the 'retirement condition'.
Those who have built up a right to the state pension by virtue of
their contributions are only awarded their pension following formal
retirement from employment (Beveridge, 1942). The retirement condition
institutionalised the dependency relationship between elderly people,
the state and the labour market. It encouraged an end to labour force
participation and established an arbitrary age as the customary retirement
age. Ironically, Beveridge had hoped that the retirement condition would
encourage workers to defer retirement:

> Making receipt of pension conditional on retirement is not intended to
> encourage or hasten retirement. On the contrary, the conditions governing
> pension should be such as to encourage every person who can go on working
> after reaching pensionable age, to go on working and to postpone retirement
> and the claiming of pension. (Beveridge, 1942, p. 96)

But in practice, it has resulted in the adoption of the pension ages as the
retirement ages. Together with the high marginal rates of taxation levied
on pensioners who take up employment by the notorious earnings rule,
it militates against the continuation of work by elderly people. More
recently, the social security system has been used to further encourage
the disengagement of older men from the labour market by awarding the
long-term rate of supplementary benefit to those over the age of 60 who
are unemployed. Originally, this was conditional on them not registering
as unemployed.

The social security system is also one of the main mechanisms through
which women's dependence on men is enforced both prior to and after
retirement. Most women still receive pensions as dependants on their
husbands' contributions and, regardless of their age, have to wait until
he reaches 65. Although the Social Security Act 1980 contained some
improvements in the status of women these are only a tentative first

step towards 'similar treatment' for women and men rather than equal treatment. Furthermore, until equality between men and women is established in the labour market it is unlikely to be realised in a social security system which is geared to the labour market. Elderly married women are less likely than men to receive a NI retirement pension in their own right and are overwhelmingly less likely to receive a pension from a former employer. As we have seen, older women are much more likely than men to live in poverty.

Subsistence principle in the state pension policy
The financing of state pensions and particularly the size of the Exchequer contribution has been the overriding political issue in post-war pensions policy. It was dominant too in the preparation of the Beveridge report. Many of the assumptions that Beveridge brought to his study of social insurance were based not on considerations of social welfare 'but on the prejudices of official economic opinion' and 'the notions of financial soundness which prevailed in Treasury circles' (Kincaid, 1973). Beveridge and the Treasury officials who scrutinised his proposals had intended that retirement pensions and other social security benefits should be self-financing according to actuarially sound insurance principles. This was to be achieved and a reserve fund established by phasing in the scheme over 21 years. However, the public pressure for retirement pensions was enormous and the 1946 National Insurance Act allowed the claiming of full benefits from the outset of the scheme (Shragge, 1984). Thus, rather than being based on the insurance principle the NI pension has always been a 'pay-as-you-go' scheme in which those in employment support those drawing pensions. The immediate post-war period also saw a sharp diminution in the Exchequer contribution to social security, from 24 per cent of total receipts in 1950 to 12 per cent in 1953 (George, 1968). But it was to rise subsequently in the 1950s as the Beveridge principle of financing pensions began to collapse and the national insurance fund went into deficit.

The response of the government to the rising costs of pensions in the early years of the scheme and worries about the projected increases in the numbers of pensioners was to set up the Phillips Committee in July 1953, 'to review the economic and financial problems involved in providing for old age, having regard to the prospective increase in the numbers of aged' (Phillips Committee, 1954, p. 1). Like the subsequent Inquiry into Provision for Retirement 1983–85, set up 30 years later as part of the general social security review (DHSS, 1985a), the Phillips Committee was primarily concerned with the long-term growth in demand for and cost of pensions and the capacity of the working population to finance the scheme. The Committee's report reaffirmed the importance of individual contributions as a measure of 'social discipline' and, among other things, recommended an increase in retirement age to 68 for men and 63 for women. In addition, while not challenging the operation of the 1946

Act, the Committee proposed a limitation on the Exchequer contribution, support for the development of occupational pensions and restriction of the Beveridge principle (if not the practice) that NI pensions should provide a subsistence minimum:

> A contributions scheme cannot be expected to provide a rate of pension which would enable everybody, whatever his circumstances, to live without other means, such a pension rate would be an extravagant use of national resources. (Phillips Committee, 1954, p. 81)

Once older people had worked a full course and fulfilled 'the obligation of service' they were to receive 'an adequate income to maintain them' (Beveridge, 1942, p. 92). In fact, this has never been the case. Partly because of the Treasury principle of 'financial soundness' accepted by Beveridge the NI pension was set at a level of bare subsistence rather than adequate maintenance. Beveridge drew on the work of Booth (1889) and Rowntree (1901) and, in turn, nutritionalists, such as Atwater in the United States, on whose work Rowntree's calculations of food needs were based. Furthermore, Beveridge allowed only 75 per cent of the scientific food value necessary for 'physical efficiency' for old-age pensioners, plus 10 per cent for special food needs. The amounts required for clothing and housing were also set lower than those of a person of working age (Shragge, 1984).

Thus, the definition of need in old age adopted by Beveridge and followed by the 1945 Labour government and all subsequent governments was an extremely conservative, not to say mean, one. Despite longstanding and widespread criticism of the pseudo-scientific basis of the calculations that Beveridge used for his assessment of food and other needs – not least that they bore little resemblance to what people actually spend their money on – they have influenced the levels of pensions and other social security benefits ever since. Not surprisingly, therefore, the single person's pension has remained at around only one-fifth of average gross earnings over the whole of the post-war period.

Further evidence may be adduced to show that the level of the state pension is low in both historical and comparative terms. When pensions are compared with the incomes of non-elderly people, post-war pensions are demonstrably lower than the relative values of pensions in the mid-nineteenth century, which were equivalent to two-thirds or more of the incomes of non-elderly working-class adults. Thus, in Thomson's words:

> In terms of pensions, an aged pensioner of mid-nineteenth century Britain was far more favoured under the 'harsh' New Poor Law than has been any twentieth century pensioner of the state'. (1984, p. 453)

Furthermore, the basic pension is considerably lower relative to earnings than those provided by most other EC countries. Thus, for example, the single man's basic pension was 23 per cent of average earnings in 1980 compared with 41 per cent in the Netherlands, 36 per cent in West

Germany and 32 per cent in France (Walker et al, 1983). This helps to explain Britain's relatively poor provision for pensioners, shown in Table 11.2, and suggests that the proposition that the country cannot afford higher pensions is a political rather than an economic judgement.

This review of employment and pension policies indicates that the economic dependency of elderly people – and therefore their poverty – has been socially engineered in order to facilitate the removal of older workers from the labour force. As a matter of social and economic policy state pensions have been set at a bare subsistence level. In the interests of narrow financial efficiency and increased profitability mass superannuation has been managed through retirement, early retirement and unemployment among older people. Age-restrictive social policies have been used by the state both to exclude older workers from the labour force and to legitimate that exclusion through retirement. This socially reconstructed relationship between age and the labour market has not only been the primary cause of poverty in old age, but has also formed the basis for the spread of a more general dependency among elderly people as well as ageism in many aspects of public policy and wider social attitudes.

CONCLUSION

The concentration of poverty and deprivation in old age has persisted despite social recognition for over a century and more than 30 years of welfare state provision. The recurrent issue of pension reform has always been dominated by concern with a narrow conception of cost: direct Exchequer expenditure. The fact that the needs of elderly people have rarely been central to discussions of pensions reform is a major failing of post-war social policy. Part of the problem is that pension policies themselves have been employed to regulate the economy and labour force rather than to meet need. The main lesson from successive pension reforms is that unless there is a fundamental restructuring of the relationship between age and the labour market, on the one hand, and the incomes of pensioners and those in employment, on the other, poverty will persist into the next century and beyond. Resources have been available to overcome poverty in old age for at least the last 40 years but the political will has not.

FURTHER READING

Hannah, L. (1986) *Inventing Retirement: The Development of Occupational Pensions in Britain.* Cambridge, CUP.

Phillipson, C. and Walker, A. (1986) (eds) *Ageing and Social Policy.* Gower, London

Shragge, E. (1984) *Pensions Policy in Britain.* Routledge and Kegan Paul, London.

Walker, A. (1980) 'The Social Creation of Poverty and Dependency in Old Age' *Journal of Social Policy*, 9, 49–75.

12

IMAGES OF AGEING

Mike Featherstone and Mike Hepworth

In this chapter we will discuss the significance of images of ageing in understanding the position of elderly people in British society. When we speak about images we are primarily concerned with public images: the representations which are found documented in historical sources and currently in use in the popular media. The emphasis, then, is on the ways of seeing, defining and describing ageing, which are and have been in public circulation and not on the private and unspoken thoughts of individuals.

One of the main concerns of this chapter is to highlight the considerable tension that can be generated between public images and the personal perceptions of elderly people. This tension is also to be found echoed in a more widespread tension existing in society between images and social realities. There is the danger that we will mistake images for reality and use images as direct evidence of the actual social relationships and activities which occur in everyday life. Yet images and reality clearly interrelate, and images, representations and classificatory schemes are clearly in operation at the everyday level. Therefore, we have to be careful how we treat evidence drawn from images. We have to ask questions about what images can tell us about the actual everyday practices which occurred at the time they were created, as well as the subsequent impact images may have had in creating an enduring tradition which is handed down to us and acts as a significant reference point in our daily lives. It is not sufficient to say, for example, that our contemporary images of ageing are drawn from Ancient Judaism (the reverence for the old, white-bearded biblical prophet) and Ancient Greece (the idealisation of youthful grace and beauty) – images which are clearly contradictory and according to Slater (1963) the source of the ambivalence towards ageing within our culture.

Rather than accept images as accurate descriptions, or ciphers for the attitudes and behaviour of elderly people, we need to look at the way in which images, both positive and negative, are used by men and women in their daily lives. We have to raise questions such as 'How are images used by different groups and classes?', 'Do different groups and classes operate with different images?', 'Which groups create, circulate and have an interest in the widespread adoption of new images?', 'How do images as power resources relate to other power resources used by groups at different phases in history?', 'How does our self-image relate to the social image, the image which others foster onto us, as people age?'. Of course, it is beyond the scope of this chapter to provide other than rudimentary answers to such questions and we are very conscious of the fragmentary evidence and the preliminary nature of research into the imagery of ageing in Britain. We do, however, seek to outline the basis for a sociological perspective and would argue that any attempt to understand the position of elderly people in Britain today has to take into account the role of images.

In order to understand the nature and effectiveness of the images of ageing which operate in contemporary British society we will adopt a broad historical viewpoint. We compare the images of the pre-industrial period, which for convenience we label 'traditional images', with those which emerged out of the processes of industrialisation and modernisation in the nineteenth century which we have called 'modern images'. In the concluding section we sketch out some of the tensions between current images of ageing, tensions which we consider will become significant in the future. However, we begin by making a number of points about the general role of images in everyday life and in particular about images of the ageing body.

IMAGES IN EVERYDAY LIFE

Images and the human body

Human beings share with other living species an embodied existence involving birth, growth, maturation and death. Yet unlike other species they have a biologically determined relative dissociation from biological mechanisms. That is, while human beings in common with other species possess equipment for unlearned and learned behaviour, in the case of humans the balance between unlearned and learned behaviour is more strongly tipped towards the latter, and indeed their very survival depends on their capacity to communicate with learned forms of knowledge. To speak of human beings as symbol-producing or knowledge-producing beings then is to emphasise their natural disposition to learn, to produce signs, signals and develop language to communicate with each other (Elias, 1978; 1987). Yet in emphasising the symbolic dimension we should not forget the body for in most forms of oral communication the co-presence of the other speaker or listener acts as a guide to the clarification of meaning through the capacity to observe bodily signals and facial expressions.

Images are a particular type of symbolic medium which we use in communication. The images of ageing which circulate in a society usually draw upon public representations of the body such as paintings, drawings, sculptures, photographs and films. The general tangibility and mimetic quality of such representations and the associated mental pictures we carry around with us clearly have an immediacy and facticity which make us think that they are real and self-evident, and ignore the fact that such representations are only able to function within a symbolic order. We make sense of them in terms of the language-based interpretive schemes and classificatory systems which operate within a given context. In different contexts, or in the social life of other groups, the same representations of the body may be given a very different meaning. For example, the wrinkle which appears on the face of a Chinese grandmother and is apparently greeted with joy by granddaughters is a sign of higher status. This may become redefined in other cultural contexts as a sign of bodily and moral decay, a sign of impending low status. Likewise, feminists today are trying to change the way we see a woman's body so that we can see it as other than a sex-object. Images of human bodies often appear self-evident in their meaning, yet their virtual facticity and tangibility depends upon the use of particular sets of everyday practical knowledge and classificatory schemes which direct us towards a specific meaning.

While images function to call forth a particular meaning in relation to the context in which they are used, they are in addition symbolically charged to evoke appropriate emotions and feeling tones. Images are often constructed in sets of polarities (heaven and hell, God and the devil, etc). When we think of images of ageing bodies, it is evident that in our culture images of youth become positively charged with connotations of beauty, energy, grace, moral fortitude and optimism, whereas images of old age become negatively charged with ugliness, idleness, degeneration and moral failure. These symbolic polarities are never final and fixed, but change historically as groups struggle to define and reconstruct images to suit their own particular purposes and advantages. This emotional weighting of images, however, does not preclude the possibility of the construction of images in a more measured and detached manner. Scientific images are conceptual schemes in which the intent is to cleanse, as far as possible, the emotional charge from the representation to achieve a higher degree of detached description and analytic clarity. Nevertheless, these like any other social images are socially constructed.

We live in a world in which everyday classificatory schemes and images are taken-for-granted forms of knowledge. These function as guides to help us to know how to act and feel. Such conceptual frameworks and images also dictate our sense of the appropriate use of the body, the style of presentation, demeanour, bearing, stance and way of sitting, as well as the appropriate taste and distaste for certain types of food, sport or exercise. Particular body images under certain circumstances may become not only points of reference in classifying other people, but actually become embodied and incorporated as people seek to mimic a particular body image or ideal. The generationally bounded nature of the body images adopted – in ways of talking, gesturing, sitting, walking, looking etc, as well as in body shape and ways of dressing – are to a large extent formed by the time youth is reached and are in many instances never entirely lost as one moves through life. The datedness of a particular body image is particularly apparent in old people, who possess fewer resources and motivation to modify their image in line with the ones which are currently enjoying popularity. Hence the very embodiment of a particular 'dated' body image can itself devalue the old person's social image independently of the perception of the actual physical effects of ageing manifest in such features as sagging flesh, wrinkling, greying hair or restricted movement, and further help to reinforce the negative stereotype.

Stereotypes in old age

In the literature of social gerontology the public images of the ageing body are usually referred to as 'stereotypes'. For example, in Barrow's textbook *Ageing, the Individual, and Society* (1986) there is a chapter on 'Stereotypes and Images' which, as is usual at the present time, draws particular attention to the perpetuation of negative stereotypes of ageing in the popular media. Similar arguments are advanced by Norman (1987) in her discussion paper on attitudes to ageing and elderly people. Terms such as 'senile', she notes, are openly derogatory but:

> still worse is the common use of 'geriatric' as a noun to describe a frail old person instead of its correct use as the branch of medical science concerned with old people and their illnesses. We do not call a woman who has just had a hysterectomy 'an obstetric' or a sick child 'a paediatric'. (Norman, 1987, p. 4)

This view, that many of the images we use to describe ageing and elderly people are in fact negative stereotypes, is always accompanied by the warning that such stereotypes are damaging to our relationships with older people. They represent a form of symbolic stigmatisation which finds its way through to practical everyday action, thereby giving meaning (in this example a negative meaning) to the experience of growing old. Ageing, then, is not reducible to biological processes of physical decline which take place in some vacuum sealed off from social life, but is shaped or constructed in terms of the symbolic imagery available to us at any given time. This is the reason social gerontologists are so concerned about the social and personal implications of words such as 'wrinkly', 'crumbly', 'gaga', 'hag', 'crone', 'witch', 'biddy', 'fogey', and of course 'geriatric'. It is not true, they imply, that 'words can never hurt us'.

The power of negative stereotypes of ageing to stigmatise is clearly grounded in the essentially symbolic nature of social life to which we have referred. The anxiety occasioned by such stereotypes is an acknowledgement of their central role in social life; we are highly dependent on stereotypes as a means of communication (Lippman, 1922). We do not, said Lippman, see first and then define but *define first and then see*. Stereotypes precede and shape our perceptions and are an inescapable consequence of living in a complex world in which a bewildering profusion of messages is generated. For Lippman, stereotypes are not inevitably negative, as the popular usage of the term often implies. They are simply a basic means of communication which help us to order potentially confusing experiences and impose some descriptive unity on them. The role of stereotypes is to make fast, firm and separate what is in reality fluid and changing (Dyer, 1979).

As reference points for human interaction, images of ageing are stereotypes which we use to categorise and thus identify a wide diversity of individual persons in terms of socially prescribed age categories. In earlier chapters it has been emphasised that ageing is a highly individual process. Although general patterns of physical change can be detected, the actual ways in which people age are determined by their specific circumstances and a host of other factors. This is one reason why the study of ageing is usually described as 'interdisciplinary' (Gilmore et al, 1981). Such categories have enormous convenience value since they help to simplify what is otherwise complex and often confusing, both to academics involved in the study of ageing and to everyone in their dealings with older people. The problem is, of course, that they do not do full justice to any particular individual who is labelled as 'ageing' or 'old' in terms of his or her observable appearance and behaviour. Thus, in Fairhurst's study of certain aspects of the ageing process as described by a number of elderly interviewees in Manchester, one man summed up the situation as follows:

> I think you'll find yourself that you reach a stage where you don't grow any older inside. Outside you do but you're perpetually 28 or something or whatever it may be – wherever you stop'. (Fairhurst, 1982)

In her introduction to her book about the lives of older women Hemmings writes:

> In my experience, younger women with an awareness of ageism tend to speak of all of us over about 45 as older women. However, women of 80 have daughters of 60, and granddaughters in their 40s. Lumping us all together in one generation means we all lose out. (Hemmings, 1985, pp. 2–3)

The perpetual tension between social categories based on generalisations about ageing and the actual personal experience of ageing in its diversity is of constant concern and increasingly so for those who work with older people. In recognition of this tension some writers find it easier to describe the ageing process as a mask or disguise which, like some trick of the make-up artist's craft, conceals, layer after layer, the timeless human personality beneath. When asked to describe at the age of 79 what it felt like to be old, the celebrated author J.B. Priestley replied:

> It is as though walking down Shaftesbury Avenue as a fairly young man, I

was suddenly kidnapped, rushed into a theatre and made to don the grey hair, the wrinkles and the other attributes of age, then wheeled on stage. Behind the appearance of age I am the same person, with the same thoughts, as when I was younger. (Puner, 1978, p. 7)

Priestley's reference to the 'appearance of age' reminds us of the primary role of physical appearance in the social construction of age categories; an importance which receives confirmation from psychologists researching the influence of appearance on human relationships (Wells, 1983; Hatfield and Sprecher, 1986; Pennington, 1986). As we shall see later, our concern with physical appearance and especially the 'appearance of age' is very much a preoccupation of modern times but it does, for all that, have deep roots in the past.

In his study of the human face, Liggett asserts that amongst the most interesting characteristics of the human face are:

those produced simply by the passage of time itself. Many of the changes brought about by age such as greying of hair and wrinkling of skin, are easy enough to see .... With loss of elasticity there comes an increasing tendency for the skin to crease under the influence of the muscles, usually in the same place, forming wrinkles and coarse folds or *rugae*, which can neither be prevented nor removed, except perhaps by surgery. Unlike some of the other marks of age, such as greying hair, they defy all attempts at concealment. As the Spanish proverb has it, 'the hair deceives, the wrinkles undeceive'. (Liggett, 1974, pp. 23–24)

As Liggett's observations indicate, it is not the wrinkles as such which are significant but the fact that they make it very difficult for people to conceal the fact that they have lived for quite a long time or that they *appear* to have lived for quite a long time, which is just as bad. They are a mask which cannot be removed: any connection they may have with the individual's personal sense of identity is the result of the ways other people react to changes in facial appearance and the social category they imply. In her trenchant account of the effects of ageing in the United States, MacDonald (1984) describes the effects of wrinkling and other outwardly visible changes associated with ageing as a process of transformation whereby women become socially invisible. On the personal level, she writes 'I lived with the never-knowing when people would turn away from me ... because they had identified me as old' (MacDonald, 1984, p. 5). When she was out with her younger friend Rich, the latter noticed significant differences in social interaction:

It is I who receive the eye contact; questions are less often addressed to her. When we go to a hardware store and Barbara asks about something, the man behind the counter looks at me when he responds. (MacDonald, 1984, p. 11)

The body, which is easier to conceal from public gaze, also reveals ineradicable evidence of the march of time. This evidence has a long history of disenchantment. There does not appear to have been a time in western culture when the sight of the naked ageing body has given much pleasure. In her study of *The Nude Male*, Walters (1978) traces the shame of the ageing body back to the ancient Greeks. Their images of the body do not include an association between bodily decrepitude and beauty:

> Homer's Priam, foreseeing the fall of Troy exclaims that the most pitiful sight of all is the body of an old man who is 'dead and down, and the dogs mutilate the grey head and the grey beard and the parts that are secret'. The fall of a young warrior is less sad, for 'though dead, still all that shows about him is beautiful', and he will be remembered so. (Walters, 1978, p. 45)

In the history of art 'the naked body has been given memorable shapes' in order to 'communicate certain ideas or states of feeling' (Clark, 1960, p. 335). In these representations of either men or women, age is not generally an object of great respect. Rarely, writes Clark, is the aged body 'grandly portrayed'. When artists have created pictorial images of the ageing body which are close to reality they have usually been motivated by the desire to evoke pity, curiosity, repulsion, stoicism, or only occasionally, as in the case of Rembrandt, dignity and nobility. It is scarcely surprising, therefore, that in Middleton's novel, *An After Dinner's Sleep*, when the elderly hero scrutinises his body after getting out of his bath he is relieved to discover he is not in too bad a shape:

> His body had not sagged into blubber; the hair on his chest, though grey, grew darker than that on his scalp. He turned his head, trunk to assess legs and buttocks, and not dissatisfied plugged in his razor. The mirror light wickedly etched wrinkles round his eyes, ruined his forehead, but his skin this morning at least looked healthy. He dragged on gardening clothes, and singing 'Prepare thyself, Zion', ran out to the kitchen, to a large mug of coffee and a folded *Guardian*, deciding that he was pleased with his life or himself. (Middleton, 1987, pp. 80–81)

The tragic belief that youth will fade and beauty is fleeting is not only borne out of experience, but stems from the traditional symbolic equation between youth, beauty and goodness. As a result of this equation, the outward and visible signs of ageing on face and body have been given a meaning which is essentially ambivalent. On the one hand ageing has never been entirely devalued. On the other hand there is not much evidence that ageing in general (as distinct from specifically honoured elderly individuals) has been regarded as a welcome biological process, either socially or personally. As the increasing quantity of research into the position of women and the social construction of gender forcibly reminds us, a stereotypically attractive physical appearance is a source of power for women who are fortunate enough to resemble the ideal but one which is destined to wane (Lakoff and Scherr, 1984). Women's power is based almost entirely on physical beauty and unlike the power of men, which is based on more enduring foundations such as wealth and occupation, it is bound to fade away. The situation of ageing and elderly women is seen to be less ambivalent than that of men (who don't of course live so long) because of their greater dependence on good looks. This state of affairs is defined by Sontag (1978) as 'the double standard of ageing'.

We shall return later to the important issue of the double standard; for the moment we wish only to underline the contribution of the particular symbolic meanings given to the changing human face and body by the images of ageing which occur with the greatest frequency in our society. In the course of their construction these images have helped to create the distance often detected between the personal experience of ageing and the stereotype or age category which is so forcefully described as a mask or disguise (Featherstone and Hepworth, 1989).

But to describe the ageing process as a mask which conceals the enduring and more youthful self is not quite the same as saying that people attempt to disguise their age. Ageing as a disguise in the sense we have used the term may be regarded as a tragic destiny, what Gonzalez-Crussi (1987) defines as 'the pangs of progressive bodily ruin', and it is one which contemporary images of ageing are increasingly trying to disregard. The struggle in today's treatment of elderly people is to fight to rediscover or rescue the person partially or totally concealed beneath the overlay of physical change brought on by that most modern enemy of the human race: chronological time.

The image of senility
Earlier we described the popular usage of the term 'geriatric' as a deroga-tory stereotype reflecting the deleterious effects on social competence which can accompany the process of physical ageing. The image of 'senility' is a frightening vision of dribbling, drooling, incontinence, an absence of physical coordination and the inability to comport oneself or to communicate coherently. It is the image of one who is less than fully human (Goffman, 1968). It is, thus stereotyped, a nightmarish vision:

> Oh God, I know my mind is going. I cannot stem the tide of sleeplessness and sorrow. Keep me safe keep me safe. I beseech thee that I may not live long to be a burden to those I love so dearly. I have tried to see my way but I have failed all round. I know nothing, I understand nothing. I only know that I want to do right, and some time to meet the dear ones again whom I have loved so much. This is an agony far far worse than death yet I know I must cling to life however useless and broken it is. (Jalland and Hooper, 1986, p. 302)

In this image of senility, or the terror of it, public and private visions of ageing have a poignant meeting place. We dread living on in a state of abject physical impairment yet somehow consciously aware of our original selves and the involuntary puppets we have ironically become. In this prevailing imagery, old age understood as senility is not so much a mask or disguise as an 'iron cage'. The self becomes imprisoned in a body which is no longer physically able to express its true identity; the afflicted individual has lost his or her power of self-control: of being able to express the self-identity that others have come over the years to expect. This loss of the ability to live up to the expectations we are aware others have of us is described with great regret in Gathorne-Hardy's (1987) account of the last years of the author Gerald Brenan who died in Spain aged over 90 years. Brenan was a highly intelligent man whose independent and vital identity is described as being progressively masked by the restrictions and impediments of illness and deep old age. Towards the end he is treated by the servant girls:

> like an object, almost with contempt. He no longer gets up to eat but is spoon-fed in his chair. He asked for wine but was briskly forbidden it. After lunch they simply picked him up like a bundle of sticks and half-carried, half-dragged him out... Nicky said it was as though he *had* died and left behind that sad, tortured, mumbling husk. One could hardly have contrived a more terrible and lonely end if one had hated him and been able to dictate it. (Gathorne-Hardy, 1987, p. 22)

This fearful image of senility as the end result of the ageing process reflects our dread of any progressive decline in our ability to control our bodies through which we express our relationships with others. We become unable to disguise the fact that we are getting older; we are in the end incapable of resisting the age-related categories society has stored up for us. In their investigation of 100 local authority residential homes, Willcocks et al (1987) show how the transition from one's own home to residential accommodation can swiftly undermine or remove completely the social and territorial props old people often utilise to maintain an independent identity. The very privacy of the British home ensures that elderly people can conceal to some extent their incapacities and limitations. Familiarity with the arrangement of the furniture and the general territory of the house can compensate an older man or woman for sensory loss and confers a power over his or her immediate environment which disappears very often with removal to a 'home'. In their own homes, where the majority of elderly people in Britain live until the end of their days, they are much more likely to be able to fulfil the expectation of an age-conscious society that 'older people should feel obliged to mask partial frailties for fear of being judged totally incapable of managing daily life' (Willcocks et al, 1987, pp. 7–8).

Reference to the social obligation of masking the frailties associated with ageing suggests that senility is itself a social construct. Any social arrangements which undermine the ability to express an independent self bring the person concerned progressively closer to the public image; 'senile'. In this sense we are looking at a self-fulfilling prophecy. The research to which we have just referred shows how it is possible for what Bromley (1977) has memorably described as the 'aversive properties of the aged person' to become more apparent in the public setting of the residential local authority home where it is impossible to conceal one's weaknesses and avoid relentless if well-meaning scrutiny. Commenting on the factors which influence our impressions of elderly people Bromley observes that it is:

> common knowledge that for many younger people, the physical appearance and behaviour of some aged persons, especially deteriorated patients in departments of geriatric medicine, have 'aversive' properties. The effects

of these characteristics may be aggravated by the unpleasant features of an institutional environment. Aged people, in other words, are often perceived as unpleasant or frightening or, at best, as pitiful. Fear, disgust, rejection and avoidance are not uncommon reactions. (Bromley, 1978, pp. 22–23)

The institutional environment, Bromley argues, constitutes a social setting where the effects of ageing on a person's expressive behaviour are accentuated and made more sharply reflexive. Their expressive weaknesses become much more apparent and because such weaknesses make interaction more difficult have the effect of masking the identity of the person who may be struggling to communicate 'normal' desires and feelings. Relevant to our concern with the role of images in understanding the ageing process is Bromley's suggestion that our first impressions of a person's expressive behaviour are important. These include:

1. a decline in spontaneity and response of posture, gesture, facial expression and eye contact which slow down interaction so that a younger person feels that communication is breaking down;
2. reduced ability to keep pace with the rapidity of the expressive behaviour of persons younger than themselves and difficulties in communicating when either misunderstand;
3. slower reactions which reduce sensitivity to social signals and which reflexively produce alterations in self-concept;
4. a reduction in mobility and sitting posture which in turn affects the range of expressive behaviours open to an older person, less control over his or her position and distance in interpersonal interaction.

The result of these limitations is that an older person becomes relatively isolated from normal interaction with inevitable consequences for the way he or she is perceived by those whose expressive skills are not impaired. Impaired social skills do not qualify a person for acceptance as a stereotypical 'normal'. An extra effort has to be made by all parties to the interaction to bring the normality of the problematic individual to light: to penetrate, as it were, the disguise. Those elderly patients who are seen to possess 'aversive properties' have lost the highly valued attributes of acceptable physical appearance, social skills, independence and expressive competence. As Bromley writes:

> In the crude cost-benefit terms of social exchange theory, the elderly patient may seem to have little or nothing to give in exchange for any services rendered by a younger person, and he is costly for the younger person to interact with. (Bromley, 1978, p. 26)

This situation is reproduced in its essentials in the film *No Surrender* where a party of grossly impaired elderly patients is taken into a Liverpool nightclub to participate in a New Year's Eve celebration. The impact of this visit is such that several of the younger (though not much younger) visitors are provoked to aggressive or tearful resentment of the slovenly and repulsive behaviour of the patients: 'Is this the future?' asks one active and still physically combative man in late-middle life; whilst an elderly woman in a state of near collapse moans 'I don't want to end up like that', demanding that the patients be taken away and hidden from sight.

It should now be apparent that if we are to describe ageing and old age we must use symbolic evaluations of the appearance and behaviour we are trying to define. In his sociological analysis of Alzheimer's disease, Gubrium (1986) shows how the behavioural changes associated with senile dementia (confusion, forgetfulness, lapses of attention, speech impairment and other reductions in function, aggressiveness, unwelcome sexual behaviour, loss of bladder and bowel control) are very similar to those associated with 'normal ageing'. In other words, diagnostic techniques are not yet sufficiently precise to be absolutely certain that the cause of disturbing behaviour in many older people is a number of pathological changes in the brain resulting from an identifiable disease rather than the ultimately 'natural' or 'normal' and unavoidable process of growing old. According to Gubrium, the whole issue is complicated by the desire to see certain of the symptoms of ageing as the product of a curable disease. It is hoped that one day research will eliminate senility which has nothing much to do with growing older.

Once again the prevailing image is that of the mask. Caregivers are advised by experts on Alzheimer's disease to struggle to discover signs of the original loved one behind the mask of senile dementia. The symbolic meaning of the body and behaviour must be carefully interpreted and reconstructed to penetrate the disguise of disease which one day, with much more research, will be curable. In common with what are seen to be the more 'normal' processes of ageing which leave individuals relatively unimpaired, Alzheimer's disease has its celebrities and exemplars. One of the most prominent of these is the late film star, Rita Hayworth, whose daughter Yasmin Khan became a key figure in the Alzheimer's movement in America. Gubrium quotes extensively from an article by Rosemary Santini and Katherine Barrett for the *Ladies' Home Journal*, January 1983, entitled 'The Tragedy of Rita Hayworth'.

Their story of Rita Hayworth's decline is accompanied by 'before and after' photographs showing the nightmarish depredations of the disease on outward appearance and demeanour. In the 'after' photograph of the star she appears to be 'an elderly, disheveled woman .... glassy-eyed and pathetic'. Occasionally her daughter catches fleeting glimpses of her mother's former self: her eyes stare past her daughter. They are clouded and uncomprehending. '"It's so hard to know what she's feeling, what's going on inside' Yasmin Khan says softly. 'I don't know what she can understand but there are fleeting moments when I am sure she's at least somewhat aware"'. (Gubrium, 1986, p. 136)

The image of the mask or disguise which is involuntarily assumed by many of us as we get older takes us to the heart of the social construction of ageing which involves a tension or balance of power between the individual and society. Skinner writes:

> Someone has said that if you want to know what it feels like to be old, you
> should smear dirt on your glasses, stuff cotton in your ears, put on heavy
> shoes that are too big for you, and wear gloves; then try to spend the day in
> a normal way. (Skinner and Vaughan, 1983, p. 38)

This is a deliberate overstatement of the difficulties facing many people
who are old but it does serve to highlight the struggle to avoid negative
stereotyping and loss of independent identity with which we are confronted as we gradually get older.

The images with which we struggle do not have a fixed shape or meaning; they change over the years, and can be manipulated and modified
within certain limits. We may be constrained by meaning but the meanings
are much more flexible than we sometimes imagine. In the sections which
follow we take a closer look at the prevailing meanings of ageing and
old age as the available evidence suggests they have emerged in Britain.

But before we move on to our examination of the central characteristics
of traditional and modern images of ageing, a final word of caution
is in order. Until recently in Britain the images of ageing were white.
Ethnicity was not an issue. Indeed, even in an ethnically plural society
such as the United States, it is only during the last decade or so that
social gerontologists have begun to 'accumulate a body of scientific
generalisations concerning ethnicity as a mediator in problems of ageing'
(Bengston, 1979, p. 10). Bengston further observes:

> Practitioners and policymakers have only recently begun to formulate
> programmes reflecting the service implications of ethnic contrasts among
> elderly Americans. Criticisms are raised frequently to the effect that both
> research and policy are insensitive, and therefore ultimately irrelevant, to cur-
> rent realities of ethnic differences amongst the aged. (Bengston, 1979, p. 10)

Times are changing in Britain too, and there are clear signs that our
images of ageing are gradually becoming enriched by accounts of the
experience of ageing from differing ethnic backgrounds. Ethnicity is now
an issue for social gerontologists in Britain as Bornat et al (1985) point
out in their *Manifesto for Old Age*. Personal accounts of the experience
of ageing include Asian women (Ford and Sinclair, 1987) and women
who have settled in Britain from Jamaica, India and Nazi Germany
(Hemmings, 1985).

TRADITIONAL IMAGES

Until comparatively recently there was a distinct tendency for images of
ageing to be blurred by a nostalgically romantic view of Britain's past
where the old were venerated for their skills and wisdom. The notion
of the 'good old days' has distorted our perceptions not only of the
treatment of elderly people in the past but also of our treatment and
attitudes in contemporary society (Laslett, 1977). We have already seen
that there is little evidence from the history of art that the naked ageing
body has been portrayed as a desirable end. We can add to this reflection

the general belief amongst historians that there was no 'golden age' of ageing (Quadagno, 1982). Those facial and bodily changes which give an aged appearance have never been venerated in themselves; the main source of reverence of elderly people in pre-industrial Britain appears to have been wealth and power (Thomas, 1976; MacFarlane, 1986).

With diminished resources of physical strength, money and social influence the ageing process left many who survived into old age totally dependent on the goodwill and charity of family or neighbours. Although, as MacFarlane (1986) shows in his study of the period 1300 to 1840, there were ideals of charitable Christian duty towards elderly people, in practice men and women who had made little provision for an independent old age could find themselves neglected and even despised. The clear message to elderly individuals was: do not lose control of your resources. Thomas (1976) notes that the ongoing process of social change tends not to improve relationships between younger and older generations. On conditions of conflicting beliefs and social change, he writes:

> old age could never in itself command respect. If some of the elderly retained authority, it was because of the material resources at their disposal. 'Old people commonly are despised' said Richard Steele, adding the significant qualification, 'especially when they are not supported with good estates'. The old man sitting at the fireplace was disregarded, but if he 'hath estate of his own to maintain himself and to pleasure his children, oh, then ... his age is honoured, his person is reverenced, his counsel is sought, his voice is obeyed'. (Thomas, 1976, pp. 247–248)

What is clear, then, is that despite the images of authoritative and respected old age in pre-industrial Britain, a society where in *theory* elderly people enjoyed power and control over younger people, the stigmatisation of old age was in *practice* a familiar feature of everyday life. To quote once again from Thomas:

> 'For any to have their understanding good, their memories and sense tolerable, their conversation acceptable, their relations kind and respectful ... this' thought John Shower in 1698, 'is a rare case and happens seldom to old people'. The verbal prosecution of the elderly is explicit in proverbial lore about old trots and old shrews: there was no fool like an old fool and nothing worse than an 'old woman'. Schoolmasters constantly forbade their charges to mock the elderly, but the effect of such prohibitions must have been diminished by the presence in Tudor textbooks of such sentences for translation as 'this dotard waseth a child again'. (Thomas, 1976, pp. 245–246)

The concept of senility as the ultimate disqualification from full social acceptability has thus deep roots in Britain's cultural history. Its images can be detected long before the emergence of geriatric medicine in the closing years of the nineteenth century.

Indeed, as Haynes (1963) has shown in her study of images of ageing in classical Rome:

> old age was felt to be a burdensome stage rather than a blessing in a man's

life, for it brought not only the loss of health but also, very often, a weakening of a man's mental powers. (Haynes, 1963, pp. 34–35)

The men whose names have been handed down to us through the ages as exemplars of a serene and pleasurable old age:

> lived a comfortable life in their villas, which overflowed with costly books, statues, and pictures, were attended by a staff of servants, and visited daily by a number of cheerful friends. They spent the days of their old age much in the same manner the upper class old men live today in Palm Springs, St Moritz, or at the French Riviera. (Haynes, 1963, p. 35)

Images of what we might now call 'successful ageing' as recorded in Cicero's classic *De Senectute* (44BC) are based, according to Haynes' analysis, on the lives of exceptionally advantaged people. This argument, when added to the findings of historians of pre-industrial Britain, leads us towards the generally accepted view that prior to the process of modernisation, which accelerated rapidly in the last century, ageing and its end result, old age, were defined in comparatively simple terms. Old people were those who, regardless of chronological age, had become helpless and dependent and thus appropriate objects of charity. The broken-down labourer could therefore be old at 40 and a woman of this age worn out by the physical hazards of constant childbearing could present all the outward appearance of what we nowadays describe as 'premature ageing' (Shorter, 1983).

Prior to the 'modernisation of the life cycle' (Gruman, 1978), elderly people are those who have become powerless and dependent. The belief that industrial society has destroyed the respect traditionally accorded to elderly people in more closely-knit rural society does not, as far as Britain is concerned, gain a great deal of support from historical researchers. Nor does the image of the 'golden age of senescence' (Haber, 1983) command much support from historians of ageing in the United States where the issue of the respect given to elderly people in the past, simply because they were old, is hotly contested (Fischer, 1978; Stone, 1977; Achenbaum, 1978a; Graebner, 1980; Haber, 1983) (see also Chapter 1). Without becoming entangled in the subtleties of historical periodisation, it seems fair to summarise the situation in the words of Haber:

> at best attitudes towards senescence have always been ambivalent and ... for the elderly who had lost status and power, the future was bleak. Grey hair, wrinkles, and increasing infirmities did indeed become signs of ridicule. Despite biblical prescriptions that called for respect for the old, one did not gladly pass into this stage of existence. (Haber, 1983, p. 7)

Behind the lack of reverence for frail and dependent elderly people, which is the most noteworthy feature of traditional images of ageing recorded by historians, can be detected an ambivalence towards ageing and death (Kastenbaum, 1974). Death in pre-industrial Britain was much more familiar and taken for granted than it is in modern society where it tends to be more hospitalised and concealed from public gaze (Ariès,

.1983; Elias, 1985). However, people with the necessary knowledge and resources have always struggled to avoid it. This tendency became particularly evident in the eighteenth century when confidence in medical science as a source of 'defences against death' (McManners, 1985) began to grow. In France there was, amongst educated people, an increasing optimism about medical progress reflected in 'increased concern with problems of health, a growing reluctance to accept illness fatalistically, and an intensified shrinking in face of pain' (McManners, 1985, p. 47). In Britain too the interest in health followed a similar pathway where it merged with the quest for youth and beauty. Eighteenth-century Britain was not:

> an era which revered grey hairs. Ageing Georgians did not try to impersonate long-bearded patriarchs: wigs and cosmetics, used even by men, were to keep an appearance of youth. The outlook of the Age of Reason led Henry Fox to bring up his son to believe that 'the young are always right, the old are always wrong. (Porter, 1982, p. 166)

The prevailing images of ageing in pre-industrial society do not suggest a tradition of interest in growing old or an optimistic prospect for old age. The growing eighteenth-century preoccupation with health, linked with a concern to prolong life, looks towards a youthful vision of life rather than its prolongation. The preferred choice has always been between youth and death and not youth followed by senility and decrepitude (Gruman, 1966; Kastenbaum, 1974). From this standpoint distinctions are made between differing images of ageing and embellishments added to the overall imagery we have described. Within the broad negative stereotype of ageing, therefore, a number of significant variations can be found.

Tamke's (1978) analysis of children's stories, songs and games in nineteenth-century England reveals three 'predominant models of the elderly'. These are:

1. wise and moral old people who are basically passive and do not take an active part in life. This is the quality most approved in the children's didactic literature. The dominant image is passivity and passionlessness: 'white-haired, slightly plump, and smiling' figures who behave affably towards the young and present themselves as self-supporting models of moral conduct;
2. old people whose behaviour does not conform to the above age-category and who do not, as we say, 'act their age'. These are the men, and much more frequently women, who behave out of character by attempting (usually pathetically) to disguise their ageing appearance and by refusing to act out the roles which are stereotypically prescribed for them in the literature. They are the women who have been described at least since the eighteenth century as 'mutton dressed as lamb'; and the men who usually appear as ageing dandies or beaux: caricatures of their former selves;
3. the group who are described by Tamke as the 'simply old'. These

people are neither good nor bad: they are the men and women who have been previously described as 'senile' or 'geriatric'. This category is 'rarely treated kindly: because they are old they are laughed at, their physical impairments are the subject of jests, and they are denied the rewards which are given to the young. They are punished simply because they are old' (Tamke, 1978, p. 64).

This threefold distinction between the 'good old', the 'bad old', and those who are simply 'past it' is one which has roots deep in history. It is not, as Tamke points out, that these images reflect the total reality of growing old in Victorian England, where ageing 'most often entailed economic misery'. They demonstrate values and beliefs about ageing which also are found in the adult literature of the period and which in turn have strong links with the past. In his report of research into attitudes towards ageing amongst a small sample of men and women in Aberdeen, Williams (1986) locates the positive and negative attitudes towards ageing that he discovered in a broader European tradition dating from pre-industrial times. This long history is noteworthy on two counts. First, the distinction that is made between a 'green old age' and 'the last stage of withering'. Second, between 'the honoured and despised old, the honoured retaining their faculties through wealth and moral effort, and the despised losing theirs through poverty and moral weakness' (Williams, 1986, p. 4).

These traditional images of ageing which we have attempted to sum-marise in this section make, we suggest, a valuable contribution to our understanding of ageing in our own society at the present time for three reasons. First, they show how age-related images, or stereotypes of ageing men and women, contain prescriptions for what we nowadays call 'successful' (positive) as distinct from 'unsuccessful' (negative) ageing. Second, in the shape of positive and negative stereotypes they provide us with some idea of the gap which may well exist between the private and personal experience of ageing and the public images in circulation. This gap makes it possible to see old age as a mask or disguise which conceals the 'real' or enduring self. Third, a comparison of the images of the past with those of our own time gives us a clearer idea of the flexibility of images which we noted in our opening observations on the role of symbols in social life. We can see that although the images with which we are most familiar are rooted in our history, they are also subject to change and can indeed be moulded and manipulated as part of attempts to change attitudes to ageing and old age in modern times.

It is to the effects of modernisation on the images we have defined as 'traditional' that we turn in the next section of this chapter.

MODERN IMAGES

When we look at old photographs, etchings, prints and paintings of people who are old we see the 'same grey hairs and deeply lined faces' (Achenbaum, 1978b, p. 9) with which we are familiar today. But, as Achenbaum indicates in his history of ageing in America since 1790, there are important differences in our perceptions of these images. We can summarise these with reference to the social changes which have reshaped our images of ageing in modern times.

Since the latter half of the nineteenth century there have emerged more elaborate programmes for defining the various stages of the ageing process (Haber, 1983) and categorising elderly men and women on an administrative basis (Cain, 1974; Roebuck, 1978; Roebuck and Slaughter, 1979; Graebner, 1980). There has also been the emergence of an enhanced awareness of the stigma of ageing or 'ageism' (Phillipson, 1982; Itzin, 1986). Taken together, these two developments are the products of modernisation which, although it is difficult to periodise with complete precision (Cowgill and Holmes, 1972; Achenbaum, 1978a; Gruman, 1978; Dowd, 1980), have fostered age consciousness on a scale which did not exist in the pre-industrial world.

The central values of modernity which are particularly relevant to our understanding of changes in the imagery of ageing are an emphasis on youthful energy in the service of social change. The processes of industrialisation and technological innovation which provide the dynamic thrust of modernisation, it is argued, render the skills and knowledge of the older generation redundant. As a consequence old people become devalued and irrelevant to the productive process (Dowd, 1980). It is this perspective on social change since the mid-nineteenth century which has persuaded some commentators that elderly people were much more valued in the pre-industrial world (Fischer, 1978). As a result of modernisation, individuals become increasingly age-conscious because the stereotypical age categories handed down from traditional society are expanded and developed by experts such as medical scientists, psychologists, economists, management consultants, social administrators, and others. The activities of these experts over the years, in the climate of urgent industrial and technological change, has gradually produced a shift in the imagery of ageing, which has percolated through into the wider society. This shift in the prevailing imagery of ageing in Britain follows developments elsewhere (particularly in the United States) and is a *gradual* process involving the social *reconstruction* of traditional images of ageing so that they will correspond to the demands of a more sophisticated world. The break with the past has never been complete, however, nor has the modernisation of ageing developed uniformly throughout the western world (Achenbaum, 1978a). Images of ageing in France, for example, differ in certain interesting ways from those found in Britain and elsewhere in the western world (Stearns, 1977; Zeldin, 1983).

It is also generally agreed that as far as changing images of ageing are concerned, the most significant developments have occurred since the First World War (Achenbaum, 1978b). Although the images of ageing with which we are now much more familiar began to appear in medical and other books of advice on how to age gracefully from the mid-nineteenth century in Britain and elsewhere (Haber, 1983; Featherstone and Hepworth, 1985a; 1985b), it is really during the inter-war years that the influence of consumer culture first began to make itself felt. The impact of this reconstructed public imagery was enhanced by changes in the political economy which placed a greater premium on the value of a younger or more youthful work force.

After the First World War, the introduction of new production methods and the effects of economic depression forced many workers to become unemployed. In this context of unsettling social ferment, the idea of retirement as an appropriate stage of life for ageing workers took a hold of the public imagination (Graebner, 1980; Phillipson, 1982). The concept of the old age pension had already been accepted. On humanitarian grounds and on grounds of expediency, retirement came to be seen as a 'natural' resting place, even a reward, for men in their sixties. During the inter-war years, too, women (many of whom were dependent on a male wage-earner) began to be treated as a distinct category who were increasingly seen as requiring special treatment (Roebuck and Slaughter, 1979).

Against this background, the images of retirement as a 'normal' consequence of reaching the age of 65 for men and 60 for women gradually emerged and added an extra layer to the traditional belief that as we get older we become more useless. The difference between traditional and modern images of old age as uselessness is that in pre-industrial Britain it resulted from the basic inability to work whereas in modern Britain, as elsewhere in advanced societies, it is determined by a bureaucratic decision based on fashionable stereotypes of ageing which have little to do with the actual capacity of many individuals to carry out productive activity (Cain, 1974). Such bureaucratic features of social policy towards older people, linked with the emergence of 'geriatric' medicine and gerontology during this century (Armstrong, 1983; Haber, 1983), have played an important part in the development of the age-consciousness which is evident at all 'stages' of the contemporary everyday life 'course' (Cohen, 1987).

We noted earlier that images of ageing are often ambivalent. On the one hand they express concern for the old and frail whilst on the other they reveal anxiety and even fear. This combination is especially evident in modern images where the balance between these ingredients varies in a number of interesting ways. To illustrate this more clearly we shall examine the increasing sensitivity about the effects of ageing on the face, the body, and thus on general physical appearance reflected in the following typical observations:

> I was in my sixties but my body and mind were still youthful – yet my face looked wrinkled, sagging, and old. I wanted a youthful face to match my limber body ... I now face the day with an eager new sense of joy. People say

I seem much more vivacious ... I used to be just as bright, but my wrinkles covered up the sparkle

I'm 60-seven but I feel vital – anywhere from 40-five to 50-five, but I resent being bound by the arbitrary measurement of time ... I have an appetite for life. (Hepworth and Featherstone, 1982, p. 3)

An examination of the main trends in images of ageing since the inter-war years shows that personal statements such as these are now possible because of four developments linked with the administrative and socio-economic changes we discussed earlier. First, advances in medical science have made us more aware of our bodies and the effects of the passage of time on the visible outer surfaces. We are becoming much more conscious, too, of the relationship between the internal state of our bodies and our external appearance. Second, the increase in life expectancy (see Chapter 1) means that in general we live into our sixties and seventies and are therefore more likely to die from diseases associated with old age. This probability has led to an upsurge in demand for medical treatments which will cure or control the diseases of age and a popular enthusiasm for techniques of prolonging active life and rejuvenation. Third, the impact of consumerism as a method of promoting mass-produced goods in terms of their capacity to enhance one's 'lifestyle'. This development has important implications for the social construction of ageing because these promotion techniques rely very heavily on an image of the consumer as a person with the youthful energy to carry on renewing his or her purchases; in effect to carry on consuming. The stylisation of consumer durables changes so rapidly nowadays that one can very quickly become out of date. Fourth, there is the expansion of the mass media which reproduce, stereotype, and circulate images at a faster pace and to a wider audience than ever before. It is now possible to close one's eyes and ears to images one does not appreciate but not possible to ignore the pervasive presence of images as such.

It is, perhaps, unnecessary to add that these processes do not work on our consciousness of ageing as separate and distinct forces of which we are always fully aware. These social influences merge together – sometimes subconsciously – so that the stereotypes we use in our conver-sations, our relationships with elderly people, and our attitudes towards ourselves as *we* grow older, contain mixed elements of folklore, medical knowledge, media images and the like. They act as *reference points* in our everyday lives and not as rigid programmes we are condemned to act out mindlessly.

To provide a more detailed illustration of the way these tendencies reveal themselves in modern images of ageing we now turn to two significant examples taken from our research into cultural aspects of ageing in contemporary Britain. First, the social construction of middle age or, as it is now generally described, 'mid-life'; and second, changing images of retirement (Featherstone and Hepworth, 1984).

Social construction of middle age

Such is the ambivalence underlying our images of ageing, ancient and modern, that it is impossible to ignore the widespread fear of what Henry (1972) poignantly described as 'deep ageing' and 'human obsolescence' which permeates handbooks and other texts on ageing. Almost without exception, the popular literature of modern ageing, and much of the academic and professional literature, conveys a sense of urgency. Time, that most precious of commodities, is running out. One of the most socially significant aspects of the social reconstruction of middle age, therefore, is the attempt to establish an ever-increasing distance between the 'middle years' (currently ranging from the mid-thirties through to the late sixties) and deep or 'geriatric' old age and death. This distance is hopefully achieved through the redefinition of 'middle age' as 'mid-life' which is increasingly portrayed from the 1920s onwards as an extendable phase of vigorous and self-fulfilling life (Hepworth and Featherstone, 1982).

This gradual shift in the public imagery of middle age involves a transformation of the traditional into the modern. In the traditional stereotype of middle age the physical changes associated with the process of growing older – putting on weight, baldness, reduced energy, impaired vision and hearing, sexual lassitude – tend to be represented as the 'normal' consequences of living for a certain number of years. In seaside postcards of the years preceding the Second World War, for example, men in middle age are usually shown as balding, paunchy, and with dangerously flushed faces. The women who have reached a similar time of life have pot bellies and protuberant backsides which bulge through bathing costumes and everyday dress. In this image the body unambiguously betrays the 'stage' in life one has reached.

At the same time there are detectable signs of class variations in body shape and comportment and their influence on the ageing process (Schwartz, 1986). We have already noted the age-consciousness of socially-advantaged men and women in eighteenth-century Britain and France. The available evidence strongly suggests that this sensitivity showed no signs of waning through the nineteenth century. From the 1850s onwards medical men were urging that 'natural' ageing was influenced by factors such as diet, work, way of life ('lifestyle' as we now call it), childbearing, and sexual activity. In particular, the attack which gained impetus under the influence of consumerism in the 1920s, on the idea that men and women should inevitably put on weight in middle age, began to receive major publicity among the literate classes. Members of fashionable society flocked to the seaside, watched their diets, swallowed pills, sweated in Turkish baths and invented taxing physical activities partly to ensure they aged in a moral way. For the assumption was gaining ground that because the body is a visible record of a person's moral character, the signs of ageing the body betrays are a true guide to the kind of moral life he or she has led.

The traditional stereotype of middle age as 'natural' and inevitable, therefore, was gradually being undermined by select groups of people and specific interests quite some time before consumerism got fully under way. But it was during the 1920s and 1930s that *mass* interest in the connections between graceful ageing, health, and physical and moral attractiveness became possible and began to exert a heightened influence on the social reconstruction of middle age. Thus, in the 1922 edition of *Old Age Deferred*, Lorand agreed it was not yet possible to create a young man out of an old one but it was:

> quite within the bounds of possibility, as we shall endeavour to demonstrate herein, to prolong our term of youthfulness by 10 or twenty years. In other words we need no longer grow old at forty or fifty .... All this can be brought about by the observance of certain hygienic measures, and by improving the functions of a certain few of the glandular structures of the body. (Hepworth and Featherstone, 1982, p. 67)

The signs of ageing in face and on physique were increasingly portrayed as visible evidence of an unwise and socially unacceptable way of life, particularly when they became noticeable during middle age. The ageing process should be deferred as long as possible: a youthful appearance was the ideal and 'premature ageing' the dreaded enemy.

An increasing faith in the ability to discriminate in terms of outward appearance between those who aged 'honourably' and those who aged 'dishonourably', as Williams (1986) puts it, became one of the cornerstones of what we have described as the 'new middle age' (Featherstone and Hepworth, 1982). The accelerating impact of consumerism during the inter-war years sharpened awareness of the central role of the body in social life and the influence of imagery on the evaluation of individuals in a world of appearances (Featherstone, 1982). Throughout this period, too, middle age was steadily presented as a time of opportunity for 'taking stock' and self-development. 'At a certain age', wrote Knopf (1932) in typical fashion, 'people have to realise that tomorrow will never come'; they must therefore abandon regret for the past and begin to live in the light of the urgent knowledge that time is running out: 'terror of the closing door' (Knopf, 1932, p. 226). The speeded-up pace of life demanded a faster reaction to life events and the capacity to continue in personal 'growth'. These pressures were seen, as we have implied throughout, to affect the lives of both men and women though their responses might be considered to vary according to the dictates of gender and their way of life.

Changes in the imagery of middle age reappeared to even greater public acclaim in Britain of the 1970s where concern over the problems of mid-life showed no signs of waning. In her study of the portrayals of ageing women in American popular film, Stoddard (1983) writes that from the 1960s film images 'became more and more sympathetic' whilst by the early 1970s middle age was represented as a crisis period for men as well as women, 'measured more in terms of self-fulfilment than ... traditional social expectations' (Stoddard, 1983, p. 121). The same picture applies to Britain in the images of mid-life (filmed or otherwise) which have been in circulation over the last decade and a half (Hepworth, 1987). But buried not too far beneath the enthusiastic celebration of potential self-fulfilment in mid-life lies the anxiety over dependent deep old age that a youth-oriented modern society can do little to dispel. For still the hope is held out that an active and vigorously extended mid-life will push the deleterious consequences of physical decline well into the background and increase the power of those who age gracefully to maintain control over their lives.

Images of retirement

Retirement has come to be portrayed as a period of refurbishment. From its first appearance in Britain in 1972, the retirement and leisure magazine *Choice* (originally entitled *Retirement Choice*) set out to dismantle the traditional image of retirement. In the second issue Lord Raglan, the president of the Pre-retirement Association, advanced the following message. Since society has arbitrarily contrived the age of retirement and its conditions, society 'should play its full part in providing pre-retirement education to help people adjust to a new way of life, at what after all is a time in life when change is proverbially difficult'. There was a crying need for a 'dramatic change in attitudes to the whole question of retirement' (Raglan, 1972). The new magazine, then, set itself the task of confronting and dismantling the traditional image of retirement which associated the end of full-time employment with passive old age. Retirement should become a positive 'stage' in life. The section on women's fashion was especially interesting during those early days on account of its militant posture towards what was called the 'dull uniform' of retirement. In an article, 'Strictly Between Women – Yes, You Can Wear These Clothes', readers were told to adopt a modern outlook. The days were gone when they could skimp on make-up and wear something old and comfortable around the house; 'Now, when your husband is going to be home most of the time, is the moment to make him sit up and take notice of your elegant new image' (*Retirement Choice*, November 1972, pp. 18–19).

In February 1973, a continuing sense of grievance was expressed over the outworn public stereotype of retirement which had a tendency, it was argued, to trap retired men and women behind a kind of metaphorical fence. 'Isn't it about time', the editor demanded, 'that the news got around that nowadays people stay younger and are not old in the same way that people were old in times of yore?'. The processes of growing old were 'inevitable enough without officialdom giving them a shove along with an outdated vocabulary'. On the inside pages of this issue was a reference to Newport and Monmouthshire Retirement Council which had issued a brochure including a lively sketch of an old man with a red nose and fringe of white hair leaping a GPO pillarbox: 'Don't be a Mouldy Oldy. Be a Lively Sixty Five!'

Between October and November 1974, the powers of the commercialised popular media were drawn upon in order to increase the impact of the magazine and attract a wider readership. The format was changed dramatically and almost out of all recognition. The title was changed from *Retirement Choice* to *Pre-Retirement Choice* (with the emphasis in bold print on the word *Choice*). The covers became glossy, featuring for the first time close-ups of celebrities from politics, show business, and the media – all of whom were ageing gracefully and some of whom expressed no intention of retiring. The accent was now on preparation for retirement planning for, by implication, a new generation of men and women in mid–life, who could not be expected to be attracted by images of retirement and old age but who might reasonably be expected to have a long-term interest in leisure planning. The avowed intention was to expand the concept of pre-retirement to include a younger readership of 'people looking ahead to retirement'. 'We shall', the publishers announced, 'be covering a wide range of topics of special interest to men and women who *know* that sooner or later they have to *fashion their lives afresh*' (*Pre-Retirement Choice*, 1974).

Between May and June 1975, the word *Pre-Retirement* was dropped from the cover leaving the title of the updated magazine as simply *Choice*. In 1978 there was a merger with the Over 50s Club and *Choice* continues to present retirement as an extended leisure lifestyle within which any infirmities that old age may bring can be managed with dignity and skill.

These changes in the image of retirement as reflected in *Choice* have clear and close connections with the social reconstruction of middle age we previously outlined. In order to expand the readership and thus more effectively communicate their message the exponents of a positive conception of retirement found it necessary to draw upon the techniques of consumer culture. To change the private vocabulary of retirement it was imperative to transform the public imagery so that it reflected the changing aspirations of new generations of retirees who see themselves and feel themselves to be far distanced from the passive and less than exhilarating traditional image of middle life as the threshold of a disengaged old age.

IMAGES OF THE FUTURE

In conclusion we believe it is important to ask: 'what are the implications of our survey of images of ageing in Britain for the future?' There are four possible future scenarios we would like to identify. First, the long-standing interest over a number of centuries in scientific approaches to longevity and rejuvenation – increasing both the length and the quality of life – shows little sign of abating. The possibility of developing technologies with which the ageing process can be slowed down and ultimately halted clearly forms the basis for some rather speculative positive images in which the problems associated with old age can be steadily eliminated. Yet as is the case with the capacity to benefit from existing techniques (cellular therapy, cosmetic surgery etc) one would expect that the ability to purchase and utilise the new expertise would be stronger in the most powerful and privileged groups who would use it to reinforce existing social inequalities and status distinctions.

Second, it is clear that in a society such as ours in which consumerism and material values are regarded as absolutely central, images of youthful beauty and energy will receive prominence. The emphasis upon flexibility, adaptability and self-expression long associated with youth is now being extended for forthcoming generations into old age. Here we can refer to the whole paraphernalia of consumer cultural artefacts and services. Jogging, exercise routines, cosmetics, health foods and fashionable leisure-wear are now marketed to elderly people to sustain health, youthful energy and the spirit of self-improvement deep into old age. The consequences for the relationships between the generations are momentous.

Third, there will still be the basis for negative images of old age to persist because of the general insensitivity and disgust often expressed towards those who lose control over their bodily functions and embody some of the aversive properties of old age. Here we have the disturbing image of old age as a dirty secret, of decrepit sub-human beings on the edge of death, who can only be physically and mentally shut away.

Finally, in addition to our heightened sensitivity and disgust for the aversive properties of old age, we should also note the counter-tendency of a more humanitarian and tolerant attitude towards minority groups such as elderly people. Over the last hundred years we have seen a shift in the balance of power between men and women, children and parents and younger and older people. Groups such as women, children and elderly people, which previously had relatively little power, have made some gains. There has also been a general diminishing of contrasts within society through an awareness of the chains of interdependencies that bind all human beings together. This increases the capacity to identify and empathise with outsiders and minority groups. Pressure groups and social movements such as the Gray Panthers are thus able to raise questions about the rights of elderly people in a more open cultural climate for minority group rights, whatever the particular sympathies and economic policies governments may choose to follow.

Of course, the realisation of this fourth scenario for old age will be difficult in the face of the third one. There are great difficulties in the way of constructing a positive image of deep old age which will help us detach ourselves from the emotional response of aversion and disgust. In all probability the future tendency will be to feature images which present old age as an active continuing phase of consumerism. Here the emphasis will be on old age not as settled, routine relaxation, but as a phase of continuous physical, mental and sexual renewal. One of the heroes of ageing in this context is Ronald Reagan, who in his seventies increased his chest measurement by over two inches through body building. Within consumer culture there will be little attention given to the problems of how to live in a post-active old age. There is then still the tendency to hide away the hideous and disturbing. Few of us can face photographs of First World War facial injuries or massively disfiguring cancers which one finds in journals on plastic surgery, without a sense of disgust, embarrassment and helplessness at these seeming abominations of human nature. Deep old age offers a similar challenge to our capacity to balance out emotional involvement and detachment, to face and explore our emotional reactions in order to better understand the old person behind the mask, for their sake and our own.

In this chapter we have highlighted the various tensions between images and realities, the lived experience and social practices they purport to represent, but usually effectively *misrepresent* in various ways which can have both negative and occasionally positive social effects. We have argued that history must not be seen as a unitary process, for elderly people have been treated in different ways in different phases. There is much research still to be done and we are conscious of the need for systematic detailed research into images of ageing which examines the production, reception and day-to-day use of images by individuals from different class, racial and gender backgrounds.

Finally, we would like to end on a point which we have stressed throughout this chapter. Human society is a process and it is dangerous to assume that attitudes towards elderly people and images of old age which currently exist enjoyed the same currency in the past or necessarily will do so in the future. Hence for all the talk about our youth-orientated society we should be aware that while the qualities associated with youthfulness have generally been valued in history, this valuation must be related to the balance of power between the generations, which undergoes periodic fluctuations (Featherstone, 1987). The large post-war 'baby boom' cohort which became the sixties generation seemed to have gained a good deal of power for youth. Yet now they are in the process of entering middle age and in the early decades of the next century they will enter old age. They will take with them different values and command financial and other power resources on a very different scale from their parents. It is this generation which will play out the tensions between the current and future images and realities of old age. This generation will shift the balance of power a little towards elderly people, if not from some sense of altruism, then on the basis of realistic foreknowledge based on the strong possibility that we too will have to cope with the vicissitudes of old age one day and therefore have an interest in furthering the reconstruction of the images and realities of old age.

FURTHER READING

Hepworth, M. and Featherstone, M. (1982) *Surviving Middle Age*. Basil Blackwell, Oxford.

Featherstone, M. and Hepworth, M. (1989) Ageing and old age: reflections in the postmodern lifecourse. In: Bytheway, B., Keil, T., Allat, P. and Bryman, A. (eds) *Becoming and Being Old. Sociological Approaches to Later Life*. Sage Publications, London.

AGEING INTO THE TWENTY-FIRST CENTURY

John Bond and Peter Coleman

Interest in the scientific study of human ageing is unlikely to diminish in the twenty-first century although emphases and foci might change. Throughout this book there has been an attempt to emphasise the normality of human ageing as a balance to the problem-oriented approach of many discussions about ageing. In Chapter 1 we identified that in the twentieth century there have been two dominant themes in social gerontology: demographic change and the role of attitudes. It is unlikely that these themes will disappear. However, we would expect other themes to become stronger. One thing is clear. Social gerontology as an academic discipline will increasingly become multidisciplinary, something which we hope this book has shown.

In this chapter we revisit some of the demographic data and consider some of the implications for the twenty-first century. Major determinants of future demographic patterns are changes in life expectancy and the effects of the physical and social environments, including the effects of medical science. The impact of future demographic patterns on social networks will be mediated by the economic and political structures in the twenty-first century. What will be the social policy response to these trends? This book has provided a rather ethnocentric view of human ageing and the answers to many such questions in the future will depend on social gerontology taking a wider comparative and historical perspective.

DEMOGRAPHIC CHANGES IN THE TWENTY-FIRST CENTURY

The prediction of the demographic structure of society in the twenty-first century is an inexact science. The size and structure of the present population and the distribution of the birth rate over time are important factors affecting the future size and structure of any population.

Birth rates are affected by the proportion of women of childbearing age. In the twentieth century this statistic has varied quite considerably as a result of a decline in mortality, particularly infant mortality, and fluctuations in the birth rate for earlier cohorts of woman of childbearing age. The two world wars each influenced the birth rate. Each war was followed by an increase in the birth rate and subsequent increases, for example, in the mid-1960s and mid-1980s, can be traced to the post-war cohort of female children reaching childbearing age. Changes in the economic and social structure have mediated this cohort effect. Changes in family size, earlier marriage and many women delaying conception have led to a stabilising of the birth rate in European countries. However, ethnic minorities within countries often have different cultural expectations about childbirth which are reflected in their birth rate distribution. An important influence on the birth rate has been the wider use of birth control but again contraceptive practice is influenced by secular and social expectations within different cultural groups. In some countries political coercion has been applied to limit the birth rate, as in China, or to increase it, as in European Russia.

Once the size of any given birth cohort is known the prediction of the size and structure of the adult population is a relatively straightforward calculation. However, mortality and migration are important influences. In the twentieth century there was a marked improvement in the infant mortality rate such that the largest single cause of death up to the age of 40 was accidents. However, with the emergence of the Human Immunodeficiency Virus (HIV) epidemic it will be increasingly difficult to predict the future size of the adult population because until the epidemiology of HIV is better understood we have little idea about the prevalence of mortality from Acquired Immune Deficiency Syndrome (AIDS) into the twenty-first century. Similarly, changes in the smoking and dietary habits of men and women may have a significant effect on mortality in middle age. We just do not know what changes in lifestyle and the environment will occur in the twenty-first century which will influence mortality rates and the subsequent demographic structure of societies.

Migration does not have such an important effect between countries although changes in 1992 to the European Community and the changes in Eastern Europe in 1989 may influence future cohorts of Europeans in ways which we cannot predict. Within countries migration has an important influence. In the late twentieth century, later-life migration between areas of a country has been estimated in Chapter 8 to be about 10 per cent of elderly people. However, as we have seen, a disproportionate number of elderly migrants move to a few relatively distinct areas. In the United Kingdom movement from urban environments to coastal and rural retirement centres has made the projection of population sizes very difficult for local planners.

However, these uncertainties should not prevent attempts to project the

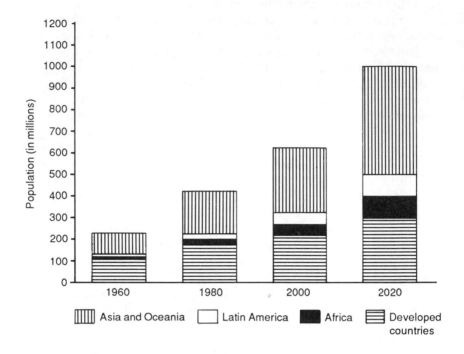

Figure 13.1 *Population aged 60 years or over, by major world regions, 1960–2020*

Sources: World Health Organisation (1989) Health of the Elderly Technical Report Series 779. Geneva. World Health Organisation, Figure 1.

structure of future populations, since the planning of health, welfare and social security provision could not be undertaken without these data. In Chapter 1 we reported the marked increase in the population of elderly people in the twentieth century. Projections beyond 30 years ahead are not usually published.

In the first 20 years of the twenty-first century the number of people aged 60 or over throughout the world is expected to increase from some 600 million to over 1000 million (WHO, 1989) and as Figure 13.1 shows the increase in Third World countries is expected to be much more marked than in Europe and North America, due mainly to the significant improvement in infant mortality in the last 30 years. Estimates for the United Kingdom indicate that within this broad age group there will be differential changes among age bands. Figure 13.2 shows the population projections for people aged 65 or over in the United Kingdom for the years 1991, 2001, 2011, 2021. The most significant feature is the increase in the numbers of people of very advanced age. Although a substantial majority of these will be women the projections for the future suggest that the current preponderance of women may slightly fall in the twenty-first century (Alderson, 1988).

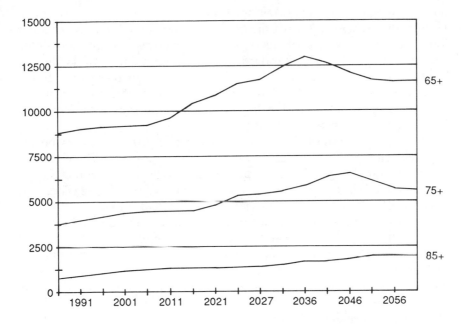

Figure 13.2 *Projected population of elderly people (in millions) in the United Kingdom 1987–2057*

Source: OPCS (1989) Population Pojections 1987–2057. Series PP2 No. 16. HMSO, London

INCREASING LIFE EXPECTANCY

Perhaps one of the most intriguing prospects in the twenty-first century is the possibility of increasing life expectancy. It is unlikely that medical science will play a major role, since as in the twentieth century it is likely to be the environment and lifestyles of individuals which have the greatest impact on longevity (McKeown, 1979). However, we would expect medical science to have an important role in increasing the quality of life of elderly people. The difficulty we face is in predicting what will be the hip replacement of the twenty-first century.

What evidence exists to suggest that life expectancy will increase during the next century? Current theories of human ageing predict that life expectancy is unlikely to increase much beyond present levels. Two explanations have been proposed (see Chapter 2). The first suggests that the limitation of lifespan is due to the cellular processes of senescence and the second suggests that there is increased societal risk of mortality from chronic disease.

Four types of evidence have been put forward to support the view that senescence will soon limit life expectancy. First, historically, the maximum human lifespan has not been observed to change except in populations where age documentation is poor and literacy rates are low. Secondly, the risk of death seems to increase as an exponential function of age. Thirdly, standard actuarial computations indicate that the elimination of cancer and heart disease would increase average life expectancy only minimally. Finally, there is experimental evidence which suggests that certain human cells are internally programmed for only a limited number of reproductions (Manton, 1982).

Within this school of thought there exist two different views on the expected changes in morbidity and mortality patterns. The optimistic view, illustrated by Fries and Crapo's rectangular curve (see Figure 13.3), sees the possibility of postponing the onset of chronic disease (Fries and Crapo, 1981). However, British and American data do not support this view (Isaacs et al, 1971; Manton, 1982). In contrast, the pessimistic view suggests that chronic illness and disability will increase as life expectancy is increased. Data from Northern Ireland on the prevalence of terminal dependency lends some support to this view (Stout and Crawford, 1988). However, an analysis of American data suggested that although more people were surviving to an advanced age there was little evidence to suggest that elderly people were more disabled than earlier cohorts (Manton, 1982).

Manton (1982) has also suggested that longitudinal ageing changes the age trajectory of mortality risks such that mortality reductions extend the productive lifespan of individuals, not by eliminating chronic disease, but by reducing its severity at any given age. The implication of these data for the twenty-first century is that the lifespan can be extended by controlling chronic diseases and there is increasing belief that the process of ageing may itself be controlled. The implication of this analysis is that medical science should increasingly turn its attention to identifying ways of preventing ill health and maintaining health in elderly people. If life expectancy is to increase in the next century individuals and society will need to control the consumption of tobacco and alcohol, improve diets, encourage healthier and more active lifestyles, and change the way societies are organised in order to eradicate environmental pollution.

PSYCHOLOGICAL CHANGE

As we have stressed before, biological decline is only one part of human ageing. Whether or not this seemingly programmed process can be manipulated, the prospects for enhancing psychological and social ageing remain vastly more significant. But our thinking on the subject remains confused. Birren and Schroots (1984) have pointed to the need for separate concepts to delineate the different processes referred to by the ambiguous term *ageing*. As it is, the outdated metaphors and negative stereotypes

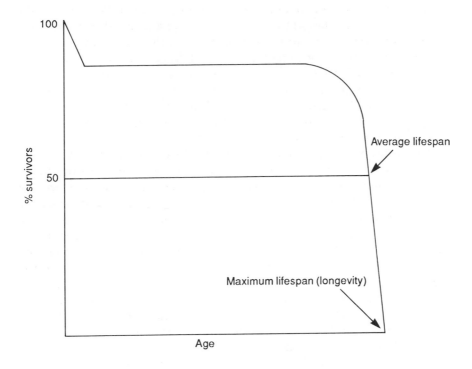

Figure 13.3   *Rectangular survival curve*

that surround the concept are a hindrance to creative thinking about the possibilities for later life.

Three terms have been proposed to encompass biological, sociological and psychological ageing: 'senescence', the process of increasing probability of dying with age; 'eldering', the process of acquiring social roles and behaviours appropriate to older age groups; and 'geronting', the self-regulation we exercise over our lives as we age (Birren and Schroots, 1984). To have a proper perspective on ageing, we need to be able to envisage an overall model that allows some processes to decline, while others stay the same and some indeed may improve.

One of the major achievements of modern studies of ageing has been to demonstrate that most of the decline in psychological functioning with age is not an inevitable product of age. That might sound a rather dull conclusion, but society has still not caught up with its implications. An underlying fault is the failure to appreciate the significance of the enormous differences in the ways people age. Previous studies had tended to hide these discrepancies by the use of measures of average tendencies which consequently presented pictures of uniform decline.

Rowe and Kahn (1987) have highlighted a distinction between what they call 'usual' ageing and 'successful' ageing. In 'usual' ageing extrinsic factors heighten the effects of biological senescence, whereas in 'success-ful' ageing extrinsic factors play a neutral or positive role. They cite the examples already referred to in Chapters 2 and 4 which demonstrate the stability of cognitive performance for many individuals who have been followed throughout the latter part of their lives. Indeed, in studies where comparisons have been made between people of equal education, 'age effects' become insignificant. They also refer to the studies discussed in Chapter 5 which show the influence of autonomy (control) and social support (connectedness) on behaviour and subjective well-being, as well as on physiological indicators.

We can go further to postulate that much of the emotional disturb-ance and health deterioration observed in elderly people is due to the failures of modern society to satisfy such needs for autonomy and for relationships. We may have created the improved material conditions to allow people to live longer, but the psychological and social conditions in old age may be much inferior to those in traditional societies. In the future we can expect psychological research to go further along this path and focus more on the variables that can maintain or increase perfor-mance throughout life. Greater sophistication in concepts is required, for example in distinguishing autonomy-enhancing and autonomy-reducing modes of support. Such distinctions are commonplace in the study of child development but not yet in the study of ageing.

Not all psychological disturbance in later life, of course, can be attributed to the character of society. Individuals become locked into unsatisfactory situations, in their relationships with others and in the circumstances of their lives, which lead eventually to psychological decline and physical illness. Many would benefit by greater access to possibilities for counselling throughout life. At present, stereotypes about older people's inability to change their ways of thinking, feeling and acting, as well as practical considerations of availability of help and its finance, stand in the way.

But at least we can envisage gerontology growing into a more truly liberating subject, less concerned with charting decline and predicting outcomes, and more with outlining possibilities to enable people to make better choices about their lives. We can expect the present theoretical barrenness of thinking about age – illuminated by a few idealistic models of successful ageing, such as Erikson's (1950) concept of integrity – to be superseded by many other ways of thinking about ageing. Ageing itself will come to be seen as a creative enterprise.

Issues of maintaining and finding meaning, and the appreciation of the characteristic achievements of a long life, such as wisdom, will probably play prominent roles in this venture (Reker and Wong, 1988). It is significant that the growth of ideas about possible ways of living open to older people has been accompanied by a greater readiness to accept the notion that old age itself has acquired certain special abilities in the process of evolution (Birren, 1988). It might appear paradoxical at first sight, but not on deeper consideration, that ideas on genetic determination and individual emancipation can go hand in hand.

We cannot judge where such developments will lead us. If we try to concretise a psychological future for old age we are likely to underestimate the impact of changing attitudes. Of all the current extrinsic factors operating in old age, public attitudes remain the most damaging. People's self-conceptions are so much moulded by the attitudes they perceive around them. Negative stereotypes die hard.

For example, Waldman and Avolio (1983) reviewed more than a dozen studies of adult performance in the work place and found little support for deterioration of performance with increasing age. Indeed, many objective measures of job performance showed improvement with age, especially for workers' performance in professional jobs. Nevertheless, supervisors rated older workers slightly worse than younger workers. Image has got in the way of reality.

We can justifiably hope that a more positive view of later life will have just as striking an effect in the contrary direction. Whereas at present a negative view of ageing itself contributes to the actual decline of many people in later life, so we can expect that images of continued potential will themselves facilitate the actualisation of much greater potential in later life.

SOCIAL CHANGE

Students of human ageing have difficulty in not considering the implications of ageing for themselves. A question we often consider is: 'What will social life be like when I'm older?' The pace of social change in the twentieth century has been phenomenal. What was life like before the computer, the motor car, universal piped water and electricity and all the other innovations of the twentieth century? Perhaps it is the science fiction writers of today who would make the better attempt at predicting the future for elderly people. If history tells us anything, the quality of life is unlikely to improve, unless 'the revolution of possibilities and hope' takes place (Maddox, 1985).

Social change is likely to occur in a number of areas of elderly people's lives, but particularly in relation to work and leisure and in family and social networks.

Work and leisure

Working life has changed dramatically in the twentieth century. For many men the physical conditions of the work place have improved and the number of hours worked has declined. Particularly in recent decades there has been a movement away from heavy manufacturing jobs toward service jobs. The technological revolution has changed the face of work in innumerable ways. For the majority of women paid work has become a lifelong activity rather than something undertaken prior to marriage or motherhood. Increasingly women have entered the labour market in areas traditionally dominated by men. However, there is still a long way to go before equality in work is achieved.

Leisure time has expanded markedly in recent years and the range of activities available to elderly men and women has increased. A major revolution of the twentieth century was the development of the television, which has become the number one leisure activity for people of all ages.

People reaching the Third Age in the twenty-first century will have experienced these rapidly changing conditions and their expectations of leisure time activities will reflect these experiences. Whether they are able to participate in leisure activities will depend, as it does today, on the resources they have available.

The age of retirement in the latter part of the twentieth century has steadily declined for many older workers (see Chapter 7). However, it is not inevitable that this decline will continue. As we move into the twenty-first century we are all more likely to change careers and jobs more often than was the experience of our peers in earlier decades. Gone are the days when we are trained for a job for life. The next century may see an emerging pattern in which the statutory retirement age is formally abolished and individuals change jobs successively until they choose to retire. Employment patterns would need to change to accommodate these possibilities by allowing for job sharing on a greater scale and sabbaticals from work for other activities including family life and education. This optimistic view, of course, depends on the equality of opportunity for all and income support being available for those who choose to retire. It is difficult to see what will be the effect of the post-industrial revolution on retirement patterns. We can be sure of one thing. It will be different!

Family life and social networks

Marriage is more popular nowadays than it has ever been. Equally so is divorce. These two social trends will have important implications for social networks in old age. Jerrome in Chapter 9 has already drawn attention to the changing balance of kin and friends in social networks. Historically children have experience of only one or two grandparents. In the future one child might have any number of parents, grandparents and great or even great-great grandparents. In China where there is a single-child policy this has had detrimental effects in the form of overweight and spoilt children who are uncontrollable at school and at home.

Once the children of the twenty-first century reach adulthood they will still have the opportunity, not available to their peers in the earlier years of the twentieth century, of interacting with grandparents and great grandparents. However, divorce has been shown to restrict access to grandchildren by grandparents (Hagestad et al, 1984). A significant change in the twenty-first century may therefore be further development in intergenerational relations.

Geographical mobility and changes in family size, however, imply a change in the balance of social networks. We have seen in Chapter 9 the increasing importance of peer networks on old age and how increasingly elderly people spend more time with friends than with kin. In the next century technological innovations may overcome some of the barriers to kin relationships created by geographical mobility.

Technological change

Technology has changed our lives, including the lives of elderly people, in the twentieth century more rapidly than in any other age. Never before has technological change intruded so much into the world of work, family life, leisure, health care, religion and education. As we move into the twenty-first century the pace of technological change is likely to increase and it will be difficult to predict its effects. We are able to predict, however, that people of all age groups will be affected.

Technological change has been reported to have undesirable outcomes: increased stress due to the faster pace of work, the increased obsolescence of older workers, the displacement of older workers, the reduction of face-to-face interaction, and the weakening of family and other social ties (Robinson et al, 1984). Some of the favourable outcomes of technological change have been identified as the reduction in physical workload, the facilitating of communication, compensation for infirmities, and the increased safety of individuals living alone. Rapid technological advances now make it possible to address realistically some human problems which were unsolvable 10 years earlier (Lesnoff-Caravaglia, 1988). Some recent practical applications of technological change which have facilitated independent living for elderly or frail people are portable telephones and personal alarm systems, alterations in lighting and heating controls and the introduction of escalators or lifts into people's homes.

Of increasing concern to gerontologists in the twenty-first century will be ways in which high and low technology can be further developed and utilised to prevent disease, assist health care organisations to deliver health care efficiently, and to foster independence among elderly people who are frail.

SOCIAL JEOPARDY

Norman (1985) has described the triple jeopardy of old age to refer to the position of elderly, black women in British society. All societies are stratified. Gender, ethnicity and age are three dimensions by which people are stratified. In our introduction we argued for not developing individual themes about the effects of gender and ethnicity on old age. We argued that because elderly people as a social group were heterogeneous it would be inappropriate to focus on gender or ethnicity issues. However, ageing in the twenty-first century will be strongly influenced by the pattern of social stratification.

Class We use class in the Weberian sense that people can be divided into groups on the basis of their relationship to the economic structure of society (Gerth and Mills, 1948). Class is a much stronger predictor of lifestyle than age and we suggest that older people have much more in common with younger people of their own class than they do with elderly people from other classes. There is little evidence in Britain to suggest that the class divisions of modern society have changed in the twentieth century (Goldthorpe, 1980) and it is unlikely that there will be any change in the twenty-first century.

Gender In Chapter 1 we reported that women have longer life expectancies than men. There are proportionately more women than men in each of the age bands over the age of 65 (see Chapter 1: Table 1.2). The implications of this for women in terms of living arrangements, social networks and poverty have been spelt out in previous chapters. Even though an optimistic view sees women as more economically independent in the twenty-first century this is unlikely to reduce the physical and emotional isolation of elderly women. Hagestad (1986) has suggested that rather than positive discrimination for women, who are the disadvantaged, we should positively discriminate in favour of men in order to redress the imbalance in the number of elderly men and women. Life in the twenty-first century could be improved for women if we encouraged men to adopt healthier lifestyles in order to improve their life expectancy. Evidence, however, suggests that rather than men adopting the healthier lifestyles of women, women are adopting the unhealthy lifestyles of men. Of course, another solution would be to encourage men to marry older women and women to marry younger men.

Ethnicity Being members of an ethnic minority implies not only that people belong to a minority culture but that they are disadvantaged by that membership. Whether you are black in Britain, Catholic in Northern Ireland or a guest worker in West Germany or France, ethnicity will play an important part in how you age. British social gerontology has seriously ignored the question of ethnicity in recent years (Fennell et al, 1988). Not only is poverty disproportionately high among ethnic minorities but the response of the dominant culture has been excessively ethnocentric. In the twenty-first century the response to the ageing of ethnic minorities will need to be flexible and responsive to the interests and needs of different minority groups.

POLITICAL CHANGE

Social change in the twenty-first century depends not only on techno-logical advance but on political change. In Chapter 1 we highlighted two important themes of social gerontology, namely demography and attitudes. In the last two decades there has been a sustained attempt to reduce high public expenditure which, current political ideology argues, is inconsistent with the efficient operation of capitalism. Estes (1986b) has argued that this ideology, in support of advanced industrial capitalism, uses the negative attitudes of society toward elderly people to justify the reduction in public expenditure and at the same time reinforces these negative attitudes by blaming demographic changes for increased public expenditure. We cannot place all the blame of negative attitudes at the door of advanced industrial capitalism because as we have seen negative attitudes toward elderly people have been an enduring feature of many societies.

Political action

One way that elderly people can protect themselves from such ideology is to develop their own group consciousness. However, as we have seen, elderly people are not a homogeneous group, they reflect the diversity of class and social and political interests of the whole of industrial society. It is therefore difficult to envisage how such a diverse group can organise themselves politically to work in their own common interest. Further, within the group of people defined as 'elderly' there are major inequalities between different cohorts. As Walker shows in Chapter 11 the 'young old', perhaps those recently retired, command more resources than those people defined as 'old old' who do not have occupational pensions and whose assets have withered away with inflation. Elderly people also have a relatively weak political base since much political activity originates through employment. Elderly people are difficult to organise politically because they do not generally meet as a group, as do for example, industrial workers, employers or students. Poor health and disability are also barriers to political participation and no formal organisation exists to represent the interests of elderly people within the major political parties. Finally, elderly people are often seen to be conservative by nature and therefore resistant to change. However, the political behaviour of those currently old may reflect experiences at earlier stages of the life cycle. The present cohort of elderly people may feel relatively advantaged, since it was this cohort which lived through two World Wars and an economic depression.

SOCIAL POLICY

If the position of older people in society relative to other groups is to improve then the twenty-first century will have to provide a very different environment for them. Obviously, the first change which will have an impact on the lives of all elderly people must be a change in attitudes. Featherstone and Hepworth in Chapter 12 were not very optimistic. There are some ways that we as individuals can change things. In our dealings with elderly people we can avoid a paternalistic approach by maximising their independence, autonomy, self-respect and dignity. We can interact with them in the way we would like younger people to interact with us when we are older by treating all people as individuals in their own right. We need to encourage elderly people themselves to think positively. However, major changes seem unlikely since as the political economy of old age has shown, elderly people are not valued within capitalist society. Once people retire from the world of work they have less productive value and so their social status is reduced.

Education

One way in which attitudes might be improved is through education. Most professionals having contact with elderly people have had little or no specialist training in the care of elderly people. Those who have tend to be health professionals whose training has been dominated by the medical model which focuses on the pathological aspects of ageing rather than normal ageing. Other workers involved with elderly people often tend to be untrained and low paid and have little professional commitment to the care of elderly people. Their attitudes will reflect those of society as portrayed by the media. In developing educational programmes for people involved with elderly people it will be important to examine the stereotypes of old age and to focus on the process of normal human ageing. Human ageing should be taught from a historical, cross-cultural and multidisciplinary perspective.

In the twenty-first century education will not be confined to the first 20 years of life but will increasingly become a lifelong process. If we are to improve attitudes it will not be sufficient to educate professional workers and carers. It will be essential for normal human ageing to become a part of a variety of educational curricula starting in schools and colleges of education for the young and moving into all kinds of educational training programmes. Faced with the challenge of eight decades of life for the majority of twenty-first century travellers young people and adults will need to be continually reminded that the quality of life in later years is a product of a lifetime.

Perhaps the most exciting prospect for elderly people currently reaching the Third Age is the increasing opportunity for education. Distant learning facilities and the University of the Third Age now make it possible for elderly people to catch up on the missed opportunities of youth and read for a degree. Although this facility currently only reaches a small minority of relatively privileged individuals there is the beginning of a trend toward continuing education for elderly people (Laslett, 1989). More emphasis on developing the skills of all ability levels is required. The work of psychologists has been paramount in highlighting the importance of continuing mental activity in old age, since both physical and mental activity are essential ingredients of a good quality of life in later years.

Income and resources

In Chapter 11 Walker highlighted the relative deprivation of elderly people, particularly elderly women. He presented data which showed that about one-third of elderly people were at or below the poverty line in contrast to some 10 per cent of people under the age of 65 and that around 90 per cent of elderly people were solely reliant on state support. Clearly, if there is to be a significant improvement in the quality of life for elderly people into the twenty-first century governments will need to plan an equitable and effective social security system. For this goal to be achieved significant changes in retirement and pension policies will be required.

Retirement policies will need to be developed which allow elderly people both access to employment and genuine choice about retirement. However, this will be difficult to achieve in a system which does not have as its primary goal the provision of employment. Thus, the promotion of full employment will be the only effective way of providing real choice to elderly workers. It is difficult to see whether the post-industrial society of the twenty-first century will be equipped to provide full employment unless some of the assumptions of advanced industrial capitalism are modified in order to promote it. Health promotion in the work place and the prevention of occupational disease and disability will be essential if elderly workers are not to be forced to retire before they wish because of ill health or disability. A flexible retirement policy coupled with a minimum pension for both men and women at the age of 60 should provide the opportunity for elderly people to choose when precisely to retire (Walker and Laczko, 1982). Adequate minimum pensions should be provided through the public sector. Public expenditure on social security would need to be increased by a reallocation of public resources. However, current political ideology, which has encouraged the development of private pensions, militates against this happening in practice.

Housing

Poverty and inadequate incomes are often associated with housing deprivation among elderly people and often reflect housing provision in earlier life. But as we saw in Chapter 8, housing deprivation is also the result of paternalistic policies with few appropriate housing options available to elderly people.

Elderly people living in the twenty-first century have a right to enjoy housing which is comfortable and which suits their individual requirements. Future policy should be developed which increases real choices for elderly people and, because the costs of home ownership are relatively high for elderly people, opportunities should be available throughout the life cycle to enable people to change tenure status. Policies are also necessary to secure the upkeep of owner-occupied property through home maintenance schemes. But in developing a housing policy for elderly people it is essential that trends toward segregated living arrangements or ghettos for elderly people should be avoided by planning for mixed housing types catering for all age groups and needs within a local community.

TOWARD THE TWENTY-FIRST CENTURY

The quality of life for elderly people in the next century will depend on a number of fundamental changes in the way that societies perceive and respond to human ageing. In this concluding chapter we have tried to identify the most crucial ones. Needless to say we have been selective in our choice. If we were to focus on just one theme it would be the theme of promoting positive attitudes. So much change could be realised if attitudes toward normal ageing and elderly people and elderly people's attitudes toward themselves were improved. However, it would be difficult to change attitudes without making some inroad into the policies advocated above.

This book is about widening the understanding of human ageing. In bringing together a number of authors of different disciplines we have identified a number of perspectives both theoretical and practical. These should be seen as complementary. However, this final chapter is somewhat speculative since we do not know what the future has on offer for us. Ecological changes may be of greater significance to all human societies in the twenty-first century than medical advances, psychological, political or social change. Those of us who are young enough will be able to see how correct we have been.

REFERENCES

Abrams, M. (1978) *Beyond Three-Score and Ten: A First Report on a Survey of the Elderly*. Age Concern, Mitcham, Surrey.

Abrams, M. (1980a) *Beyond Three-Score and Ten: A Second Report on a Survey of the Elderly*. Age Concern Research Unit, Mitcham, Surrey.

Abrams, M. (1980b) Transitions in middle and later life. In: Johnson, M.L. (ed.) *Transitions in Middle and Later Life*. British Society for Gerontology, London.

Abrams, M. (not dated) *People in their Late Sixties: a Longitudinal Survey of Ageing. Survivors and Non-survivors*, Part I. Age Concern Research Unit, Mitcham, Surrey.

Achenbaum, W.A. (1978a) Essay: old age and modernisation, *The Gerontologist*, **18**, 307–312.

Achenbaum, W.A. (1978b) *Old Age in the New Land: The American Experience Since 1790*. Johns Hopkins University Press, Baltimore and London.

Adam, R. (1967) The role of the grandmother today. In: Owen, R. (ed.) *Middle Age*. BBC, London, pp. 141–148.

Ade-Ridder, L. and Brubaker, T. (1983) The quality of long-term marriage. In: Brubaker, T.H. (ed.) *Family Relationships in Later Life*. Sage, CA, pp. 21–30.

Akhtar, A.J., Broe, G.A., Crombie, C., McLean, W.M.R., Andrews, G.R. and Caird, F.I. (1973) Disability and dependence in the elderly at home. *Age and Ageing*, **2**, 102–111.

Alderson, M. (1988) Demographic and health trends in the elderly. In: Wells, N. and Freer, C. (eds) *The Ageing Population. Burden or Challenge?* Macmillan, Basingstoke, pp. 87–102.

All Faiths for One Race, (1981) *Elders of the Minority Ethnic Groups*, AFFOR, Birmingham.

Allan, G. (1986) Friendship and care for elderly people. *Ageing and Society*, **6**, 1–12.

Allen, I. (1983) The elderly and their informal carers. In: DHSS (ed.) *Elderly People in the Community – their Service Needs*. HMSO, London, pp. 70–92.

Allon-Smith, R.D. (1982) The evolving geography of the elderly in England. In: Warnes, A.M. (ed.) *Geographical Perspectives on the Elderly*. Wiley, London, pp. 35–52.

Altergott, K. (1985) Marriage, gender and social relations in later life. In: Peterson, W. and Quadagno, J. (eds) *Social Bonds in Later Life*. Sage, Beverly Hills, pp. 51–70.

Amos, G. (ed.) (1980) *Home from Hospital – To What?* Community Care Project, Birmingham.

Anderson, M. (1971) Family, household and the industrial revolution. In: Anderson, M. (ed.) *The Family*. Penguin, London, pp. 78–96.

Anderson, R. and Cartwright, A. (1986) The use of medicine by older people. In: Dean, K., Hickey, T. and Holstein, B.E. (eds) *Self-care and Health in Old Age. Health Behaviour. Implications for Policy and Practice*. Croom Helm, London, pp. 167–203.

Anderson, W.F. and Cowan, N. (1956) Work and retirement: influences on the health of older men. *The Lancet*, **ii**, 1344–1347.

Andrews, G.R., Cowan, N.R. and Anderson, W.F. (1971) The practice of geriatric medicine in the community. In: McLachlan, G. (ed.) *Problems and Progress in Medical Care, Fifth Series*. Oxford University Press, London, pp. 57–86.

Antonovsky, A. (1979) *Health, Stress and Coping*. Jossey-Bass, London.

Archer, J.L. (1982) Discovering a philosophy for working with the elderly mentally infirm. *Social Work Service* (Department of Health and Social Security), Summer 1982, 43–49.

Ariès, P. (1983) *The Hour of Our Death*. Penguin, Harmondsworth.

Armstrong, D. (1983) *Political Anatomy of the Body: Medical Knowledge in Britain in the Twentieth Century*. Cambridge University Press, Cambridge.

Atchley, R. (1971) Retirement and leisure participation. *The Gerontologist*, **11**, 13–17.

Atchley, R. (1976) Selected social and psychological differences between men and women in later life. *Journal of Gerontology*, **31**, 204–211.

Atkinson, D.A., Bond, J. and Gregson, B.A. (1986) The dependency characteristics of older people in long term institutional care. In: Phillipson, C., Bernard, M. and Strang, P. (eds), *Dependency and Interdependency in Old Age – Theoretical Perspectives and Policy Alternatives*. Croom Helm, London, pp. 257–269.

Audit Commission (1985) *Managing Social Services for the Elderly More Effectively*. HMSO, London.

Auer, J. (1987) Psychological aspects of elderly dialysis patients. In: Monkhouse, P. and Stevens, E. (eds) *Aspects of Renal Care I*. Baillière, Tindall, London.

Baikie, E. (1984) Sexuality and the elderly. In: Hanley, I. and Hodge, J. (eds) *Psychological Approaches to the Care of the Elderly*. Croom Helm, London, pp. 237–254.

Baker, D.E. (1978) Attitudes of Nurses to the Care of the Elderly. Unpublished PhD Thesis, University of Manchester.

Baldwin, S. and Cooke, K. (1984) *How Much is Enough?* Family Policy Studies Centre, London.

Baltes, M.M. and Baltes, P.B. (eds) (1986) *The Psychology of Control and Aging*. Lawrence Erlbaum, Hillsdale, New Jersey.

Baltes, P.B., Reese, H.W. and Nesselroade, J.R. (1977) *Life-Span Developmental Psychology: Introduction to Research Methods*. Wadsworth, Belmont, CA.

Baltes, P.B., Reese, H.W. and Lipsitt, L.P. (1980) Life-span developmental psychology. *Annual Review of Psychology*, **31**, 65–110.

Bankoff, E. (1981) Effects of friendship support on the psychological well-being of widows. In: Lopata, H. and Maines, D. (eds) *Research in the Interweave of Social Roles: Friendship*, Vol. 2. JAI Press, Greenwich, Connecticut, pp. 109–139.

Barlow, D.H. and Hersen, M. (1984) *Single Case Experimental Designs: Strategies for Studying Behaviour Change*. Pergamon Press, New York.

Barnes, C. (1980) *The Relentless Tide: A Study of Admissions into Homes for the Elderly*. Social Services Department, Training and Development Division, Surrey County Council.

Barrow, G.M. (1986) *Ageing, the Individual and Society*, 3rd edition. West Publishing Co., St Paul, New York.

Barrowclough, C. and Fleming, I. (1986) *Goal Planning with Elderly People. Making Plans to Meet Individual Needs. A Manual of Instruction*. Manchester University Press, Manchester.

Barsby, S.L. and Cox, D.R. (1975) *Interstate Migration of the Elderly*. Heath-Lexington, Toronto.

Batchelor, L.R.C. and Napier, M.B. (1953) Attempted suicide in old age. *British Medical Journal*, **2**, 1186–1190.

Bebbington, A. (1979) Changes in the provision of social services to the elderly in the community over 14 years. *Social Policy and Administration*, **13**, 111–123.

Becker, H.S. (1963) *Outsiders. Studies in the Sociology of Deviance*. Free Press, New York.

Bender, M. and Norris, A. (1987) *Groupwork with the Elderly*. Winslow Press, London.

Bengtson, V.L. (1979) Ethnicity and ageing: problems and issues in current social science inquiry. In: Gelfand, D.E. and Kutzik, A.J. (eds) *Ethnicity and Ageing Theory, Research and Policy*. Springer, New York, pp. 9–31.

Bengtson, V. (1986) Ageing, families and socio-cultural change. Unpublished paper presented to King's College Institute of Gerontology, London, March.

Bengtson, V. and Kuypers, J. (1985) The family support cycle. In: Munnichs, J., Mussen,

P., Olbrich, E. and Coleman, P. (eds) *Lifespan and Change in a Gerontological Perspective*. Academic Press, CA, pp. 257–274.

Bengtson, V., Olander, E. and Haddad, A. (1976) The generation gap and ageing family members: toward a conceptual model. In: Gubrium, J. (ed.) *Time, Roles and Self in Old Age*. Behavioural Publications, New York, pp. 237–263.

Bengtson, V.L., Cuellar, J.B. and Ragan, P.K. (1977) Stratum contrasts and similarities in attitudes towards death. *Journal of Gerontology*, **32**, 76–88.

Bergin, A.E. (1983) Religiosity and mental health: a critical re-evaluation and meta-analysis. *Professional Psychology: Research and Practice*, **14**, 170–184.

Berkeley, J.S. (1976) Reasons for referral to hospital. *Journal of the Royal College of General Practitioners*, **26**, 293–296.

Berkman, L.P. and Syme, S. (1979) Social network, host resistance and mortality. *American Journal of Epidemiology*, **100**, 186–204.

Bernard, J. (1976) Homosociality and female depression. *Journal of Social Issues*, **32**, 4, 213–238.

Berthoud, R. (1984) *The Reform of Supplementary Benefit*, Working Papers. Policy Studies Institute, London.

Beveridge, Sir W. (1942) *Social Insurance and Allied Services*, Cmnd. 6404. HMSO, London.

Birren, J.E. (1988) A contribution to the theory of the psychology of aging: as a counterpart of development. In: Birren, J.E. and Bengtson, V.L. (eds) *Emergent Theories of Aging*. Springer, New York, pp. 153–176.

Birren, J.E. and Schroots, G.F. (1984) Steps to an ontogenetic psychology. *Academic Psychology Bulletin*, **6**, 177–190.

Birren, J.E., Butler, R.N., Greenhouse, S.W., Sokoloff, L. and Yarrow, M.R. (eds) (1963) *Human Aging: A Biological and Behavioral Study*. Publication No. (HSM) 71-9051. US Government Printing Office, Washington, DC.

Birren, J.E., Woods, A.M. and Williams, M.V. (1979) Speed of behaviour as an indicator of age changes and the integrity of the nervous system. In: Hoffmeister, F. and Muller, C. (eds) *Brain Function in Old Age*. Springer-Verlag, Berlin.

Blaikie, A. and MacNicol, J. (1989) Ageing and social policy: a twentieth century dilemma. In: Warnes, A. (ed.) *Human Ageing and Later Life: Multidisciplinary Perspectives*. Edward Arnold, London, pp. 69–82.

Blakemore, K. (1983) Ageing in the inner city: a comparison of old blacks and whites. In: Jerrome, J. (ed.) *Ageing in Modern Society*. Croom Helm, London, pp. 81–103.

Blau, P. (1964) *Exchange and Power in Social Life*. Wiley, New York.

Blau, Z. (1973) *Old Age in a Changing Society*. Franklin Watts, New York.

Blum, J.E. and Tross, S. (1980) Psychodynamic treatment of the elderly: a review of issues in theory and practice. In: Eisdorfer, C. (ed.) *Annual Review of Gerontology and Geriatrics*, **1**, 204–234.

Blumer, H. (1969) *Symbolic Interactionism: Perspective and Method*. Prentice Hall, Englewood Cliffs, NJ.

Boldy, D. (1976) A study of the wardens of grouped dwellings for the elderly. *Social and Economic Administration*, **10**, 59–67.

Boleat, M. (1986) *Housing in Britain*. Building Societies Association, London.

Bond, J. (1987) Psychiatric illness in later life. A study of prevalence in a Scottish population. *International Journal of Geriatric Psychiatry*, **2**, 39–58.

Bond, J. and Bond, S. (1986) *Sociology and Health Care. An Introduction for Nurses and other Health Care Professionals*. Churchill Livingstone, Edinburgh.

Bond, J. and Bond, S. (1987) Developments in the provision and evaluation of long-term care for dependent old people. In: Fielding, P. (ed.) *Research in the Nursing Care of Elderly People*. Wiley, Chichester, pp. 47–85.

Bond, J. and Carstairs, V. (1982) *Services for the Elderly: A Survey of the Characteristics and Needs of a Population of 5,000 Old People, Scottish Health Service Studies No. 42*. Scottish Home and Health Department, Edinburgh.

Bond, J., Atkinson, A., Gregson, B., Hughes, P. and Jeffries, L. (1989a) *Evaluation of*

Continuing-Care Accommodation for Elderly People. Report No.38. Vol.4. The 1984 and 1987 Surveys of Continuing-Care Institutions in Six Health Authorities. Health Care Research Unit, University of Newcastle upon Tyne.

Bond, J., Gregson, B., Atkinson A. and Hally, M.R. (1989b) *Evaluation of Continuing-Care Accommodation for Elderly People. Report No.38. Vol.2. The Randomised Controlled Trial of the Experimental NHS Nursing Homes and Conventional Continuing-Care Wards in NHS Hospitals.* Health Care Research Unit, University of Newcastle upon Tyne.

Bond, J., Bond, S., Donaldson, C., Gregson, B. and Atkinson, A. (1989c) *Evaluation of Continuing-Care Accommodation for Elderly People. Report No.38. Vol.7. Overview of an Evaluation of Continuing-Care Accommodation for Elderly People.* Health Care Research Unit, University of Newcastle upon Tyne.

Booth, C. (1889) *Life and Labour of the People in London.* Macmillan, London.

Booth, C. (1892) *Pauperism: A Picture; and the Endowment of Old Age; An Argument.* Macmillan, London.

Booth, C. (1894) *The Aged Poor: Condition.* Macmillan, London.

Booth, T. (1985) *Home Truths: Old People's Homes and the Outcome of Care.* Gower, Aldershot.

Booth, T. and Phillips, D. (1987) Group living in homes for the elderly. A comparative study of outcomes of care. *British Journal of Social Work,* 17, 1–20.

Bornat, J., Phillipson, C. and Ward S. (1985) *A Manifesto for Old Age.* Pluto, London.

Bosanquet, N. (1978) *A Future for Old Age.* Temple Smith/New Society, London.

Bottomore, T.B. and Rubel, M. (eds) (1965) *Karl Marx: Selected Writings in Sociology and Social Philosophy.* Penguin, Harmondsworth.

Botwinick, J. (1984) *Aging and Behavior: A Comprehensive Integration of Research Findings,* 2nd edition. Springer, New York.

Botwinick, J. and Storandt, M. (1980) Recall and recognition of old information in relation to age and sex. *Journal of Gerontology,* **35**, 70–76.

Bowlby, J. (1965) *Child Care and the Growth of Love,* 2nd edition. Penguin, Harmondsworth.

Bowlby, J. (1980) *Attachment and Loss. Volume three. Loss: Sadness and Depression.* Hogarth, London.

Bowles, N.L. and Poon, L.W. (1982) An analysis of the effect of aging on recognition memory. *Journal of Gerontology,* **37**, 212–219.

Bowling, A. and Cartwright, A. (1982) *Life After a Death: a Study of the Elderly Widowed.* Tavistock, London.

Bradshaw, J. and O'Higgins, M. (1984) *Equity, Income Equality and the Life Cycle: An Analysis for 1971, 1976 and 1982.* University of York, mimeo.

Braithwaite, V.A. and Gibson, D.M. (1987) Adjustment to retirement: what we know and what we need to know. *Ageing and Society,* **7**, 1–18.

Braverman, H. (1974) Labour and monopoly capital: the degradation of work in the twentieth century. Monthly Review Press, New York.

Brayne, C. and Ames, D. (1988) The epidemiology of mental disorder in old age. In: Gearing, B., Johnson, M.L. and Heller, T. (eds) *Mental Health Problems in Old Age.* Wiley, Chichester, pp. 10–26.

Briggs, R. (1985) Acute confusion. In: Lye, M. (ed.) *Acute Geriatric Medicine.* MTP Press, Lancaster, pp. 113–134.

Brocklehurst, J.C. (ed.) (1975) *Geriatric Care in Advanced Societies.* MTP Press, Lancaster.

Brocklehurst, J.C. (1978) Geriatric services and the day hospital. In: Brocklehurst, J.C. (ed.) *Text Book of Geriatric Medicine and Gerontology, Second Edition.* Churchill Livingstone, Edinburgh, pp. 747–762.

Brocklehurst, J.C., Carty, M.H., Leeming, J.T. and Robinson, J.M. (1978) Medical screening of old people accepted for residential care. *Lancet,* **iii**, 141–143.

Brody, E. (1979) Aged parents and aging children. In: Ragan, P.K. (ed.) *Ageing Parents.* California, University of California Press, pp. 267–287.

Brody, J.A. (1985) Prospects for an ageing population. *Nature,* **315**, 463–466.

Bromley, D.B. (1977) Speculations in social and environmental gerontology. In: Carver,

V. and Liddiard, P. (eds) *An Ageing Population: A Reader and Sourcebook*. Hodder and Stoughton/The Open University Press, Sevenoaks, pp. 50–57.

Bromley, D.B. (1978) Approaches to the study of personality changes in adult life and old age. In: Isaacs, A.D. and Post, F. (eds) *Studies in Geriatric Psychiatry*. Wiley, Chichester, pp. 17–40.

Bromley, D.B. (1986) *The Case-study Method in Psychology and Related Disciplines*. Wiley, Chichester.

Bromley, D.B. (1990) *Behavioural Gerontology: Central Issues in the Psychology of Ageing*. Wiley, Chichester.

Brown, G.W. and Harris, T. (1978) *Social Origins of Depression: a Study of Psychiatric Disorder in Women*. Tavistock, London.

Brown, G.W., Andrews, B., Harris, T., Adler, Z. and Bridge, L. (1986) Social support, self-esteem and depression. *Psychological Medicine*, **16**, 813–831.

Brown, R.A. (1957) Age and 'paced' work. *Occupational Psychology*, **31**, 11–20.

Brubaker, T. (1983) *Family Relationships in Later Life*. Sage, Beverly Hills, CA.

Brubaker, T. (1985) *Later Life Families*. Sage, Beverly Hills, CA.

Bruning, H. and Hesselink, J.K. (1986) *Omgaan met Sterven*. Zorn, Leiden.

Bulcroft, K. and Bulcroft, R. (1985) Dating and courtship in later life. In: Peterson, W. and Quadagno, J. (eds) *Social Bonds in Later Life*. Sage, Beverly Hills, CA, pp. 115–126.

Bulmer, M. (1986) *Neighbours: The Work of Philip Abrams*. Cambridge University Press, Cambridge.

Burgess, E.W. (1925) The growth of the city: an introduction to a research project. In: Park, R.E., Burgess, E.W. and McKenzie, R.D. (eds) *The City*. University of Chicago Press, 1967, pp. 47–62.

Burnside, I. (1975) *Sexuality and Ageing*. Andrus Gerontology Centre, Los Angeles.

Burrow, J.A. (1986) *The Ages of Man: A Study in Medieval Writing and Thought*. Clarendon Press, Oxford.

Burton, L. and Bengtson, V. (1985) Black grandmothers. In: Bengtson, V. and Robertson, J. (eds) *Grandparenthood*. Sage, Beverly Hills, CA, pp. 61–78.

Busse, E.W. (1985) Normal aging: the Duke longitudinal studies. In: Bergener, M., Ermini, M. and Staheline, H.B. (eds) *Thresholds in Aging*. Academic Press, New York, pp 215–230.

Butcher, H. and Crosbie, D. (1978) *Pensioned Off*. University of York, Community Development Project Unit.

Butler, A. and Tinker, A. (1983) Integration or segregation: housing in later life. In: *Elderly People in the Community: Their Service Needs*. HMSO, London.

Butler, A., Oldman, C. and Greve, J. (1983) *Sheltered Housing for the Elderly*. Allen and Unwin, London.

Butler, R.N. (1963) The Life Review: an interpretation of reminiscence in the aged. *Psychiatry*, **26**, 65–76.

Byrne, D.S., Harrisson, S.P., Keithley, J. and McCarthy, P. (1986) *Housing and Health. The Relationship between Housing Conditions and the Health of Council Tenants*. Gower, Aldershot.

Bytheway, W. (1986) Making way: the disengagement of older workers. In: Phillipson, C., Bernard, M. and Strang, P. (eds) *Dependency and Interdependency in Old Age: Theoretical Perspectives and Policy Alternatives*. Croom Helm, London, pp. 315–326.

Bytheway, W. and James, L. (1978) *The Allocation of Sheltered Housing*. University College, Swansea.

Cain, L.D. (1974) The growing importance of legal age in determining the status of the elderly. *The Gerontologist*, **14**, 167–174.

Callahan, E.J., Brasted, W.S. and Granados, J.L. (1983) Fetal loss and sudden infant death: grieving and adjustment for families. In: Callahan, E.J. and McCluskey, K.A. (eds) *Life-span Developmental Psychology: Nonnormative Life Events*. Academic Press, New York, pp. 161–182.

Cameron, P., Stewart, L. and Biber, H. (1973) Consciousness of death across the life-span. *Journal of Gerontology*, **28**, 92–95.

Carp, F.M. (1966) *A Future for the Aged: Victoria Plaza and its Residents*. University of Texas Press, Austin.

Carp, F.M. (1968) Person-situation congruence in engagement. *The Gerontologist*, **8**, 184–188.

Carp, F.M. (1969) Senility or garden-variety maladjustment. *Journal of Gerontology*, **24**, 203–208.

Carstairs, V. and Morison, M. (1971) *The Elderly in Residential Care. Report of a Survey of Homes and their Residents. Scottish Health Service Studies No. 19*. Scottish Home and Health Department, Edinburgh.

Cartwright, A., Hockey, L. and Anderson, J. (1973) *Life Before Death*. Routledge and Kegan Paul, London.

Cattell, R. (1971) *Abilities: Their Structure, Growth and Action*. Houghton Mifflin, New York.

Cavan, R.S., Burgess, E.W., Havighurst, R.J. and Goldhammer, H. (1949) *Personal Adjustment in Old Age*. Science Research Associates, Chicago.

Central Statistical Office (1985) *Social Trends 15*. HMSO, London.

Central Statistical Office (1988) *Social Trends 18*. HMSO, London.

Centre for Policy on Ageing (1984) *Home Life: A Code of Practice for Residential Care*. CPA, London.

Challis, D. and Knapp, M. (1980) *An Examination of the PGC Morale Scale in an English Context*. Discussion paper 168, University of Kent at Canterbury, Personal Social Services Research Unit.

Cherlin, A. and Furstenberg, F. (1985) Styles and strategies of grandparenting. In: Bengtson, V. and Robertson, J. (eds) *Grandparenthood*. Sage, Beverly Hills, CA, pp. 97–116.

Chown, S.M. (1962) Rigidity and age. In: Tibbitts, C. and Donahue, W. (eds) *Social and Psychological Aspects of Aging*. Columbia University Press, New York.

Chown, S. (1981) Friendship in old age. In: Duck, S. and Gilmour, R. (eds) *Personal Relationships*, Vol. 2. Academic Press, London, pp. 231–246.

Cicirelli, V. (1985) The role of siblings as family caregivers. In: Sauer, W. and Coward, R. (eds) *Social Support Networks and Care of the Elderly*. Springer, New York, pp. 93–107.

Clark, K. (1960) *The Nude: A Study of Ideal Art*. John Murray, London.

Clark, M. (1972) Cultural values in later life. In: Cowgill, D.O. and Holmes, L.D. (eds) *Aging and Modernisation*. Appleton-Century-Crofts, New York, pp. 263–274.

Clark, M. and Anderson, B. (1967) *Culture and Ageing*. C. Thomas, Illinois.

Clark, R. and Spengler, J. (1980) Dependency ratios: their use in economic analysis. In: Simon, J. and Devanzo, J. (eds) *Research in Population Economics*. Vol 2, JAI Press, Greenwich, Connecticut, pp. 63–76.

Clarke, L. (1984) *Domiciliary Services for the Elderly*. Croom Helm, London.

Clayton, V. (1975) Erikson's theory of human development as it applies to the aged: wisdom as contradictive cognition. *Human Development*, **18**, 119–128.

Clayton, V.P. and Birren, J.E. (1980) The development of wisdom across the life-span: a re-examination of an ancient topic. In: Baltes, P.B. and Brim, O.G. Jr. (eds) *Life-Span Development and Behaviour, Volume 3*. Academic Press, New York.

Cohen, G. (1987) *Social Change and the Life Course*. Tavistock, London and New York.

Cohen, G. and Faulkner, D. (1984) Memory in old age: 'good in parts'. *New Scientist*, 11 October, pp. 49–51.

Coid, J. and Crome, P. (1986) Bed blocking in Bromley. *British Medical Journal*, **292**, 1253–1256.

Cole, D. with Utting, W. (1962) *The Economic Circumstances of Old People*. Codicote Press, Welwyn, Hertfordshire.

Coleman, P.G. (1983) Cognitive functioning and health. In: Birren, J.E., Munnichs, J.M.A., Thomae, H. and Marois, M. (eds) *Ageing: A Challenge to Science and Society. Volume 3: Behavioural Sciences and Conclusions*. Oxford University Press, Oxford, pp. 57–67.

Coleman, P.G. (1984a) The Netherlands: poverty and disability in old age. In: Walker, R., Lawson, R. and Townsend, P. (eds) *Responses to Poverty: Lessons from Europe.* Heinemann, London, pp. 266–282.

Coleman, P.G. (1984b) Assessing self esteem and its sources in elderly people. *Ageing and Society*, **4**, 117–135.

Coleman, P.G. (1986) *Ageing and Reminiscence Processes: Social and Clinical Implications.* Wiley, Chichester.

Coleman, P.G. (1990) Religion, ageing and adjustment: questions for research. *Generations, Bulletin of the British Society of Gerontology.* In press.

Coleman, P.G. and McCulloch, A.W. (1985) The study of psychosocial change in late life: some conceptual and methodological issues. In: Munnichs, J.M.A., Mussen, P., Olbrich, E. and Coleman, P.G. (eds) *Life-span and Change in a Gerontological Perspective.* Academic Press, Orlando, CA, pp. 239–255.

Comfort, A. (1960) Discussion Session 1. Definition and universality of aging. In: B.L. Strehler (ed.) *The Biology of Aging.* American Institute of Biological Sciences, Washington, pp. 3–13.

Comfort, A (1977) *A Good Age.* Mitchell Beazley, London.

Copeland, J.R.M., Kelleher, M.J., Kellett, J.M., Barron, G., Cowan, D.W. and Gourlay, A.J. (1975) Evaluation of a psychogeriatric service: the distinction between psychogeriatric and geriatric patients. *British Journal of Psychiatry*, **126**, 21–29.

Copeland, J.R.M., Kelleher, M.J., Smith, A.M.R. and Devlin, P. (1986) The well, the mentally ill, the old and the old old: a community survey of elderly persons in London. *Ageing and Society*, **6**, 417–433.

Copeland, J.R.M., Dewey, M.E., Wood, N., Searle, R., Davidson, A. and McWilliam, C. (1987) Range of mental illness amongst the elderly in the community. Prevalence in Liverpool using the GMS-AGECAT package. *British Journal of Psychiatry*, **150**, 815–823.

Corson, J.H. and McConnell, J.W. (1956) *Economic Needs of Older People.* Twentieth Century Fund, New York.

Costa, P.T. and McCrae, R.R. (1978) Age differences in personality structure revisited. *International Journal of Aging and Human Development*, **8**, 131–142.

Covell, B. and Angus, M.M. (1980) A comparison of the characteristics of elderly patients admitted to acute medical and geriatric wards. *Health Bulletin*, **38**, 64–70.

Cowgill, D.O. (1984) The disengagement of an aging activist: the making and unmaking of a gerontologist. In: Spicker, S.F. and Ingman, S.R. (eds) *Vitalizing Long-Term Care.* Springer, New York, pp. 221–228.

Cowgill, D.O. and Holmes, L.D. (eds) (1972) *Aging and Modernization.* Appleton, New York.

Craik, F.I.M. (1977) Age differences in human memory. In: Birren, J.E. and Schaie, K.W. (eds) *Handbook of the Psychology of Aging.* Van Hostrand Reinhold, New York, pp. 384–420.

Craik, F.I.M. and McDowd, J. (1987) Age differences in recall and recognition. *Journal of Experimental Psychology: Learning, Memory and Cognition*, **13**, 473–479.

Craven, E., Rimmer, L. and Wicks, M. (1982) *Family Issues and Public Policy.* Study Commission on the Family, London.

Crawford, M. (1971) Retirement and disengagement. *Human Relations*, **20**, 255–278.

Crawford, M. (1972a) Retirement and role playing. *Sociology*, **6**, 217–236.

Crawford, M. (1972b) Retirement as a psychological crisis. *Journal of Psychosomatic Research*, **16**, 375–380.

Creech, J. and Babchuk, N. (1985) Affectivity and the interweave of social circles. In: Peterson, W. and Quadagno, J. (eds) *Social Bonds in Later Life.* Sage, Beverly Hills, CA, pp. 129–142.

Cribier, F. (1975) Retirement migration in France. In: Prothera, R.M. and Koszinski, E. (eds) *People on the Move.* Methuen, London, pp. 360–373.

Cribier, F. (1981) Changing retirement patterns of the seventies: the example of a generation of Parisian salaried workers. *Ageing and Society*, **1**, 51–73.

Crosby, I. and Traynor, J. (1985) *In Our Care: A Handbook of Workshop Activities for Those Caring for Older People*. Help the Aged Education Department, London.

Cuber, J. and Haroff, P. (1963) The more total view: relationships among men and women of the upper middle class. *Journal of Marriage and Family Living*, **25**, 140–145.

Cuff, E.C. and Payne, G.C.F. (1984) *Perspectives in Sociology*, 2nd edition. Allen and Unwin, London.

Cumming, E. and Henry, W. (1961) *Growing Old: the Process of Disengagement*. Basic Books, New York.

Cunningham-Burley, S. (1984) We don't talk about it... *Sociology*, **18**, 325–338.

Currie, C.T., Smith, R.G. and Williamson, J. (1979) Medical and nursing needs of elderly patients admitted to acute medical beds. *Age and Ageing*, **8**, 149–151.

Dale, A., Evandrou, M. and Arber, S. (1987) The household structure of the elderly population in Britain. *Ageing and Society*, **7**, 37–56.

Dant, T. (1988) Dependency and old age: theoretical accounts and practical understandings. *Ageing and Society*, **8**, 171–188.

Davies, A.D.M. (1982) Research with elderly people in long-term care: some social and organisational factors affecting psychological interventions. *Ageing and Society*, **2**, 285–298.

Davies, B. and Knapp, M. (1981) *Old People's Homes and the Production of Welfare*. Routledge and Kegan Paul, London.

Davies, B. and Knapp, M. (1987) *Matching Resources to Community Needs*. Gower, Aldershot.

Department of Employment (1980) *Job Release Schemes*. Department of Employment, London.

Department of Environment (1983) *English Housing Condition Survey, 1981*. HMSO, London.

Department of Health and Social Security (1978) *A Happier Old Age: a Discussion Document on Elderly People in Our Society*. HMSO, London.

DHSS (1981) *Growing Older*, Cmnd 8173. HMSO, London.

DHSS (1983a) *Low Income Families – 1981*. DHSS, London.

DHSS (1983b) *The Experimental National Health Service Nursing Homes for Elderly People. An Outline*. DHSS, London.

DHSS (1984) *Population, Pension Costs and Pensioners' Incomes: Background Paper for the Inquiry into Provision for Retirement*. HMSO, London.

DHSS (1985a) *Reform of Social Security*, Cmnd 9517. HMSO, London.

DHSS (1985b) *Social Security Statistics 1984*. HMSO, London.

DHSS (1985c) *Reform of Social Security: Technical Annex*. HMSO, London.

DHSS (1985d) *Reform of Social Security: Programme for Action*, Cmnd 9691. HMSO, London.

DHSS (1985e) *Health and Personal Social Services Statistics*. HMSO, London.

DHSS (1988) *Low Income Families – 1985*. DHSS, London.

Dex, S. (1985) *The Sexual Divisions of Work*. Wheatsheaf Books, Brighton.

Dex, S. and Phillipson, C. (1986) Social policy and the older worker. In: Phillipson, C. and Walker, A. *Ageing and Social Policy*. Gower, Aldershot, pp. 45–60.

Dibner, A.S. (1975) The psychology of normal ageing. In: Spencer, M.G. and Dorr, C.J. (eds) *Understanding Ageing: A Multi-disciplinary Approach*. Appleton-Century-Crofts, New York.

Dick, D. (1985) The institutional trap. *Nursing Times*, **81**, 47–48.

Dittmann-Kohli, F. (1988) Sinndimensionen des Lebens in Frühen und Späten Erwachsenenalter. In: Bierhoff, H.W. and Nienhaus, R. (eds) *Psychogerontologie*. Universität Marburg, Marburg.

Dittmann Kohli, F. and Baltes, P.B. (1990) Toward a neofunctionalist concept of adult intellectual development: wisdom as a prototypical case of intellectual growth. In:

Alexander, C. and Langer, E. (eds) *Higher Stages of Human Development*. Oxford University Press, New York, 54–77.

Donahue, W., Orbach, H.L. and Pollak, O. (1960) Retirement: the emerging social pattern. In: Tibbitts, C. (ed.) *Handbook of Social Gerontology*. University of Chicago Press, Chicago.

Dono, J., Falbe, C., Kail, B., Litwak, E., Sherman, R. and Siegel, D. (1979) Primary groups in old age. *Research on Ageing*, **1.4**, 403–433.

Dowd, J.J. (1980) *Stratification Among the Aged*. Brooks/Cole, Monterey, CA.

Durkheim, E. (1897) *Suicide. A Study in Sociology*. Routledge and Kegan Paul, London, 1952 edn.

Dyer, R. (1979) The role of stereotypes. In: Cook, J. and Lewington, M. (eds) *Images of Alcoholism*. BFI, London.

Eastman, M. (1982) Granny battering: a hidden problem. *Community Care*, **413**, 12–13.

Eastman, M. (1985) *Old Age Abuse*. Age Concern, London.

Edwards, A.E. and Vine, D.B. (1963) Personality changes with age: their dependency on concomitant intellectual decline. *Journal of Gerontology*, **18**, 182–184.

Eisdorfer, C. and Wilkie, F. (1973) Intellectual changes with advancing age. In: Jarvick, L.F., Eisdorfer, C. and Blum, J.E. (eds) *Intellectual Functioning in Adults*. Springer, New York.

Elias, N. (1978) *What is Sociology?* translated by S. Mennell, Hutchinson, London.

Elias, N. (1985) *The Loneliness of the Dying*. Basil Blackwell, Oxford.

Elias, N. (1987) On human beings and their emotions: a process sociological essay. *Theory, Culture & Society*, **4**, 287–316.

Emerson, A.R. (1959) The first year of retirement. *Occupational Psychology*, **33**, 197–208.

Equal Opportunities Commission (1982) *The Experience of Caring for Elderly and Handicapped Dependants: Survey Report*. EOC, Manchester.

Erikson, E.H. (1965) *Childhood and Society*. Penguin, Harmondsworth. First published 1950.

Erikson, E.H. (1978) Reflections on Dr Borg's life cycle. In: Erikson, E.H. (ed.) *Adulthood*. Norton, New York.

Erikson, E.H. (1982) *The Life Cycle Completed: A Review*. Norton, New York.

Erikson, E.H., Erikson, J.M. and Kivnick, H.Q. (1986) *Vital Involvement in Old Age: the Experience of Old Age in Our Time*. Norton, New York.

Estes, C. (1979) *The Aging Enterprise*. Jossey-Bass, San Francisco.

Estes, C. (1986a) The politics of aging in America. *Ageing and Society*, **6**, 121–134.

Estes, C.L. (1986b) The politics of ageing in America. In: Phillipson, C., Bernard, M. and Strang, P. (eds) *Dependency and Interdependency in Old Age – Theoretical Perspectives and Policy Alternatives*. Croom Helm, London, pp. 15–29.

Estes, C.L., Swan, J.S. and Gerard, L.E. (1982) Dominant and competing paradigms in gerontology. *Ageing and Society*, **2**, 151–164.

Evans, G.J., Hodkinson, H.M. and Mezey, A.G. (1971) The elderly sick: who looks after them. *Lancet*, **iii**, 539–541.

Evans, J.G. (1981) Hospital care of the elderly. In: Shegog, R. (ed.) *The Impending Crisis for Old Age*. Oxford University Press, Oxford, pp. 133–146.

Evers, H.K. (1981) The creation of patient careers in geriatric wards: aspects of policy and practice. *Social Science and Medicine*, **15A**, 581–588.

Eversley, D. (1982) Some new aspects of ageing in Britain. In: Hareven, T. and Adams, K. *Ageing: Life Course Transitions*. Tavistock, London, pp. 245–266.

Fairhurst, E. (1982) 'Growing old gracefully' as opposed to 'mutton dressed as lamb': the social construction of recognising older women. Paper presented to the British Sociological Association Annual Conference, University of Manchester.

Falkingham, J. (1987) *Britain's ageing population: the engine behind increased dependency?* Suntory Toyota International Centre for Economics and Related Disciplines, London School of Economics.

Family Policy Studies Centre (1984a) *The Forgotten Army: Family Carers and Elderly People*. FPSC, London.

Family Policy Studies Centre (1984b) *The Family Today: Continuity and Change*. FPSC, London.

Farrow, S.C., Rablen, M.R. and Silver, C.P. (1976) Geriatric admissions in East London, 1962–1972. *Age and Ageing*, 5, 49–55.

Featherstone, M. (1982) The body in consumer culture. *Theory, Culture & Society*, 1, 18–33.

Featherstone, M. (1987) Leisure, symbolic power and the life course. In: Jary, D., Horne, S. and Tomlinson, A. (eds) *Sport, Leisure and Social Relations*. Routledge, London, pp. 113–138.

Featherstone, M. and Hepworth, M. (1982) Ageing and inequality: consumer culture and the new middle age. In: Robbins, D. (ed.) *Rethinking Social Inequality*. Gower, Aldershot, pp. 97–126.

Featherstone, M. and Hepworth, M. (1984) Changing images of retirement: an analysis of representations of ageing in the popular magazine 'Retirement Choice'. In: Bromley, D.B. (ed.) *Gerontology: Social and Behavioural Perspectives*. Croom Helm/British Society of Gerontology, London, pp. 219–224.

Featherstone, M. and Hepworth, M. (1985a) The history of the male menopause 1848–1936. *Maturitas*, 7, 249–257.

Featherstone, M. and Hepworth, M. (1985b) The male menopause: lifestyle and sexuality. *Maturitas*, 7, 235–246.

Featherstone, M. and Hepworth, M. (1989a) *Surviving Middle Age*. Basil Blackwell, Oxford.

Featherstone, M. and Hepworth, M. (1989b) Ageing and old age: reflections in the postmodern lifecourse. In: Bytheway, B., Keil, T., Allat, P. and Bryman, A. (eds) *Becoming and Being Old. Sociological Approaches to Later Life*. Sage Publications, London.

Feneley, R.C.L. and Blannin, J.P. (1984) *Incontinence*. (Patient Handbook: 18). Churchill Livingstone, Edinburgh, London, Melbourne and New York.

Fennell, G., Phillipson, C. and Evers, H. (1988) *The Sociology of Old Age*. Open University Press, Milton Keynes.

Field, D. and Honzik, M.P. (1981) Personality and Accuracy of Retrospective Reports of Aging Women. Paper presented at the International Congress of Gerontology, Hamburg, July.

Fillenbaum, G. (1984) *The Wellbeing of the Elderly: Approaches to Multidimensional Assessment*. World Health Organisation offset publication no.84, Geneva.

Finlay, D.E., Bayles, T.B., Rosen, C. and Milling, J. (1983) Effects of chair design, age and cognitive status on mobility. *Age and Ageing*, 12, 329–331.

Finlinson, R. (1985) Chronic illness and care provision: A study of Alzheimer's disease. In: Peterson, W.A. and Quadagno, J. (eds) *Social Bonds in Later Life*. Sage, Beverly Hills, CA, pp. 325–347.

Fischer, C.S. (1977) *Networks and Places*. Free Press, New York.

Fischer, D.H. (1978) *Growing Old in America*. Oxford University Press, New York.

Fiske, M. and Chiriboga, D. (1985) The interweaving of societal and personal change in adulthood. In: Munnichs, J.M.A., Mussen, P., Olbrich, E. and Coleman, P.G. (eds) *Life-Span and Change in a Gerontological Perspective*. Academic Press, Orlando, CA, pp. 177–209.

Flavell, J.H. (1963) *The Developmental Psychology of Jean Piaget*. Van Nostrand Reinhold, New York.

Fleiss, A. (1985) *Home Ownership Alternatives for the Elderly*. HMSO, London.

Fletcher, R. (1962) *The Family and Marriage*. Penguin, Harmondsworth.

Folkman, S. and Lazarus, R.S. (1988) Coping as a mediator of emotion. *Journal of Personality and Social Psychology*, 54, 466–475.

Folkman, S., Lazarus, R.S., Pimley, S. and Novacek, J. (1987) Age differences in stress and coping processes. *Psychology and Aging*, 2, 171–184.

Ford, G.G. (1986) Illness behaviour in the elderly. In: Dean, K., Hickey, T. and Holstein, B.E. (eds) *Self-care and Health in Old Age. Health Behaviour. Implications for Policy and Practice.* Croom Helm, London, pp. 130–166.

Ford, J. and Sinclair, R. (1987) *Sixty Years On: Women Talk About Old Age.* The Women's Press, London.

Foster, E.M., Kay, D.W.K. and Bergmann, K. (1976) The characteristics of old people receiving and needing domiciliary services: the relevance of psychiatric diagnosis. *Age and Ageing,* **5,** 245–255.

Fox, J.A. (1976) Women, Work and Retirement. Ph.D Thesis. Duke University, Durham USA.

Francis, D. (1981) Adaptive strategies of the elderly in England and Ohio. In: Fry, C. (ed.) *Dimensions: Ageing, Culture and Health.* J.P. Bergin, New York, pp. 85–107.

Francis, D. (1984) *Will You Still Need Me, Will You Still Feed Me, when I'm 84?* Indiana University Press, Bloomington.

Frankl, V.E. (1963) *Man's Search for Meaning: an Introduction to Logotherapy.* Pocket Books, New York.

von Franz, M. (1986) *On Dreams and Death: A Jungian Perspective.* Shambhala, Boston.

Freden, L. (1982) *Psychosocial Aspects of Depression: No Way Out?.* Wiley, Chichester.

Freer, C. (1988) Old myths: frequent misconceptions about the elderly. In: Wells, N. and Freer, C. (eds) *The Ageing Population. Burden or Challenge.* Macmillan, Basingstoke.

Freter, H.J., Kohli, M. and Wolf, J. (1987) *Early Retirement and Work after Retirement – Implications for the Structure of the Work Society.* Freie Universitat Berlin, Mimeo, Federal Republic of Germany.

Friedmann, E. and Orbach, H. (1974) Adjustment to retirement. In: Arieti, S. (ed.) *The Foundations of Psychiatry, Vol 1.* Basic Books, New York, pp. 609–647.

Fries, J.F. (1980) Aging, natural death and the compression of morbidity. *New England Journal of Medicine,* **303,** 130–135.

Fries, J.F. and Crapo, L.M. (1981) *Vitality and Aging. Implications of the Rectangular Curve.* W H Freeman, San Francisco.

Frisch, M. (1975) *Montauk.* Suhrkamp, Frankfurt.

Froggatt, A. (1988) Self-awareness in early dementia. In: Gearing, B., Johnson, M. and Heller, T. (eds) *Mental Health Problems in Old Age.* Wiley, Chichester, pp. 131–136.

Fry, P.F. (1983) Structured and unstructured reminiscence training and depression among the elderly. *Clinical Gerontologist,* **1,** 15–37.

Gardiner, R. (1975) The identification of the medical and social needs of the elderly in the community: a pilot survey. *Age and Ageing,* **4,** 181–187.

Garland, J. (1985) Adaptation skills in the elderly, their supporters and carers. In: Davis, H. and Butcher, P. (eds) *Sharing Psychological Skills: Training Non-psychologists in the Use of Psychological Techniques.* The British Psychological Society, Leicester, pp. 61–68.

Garland, J. (1987) Working with the elderly. In: Marzillier, J.S. and Hall, J. (eds) *What Is Clinical Psychology?* Oxford University Press, Oxford, pp. 163–188.

Gathorne-Hardy, J. (1987) The final chapter. *Observer Review,* 3 March, 21–22.

Gaullier, X. (1982) Economic crisis and old age: old age policies in France. *Ageing and Society,* **2,** 165–182.

Gelding, P. and Newell, D.J. (1972) Hospital beds for the elderly. In: McLachlan, G. *Problems and Progress in Medical Care, Sixth Series.* Oxford University Press, Oxford, pp. 133–145.

George, L.K. (1980) *Role Transitions in Later Life.* Brooks/Cole, Monterey, CA.

George, L.K. (1981) Subjective well-being: conceptual and methodological issues. *Annual Review of Gerontology and Geriatrics,* **2,** 345–382.

George, V. (1968) *Social Security: Beveridge and After.* Routledge and Kegan Paul, London.

Gergen, K.J. (1980) The emerging crisis in life-span developmental theory. In: Baltes, P.B. and Brim. O.G. (eds) *Life-Span Development and Behavior Vol.3.* Academic Press, New York, pp. 129–168.

Gerth, H.H. and Mills. C.W. (1948) *From Max Weber: Essays in Sociology.* Routledge and Kegan Paul, London.

Giles, H. and Johnson, P. (1981) The role of language in ethnic group relations. In: Turner, J.C. and Giles, H. (eds) *Intergroup Behaviour.* Basil Blackwell, Oxford.

Gilhome-Herbst, K.R. (1976) Communication problems of the elderly deaf. In: *Deafness in the Elderly.* Age Concern, London.

Gilhome-Herbst, K.R. (1983) Psychosocial consequences of disorders of hearing in the elderly. In: Hinchcliffe, R. *Medicine in Old Age: Hearing and Balance.* Churchill Livingstone, Edinburgh.

Gilhome-Herbst, K.R. and Humphrey, C. (1980) Hearing impairment and mental state in the elderly living at home. *British Medical Journal*, **281**, 903–905.

Gilhooly, M. (1987) Senile dementia and the family. In: Orford, J. (ed.) *Coping with Disorder in the Family.* Croom Helm, London, pp. 138–168.

Gilleard, C.J. (1984) *Living with Dementia: Community Care of the Elderly Mentally Infirm.* Croom Helm, London.

Gilleard, C.J., Pattie, A.H. and Dearman, G. (1980) Behavioural disabilities in psychogeriatric patients and residents of old people's homes. *Journal of Epidemiology and Community Health*, **34**, 106–110.

Gilmore, A.J.J., Svanborg, A., Marois, M., Beattie, Jr, W.M. and Piotrowski, J. (eds) (1981) *Ageing: A Challenge to Science and Society.* Oxford University Press, Oxford, New York, Toronto.

Godber, C., Rosenvinge, H., Wilkinson, D. and Smithies, J. (1987) Depression in old age: prognosis after E.C.T. *International Journal of Geriatric Psychiatry*, **2**, 19–24.

Goffman, E. (1961) *Asylums: Essays on the Social Situation of Mental Patients and Other Inmates.* Anchor, New York.

Goffman, E. (1968) *Stigma: Notes on the Management of Spoiled Identity.* Penguin, Harmondsworth.

Goffman, E. (1971) *The Presentation of Self in Everyday Life.* Penguin, Harmondsworth.

Golant, S.M. (1977) Spatial context of residential moves by elderly persons. *International Journal of Ageing and Human Development*, **8**, 279–289.

Goldberg, E.M. and Connelly, N. (1982) *The Effectiveness of Social Care for the Elderly: An Overview of Recent and Current Evaluative Research.* Heinemann, London.

Goldthorpe, J.H. (1980) *Social Mobility and Class Structure in Modern Britain.* Clarendon Press, Oxford.

Gonzalez-Crussi, F. (1987) *Three Forms of Sudden Death, and Other Reflections on the Grandeur and Misery of the Body.* Picador, London.

Gottsdanker, R. (1982) Age and simple reaction time. *Journal of Gerontology*, **37**, 342–348.

Government Actuary (1978) *Occupational Pension Schemes 1975.* HMSO, London.

Government Actuary (1986) *Occupational Pension Schemes 1983.* HMSO, London.

Graebner, W. (1980) *A History of Retirement: the Meaning and Function of an American Institution, 1885–1978.* Yale University Press, New Haven and London.

Graff, T.O. and Wiseman, R.F. (1978) Changing concentrations of older Americans. *The Geographical Review*, **63**, 379–393.

Graham, H. and Livesley, B. (1983) Can re-admission to a geriatric medical unit be prevented? *Lancet*, **i**, 404–406.

Gray, B. and Johnson, M.L. (eds) Up the long track: poems of ageing. Unpublished.

Gruer, R. (1975) *Needs of the Elderly in the Scottish Borders. Scottish Health Service Studies No. 33.* Scottish Home and Health Department, Edinburgh.

Gruman, G.J. (1966) A history of ideas about the prolongation of life: the evolution of prolongivity hypotheses to 1800. *Transactions of the American Philosophical Society*, **56**, 65–110.

Gruman, G.J. (1978) Cultural origins of present-day 'ageism': the modernisation of the life cycle. In: Spicker, S.F. (ed.) *Ageing and the Elderly: Humanistic Perspectives in Gerontology*, Humanistic Press, New York, pp. 359–387.

Grundy, E. (1987) Retirement migration and its consequences in England and Wales.

Ageing and Society, **7**, 57–82.

Gubrium, J.F. (1975) Being single in old age. *Ageing and Human Development*, **6**, 29–41.

Gubrium, J.F. (1986) *Oldtimers and Alzheimer's: The Descriptive Organization of Senility*. JAI Press, London.

Gubrium, J.F. and Lynott, R.J. (1983) Rethinking life satisfaction. *Human Organization*, **42**, 30–38.

Gubrium, J.F. and Lynott, R.J. (1985) Alzheimer's disease as biographical work. In: Peterson, W.A. and Quadagno, J. (eds) *Social Bonds in Later Life*. Sage, Beverly Hills, CA, pp. 349–367.

Guillemard, A.M. (ed.) (1983) *Old Age and the Welfare State*. Sage, London.

Guillemard, A.M. (1986) Social policy and ageing in France. In: Phillipson, C. and Walker, A. (eds) *Ageing and Social Policy: A Critical Assessment*. Gower, Aldershot, pp. 263–279.

Gumpert, M. (1950) *You Are Younger Than You Think*. Hammond, Hammond, London.

Gunn, P.A. (1986) Legislating filial piety: the Australian experience. *Ageing and Society*, **6**, 135–167.

Guralnik, J.M., Brock, D.B. and Brody, J.A. (1987) The changing demography of the elderly in the United States. In: Caird, F. and Evans, J.G. (eds) *Advanced Geriatric Medicine 6*. Wright, Bristol, pp. 3–20.

Gurland, B.J. (1976) The comparative frequency of depression in various adult age groups. *Journal of Gerontology*, **31**, 283–292.

Gurland, B.J. and Toner, J.A. (1982) Depression in the elderly: a review of recently published studies. *Annual Review of Gerontology and Geriatrics*, **3**, 228–265.

Gurland, B.J., Dean, L., Cross, P. and Golden, R. (1980) The epidemiology of depression and dementia in the elderly: the use of multiple indicators of these conditions. In: Cole, J.O. and Barrett, J.E. (eds) *Psychopathology in the Aged*. Raven Press, New York, pp. 37–60.

Gurland, B.J., Copeland, J., Kuriansky, J., Kelleher, M., Sharpe, L. et al (1983) *The Mind and Mood of Ageing. Mental Health Problems of the Community Elderly in New York and London*. Croom Helm, London.

Gutmann, D.L. (1964) An exploration of ego configurations in middle and later life. In: Neugarten, B.L. (ed.) *Personality in Middle and Later Life*. Atherton Press, New York.

Gutmann, D.L. (1980) Psychoanalysis and aging: a developmental view. In: Greenspan, S.I. and Pollock, G.H. (eds) *The Course of Life: Psychoanalytic Contributions towards Understanding Personality Development. Volume III: Adulthood and the Aging Process*. US Department of Health and Human Services, Washington DC, pp. 489–517.

Gutmann, D.L. (1987) *Reclaimed Powers: Towards a New Psychology of Men and Women in Later Life*. Basic Books, New York.

Gutmann, D.L., Griffin, B. and Grunes, J. (1982) Developmental contributions to the late-onset affective disorder. In: Brim, G.B. and Baltes, P.B. (eds) *Life-Span Development and Behaviour, Vol 4*. Academic Press, New York.

Haber. C. (1983) *Beyond 60-Five: The Dilemma of Old Age in America's Past*. Cambridge University Press, Cambridge.

Hagestad, G. (1985) Continuity and connectedness. In: Bengtson, V. and Robertson, J. (eds) *Grandparenthood*. Sage, Beverly Hills, CA, pp. 31–48.

Hagestad, G.O. (1986) Challenges and opportunities of an ageing society. In: Phillipson, C., Bernard, M. and Strang, P. (eds) *Dependency and Interdependency in Old Age – Theoretical Perspectives and Policy Alternatives*. Croom Helm, London, pp. 1–14.

Hagestad, G.O., Smyer, M.A. and Stierman, K.L. (1984) Parent-child relations in adulthood: the impact of divorce in middle age. In: Cohen, R., Weissman, S. and Cohler, B. (eds) *Parenthood: Psychodynamic Perspectives*. Guildford Press, New York.

Haight, B.K. (1988) The therapeutic role of a structured life review process in homebound elderly subjects. *Journal of Gerontology*, **43**, pp. 40–44.

Hall, M. (1988) Geriatric medicine today. In: Wells, N. and Freer, C. (eds) *The Ageing*

Population. Burden or Challenge? Macmillan, London, pp. 65–86.

Hanley, I.G. (1981) The use of signposts and active training to modify ward disorientation in elderly patients. *Journal of Behaviour Therapy and Experimental Psychiatry*, **12**, 241–247.

Hanley, I. and Baikie, E. (1984) Understanding and treating depression in the elderly. In: Hanley, I. and Hodge, J. (eds) *Psychological Approaches to the Care of the Elderly*. Croom Helm, London, pp. 213–236.

Hannah, L. (1986) *Inventing Retirement. The Development of Occupational Pensions in Britain.* Cambridge University Press, Cambridge.

Hare, E.H. and Shaw, G.K. (1965) *Mental Health on a New Housing Estate.* Maudsley Monograph 12. Oxford University Press, London.

Hareven, T.K. (1977) Family time and historical time. *Daedalus*, **106**, 57–70.

Harris, A.I. (1968) *Social Welfare for the Elderly. Government Social Survey No. SS366.* HMSO, London.

Harris, C. (1983) Associational participation in old age. In: Jerrome, D. (ed.) *Ageing in Modern Society*. Croom Helm, London, pp. 14–24.

Harwood, E. and Irvine, K.L. (1985) Psychological Significance of the University of Queensland Longitudinal Study of Ageing: Retrospect and Perspective in the Twentieth Year. Paper given at the XIIIth International Congress of Gerontology, New York.

Hatfield, E. and Sprecher, S. (1986) *Mirror, Mirror: The Importance of Looks in Everyday Life.* State University of New York Press, New York.

Havighurst, R.J. (1963) Successful ageing. In: Williams, R.H., Tibbitts, C. and Donahue, W. (eds) *Processes of Ageing, Volume 1*. Atherton, New York, pp. 299–320.

Havighurst, R.J. and Glasser, R. (1972) An exploratory study of reminiscence. *Journal of Gerontology*, **27**, 235–253.

Hayflick, L. and Moorhead, P.S. (1961) The serial cultivation of human diploid cell strains. *Experimental Cell Research*, **25**, 585–621.

Haynes, M.S. (1963) The supposedly golden age for the aged. *The Gerontologist*, **3**, 26–35.

Hazan, H. (1980) *The Limbo People: A Study of the Constitution of the Time Universe among the Aged*. Routledge and Kegan Paul, London.

Health Education Council (1986) *Who Cares? Information and Support for the Carers of Confused People*. HEC, London.

Hedström, P. and Ringen, S. (1987) Age and income in contemporary society: a research note. *Journal of Social Policy*, **16**, 227–239.

Heinemann, G. (1985) Interdependence in informal support systems. In: Peterson, W. and Quadagno, J. (eds) *Social Bonds in Later Life*. Sage, Beverly Hills, CA, pp. 165–186.

Help the Aged (1981) *Recall: a Handbook*. Help the Aged Education Department, London.

Hemmings, S. (1985) *A Wealth of Experience: the Lives of Older Women*. Pandora Press, London.

Henderson, A.S. (1989) Psychiatric epidemiology and the elderly. *International Journal of Geriatric Psychiatry*, **4**, 249–253.

Hendricks, J. and Hendricks, C.D. (1977) *Ageing in Mass Society*. Winthrop, Cambridge, Mass.

Henry, J. (1972) *Culture Against Man*. Penguin, Harmondsworth.

Henwood, M. and Wicks, M. (1985) Community care family trends and social change. *The Quarterly Journal of Social Affairs*, **4**, 357–371.

Hepworth, M. (1987) The mid life phase. In: Cohen, G. (ed.) *Social Change and the Life Course*. Tavistock, London and New York.

Hepworth, M. and Featherstone, M. (1982) *Surviving Middle Age*. Basil Blackwell, Oxford.

Heron, A. (1962) Preparation for retirement: a new phase in occupational development. *Occupational Psychology*, **37**, 1–9.

Heron, A. (1963) Retirement attitudes among industrial workers in the 6th decade of life. *Vita Humana*, **5**, 152–159.

Heron, A. and Chown, S.M. (1967) *Age and Function*. Churchill Press, London.

Hess, B. (1979) Sex roles, friendship and the life course. *Research on Ageing*, **1**, 494–515.

Hess, B. and Soldo, B. (1985) Husband and wife networks. In: Sauer, W. and Coward, R. (eds) *Social Support Networks and Care of the Elderly*. Springer, New York, pp. 67–92.

Hinton, J.M. (1975) The influence of previous personality on reactions to having terminal cancer. *Omega*, **6**, 95–111.

Hirsch, F. (1977) *Social Limits to Growth*. Routledge and Kegan Paul, London.

Hochschild, A. (1975) *The Unexpected Community*. Prentice-Hall, New York.

Hodkinson, H.M., Evans, G.J. and Mezey, A.G. (1972) Factors associated with the misplacement of elderly patients in geriatric and psychiatric hospitals. *Gerontologia Clinica*, **14**, 267–273.

Holahan, C.K., Holahan, C.J. and Belk, S. (1984) Adjustment in aging: the roles of life stress, hassles and self-efficacy. *Health Psychology*, **3**, 315–328.

Holden, U.P. and Woods, R.T. (1988) *Reality Orientation: Psychological Approaches to the 'Confused' Elderly*. Churchill Livingstone, Edinburgh.

Holliday, S.G., Burnaby, H.C. and Chandler, M.J. (1986) *Wisdom: Explorations in Adult Competence*. Karger, Basle.

Hollingshead, A.B. and Redlich, F.C. (1958) *Social Class and Mental Illness: A Community Study*. Wiley, New York.

Hooper, F.H., Hooper, J.O. and Colbert, K.K. (1984) *Personality and Memory Correlates of Intellectual Functioning: Young Adulthood to Old Age*. Karger, Basle.

Houts, P.S. and Scott, R.A. (1976) *Individualized Goal Planning in Nursing Care Facilities*. Department of Behavioural Science, Pennsylvania State University College of Medicine, Hershey, Penn.

Hudson, B.L. and Macdonald, G.M. (1986) *Behavioural Social Work: An Introduction*. Macmillan Education, Basingstoke.

Hufton, O.H. (1974) *The Poor in Eighteenth Century France*. Oxford University Press, Oxford.

Hunt, A. (1970) *The Home Help Service in England and Wales*. HMSO, London.

Hunt, A. (1978) *The Elderly at Home: a Study of People Aged 60-Five and Over Living in the Community in England in 1976*. OPCS, London.

Huppert, F. and Tym, E. (1986) Clinical and neuropsychological assessment of dementia. *British Medical Bulletin*, **42**, 11–18.

Hussian, R.A. (1981) *Geriatric Psychology: A Behavioural Perspective*. Van Nostrand Reinhold, New York.

Huyck, M. (1977) Sex and the older woman. In: Troll, L., Israel, J. and Israel, K. (eds) *Looking Ahead: A Woman's Guide to the Problems and Joys of Growing Older*. Prentice-Hall, New Jersey, pp. 43–58.

Isaacs, B., Gunn, J., McKechan, A., McMillan, I. and Neville, Y. (1971) The concept of predeath. *Lancet*, **1**, 1115–1119.

Isaacs, B. and Neville, Y. (1975) *The Management of Need in Old People. Scottish Home and Health Service Studies No. 34*. Scottish Home and Health Department, Edinburgh.

Isaacs, B., Livingstone, M. and Neville, Y. (1972) *Survival of the Unfittest: A Study of Geriatric Patients in Glasgow*. Routledge and Kegan Paul, London.

Itzin, C. (1986) Ageism awareness training: a model for groupwork. In: Phillipson, C., Bernard, M. and Strang, P. (eds) *Dependency and Interdependency in Old Age: Theoretical Perspectives and Policy Alternatives*. Croom Helm, London, pp. 114–139.

Jacobson, D. (1974) Rejection of the retiree role: a study of female industrial workers in their 50s. *Human Relations*, **27**, 477–491.

Jacoby, R.J. (1981) Depression in the elderly. *British Journal of Hospital Medicine*, **25**, 40–47.

Jalland, P. and Hooper, J. (eds) (1986) *Women from Birth to Death. The Female Life Cycle in Britain, 1830–1914*. The Harvester Press, Brighton.

Jeffery, D.P. (1986) The systems approach to changing practice in residential care. In: Hanley, I. and Gilhooly, M. (eds) *Psychological Therapies for the Elderly*. Croom Helm, London, pp. 124–150.

Jenkins, J., Felce, D., Lunt, B. and Powell, E. (1977) Increasing engagement in activity of residents in old people's homes by providing recreational materials. *Behaviour Research and Therapy*, **15**, 429–434.

Jerrome, D. (1981) The significance of friendship for women in later life. *Ageing and Society*, **1**, 175–197.

Jerrome, D. (1983) Lonely women in a friendship club. *British Journal of Guidance and Counselling*, **11.1**, 10–20.

Jerrome, D. (1984) Good company: the sociological implications of friendship. *Sociological Review*, **32**, 696–718.

Jerrome, D. (1986) Me Darby, you Joan. In: Phillipson, C., Bernard, M. and Strang, P. (eds) *Dependency and Interdependency in Old Age – Theoretical Perspectives and Policy Alternatives*. Croom Helm, London, pp. 348–358.

Johnson, C. (1985) Grandparenting options in divorcing families. In: Bengtson, V. and Robertson, J. (eds) *Grandparenthood*. Sage, Beverly Hills, CA, pp. 81–96.

Johnson, D.E. (1958) A depressive retirement syndrome. *Geriatrics*, **13**, 314–319.

Johnson, F. and Aries, E. (1983) The talk of women friends. *Women's Studies International Forum*, **6**, 353–361.

Johnson, M.L. (1972) Self perception of need amongst the elderly: an analysis of illness behaviour. *Sociological Review*, **20**, 521–531.

Johnson, M.L. (1982) Implications of greater activity in later life. In: Fogarty, M. (ed.) *Retirement Policy – the Next Fifty Years*. Heinemann, London, pp. 138–156.

Johnson, M. (1986) Ageing as a labelling phenomenon. In: Dean, K., Hickey, T. and Holstein, B.E. (eds) *Self-care and Health in Old Age. Health Behaviour. Implications for Policy and Practice*. Croom Helm, London, pp. 12–34.

Johnson, M.L., di Gregorio, S. and Hughes, B. (1981) *Ageing, Needs and Nutrition*. Policy Studies Institute, London.

Johnson, P. (1987) *Structured Dependency of the Elderly: A Critical Note*. Centre for Economic Policy Research, London.

Johnson, P., Conrad, C. and Thomson, D. (1989) *Workers versus Pensioners*. Manchester University Press in association with The Centre for Economic Policy Research, Manchester.

Jones, D. (1980) Gossip. *Women's Studies International Forum*, **3**, 139–198.

Judge, K., Knapp, M. and Smith, J. (1983) The comparative costs of public and private residential homes for the elderly. *DHSS Seminar Papers on Residential Research*. DHSS, London.

Jung, C.G. (1972) The transcendent function. In: Read, H., Fordham, M., Adler, G. and McGuire, W. (eds) *The Structure and Dynamics of the Psyche, 2nd edition, Volume 8 of the Collected Works of C.G. Jung*. Routledge and Kegan Paul, London.

Kahana, E. (1982) A congruence model of person-environment interaction. In: Lawton, M.P., Windley, P.G. and Byerts, T.O. (eds) *Aging and the Environment: Theoretical Approaches*. Springer, New York, pp. 97–121.

Kahana, B. and Kahana, E. (1983) Stress reactions. In: Lewinsohn, P.M. and Teri, L. (eds) *Clinical Geropsychology: New Directions in Assessment and Treatment*. Pergamon Press, New York, pp. 139–169.

Kalish, R.A. (1985) The social context of death and dying. In: Binstock, R.H. and Shanas, E. (eds) *Handbook of Aging and the Social Sciences*. Van Nostrand Reinhold, New York, pp. 149–170.

Kalish, R.A. and Reynolds, D.K. (1976) *Death and Ethnicity: a Psychocultural Study*. University of Southern California Press, Los Angeles.

Karn, V.A. (1977) *Retiring to the Seaside*. Routledge and Kegan Paul, London.

Kastenbaum, R. (1974) On death and dying. *Journal of Geriatric Psychiatry*, **7**, 94–107.

Kastenbaum, R. and Alsenberg, R. (1976) *The Psychology of Death*. Springer, New York.

Kay, D.W., Beamish, P. and Roth, M. (1964) Old age mental disorders in Newcastle upon Tyne I. *British Journal of Psychiatry*, **110**, 146–158.

Kay, D.W.K., Henderson, A.S., Scott, R., Wilson, J., Rickwood, D. and Grayson, D.A. (1985)

Dementia and depression among the elderly living in the Hobart community: the effect of the diagnostic criteria on the prevalence rates. *Psychological Medicine*, **15**, 771–788.

Keith, D.M. (1979) Life changes and perceptions of life and death among older men and women. *Journal of Gerontology*, **34**, 870–878.

Keith, J. (1977) *Old People, New Lives: Community Creation in a Retirement Residence.* University of Chicago Press, Chicago.

Keith, J. (1982) *Old People as People.* Little and Brown, Boston and Toronto.

Kendrick, D.C. (1982) Why assess the aged. A clinical psychologist's view. *British Journal of Clinical Psychology*, **21**, 47–54.

Kerckhoff, A.C. (1964) Husband–wife expectations and reactions to retirement. *Journal of Gerontology*, **19**, 510–516.

Kidd, C.B. (1962) Misplacement of the elderly in hospital. *British Medical Journal*, **4**, 1491–1495.

Kilroy, B. (1982) Public expenditure on housing. In: Walker, A. (ed.) *Public Expenditure and Social Policy.* Heinemann, London, pp. 113–136.

Kincaid, J. (1973) *Poverty and Inequality in Britain.* Penguin, Harmondsworth.

King, A. (1911) Prayers during the long struggle. In: Jalland, P. and Hooper, J. (eds) *Women from Birth to Death: the Female Life Cycle in Britain 1830–1914.* The Harvester Press, Brighton, 1986, p. 302.

King, G.B. and Stearns, P. (1981) The retirement experience as a policy factor. *Journal in Social History*, 14, 589–625.

King's Fund Centre (1986) *Living Well into Old Age: Applying Principles of Good Practice to Services for People with Dementia.* Project paper no. 63. King's Fund Publishing Office, London.

Kirkwood, T.B.L. (1977) Evolution of ageing. *Nature*, **270**, 301–304.

Kitchener, K.S. (1983) Cognition, metacognition, and epistemic cognition: a three-level model of cognitive processing. *Human Development*, **26**, 222–232.

Kitwood, T. (1988) The contribution of psychology to the understanding of senile dementia. In: Gearing, B., Johnson, M. and Heller, T. (eds) *Mental Health Problems in Old Age.* Wiley, Chichester, pp. 123–130.

Knopf, O. (1932) *The Art of Being a Woman.* Rider, London.

Koenig, H.G., George, L.K. and Siegler, I.C. (1988) The use of religion and other emotion-regulating coping strategies among older adults. *The Gerontologist*, **28**, 303–310.

Kolhi, M., Rosenow, J. and Wolf, J. (1983) The social construction of ageing through work: economic structure and life world. *Ageing and Society*, **3**, 23–42.

Kornhaber, (1985) Grandparenthood and the new social contract. In: Bengtson, V. and Robertson, J. (eds) *Grandparenthood.* Sage, Beverly Hills, CA, pp. 159–172.

Kosberg, J. (ed.) (1983) *Abuse and Maltreatment of the Elderly: Causes and Interventions.* John Wright, Boston.

Kramer, D.A. (1983) Post-formal operations? A need of further conceptualisation. *Human Development*, **25**, 91–105.

Krasner, J. (1977) Treatment of the elderly person. In: Fabrikant, B., Barron, J. and Krasner, J. (eds) *To Enjoy is to Live.* Nelson Hall, Chicago.

Krause, N. (1987) Life stress, social support and self-esteem in an elderly population. *Psychology and Ageing*, **2**, 349–356.

Kruse, A. (1989) Coping with chronic disease and elder abuse. In: Wolf, R.S. and Bergman, S. (eds) *Stress, Conflict and Abuse of the Elderly.* JDC-Brookdale Institute of Gerontology and Adult Human Development, Jerusalem.

Kubler-Ross, E. (1969) *On Death and Dying.* Macmillan, New York.

Kuhn, M. (1986) Prologue: social and political goals for an ageing population. In: Phillipson, C., Bernard, M. and Strang, P. (eds) *Dependency and Interdependency in Old Age: Theoretical Perspectives and Policy Alternatives.* Croom Helm, London.

Kuypers, J.A. and Bengtson, V.L. (1973) Social breakdown and competence. A model of normal ageing. *Human Development*, **16**, 181-201.

Kuypers, J.A. and Bengtson, V.L. (1983) Toward competence in the older family. In: Brubaker, T. (ed.) *Family Relationships in Later Life*. Sage, Beverly Hills, CA, pp. 211–228.

Labouvie-Vief, G. (1985) Intelligence and cognition. In: Birren, J.E. and Schaie, K.W. (eds) *Handbook of the Psychology of Aging*, 2nd edition. Van Nostrand Reinhold, New York.

Labouvie-Vief, G. and Blanchard-Fields, F. (1982) Cognitive ageing and psychological growth. *Ageing and Society*, **2**, 183–209.

Labouvie-Vief, G., Hoyer, W.J., Baltes, M.M. and Baltes, P.B. (1974) Operant analysis of intellectual behaviour in old age. *Human Development*, **17**, 259–272.

Laczko, F. and Walker, A. (1985) Excluding older workers from the labour force: early retirement policies in Britain, France and Sweden. In: Brenton, M. and Jones, C. (eds) *Year Book of Social Policy in Britain 1984*. Routledge and Kegan Paul, London, pp. 100–122.

Laing, W. (1987) *Laing's review of private health care*, Laing and Buisson, London.

Laing, W. (1988) *Laing's Review of Private Health Care*. Laing and Buisson, London.

Lakoff, R.T. and Scherr, R.L. (1984) *Face Values: The Politics of Beauty*. Routledge and Kegan Paul, London.

Langer, E.J. (1983) *The Psychology of Control*. Sage, Beverly Hills, CA.

Langley, E.E. and Simpson, J.H. (1970) Misplacement of the elderly in geriatric and psychiatric hospitals. *Geronotologia Clinica*, **12**, 149–163.

Larder, D., Day, P. and Klein, R. (1986) *Institutional Care for the Elderly: the Geographical Distribution of the Public/Private Mix in England*. Bath Social Policy Papers, No. 10. University of Bath, Bath.

Larson, R. (1978) Thirty years of research on the subjective well-being of older Americans. *Journal of Gerontology*, **33**, 109–125.

Laslett, P. (1976) Societal development and aging. In: Binstock, R.H. and Shanas, E. (eds) *Handbook of Aging and the Social Sciences*. Van Nostrand Reinhold, New York, pp. 87–116.

Laslett, P. (1977) *Family Life and Illicit Love in Earlier Generations: Essays in Historical Sociology*. Cambridge University Press, Cambridge.

Laslett, P. (1987) The emergence of the Third Age. *Ageing and Society*, **7**, 133–160.

Laslett, P. (1989) *A Fresh Map of Life: The Emergence of the Third Age*. Weidenfeld and Nicolson, London.

Law, C.M. and Warnes, A.M. (1973) The movement of retired people to seaside resorts: a study of Morecambe and Llandudno. *Town Planning Review*, **44**, 373–390.

Law, C.M. and Warnes, A.M. (1975) Life begins at sixty: the increase in regional retirement migration. *Town and Country Planning*, **43**, 531–534.

Law, C.M. and Warnes, A.M. (1980) The characteristics of retired migrants. In: Herbert, D.T. and Johnston, R.J. (eds) *Geography and the Urban Environment. Progress in Research and Applications, Volume III*. Wiley, Chichester, pp. 175–222.

Law, C.M. and Warnes, A.M. (1982) The destination decision in retirement migration. In: Warnes, A.M. (ed.) *Geographical Perspectives on the Elderly*. Wiley, Chichester, pp. 53–81.

Lawton, M.P. (1975) The Philadelphia Geriatric Center morale scale: a revision. *Journal of Gerontology*, **30**, 85–89.

Lawton, M.P. (1980) *Environment and Aging*. Brooks-Cole, Monterey, CA.

Lawton, M.P. (1982) Competence, environmental press and the adaptation of older people. In: Lawton, M.P., Windley, P.G. and Byerts, T.O. (eds) *Aging and the Environment: Theoretical Approaches*. Springer, New York, pp. 33–59.

Lawton, M.P. (1984) The varieties of well-being. In: Malatesta, C.Z. and Izard, C.E. (eds) *Emotion in Adult Development*. Sage, Beverly Hills, CA, pp. 67–84.

Lawton, M.P. and Nahemow, L. (1973) Ecology and the aging process. In: Eisdorfer, C. and Lawton, M.P. (eds) *The Psychology of Adult Development and Aging*. American Psychological Association, Washington, pp. 619–674.

Lawton, M.P. and Yaffe, S. (1970) Mortality, morbidity and voluntary change of residence by older people. *Journal of the American Geriatric Society*, **20**, 821–831.

Lazarus, R. (1966) *Psychological Stress and the Coping Process*. McGraw–Hill, New York.

Lazarus, R.S. and DeLongis, A. (1983) Psychological stress and coping in aging. *American Psychologist*, 245–254.

Lazarus, R., Averill, J. and Opton, E. (1974) The psychology of coping: issues of research and assessment. In: Coelho, G., Hamburg, D. and Adams, J. *Coping and Adaptation*. Basic Books, New York, pp. 249–315.

Le Gros Clark, F. (1966) *Work, Age and Leisure*. Michael Joseph, London.

Leech, K. (1977) *Soul Friend: a Study of Spirituality*. Sheldon, London.

Lefebvre, H. (1968) *The Sociology of Marx*. Pantheon Books, New York.

Lehr, U.M. (1982) Depression und 'Lebensqualitaet' im Alter-Korrelate negativer und positiver Gestimmtheit. *Zeitschrift für Gerontologie*, **15**, 241–249.

Lehr, U. and Thomae, H. (eds) (1987) *Formen seelischen Alterns*. Ferdinand Enke Verlag, Stuttgart.

Lemke, S. and Moos, R.H. (1986) Quality of residential settings for elderly adults. *Journal of Gerontology*, **41**, 268–276.

Lesnoff-Caravaglia, G. (ed.) (1988) *Aging in a Technological Society*. Human Sciences Press, New York.

Levin, E., Sinclair, I. and Gorbach, P. (1988) *Families, Services and Confusion in Old Age*. Gower, Aldershot.

Levinson, D.J., Darrow, D.N., Klein, E.B., Levinson, M.H. and McKee, B. (1978) *The Seasons of a Man's Life*. Knopf, New York.

Lieberman, M.A. and Falk, J.M. (1971) The remembered past as a source of data for research on the life cycle. *Human Development*, **14**, 132–141.

Lieberman, M.A. and Tobin, S.S. (1983) *The Experience of Old Age: Stress, Coping and Survival*. Basic Books, New York.

Liggett, J. (1974) *The Human Face*. Constable, London.

Lindesay, J., Briggs, K. and Murphy, E. (1989) The Guy's/Age Concern Survey. Prevalence rates of cognitive impairment, depression and anxiety in an urban elderly community. *British Journal of Psychiatry*, **155**, 317–329.

Linn, M.W., Hunter, K. and Harris, R. (1980) Symptoms for depression and recent life events in the community elderly. *Journal of Clinical Psychology*, **36**, 675–682.

Lipman, A. and Longino, C. (1981) Family support networks in two life-care communities. Paper presented at the XIIth International Congress of Gerontology, Hamburg.

Lipman, A. and Slater, R. (1977) Homes for old people. Toward a positive environment. *The Gerontologist*, **17**, 146–156.

Lippman, W. (1922) *Public Opinion*. Macmillan, New York.

Litwak, E. and Szelenyi, I. (1969) Primary group structures and their functions: kin, neighbours and friends. *American Sociological Review*, **34**, 465–472.

Logan, W.P.D. (1953) Work and age: statistical considerations. *British Medical Journal*, **2**, 1190–1193.

Lohmann, N. (1980) Life satisfaction research in aging: implications for policy development. In: Datan, N. and Lohmann, N. (eds) *Transitions of Aging*. Academic Press, New York.

Long, J. (1987) Continuity as a basis for change: leisure and male retirement. *Leisure Studies*, **6**, 55–70.

Lopata, H. (1979) *Women as Widows*. Elsevier North Holland, New York.

Lopata, H. (1980) The widowed family member. In: Datan, N. and Lohmann, N. (eds) *Transitions of Ageing*. Academic Press, New York, pp. 93–118.

Lorand, A. (1922) *Old Age Deferred: The Causes of Old Age and Its Postponment by Hygienic and Therapeutic Measures*. Davis, Philadelphia.

Lowenthal, M. and Haven, C. (1968) Interaction and adaptation: intimacy as a critical variable. *American Sociological Review*, **33**, 20–30. Also in: Neugarten, B.L. (ed.) *Middle Age and Aging*. University of Chicago Press, Chicago, pp. 390–400.

Lowrey, S. and Briggs, R. (1988) Boom in private rest homes in Southampton: impact on the elderly in residential care. *British Medical Journal*, **296**, 541–543.

Luker, K.A. (1982) *Evaluating Health Visiting Practice*. Royal College of Nursing, London.

Luker, K.A. and Perkins, E.S. (1987) The elderly at home: service needs and provision. *Journal of the Royal College of General Practitioners*, **37**, 248–250.

Maas, H.S. (1985) The development of adult development: recollections and reflections. In: Munnichs, J.M.A., Mussen, P., Olbrich, E. and Coleman, P.G. (eds) *Life-Span and Change in a Gerontological Perspective*. Academic Press, Orlando, CA, pp. 161–175.

Maas, H.S. and Kuypers, J.A. (1974) *From Thirty to Seventy: A 40-Year Longitudinal Study of Adult Life Styles and Personality*. Jossey-Bass, San Francisco.

MacDonald, B. with Rich, C. (1984) *'Look Me in the Eye': Old Women, Ageing and Ageism*. The Women's Press, London.

MacFarlane, A. (1986) *Marriage and Love in England: Modes of Reproduction 1300–1840*. Basil Blackwell, Oxford.

MacIntyre, S. (1977) Old age as a social problem. In: Dingwall, R., Heath, C., Reid, M. and Stacey, M. (eds) *Health Care and Health Knowledge*. Croom Helm, London, pp. 41–63.

Mack, J. and Lansley, S. (1985) *Poor Britain*. Allen and Unwin, London.

Maddox, G.L. (1966) Retirement as a social event. In: McKinney, J.C. and de Vyer, F.T. (eds) *Aging and Social Policy*. Appleton Century-Croft, New York.

Maddox, G.L. (1968) Persistence of life style among the elderly: a longitudinal study of patterns of social activity in relation to life satisfaction. In: Neugarten, B.L. (ed.) *Middle Age and Aging*. University of Chicago Press, Chicago, pp. 181–183.

Maddox, G.L. (1985) Constructing the future of ageing. In: Coleman, M.T., Smith, B.K. and Warren, C. (eds) *Looking Forward: Texas and its Elderly*. Hogg Foundation for Mental Health, University of Texas, Austin.

Maddox, G.L. and Douglass, E.B. (1973) Self-assessment of health: a longitudinal study of elderly subjects. *Journal of Health and Social Behaviour*, **14**, 87–93.

Maddox, G.L. and Douglass, E.B. (1974) Aging and individual differences: a longitudinal analysis of social, psychological and physiological indicators. *Journal of Gerontology*, **29**, 555–563.

Maeda, D. (1978) Ageing in eastern society. In: Hobman, D. (ed.) *The Social Challenge of Ageing*. Croom Helm, London, pp. 55–70.

Malinowski, B. (1922) *Argonauts of the Western Pacific*. Routledge and Kegan Paul, London.

Manton, K.G. (1982) Changing concepts of morbidity and mortality in the elderly population. *Milbank Memorial Fund Quarterly/Health and Society*, **60**, 183–244.

Markides, K. and Cooper, C. (eds) (1987) *Retirement in Industrialised Societies*. Wiley, Chichester.

Marks, J. (1975) *Home Help*. Bell and Sons, London.

Martin, J. and Roberts, C. (1984) *Women and Employment: A Lifetime Perspective*. HMSO, London.

Martin, J., Meltzer, H. and Elliot, D. (1988) *The Prevalence of Disability Among Adults. OPCS Surveys of Disability in Great Britain, Report No.1*. HMSO, London.

Matza, D. (1969) *Becoming Deviant*. Prentice-Hall, Englewood Cliffs, NJ.

Maugham, S. (1959) *Points of View*. (Cited by Butler, R.N. (1963) op. cit.)

Maule, M.M., Milne, J.S. and Williamson, J. (1984) Mental illness and physical health in older people. *Age and Ageing*, **13**, 349–356.

Mauss, M. (1925) *The Gift*. Cohen and West, 1966 (English translation).

Maynard-Smith, J. (1962) Review lectures on senescence. 1. The causes of ageing. *Proceedings of the Royal Society of London, Series B*, **157**, 115–127.

Mays, N. (1983) Elderly South Asians in Britain: a survey of relevant literature and themes for future research. *Ageing and Society*, **3**, 71–98.

McArdle, C., Wylie, J.C. and Alexander, W.D. (1975). Geriatric patients in an acute medical ward. *British Medical Journal*, **4**, 568–569.

McGoldrick, A. and Cooper, C. (1980) Voluntary early retirement: taking the decision. *Employment Gazette*, August, 859–864.

McGoldrick, A. (1984) *Equal Treatment in Occupational Pension Schemes*. Equal Opportunities Commission, Manchester.

McGoldrick, A. (1989) Stress, early retirement and health. In: Markides, K. and Cooper, C. *Aging, Stress and Health*. Wiley, Chichester, pp. 91–118.

McKechnie, A.A. (1972) A point prevalance study of a long term hospital population. *Health Bulletin*, **31**, 250–258.

McKeown, T. (1979) *The Role of Medicine. Dream, Mirage or Nemesis?* Basil Blackwell, Oxford.

McKeown, T. and Cross, K.W. (1969) Responsibilities of hospitals and local authorities for elderly patients. *British Journal of Preventive and Social Medicine*, **23**, 34–39.

McMahon, A.W. and Rhudick, P.J. (1964) Reminiscing: adaptational significance in the aged. *Archives of General Psychiatry*, **10**, 292–298.

McManners, J. (1985) *Death and the Enlightenment: Changing Attitudes to Death Amongst Christians and Unbelievers in Eighteenth Century France*. Oxford University Press, Oxford.

Mead, G.H. (1964) In: Strauss, A. (ed.) *On Social Psychology: Selected Papers*. University of Chicago Press, Chicago.

Means, R. (1984) *Meals on Wheels*. School for Advanced Urban Studies, Bristol.

Mendelson, M.A. (1974) *Tender Loving Greed: How the Incredibly Lucrative Nursing Home 'Industry' Is Exploiting America's Old People and Defrauding Us All*. Alfred A. Knopf, New York.

Merriam, S. (1980) The concept and function of reminiscence: a review of the research. *The Gerontologist*, **20**, 604–609.

Mertens, F. and Wimmers, M. (1987) Life-style of older people: improvement or threat to their health? *Ageing and Society*, **7**, 329–343.

Merton, R. (1968) *Social Theory and Social Structure*. Free Press, New York.

Michaud, E. (1986) Old age in a rural English village. Unpublished paper presented at a workshop on The Anthropology of Client Groups, London.

Middleton, S. (1987) *An After Dinner's Sleep*. Methuen, London.

Midwinter, E. (1987) *Redefining Old Age*. Centre for Policy on Ageing, London.

Miles, W.R. (1931) Measures of certain human abilities throughout the life-span. *Proceedings of the National Academy of Science*, **17**, 627–633.

Miller, E.J. and Gwynne, G.V. (1972) *A Life Apart. A Pilot Study of Residential Institutions for the Physically Handicapped and the Young Chronic Sick*. Tavistock, London.

Mills, C.W. (1959) *The Sociological Imagination*. Penguin, Harmondsworth, 1970.

Ministry of Pensions and National Insurance Report (1954) *Reasons Given for Retiring or Continuing at Work*. HMSO, London.

Ministry of Pensions and National Insurance (1966) *Financial and Other Circumstances of Retirement Pensioners*. HMSO, London.

Minkler, M. (1981) Research on the health effects of retirement: an uncertain legacy. *Journal of Health and Social Behaviour*, **22**, 117–130.

Minkler, M. and Estes, C. (eds) (1984) *Readings in the Political Economy of Aging*. Baywood Publishing, Farmingdale, New York.

Moos, R.H., Gauvain, M., Lemke, S., Max, W. and Mehren, B. (1979) Assessing the social environments of sheltered care settings. *The Gerontologist*, **19**, 74–82.

Morgan, K.O. (1984) *Labour in Power*. Oxford University Press, Oxford.

Morgan, K., Dallosso, H.M., Arie, T., Byrne, E.J., Jones, R. and Waite, J. (1987) Mental health and psychological well-being among the old and very old living at home. *British Journal of Psychiatry*, **150**, 801–807.

Munnichs, J.M.A. (1966) *Old Age and Finitude*. Karger, Basle.

Munnichs, J.M.A. (1976) Dependency, interdependency and autonomy: an introduction. In: Munnichs, J.M.A. and van den Heuval, W.J.A. (eds) *Dependency and Interdependency in Old Age*. Martinus Nijhoff, The Hague, pp. 3–8.

Munnichs, J.M.A. (1987) Ageing and Meaning: Some Reflections. Paper given at an international workshop on 'Ageing and meaning', University of Nijmegen.

Munnichs, J.M.A., Mussen, P., Olbrich, E. and Coleman, P.G. (eds) (1985) *Life-Span and Change in a Gerontological Perspective*. Academic Press, Orlando, CA.

Murie, A. (1983) *Housing Inequality and Deprivation*. Heinemann, London.

Murphy, E. (1982) Social origins of depression in old age. *British Journal of Psychiatry*, **141**, 135–142.

Murphy, E. (1983) The prognosis of depression in old age. *British Journal of Psychiatry*, **142**, 111–119.

Murphy, G. (1986) 'Over the hill and far away': the production of a video-assisted training package. In: Hanley, I. and Gilhooly, M. (eds) *Psychological Therapies for the Elderly*. Croom Helm, London, pp. 151–162.

Mussen, P. (1985) Early adult antecedents of life satisfaction at age 70. In: Munnichs, J.M.A., Mussen, P., Olbrich, E. and Coleman, P.G. (eds) *Life-span and Change in a Gerontological Perspective*. Academic Press, CA, pp. 45–61.

Myerhoff, B. (1978) *Number our Days*. Simon and Schuster, New York.

Nadelson, T. (1969) A survey of the literature on the adjustment of the aged to retirement. *Journal of Geriatric Psychiatry*, **3**, 3–20.

National Institute for Social Work (1988) *Residential Care. A Positive Choice*. Report of the Independent Review of Residential Care, chaired by G. Wagner. HMSO, London.

Naylor, G.F.K. and Harwood, E. (1977) Das akademische Lernen bei alten Menschen. *Aktuelle Gerontologie*, **7**, 397–400.

Neisser, U. (1982) *Memory Observed: Remembering in Natural Contexts*. Freeman, San Fransisco.

Neugarten, B.L. (ed.) (1964) *Personality in Middle and Later Life*. Atherton Press, New York.

Neugarten, B.L. (1977) Personality and aging. In: Birren, J.E. and Schaie, K.W. (eds) *Handbook of the Psychology of Aging*. Van Nostrand Reinhold, New York, pp. 626–649.

Neugarten, B.L. (1979) Time, age and the life cycle. *The American Journal of Psychiatry*, **136**, 887–894.

Neugarten, B.L., Havighurst, R.J. and Tobin, S.S. (1961) The measurement of life satisfaction. *Journal of Gerontology*, **16**, 134–143.

Neugarten, B.L., Havighurst, R.J. and Tobin, S.E. (1968) Personality and patterns of aging. In: Neugarten, B.L. (ed.) *Middle Age and Aging*. University of Chicago Press, Chicago, pp. 173–177.

New Society (1982) The Family Pack, editorial. *New Society*, **62**, 1039.

Newson, J. and Newson, E. (1965) *Patterns of Infant Care*. Penguin, Harmondsworth.

Newton, N.A., Brauer, D., Gutmann, D.L. and Grunes, J. (1986) Psychodynamic therapy with the aged. A review. In: Brink, T.L. (ed.) *Clinical Gerontology*. Haworth Press, New York, pp. 205–229.

Neysmith, S.M. and Edwardh, J. (1984) Economic dependency in the 1980s: its impact on the third world elderly. *Ageing and Society*, **4**, 21–44.

Nies, H. and Munnichs, J. (1986) *Sinngebung und Altern*. Deutsches Zentrum für Altersfragen, Berlin.

Norman, A. (1980) *Rights & Risk: A Discussion Document on Civil Liberty in Old Age*. National Corporation for the Care of Old People, London.

Norman, A. (1985) *Triple Jeopardy: Growing Old in a Second Homeland*. Centre for Policy on Ageing, London.

Norman, A. (1987) *Aspects of Ageism: A Discussion Paper*. Centre for Policy on Ageing, London.

Norris, A. (1987) *Reminiscence with Elderly People*. Winslow Press, London.

O'Rand, A.M. and Henretta, J.C. (1982) Midwife work history and the retirement income of older single and married women. In: Szinovacz (ed.) *Women's Retirement: Policy Implications for Recent Research*. Sage, Beverly Hills, CA, pp. 25–44.

Office of Population, Censuses and Surveys (1982) *General Household Survey 1980*. HMSO, London.

Office of Population, Censuses and Surveys (1984a) *General Household Survey 1983*. HMSO, London.

Office of Population, Censuses and Surveys (1984b) *Population Projections. 1981–2021*, Series PP2, No.12. HMSO, London.

Office of Population, Censuses and Surveys (1984c) *Census Guide No.1*. HMSO, London.

Office of Population, Censuses and Surveys and Registrar General Scotland (1983) *Census 1981. Persons of Pensionable Age. Great Britain*. HMSO, London and Edinburgh.

Olbrich, E. (1985) Coping and development in the later years: a process-oriented approach to personality and development. In: Munnichs, J.M.A., Mussen, P., Olbrich, E. and Coleman, P.G. (eds) *Life-Span and Change in a Gerontological Perspective*. Academic Press, Orlando, pp. 133–155.

Olbrich, E. and Thomae, H. (1978) Empirical findings to a cognitive theory of aging. *International Journal of Behavioral Development*, **1**, 67–84.

Olsen, H. and Hansen, G. (1981) *Living Conditions of the Aged 1977*. National Institute of Social Research, Copenhagen.

Orgel, L.E. (1970) The maintenance of the accuracy of protein synthesis and its relevance to ageing: a correction. *Proceedings of the National Academy of Science (USA)*, **67**, 1476–1479.

Orwell, G. (1939) *Coming Up for Air*. Gollancz, London, republished (1962) by Penguin, Harmondsworth.

Pahl, R.E., Flynn, R. and Buck, N.H. (1983) *Structure and Processes of Urban Life*. 2nd edition. Longman, London.

Palmore, E.B. (ed.) (1970) *Normal Aging*. Duke University Press, Durham, North Carolina.

Palmore, E.B. (ed.) (1974) *Normal Aging II*. Duke University Press, Durham, North Carolina.

Palmore, E.B. (1978) Compulsory versus flexible retirement: issues and facts. In: Carver, V. and Liddeard, P. (eds) *An Ageing Population*. Hodder and Stoughton, Sevenoaks, pp. 87–93.

Palmore, E.B. and Kivett, V. (1977) Change in life satisfaction: a longitudinal study of persons aged 46–70. *Journal of Gerontology*, **32**, 311–316.

Palmore, E.B. and Luikart, C. (1972) Health and social factors related to life satisfaction. *Journal of Health and Social Behaviour*, **13**, 68–80.

Palmore, E.G., Burchett, B., Fillenbaum, G., George, L. and Wallman, L. (1985) *Retirement: Causes and Consequences*. Springer, New York.

Panel on Nutrition of the Elderly (1972). A nutrition survey of the elderly. Department of Health and Social Security, Reports on Health and Social Subjects No.3. HMSO, London.

Parker, G. (1985) *With Due Care and Attention. A Review of Research on Informal Care*. Family Policy Studies Centre, London.

Parker, S. (1980) *Older Workers and Retirement*. HMSO, London.

Parkes, C.M. (1986) *Bereavement: Studies of Grief in Adult Life*. 2nd edition. Tavistock, London.

Parnes, H. and Less, L. (1983) *From Work to Retirement: The Experience of a National Sample of Men*. Center for Human Resource Research, mimeo, Ohio State University.

Parry, G. and Brewin,. C.R. (1988) Cognitive style and depression: symptom-related, event-related or independent provoking factor? *British Journal of Clinical Psychology*, **27**, 23–35.

Parsons, P.L. (1965) Mental health of Swansea's old folk. *British Journal of Preventive and Social Medicine*, **19**, 43–47.

Parsons, T. (1942) Age and sex in the social structure of the United States. *American Sociological Review*, **7**, 604–616.

Peace, S. (1981) *An International Perspective on the Status of Older Women*. International

Federation on Ageing, Washington.

Peace, S. (1986) The forgotten female: social policy and older women. In: Phillipson, C. and Walker A. (eds) *Ageing and Social Policy: A Critical Assessment*. Gower, Aldershot, pp. 61–86.

Peck, R.C. (1968) Psychological developments in the second half of life. In: Neugarten, B.L. (ed.) *Middle Age and Aging*. University of Chicago Press, Chicago, pp. 88–92.

Pennington, D.R. (1986) *Essential Social Psychology*. Edward Arnold, London.

Perlmutter, M. and Mitchell, D.B. (1982) The appearance and disappearance of age differences in adult memory. In: Craik, F.I.M. and Trehub, S. (eds) *Aging and Cognitive Processes*. Plenum Press, New York, pp. 127–144.

Phillips Committee (1954) *Report of the Committee on the Economic and Financial Problems of the Provision for Old Age, Cmnd 993*. HMSO, London.

Phillipson, C. (1982) *Capitalism and the Construction of Old Age*. Macmillan, London.

Phillipson, C. (1987) The transition to retirement. In: Cohen, G. (ed.) *Social Change and the Life Course*. Tavistock, London, pp. 156–183.

Phillipson, C. and Strang, P. (1983) *Pre-Retirement Education: A Longitudinal Evaluation*. Department of Adult Education, University of Keele, Stoke-on-Trent.

Phillipson, C. and Walker, A. (1986) *Ageing and Social Policy*. Gower, Aldershot.

Pifer, A. and Bronte, L. (eds) (1987) *Our Ageing Society*. W.W. Norton, New York.

Pilisuk, M. and Parks, S.H. (1986) *The Healing Web: Social Networks and Human Survival*. University Press of New England, Hanover, New Hampshire.

Pincus, A. and Wood, V. (1970) Methodological issues in measuring the environment in institutions for the aged and its impact on residents. *Ageing and Human Development*, **1**, 117–126.

Plank, D. (1977) *Caring for the Elderly: Report of a Study of Various Means of Caring for Dependent Elderly People in Eight London Boroughs*, London Council Research Memorandum, RM512. GLC, London.

Pleck, J. (1975) Man to man: is brotherhood possible? In: Glazer-Malbin, N. (ed.) *Old Family, New Family*. Van Nostrand, New York, pp. 230–244.

Political and Economic Planning (1948) *Population Policy in Great Britain*. PEP, London.

Porter, R. (1982) *English Society in the Eighteenth Century*. Penguin, Harmondsworth.

Post, F. and Shulman, K. (1985) New views on old age affective disorders. In: Arie, T. (ed.) *Recent Advances in Psychogeriatrics*. Churchill Livingstone, Edinburgh, pp. 119–140.

Pottle, S. (1984) Developing a network-orientated service for elderly people and their carers. In: Treacher, A. and Carpenter, J. (eds) *Using Family Therapy: A Guide for Practitioners in Different Professional Settings*. Basil Blackwell, Oxford, pp. 149–165.

Powell, C. and Crombie, A. (1974) The Kilsyth Questionnaire: a method of screening elderly people at home. *Age and Ageing*, **3**, 23–28.

Pratt, H.J. (1976) *The Politics of Old Age*, University of Chicago, Chicago.

Pratt, J.D. and Wood, L.E. (1984) Cognition and elderly people. *Ageing and Society*, **4**, 273–304.

Pre-Retirement Choice (1974) October.

Puner, M. (1974) *To the Good Long Life*. Macmillan, London.

Puner, M. (1978) *To the Good Long Life: What we Know About Growing Old*. Macmillan/The Open University, London.

Quadagno, J. (1982) *Ageing in Early Industrial Society: Work, Family and Social Policy in 19th Century England*. Academic Press, London.

Qureshi, H. (1986) Responses to dependency: Reciprocity and power in family relations. In: Phillipson, C., Bernard, M. and Strang, P. (eds) *Dependency and Interdependency in Old Age – Theoretical Perspectives and Policy Alternatives*. Croom Helm, London, pp. 167–179.

Rabbitt, P.M.A. (1980) A fresh look at changes in reaction times in old age. In: Stein, D. (ed.) *The Psychobiology of Ageing: Problems and Perspectives*. Elsevier/North Holland, New York.

Rabbitt, P.M.A. (1981) Talking to the old. *New Society*, 22 January, pp. 141–142.

Rabbitt, P.M.A. (1982a) How to assess the aged? An experimental psychologist's view. Some comments on Dr Kendrick's paper. *British Journal of Clinical Psychology*, **21**, 55–59.

Rabbitt, P.M.A. (1982b) How do old people know what to do next? In: Craik, F.I.M. and Trehub, S. (eds) *Aging and Cognitive Processes*. Plenum Press, New York, pp. 79–98.

Rabbitt, P.M.A. (1984) Investigating the grey areas. *Times Higher Education Supplement*, 1 June, 14.

Rabbitt, P.M.A. (1985) An age decrement in the ability to ignore irrelevant information. *Journal of Gerontology*, **20**, 233–238.

Rabbitt, P.M.A. (1988) Social psychology, neuroscience and cognitive psychology need each other; (and Gerontology needs all three of them). *The Psychologist: Bulletin of the British Psychological Society*, **12**, 500–506.

Rabinowitz, J.C. and Ackerman, B.P. (1982) General encoding of episodic events by elderly adults. In: Craik, F.I.M. and Trehub, S. (eds) *Aging and Cognitive Processes*. Plenum Press, New York, pp. 145–154.

Raglan, Lord (1972) *Retirement Choice*, **2**.

Rapoport, R. and Rapoport, R. (1977) *Fathers, Mothers and Others*. Routledge and Kegan Paul, London.

Ratna, L. and Davis, J. (1984) Family therapy with the elderly mentally ill. Some strategies and techniques. *British Journal of Psychiatry*, **145**, 311–315.

Rebok, G.W. and Hoyer, W.J. (1977) The functional context of elderly behaviour. *The Gerontologist*, **17**, 27–34.

Reichard, S., Livson, F. and Peterson, P.G. (1962) *Aging and Personality*. Wiley, New York.

Reker, G.T. and Wong, P.T.P. (1988) Aging as an individual process: toward a theory of personal meaning. In: Birren, J.E. and Bengtson, V.L. (eds) *Emergent Theories of Aging*. Springer, New York, pp. 214–246.

Reker, G.T., Peacock, E.J. and Wong, P.T.P. (1987) Meaning and purpose in life and well-being: a life-span perspective. *Journal of Gerontology*, **42**, 44–49.

Renshaw, J., Hampson, R., Thomason, C., Darton, R., Judge, K. and Knapp, M. (eds) (1988) *Care in the Community: The First Steps*. Gower, Aldershot.

Report of the Royal College of Physicians of London by the College Committee on Geriatrics (1981) Organic mental impairment in the elderly. Implications for research, education and the provision of services. *Journal of the Royal College of Physicians of London*, **15**, 141–167.

Report of the Royal Commission on the Poor Laws (1834) *Report of the Royal Commission on the Poor Laws and Relief of Distress*. HMSO, London.

Retirement Choice (1972) 1 and 2 November.

Rex, J. and Moore, R. (1967) *Race, Community and Conflict*. Oxford University Press, Oxford.

Richardson, I.M. (1956) Retirement: A socio-medical study of 244 men. *Scottish Medical Journal*, **1**, 381–391.

Riegel, K.F. (1973) Dialectical operations: the final period of cognitive development. *Human Development*, **16**, 346–370.

Riegel, K.F. (1977) History of psychological gerontology. In: Birren, J.E. and Schaie, K.W. (eds) *Handbook of the Psychology of Aging*. Van Nostrand Reinhold, New York, pp. 70–102.

Riegel, K.F. and Riegel, R.M. (1972) Development, drop and death. *Developmental Psychology*, **6**, 306–319.

Riley, M.W., Johnson, M. and Foner, A. (1968) *Aging and Society: An Inventory of Research Findings*. Russell Sage Foundation, New York.

Ritchie, J. and Barrowclough, R. (1983) *Paying for Equalisation*. EOC, Manchester.

Robb, S.S., Stegman, C.E. and Wolanin, M.O. (1986) No research versus research with compromised results: a study of validation therapy. *Nursing Research*, **35**, 113–118.

Robinson, P.K., Livingston, J. and Birren, J. (eds) (1984) *Aging and Technological Advances.* Plenum, New York.

Robson, B.T. (1975) *Urban Social Areas.* Oxford University Press, Oxford.

Robson, P. (1980) *Profiles of the Elderly: 7, Their Housing, Vol.5.* Age Concern, London.

Rodin, J. (1986) Aging and health: effects of the sense of control. *Science,* **233**, 1271–1276.

Roe, P. and Gueillem, V. (1978) The need for medical supervision in homes. *Health and Social Services Journal,* Feb. **10**, 168–169.

Roebuck, J. (1978) When does 'old age' begin?: The evolution of the English definition. *Journal of Social History,* **12**, 416–428.

Roebuck, J. and Slaughter, J. (1979) Ladies and pensioners: Stereotypes and public policy affecting old women in England, 1880–1940. *Journal of Social History,* **13**, 105–114.

Rose, A.M. (1965a) A current theoretical issue in social gerontology. In: Rose, A.M., Arnold, M. and Peterson, W.A. *Older People and their Social Worlds.* F.A. Davis, Philadelphia, pp. 359–366.

Rose, A.M. (1965b) The subculture theory of aging: A framework for research in social gerontology. In: Rose, A.M., Arnold, M. and Peterson, W.A. *Older People and their Social Worlds.* F.A. Davis, Philadelphia, pp. 3–16.

Rose, E. (1978) *Housing for the Aged.* Saxon House, Farnborough.

Rose, E. (1982) *Housing Needs and the Elderly.* Gower, Aldershot.

Rosow, I. (1967) *Social Integration of the Aged.* Free Press, New York.

Rosow, I. (1974) *Socialization to Old Age.* University of California Press, Berkeley.

Rosow, I. (1977) Morale: concept and measurement. In: Nydegger, C.N. (ed.) *Measuring Morale: a Guide to Effective Measurement.* Gerontological Society, Washington DC.

Rosser, C. and Harris, C. (1965) *The Family in Social Change.* Routledge and Kegan Paul, London.

Rossiter, C. and Wicks, M. (1982) *Crisis or Challenge? Family Care, Elderly People and Social Policy.* Study Commission on the Family, London.

Rothwell, N., Britton, P.G. and Woods, R.T. (1983) The effect of group living in a residential home for the elderly. *British Journal of Social Work,* **13**, 639–643.

Rowe, J.W. and Kahn, R.L. (1987) Human aging: usual and successful. *Science,* **237**, 143–149.

Rowles, G. (1980) Toward a geography of growing old. In: Buttimer, A. and Seamon, D. (eds) *The Human Experience of Space and Place.* Croom Helm, London, pp. 55–72.

Rowles, G. (1981) The surveillance zone as meaningful space for the aged. *The Gerontologist,* **21**, 304–311.

Rowntree, B.S. (1901) *Poverty: A Study of Town Life.* Macmillan, London.

Royal College of Physicians of London (1981) Organic mental impairment in the elderly. Implications for research, education and the provision of services. Report by the College Committee on Geriatrics. *Journal of the Royal College of Physicians of London,* **15**, 141–167.

Royal Commission on the Distribution of Income and Wealth (1978) *Lower Incomes, Cmnd 7175.* HMSO, London.

Royal Commission on Population (1949) *Report.* HMSO, London.

Rubin, S.G. and Davies, G.H. (1975) Bed blocking by elderly patients in general wards. *Age and Ageing,* **4**, 142–147.

Ryff, C.D. (1984) Personality development from the inside: the subjective experience of change in adulthood and aging. In: Baltes, P.B. and Brim, O.G. (eds) *Life-Span Development and Behavior Vol. 6.* Academic Press, New York, pp. 243–279.

Ryff, C.D. and Heincke, S.G. (1983) Subjective organisation of personality in adulthood and aging. *Journal of Personality and Social Psychology,* **44**, 807–816.

Sackville-West, V. (1931) *All Passion Spent.* Hogarth Press, London.

Salthouse, T.A. (1987) The role of experience in cognitive aging. In: Schaie, K.W. and Eisdorfer, C. (eds) *Annual Review of Gerontology and Geriatrics,* **7**, 135–158.

Savage, R.D., Britton, P.G., Bolton, N. and Hall, E.H. (1973) *Intellectual Functioning in the Aged*. Methuen, London.

Savage, R.D., Gaber, L.B., Britton, P.G., Bolton, N. and Cooper, A. (1977) *Personality and Adjustment in the Aged*. Academic Press, London.

Schaie, K.W. (1977–78) Towards a stage theory of adult cognitive development. *Journal of Aging and Human Development*, **8**, 129–138.

Schaie, K.W. and Labouvie-Vief, G. (1974) Generational versus ontogenetic components of change in adult cognitive behaviour: a fourteen year cross-sequential study. *Developmental Psychology*, **10**, 305–320.

Schaie, K.W. and Marquette, B. (1972) Personality in maturity and old age. In: Dreger, R.M. (ed.) *Multivariate Personality Research: Contributions to the Understanding of Personality in Honour of Raymond B. Cattell*. Clautors, Louisiana.

Schaie, K.W. and Strother, C.R. (1968) A cross-sequential study of age changes in cognitive behaviour. *Psychological Bulletin*, **70**, 671–680.

Scheff, T.J. (1964) The societal reaction to deviance: Ascriptive elements in the psychiatric screening of mental patients in a Midwestern State. *Social Problems*, **11**, 401–413.

Scheff, T. (1974) The labelling theory of mental illness. *American Sociological Review*, **39**, 444–452.

Scheidt, R.J. and Windley, P.G. (1985) The ecology of aging. In: Birren, J.E. and Schaie, K.W. (eds) *Handbook of the Psychology of Aging*. Van Nostrand Reinhold, New York, pp. 245–258.

Schneider, W.F. (1987) Die psychische und soziale Situation von Hochbetagten. In: Lehr, U. and Thomae, H. (eds) *Formen Seelischen Alterns, Ergebnisse und Eindrücke vom 8 Untersuchungsdurchgang*. Enke, Stuttgart, pp. 196–227.

Schooler, K.K. (1982) Response of the elderly to environment. A stress-theoretical perspective. In: Lawton, M.P., Windley, P.G. and Byerts, T.O. (eds) *Aging and the Environment: Theoretical Approaches*. Springer, New York, pp. 80–96.

Schutz, A. (1972) *The Phenomenology of the Social World*. Heinemann, London.

Schwartz, A.N. (1975) An observation on self esteem as the linchpin of quality of life for the aged. *The Gerontologist*, **15**, 470–472.

Schwartz, H. (1986) *Never Satisfied: A Cultural History of Diets, Fantasies and Fat*. Free Press/Collier Macmillan, New York and London.

Seabrook, J. (1980) *The Way We Are*. Age Concern England, Mitcham, Surrey.

Seiden, A. and Bart, P. (1975) Woman to woman. In: Glazer-Malbin, N. (ed.) *Old Family, New Family*. Van Nostrand, New York, pp. 189–228.

Selye, H. (1976) *The Stress of Life*. McGraw-Hill, New York.

Shanas, E. (1979) Social myth as hypothesis: the case of the family relationships of old people. *Gerontology*, **19**, 3–9.

Shanas, E. (1980) Older people and their families: the new pioneers. *Journal of Marriage and the Family*, **42**, 9–15.

Shanas, E., Townsend, P., Wedderburn, D., Friis, H., Milhoj, P. and Stehouwer, J. (1965) *Old People in Three Industrial Societies*. Routledge and Kegan Paul, London.

Sharp, A.D. (1988) The Impact of Ageing upon the Attitudes and Behaviour of Elderly Residents in McCarthy and Stone Private Sheltered Housing. Unpublished PhD thesis. University of Southampton.

Shaw, L.B. (1984) Retirement plans of middle-aged married women. *The Gerontologist*, **24**, 154–159.

Sheehy, G. (1976) *Passages: Predictable Crises of Adult Life*. Dutton, New York.

Sheldon, J.H. (1948) *The Social Medicine of Old Age*. Oxford University Press, Oxford.

Shephard, R.J. (1978) *Physical Activity and Ageing*. Croom Helm, London.

Sherman, E. (1981) *Counseling the Aging: an Integrative Approach*. Free Press, New York.

Shorter, E. (1983) *A History of Women's Bodies*. Allen Lane, London.

Shragge, E. (1984) *Pensions Policy in Britain*. Routledge and Kegan Paul, London.

Siegler, I.C. (1980) The psychology of adult development and aging. In: Busse, E.W. and Blazer, D.G. (eds) *Handbook of Geriatric Psychiatry*. Van Nostrand Reinhold, New York, pp. 169–221.

Siegler, I.C. (1983) Psychological aspects of the Duke longitudinal studies. In: Schaie, K.W. (ed.) *Longitudinal Studies of Adult Psychological Development*. The Guildford Press, New York.

Siegler, I.C. and Botwinick, J. (1979) A long-term longitudinal study of the intellectual ability of older adults – the matter of selective subject attrition. *Journal of Gerontology*, **34**, 242–248.

Simenon, G. (1976) *The Cat in Ninth Omnibus Edition*. Penguin, Harmondsworth.

Simpson, I.H. and McKinney, J.C. (1966) *Social Aspects of Ageing*. Duke University Press, Durham, North Carolina.

Sixsmith, A.J. (1986) Independence and home in later life. In: Phillipson, C., Bernard, M. and Strang, P. (eds) *Dependency and Interdependency in Old Age – Theoretical Perspectives and Policy Alternatives*. Croom Helm, London, pp. 338–347.

Skinner, B.F. and Vaughan, M.E. (1983) *Enjoy Old Age: A Programme of Self-management*. Hutchinson, London.

Skultans, V. (1979) *English Madness: Ideas on Insanity 1580–1890*. Routledge and Kegan Paul, London.

Slater, P. (1963) Cultural attitudes towards the aged. *Geriatrics*, **18**.

Smith, H.W. (1975) *Strategies of Social Research. The Methodological Imagination*. Prentice-Hall, Englewood Cliffs, NJ.

Smith, P.B. and Smith, L.J. (1987) *Continence and Incontinence: Psychological Approaches to Development and Treatment*. Croom Helm, London.

Sommer, R. and Ross, H. (1958) Social interaction on a geriatric ward. *International Journal Social Psychiatry*, **4**, 128–133.

Sontag, S. (1978) The double standard of ageing. In: Carver, V. and Liddiard, P. (eds) *An Ageing Population: A Reader and Sourcebook*. Hodder and Stoughton, Open University Press, Sevenoaks, pp. 72–78.

Stearns, P. (1977) *Old Age in European Society: The Case of France*. Croom Helm, London.

Stevenson, O. (1980) A special relationship. *New Age*, Summer, 18–22.

Stieglitz, E.J. (1949) *The Second Forty Years*. Staples Press, London.

Stoddard, K.M. (1983) *Saints and Shrews: Women and Ageing in American Popular Film*. Greenwood Press, London.

Stokes, G. (1986a) *Shouting and Screaming*. Winslow Press, London.

Stokes, G. (1986b) *Wandering*. Winslow Press, London.

Stokes, G. (1986c) *Aggression*. Winslow Press, London.

Stokes, G. (1986d) *Incontinence and Inappropriate Urinating*. Winslow Press, London.

Stone, L. (1977) Walking over Grandma. *The New York Review of Books*, **24** (12 May), 26–29.

Stone, R. and Minkler, M. (1984) The socio-political context of women's retirement. In: Minkler, M. and Estes, C. (eds) *Political Economy of Aging*. Baywood, New York, pp. 225–238.

Stott, M. (1981) *Ageing for Beginners*. Basil Blackwell, Oxford.

Stout, R.W. and Crawford, V. (1988) Active-life expectancy and terminal dependency: trends in long-term geriatric care over 33 years. *Lancet*, **i**, 281–283.

Strehler, B.L. (1962) *Time, Cells and Aging*. Academic Press, New York and London.

Streib, G.F. and Schneider, C.J. (1971) *Retirement in American Society*. Cornell University Press, Ithaca, NY.

Sugarman, L. (1986) *Life-Span Development. Concepts, Theories and Interventions*. Methuen, London.

Szasz, T.S. (1971) *The Manufacture of Madness*. Routledge and Kegan Paul, London.

Talland, G.A. (1965) Three estimates of the word span and their stability over the adult years. *Quarterly Journal of Experimental Psychology*, **17**, 301–307.

Tamke, S.S. (1978) Human values and ageing: the perspective of the Victorian nursery. In: *Ageing and the Elderly: Humanistic Perspectives in Gerontology*.

Taylor, R. and Ford, G. (1983) Inequalities in old age. *Ageing and Society*, **3**, 183–208.

Thane, P. (1978) The muddled history of retiring at 60 and 65. *New Society*, 3 August, 234–236.

Thane, P. (1985) Old age in Victorian Britain. *New Age*, **30**, 11–12.

Thane, P. (1987) *Economic Burden or Benefit? A Positive View of Old Age.* Centre for Economic Policy Research, London.

Thomae, H. (ed.) (1976) *Patterns of Aging: Findings from the Bonn Longitudinal Study of Aging.* Karger, Basle.

Thomae, H. (1983) *Alternsstile and Altersschicksale.* Hans Huber, Berne.

Thomae, H. (1986) Response hierarchies related to different areas of life stress. In: Angleitner, A., Furnham, A. and Van Heck, G. (eds) *Personality Psychology in Europe Vol.2.* Swets and Zeitlinger, Lisse, pp. 47–62.

Thomas, K. (1976) Age and authority in early modern England. *Proceedings of the British Academy*, **62**, 205–248.

Thompson, C. and West, P. (1984) The public appeal of sheltered housing. *Ageing and Society*, **4**, 305–326.

Thomson, D. (1983) Workhouse to nursing home: residential care of elderly people in England since 1840. *Ageing and Society*, **3**, 41–69.

Thomson, D. (1984) The decline of social welfare: falling state support for the elderly since early Victorian times. *Ageing and Society*, **4**, 451–482.

Thornton, S. and Brotchie, J. (1987) Reminiscence: a critical review of the empirical literature. *British Journal of Clinical Psychology*, **26**, 93–111.

Tibbitts, C. (1954) Retirement problems in American society. *American Journal of Sociology*, **59**, 301–308.

Timaeus, I. (1986) Families and households of the elderly population. *Ageing and Society*, **6**, 271–293.

Tinker, A. (1984) *Staying at Home: Helping Elderly People.* HMSO, London.

Tinker, A. (1987) A review of the contribution of housing to policies for the frail elderly. *International Journal of Geriatric Psychiatry*, **2**, 3–17.

Tissue, T. (1972) Another look at self-rated health among the elderly. *Journal of Gerontology*, **27**, 91–94.

Titmuss, R.M. (1963) *Essays on 'the Welfare State'*, 2nd edition. Allen and Unwin, London.

Titmuss, R.M. (1970) *The Gift Relationship: from Human Blood to Social Policy.* Allen and Unwin, London.

Todd, A.T. (1946) *Medical Aspects of Growing Old.* John Wright, Bristol.

Townsend, P. (1955) The anxieties of retirement. *Transactions of the Association of Industrial Medical Officers*, **5**, 1.

Townsend, P. (1957) *The Family Life of Old People.* Routledge and Kegan Paul, London.

Townsend, P. (1962) *The Last Refuge – A Survey of Residential Institutions and Homes for the Aged in England and Wales.* Routledge and Kegan Paul, London.

Townsend, P. (1965) On the likelihood of admission to an institution. In: Shanas, E. and Streib, G.F. (eds), *Social Structure and the Family Generational Relations.* Prentice Hall, Englewood Cliffs, NJ, pp. 163–187.

Townsend, P. (1973) The needs of the elderly and the planning of hospitals. In: *Needs of the Elderly for Health and Welfare Services.* Institute of Biometry and Community, University of Exeter, pp. 47–70.

Townsend, P. (1979) *Poverty in the United Kingdom. A Survey of Household Resources and Standards of Living.* Penguin, Harmondsworth.

Townsend, P. (1981) The structured dependency of the elderly: creation of social policy in the twentieth century. *Ageing and Society*, **1**, 5–28.

Townsend, P. (1986) Ageism and social policy. In: Phillipson, C. and Walker, A. (eds) *Ageing and Social Policy.* Gower, Aldershot, pp. 15–44.

Townsend, P. (1989) The social and economic hardship of elderly people in London: new evidence from a survey and a discussion of the influence of social policy upon current trends. *Generations*, **9**, 10–30.

Townsend, P. and Wedderburn, D. (1965) *The Aged in the Welfare State. Occasional Papers on Social Administration, No.14*. Bell, London.

Townsend, P. with Corrigan, P. and Kowarzik, U. (1987) *Poverty and Labour in London*. Low Pay Unit, London.

Troll, L. and Smith, J. (1976) Attachment through the lifespan. *Human Development*, **19**, 156–170.

Tunstall, J. (1966) *Old and Alone*. Routledge and Kegan Paul, London.

Twining, C. (1988) *Helping Older People: a Psychological Approach*. Wiley, Chichester.

United Nations (1985) *The World Ageing Situation: Strategies and Policies*. United Nations, New York.

Vetter, N. (1981) Urinary incontinence in the elderly at home. *Lancet*, 1275–1277.

Victor, C.R. (1987) *Old Age in Modern Society*. Croom Helm, London.

Wade, B., Sawyer, L. and Bell, J. (1983) *Dependency with Dignity, Occasional Papers on Social Administration, No. 68*. Bedford Square Press, London.

Waldman, D.S. and Avolio, B.S. (1983) *Enjoy Old Age*. Norton, New York.

Walker, A. (1980) The social creation of poverty and dependence in old age. *Journal of Social Policy*, **9**, 49–75.

Walker, A. (1981) Towards a political economy of old age. *Ageing and Society*, **1**, 73–94.

Walker, A. (1982a) The social consequences of early retirement. *Political Quarterly*, **53**, 61–72.

Walker, A. (1982b) Dependency and old age. *Social Policy and Administration*, **16**, 115–135.

Walker, A. (1983) Social policy and elderly people in Great Britain: the construction of dependent social and economic status in old age. In: Guillemard, A. (ed.) *Old Age and the Welfare State*. Sage, London, pp. 143–167.

Walker, A. (1985) Early retirement: release or refuge from the labour market? *The Quarterly Journal of Social Affairs*, **1**, 211–229.

Walker, A. (1986a) The politics of ageing in Britain. In: Phillipson, C., Bernard, M. and Strang, P. (eds) *Dependency and Interdependency in Later Life: Theoretical Perspectives and Policy Alternatives*. Croom Helm, London, pp. 30–45.

Walker, A. (1986b) The growth of poverty among the elderly population and the reasons for low take up of benefits. In: *Poverty and Older People*, Age Concern Scotland, Edinburgh, pp. 8–20.

Walker, A. (1986c) Pensions and the production of poverty in old age. In: Phillipson, C. and Walker, A. (eds) *Ageing and Social Policy*. Gower, Aldershot, pp. 184–216.

Walker, A. (1987) The poor relation: poverty among old women. In: Glendinning, C. and Millar, J. (eds) *Women and Poverty in Britain*. Wheatsheaf Books, Brighton, pp. 178–198.

Walker, A. and Laczko, F. (1982) Early retirement and flexible retirement. In: House of Commons Social Services Committee, *Age of Retirement*, HC 26-II, HMSO, London, pp. 211–229.

Walker, A., Noble, I. and Westergaard, J. (1985) From secure employment to labour market insecurity: the impact of redundancy on older workers in the steel industry. In: Roberts, B., Finnegan, R. and Gallie, D. (eds) *New Approaches to Economic Life*. Manchester University Press, Manchester.

Walker, A. and Phillipson, C. (1986) Introduction. In: Phillipson, C. and Walker, A. (eds) *Ageing and Social Policy. A Critical Assessment*. Gower, Aldershot, pp. 1–12.

Walker, A. and Phillipson, C. (eds) (1986) *Ageing and Social Policy*. Gower, Aldershot.

Walker, A. and Walker, C. (1987) (eds) *The Growing Divide*. Child Poverty Action Group, London.

Walker, R. (1986) Progress in private sheltered housing. *Housing and Planning Review. Housing and Elderly People*, **41**, 25–26.

Walker, R., Lawson, R. and Townsend, P. (1983) *Responses to Poverty: Lessons from Abroad*. Heinemann, London.

Walters, M. (1978) *The Nude Male*. Paddington Press, New York and London.

Warnes, A. and Law, C. (1985) Elderly population distributions and housing prospects in Britain. *Town Planning Review*, **56**, 292–313.

Warnes, A., Howes, D. and Took, L. (1985) Intimacy at a distance under the microscope. In: Butler, A. (ed.) *Ageing; Recent Advances and Creative Responses*. Croom Helm, London, pp. 98–112.

Warrington, E.K. and Sanders, H.I. (1971) The fate of old memories. *Quarterly Journal of Experimental Psychology*, **24**, 432–442.

Wattis, J. and Church, M. (1986) *Practical Psychiatry in Old Age*. Croom Helm, London.

Weaver, T., Willcocks, D.M. and Kellaher, L.A. (1985) *The Pursuit of Profit and Care: Patterns and Processes in Private Residential Homes for Old People*. Polytechnic of North London, Centre for Environmental and Social Studies in Ageing.

Weber, M. (1930) *The Protestant Ethic and the Spirit of Capitalism*. Allen and Unwin, London.

Wechsler, D. (1944) *The Measurement of Adult Intelligence*, 3rd edition. Williams and Wilkins, Baltimore, MD.

Weg, R. (1983a) *Sexuality in the Later Years: Roles and Behaviour*. Academic Press, New York.

Weg, R.B. (1983b) The physiological perspective. In: Weg, R.B. (ed.) *Sexuality in the Later Years: Roles and Behavior*. Academic Press, New York, pp. 40–80.

Welford, A.T. (1958) *Ageing and Human Skill*. Oxford University Press, London.

Welford, A.T. (1976) Thirty years of psychological research on age and work. *Journal of Occupational Psychology*, **49**, 129–138.

Wells, B.W.P. (1983) *Body and Personality*. Longman, London and New York.

Wenger, G.C. (1984) *The Supportive Network*. Allen and Unwin, London.

Wenger, G.C. (1986) A longitudinal study of changes and adaptations in the support networks of Welsh elderly over 75. *Journal of Cross-Cultural Gerontology*, **1**, 277–304.

Wenger, G.C. (1987a) *Support Networks: Change and Stability*. Second Report of a follow-up study of elderly people in North Wales. The Centre for Social Policy Research and Development, University College of North Wales, Bangor.

Wenger, G.C. (1987b) *Relationships in Old Age – Inside Support Networks*. Third Report of a follow-up study of elderly people in North Wales. The Centre for Social Policy Research and Development, University College of North Wales, Bangor.

Wenger, G.C. (1987c) Dependence, independence and reciprocity after 80. *Journal of Aging Studies*, **1**, 355–377.

Wermal, M.T. and Gelbaum, S. (1945) Work and retirement in old age. *American Journal of Sociology*, **51**, 16–21.

Wheeler, R. (1982) Staying put: a new development in policy. *Ageing and Society*, **2**, 299–329.

Wheeler, R. (1986) Housing policy and elderly people. In: Phillipson, C. and Walker, A. (eds) *Ageing and Social Policy. A Critical Assessment*. Gower, Aldershot, pp. 217–233.

Wicks, M. (1978) *Old and Cold*. Heinemann, London.

Wicks, M. (1989) Community care: the challenge for social policy. *Generations*, **9**, 31–46.

Wicks, M. and Henwood, M. (1988) The social and demographic circumstances of elderly people. In: Gearing, B., Johnson, M.L. and Heller, T. (eds) *Mental Health Problems in Old Age*. Wiley, Chichester, pp. 57–66.

Wicks, M. and Rossiter, C. (1982) *Crises or Challenge? Family Care, Social Policy and Elderly People*. Study Commission on the Family, London.

Wilcock, G.K., Gray, J.A.M. and Pritchard, P.M.M. (1982) *Geriatric Problems in General Practice*. Oxford University Press, Oxford.

Wilkin, D. Conceptual problems in dependency research. *Social Science and Medicine*, **24** 867–873.

Wilkin, D., Mashiah, T. and Jolley, D.J. (1978) Changes in behavioural characteristics of elderly populations of local authority homes and long-stay hospital wards, 1976–77. *British Medical Journal*, **2**, 1274–1276.

Willcocks, D., Peace, S. and Kellaher, L. (1987) *Private Lives in Public Places: A Research-based Critique of Residential Life in Local Authority Old People's Homes*. Tavistock, London.

Williams, G. (1988) Private sector provision of sheltered housing – meeting needs or reflecting demand? Paper presented at British Society of Gerontology Annual Conference, University College, Swansea, 23–25 September.

Williams, J.M.G. (1984) *The Psychological Treatment of Depression: A Guide to the Theory and Practice of Cognitive Behaviour Therapy*. Croom Helm, London.

Williams, R. (1986) Images of Age and Generation. Paper presented at the British Sociological Association Annual Conference, Loughborough University.

Williams, R.H. and Wirths, C.G. (1965) *Lives Through the Years*. Aldine-Atherton, Chicago.

Williamson, J. (1979) Notes on the historical development of geriatric medicine as a medical speciality. *Age and Ageing*, **8**, 144–148.

Williamson, J., Stokoe, I.H., Gray, S., Fisher, M., Smith A., McGhee, A. et al (1964) Old people at home: their unreported needs. *Lancet*, **i**, 1117–1120.

Willmott, P. and Young, M. (1962) *Family and Kinship in East London*. Penguin, Harmondsworth.

Willner, P. (1985) *Depression: A Psychobiological Synthesis*. Wiley, Chichester.

Wilson, B.A. and Moffat, N. (1984) *Clinical Management of Memory Problems*. Croom Helm, London.

Wirz, H.M. (1982) Sheltered housing. In: Lishman, J. (ed.) *Research Highlights No.3: Developing Services for the Elderly*. University of Aberdeen, Department of Social Work, pp. 87–102.

Wolfensberger, W. (1972) *Normalisation: One Principle of Normalisation in Human Services*. Leonard Crainford, Toronto.

Woods R.T. (1987) Problems in the elderly: treatment. In: Lindsay, S. and Powell, G. (eds) *A Handbook of Clinical Adult Psychology*. Gower, Aldershot, pp. 400–419.

Woods, R.T. and Britton, P.G. (1985) *Clinical Psychology with the Elderly*. Croom Helm, London.

World Health Organization (1989) *Health of the Elderly. Report of a WHO Expert Committee, Technical Report Series, 779*. WHO, Geneva.

Wright, F. (1986) *Left to Care Alone*. Gower, Aldershot.

Young, M. and Willmott, P. (1957) *Family and Kinship in East London*. Routledge and Kegan Paul, London.

Young, M. and Willmott, P. (1973) *The Symmetrical Family. A Study of Work and Leisure in the London Region*. Routledge and Kegan Paul, London.

Zabalza, A., Pissarides, C. and Barton, M. (1980) Social security and the choice between full-time and part-time work and retirement. *Journal of Public Economics*, **14**, 245–276.

Zacks, R.T. (1982) Encoding strategies used by young and elderly adults in a keeping track task. *Journal of Gerontology*, **37**, 203–211.

Zeisel, J., Epp, G. and Demos, S. (1977) *Low-rise Housing for Older People*. HUD-483 (TQ.)-76. US Dept. of Housing and Urban Development, US Government Printing Office, Washington, DC.

Zeldin, T. (1983) *The French*. Collins, London.

Index

Index compiled by Meg Davies (Society of Indexers)